Rare as Hens' Teeth

Donna Alvermann
Connie A. Bridge
Barbara A. Schmidt
Lyndon W. Searfoss
Peter Winograd

D.C. Heath and Company
HEATH Lexington, Massachusetts   Toronto, Ontario

Acknowledgments

Grateful acknowledgment is made for permission to reprint the following copyrighted material.

Adoff, Arnold. "The Baker," from *Eats*. Copyright © 1979 by Arnold Adoff. Reprinted by permission of Lothrop, Lee & Shepard Books (a division of William Morrow & Company).

Adoff, Arnold. "Tornado," copyright © 1976, 1977, by Arnold Adoff. Reprinted by permission of Delacorte Press.

Alexander, Sue. "The Case of the Kidnapped Nephew," from *Whatever Happened to Uncle Albert? And Other Puzzling Plays*, by Sue Alexander. Copyright © 1980 by Sue Alexander. Reprinted by permission of Ticknor & Fields/Clarion Books, a Houghton Mifflin Company.

Allen, Mary Emma. "In the Footsteps of the Pioneers," from *The Oregon Trail*. Copyright © 1986 by Mary Emma Allen. Reprinted by permission of the Author.

Anderson, Don. "Have You Thanked a Green Plant Today?" Reprinted from the *Saturday Evening Post* by permission. Copyright © 1973 by the Curtis Publishing Company.

Blackmore, Vivien. *Why Corn Is Golden: Stories About Plants*. Adapted by Vivien Blackmore. Translation copyright © 1984 by Organización Editorial Novaro, S.A., reprinted by permission of Little, Brown and Company.

Caras, Roger. "Planning Your Zoo," from *A Zoo in Your Room*. Copyright © 1975 by Roger Caras. Reprinted by permission of Roberta Pryor, Literary Agent.

Chaback, Elaine, and Pat Fortunato. "Give Yourself Some Help," from *The Official Kid's Survival Kit: How to Do Things On Your Own*. Copyright © 1981 by Elaine Chaback and Pat Fortunato; reprinted by permission of Little, Brown and Company.

Childcraft. "Why Leaves Are Green" from *The Green Kingdom,* Volume 6, of *Childcraft—The How and Why Library*. Copyright © 1985 by World Book, Inc. Reprinted by permission of World Book, Inc.

Clapp, Patricia. "I Will Become a Doctor," an adaptation of *Dr. Elizabeth: A Biography of the First Woman Doctor*, by Patricia Clapp. Copyright © 1974 by Patricia Clapp. Reprinted by permission of Lothrop, Lee & Shepard Books (a division of William Morrow & Company).

Cobb, Vicki. "Science Puzzles," from *Bet You Can't*. Copyright © 1980 by Vicki Cobb and Kathy Darling. Reprinted by permission of William Morrow & Company.

Cohen, Barbara. "A Ball for Davy," adapted from pages 69–92 of *Thank You, Jackie Robinson*, copyright © 1974 by Barbara Cohen. Adapted by permission of Lothrop, Lee & Shepard Books (a division of William Morrow & Company).

Davis, Hubert. "Weather Lore." Reprinted from *A January Fog Will Freeze a Hog*, by Hubert Davis. Copyright © 1977 by Hubert Davis; used by permission of Crown Publishers, Inc.

DeJong, Meindert. "Break Down the Mountains," from *The House of Sixty Fathers*, by Meindert DeJong. Copyright © 1956 by Meindert DeJong. Reprinted by permission of Harper and Row, Publishers, Inc.

Eberly, Susan Schoon. "The Care and Feeding of Your Family Tree" is reprinted from *Cricket* magazine, November 1986, by permission.

Fernández, Damián. "A Family Secret," from *Kikirikí*, copyright © 1981 by Damián Fernández. Reprinted by permission of Revista Chicano-Riquena, University of Houston.

Francis, Robert. "The Base Stealer," from *The Orb Weaver*, by Robert Francis, copyright © 1960, is reprinted by permission of Wesleyan University Press.

Gardiner, John Reynolds. "A Plant Person." Adapted from *Top Secret*, by John Reynolds Gardiner. Copyright © 1984 by John Reynolds Gardiner. Reprinted by permission of Little, Brown and Company.

Gilson, Jamie. "Twister," an abridgment of *Do Bananas Chew Gum?* by Jamie Gilson. Copyright © 1980 by Jamie Gilson. Reprinted by permission of Lothrop, Lee & Shepard Books (a division of William Morrow & Company).

Greene, Bette. "The Calf-Raising Contest," from *Philip Hall Likes Me. I Reckon Maybe*. Copyright © 1974 by Bette Greene, reprinted by permission of the Author.

Greenfield, Eloise. "Harriet Tubman," from *Honey, I Love and Other Poems*, by Eloise Greenfield (Thomas Y. Crowell). Copyright © 1978 by Eloise Greenfield. Reprinted by permission of Harper and Row, Publishers, Inc.

Greer, Gery, and Bob Ruddick. "Back to the Middle Ages," from *Max and Me and the Time Machine*, by Gery Greer and Bob Ruddick. Copyright © 1983 by Gery Greer and Bob Ruddick. Reprinted by permission of Harcourt Brace Jovanovich, Inc.

(Continued on page 592)

Published simultaneously in Canada

Printed in the United States of America

International Standard Book Number: 0-669-11479-O

4   5   6   7   8   9   0

Table of Contents

Marvelous Machines

Sizing It Up

Storm Warning

Food for Thought

Help!

Plant People

Simple Solutions

Winners All

Land of the Brave

Older, but Wiser

Baseball Fever

Fur, Fins, and Feathers

Against All Odds

TV or Not TV?

Family Ties

Up From the Sea

Rare as Hens' Teeth

In one day, three hundred inventors take their inventions to the U.S. Patent Office; 180 of them are granted a patent. Fewer than three of them ever make any money from their invention.

from IN ONE DAY *by Tom Parker*

Marvelous Machines

WHAT ISIT?

from DANNY DUNN, INVISIBLE BOY
by Jay Williams and Raymond Abrashkin

"I wish there was a secret of invisibility," said Irene, "and that I knew it. It would be awfully useful for my science project."

Irene was doing a study of birds and in particular, since it was late spring, of their nesting habits.

"How's it coming?" Danny asked.

"I'm almost finished with my field notes," said Irene. "I'll have to start putting the whole thing together pretty soon, making the charts and displays. My father loaned me a spotting scope and a pair of binoculars so that I've been able to watch the birds pretty well. But you know, there are so many leaves that it's hard to see them in their nests. If I could get right up to them without being noticed—"

"Maybe we can ask Professor Bullfinch if he knows how it can be done," Dan said. "Visibility is because light bounces off things, you know. So maybe there's a way of getting light to go around things, instead, and then you wouldn't see them."

"Let's go ask him now," said Joe. "This is interesting."

When the three friends got to the Professor's house, Danny explained their conversation.

"Do you think, Professor," he said, "it would be possible to make somebody really invisible?"

"By camouflage," said the Professor. "If you wanted to be invisible in a forest, the best way would be to look like a tree. Another way is to be so visible that nobody notices you. As in Edgar Allan Poe's story 'The Purloined Letter'—"

"I read that," Joe said. "You mean, someone didn't want a letter to be found, so he left it right out in plain sight on the mantelpiece, and nobody saw it."

"That's not real invisibility," Danny protested. "Well, I suppose it is in a way, but it isn't what I mean. I mean, being able to walk around in a room full of people without being seen, for instance."

"I don't think so, Dan," the Professor said. "The problem is in the nature of light. We see because light bounces off things and returns to our eyes. We might make mechanisms which are hard to see, but we couldn't do it to living things, like people."

Dan's face fell. He had already made up his mind that the Professor could solve the problem.

"Oh, well," said Irene. "It was fun thinking about it, anyway."

The Professor chuckled. "There is another way," he said. "You could do it by inventing a machine that would be the next best thing to invisibility."

"I don't get it," Danny said.

Irene shook her head. "Neither do I. What's the next best thing to being invisible, Professor?"

"What I'm thinking of," replied Professor Bullfinch, "is a tiny device full of sensors which would pick up the signals of light and sound and touch and send them back to a receiving station. You've all seen spy stories on television in which a 'bug' is put somewhere in a room and sends back voice signals to a listener. If it's small enough, it isn't noticed. Well, if you could make sensors tiny enough, they could send back the images and the touch of things, as well as sounds. Then, if you had the right equipment to receive the information, it would be just as if you were standing invisibly in that room."

"It sounds like a swell idea to me, Professor," said Danny. "What about making a machine like that?"

Professor Bullfinch shook his head. "Not just yet, Dan. We haven't the necessary materials to make switches and amplifiers small enough to be practical. Maybe some day—"

Several weeks later the three friends were walking home together after baseball practice. Irene said, "I'll have

4

to go right home. I have to finish up my charts for the science exhibition tomorrow. I just have an hour's work and I want to get it done."

"My project's finished," Danny said. "So I'll help you."

"And I'll watch," said Joe. "There's something soothing about watching other people work."

They went to Irene's house and up to her room. All the flat surfaces—the desk, table, bed, bureau—were covered with sheets of cardboard on which she had mounted photos and drawings of birds, or illustrated charts showing the nesting cycle of the Northern oriole from the building of the nest to the final flight of the young birds. There was also a branch set into a wooden stand with an oriole's nest hanging from it. Any free space was taken up by marking pens, paste, scissors, magazines, and reference books.

"The biggest problem about this project," said Joe, "is where do we sit down?"

Irene cleared some sheets of paper from a chair. "You can sit there," she said. "And since I know you're pretty good at lettering, you can start printing at the top of this sheet, *Third Week.*"

Joe groaned. "I might have known it. Some people just can't stand to see a person enjoying himself."

They got to work, and for a time all was quiet. The delicious smell of the newly mowed lawn came to them through the open window, just outside of which hovered a dragonfly on glittering wings. Now and then a bird called.

At last, Danny said to Irene, "I've been thinking . . . Does it bother you much to be the only girl on the baseball team?"

"Some," Irene admitted. "I get the feeling that everybody is looking twice as hard at me as at anyone else. They expect me to do worse than everybody else—or maybe better. Either way, it makes me nervous."

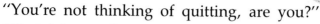

"You're not thinking of quitting, are you?"

"Certainly not."

"Good. Don't let it get you down."

Joe tipped his head back to admire his neat lettering. "You know, it's funny," he said. "There'll be boys and girls with exhibits in the science show—if there were only boys, people would think it was peculiar. So why should they think it's so strange if there are boys and girls playing baseball together?"

"It's because girls aren't supposed to be good at games," said Irene.

"No, that's not it, because girls do play all the games boys do and everybody knows it."

"Well, boys are supposed to be better at them."

"Whoever made up that rule didn't know about me," Joe protested. "The only game I'm good at is checkers."

They went on working and were just finishing up when Mrs. Miller called up the stairs, "Irene! Telephone!"

Irene ran off to answer it. She returned with a bewildered look.

"That was Professor Bullfinch," she said. "He wants us all to come to the lab right away." She hesitated, and then added, "And he said, 'Tell Joe I'm no good at games, either.'"

Joe's mouth dropped open. Danny said, "How did he know?"

"Let's go find out," said Irene.

They found the Professor seated on a high stool before one of the laboratory benches, writing busily in a notebook. He glanced up as they charged through the door opening to the back yard.

"Ah," he said, "the only girl on the team. I'm glad you're not thinking of quitting."

They gaped at him in astonishment. He went on, "I like your lettering, Joe. In fact, Irene, the whole display looks very attractive."

"How did you—?" Danny stuttered. "Where were you—?"

"Right there in Irene's room with you." The Professor chuckled. "But I never left this spot."

He stood up and touched a curious-looking device which they now noticed on the bench beside him. It resembled a crash helmet, with a visor that projected to cover the whole face of the wearer. Next to it was a pair of clumsy gauntlets. Cables connected both helmet and gauntlets with a metal box, on the front of which was a kind of miniature piano keyboard and a couple of small knobs.

"This," he said impressively, "is an invisibility simulator with intromittent transmission."

There was a long moment of silence, and then Joe said, "A which what? I never heard of such a thing."

"Yes, you have," said Danny excitedly. "We all have. I know what it is. It's the thing you told us about a long time ago, right here in the lab, isn't it Professor?"

Professor Bullfinch nodded. "I suggested, you remember, that something might be made that would be just as good as being invisible. But I told you we didn't have the right materials to make sensory devices, switches, or amplifiers small enough. Well, now we have—thanks to dunnite."

"Dunnite?"

"The stuff you produced by accident, when you melted Dr. Grimes's crystals. It is amazing—the best semiconductor I've ever tested. It allowed me to make ultra-microscopic transistors."

He reached across the helmet and picked up something small and glittering.

"A dragonfly!" said Irene.

"Not really," said the Professor. "It only looks like a dragonfly. It's the sensory probe."

He handed it over so they could inspect it. It was made of light, clear plastic, through which they could see that its insides were packed with the tiniest machinery imaginable. The wings were rigid, and covered with a design of very fine wires.

"I'll explain how it works," the Professor continued. "The 'dragonfly' flies by jets of compressed air. Also, since it's so light in weight, it can operate like a glider, taking advantage of air currents. The wings are also antennae for receiving power, which is beamed to it by microwave.

"The 'dragonfly' can be flown to a particular spot. There, it picks up sensory data—images, sounds, and touch—and broadcasts them back by microwave to screens and receivers inside the helmet and gloves. So by sending it to Irene's windowsill, I was able to watch you and listen to you as if I were there myself."

Danny gave a long whistle. Then he burst out, "Can we—"

The Professor laughed. "—Try it? I knew you'd ask that. Yes, you can, my boy. You all can. But first I must give you some instruction in operating it. It's not easy."

"What is it called?" Joe said. "An invisibility—?"

"—simulator with intromittent transmission. In other words it imitates invisibility by sending back signals."

"Yes. Isit."

"Yes, it is," said the Professor, looking puzzled.

"No, I mean Isit is what it is."

Professor Bullfinch blinked. "You're confusing me, Joe. It is what it is, isn't it?"

"Sure it is. It's Isit," said Joe. "Invisibility Simulator with Intromittent Transmission. I-S-I-T."

"Of course," said the Professor. "I see what you mean. A good name. I hearby christen it Isit." He shook his head. "I hope I can keep this straight in my own mind. Isit is *it*."

Professor Bullfinch pulled the high stool over so that it was in front of the machine. "Who is to go first?" he said.

"I think Danny should," said Irene. "You wouldn't have the thing at all if he hadn't melted those crystals."

"That's no reason for going first," Danny retorted. "It was an accident even though it worked out all right. Why don't we just draw straws?"

"That's the fairest way," agreed the Professor.

He rummaged around on the table and found a wire cutter. From a piece of copper wire, he snipped three bits of different lengths. "Shortest goes first," he said. He held them out between his fingers so that only the ends showed.

They all drew at the same time. Irene's was the shortest. Next came Dan, then Joe.

"I'm just as glad to be the last," Joe said. "That way, I'll find out what *not* to do."

The Professor made Irene sit on the stool. He helped her pull the gauntlets over her hands.

"They'll feel awkward at first, but you'll get used to them," he said. "The general idea is easy enough. These levers move the wings so that you can make the dragonfly rise, dip, or turn in the air. Put your thumbs on the buttons in the knobs. Those control the airjets. Got that?"

Irene nodded.

"Now I'll put the helmet on you. I'll switch on the sensors myself, at the keyboard. Take a minute and get ready."

Inside the helmet, all was dark. Irene felt an instant of panic, as if she were shut up in a closet. She had difficulty breathing and little golden dots swirled before her eyes.

"I'm pressing the keys," said the Professor. "Don't be frightened. Everything will seem rather strange."

It was more than strange. She seemed to be looking across a great gray space with a jumble of mountainous shapes rising on either side. Although she could still feel the control levers in her hands, she also seemed to be touching something hard and flat.

"I don't know where I am!" she said.

"Take it easy," the Professor said soothingly. "You are looking at four curved screens inside the helmet, and seeing through the lenses of the dragonfly's eyes. It's lying on the lab bench, so you may feel a little mixed up at first."

As he spoke, Irene began to sort out what she was seeing. She could make out, now, that the gray was the stone surface of the worktable, and that the shapes around her were notebooks and pieces of apparatus. The control box for Isit towered up beside her.

"Now, then," the Professor went on, "the dragonfly also has a set of hooks, or claws, under its body. You can

use these to have it cling to things or even to pick up small objects. Squeeze your hands around the knobs and that will make the claws close. Try it.''

Irene did so and felt as if her fingernails were scraping along the hard surface.

''Very good. I saw them move,'' said the Professor. ''Now you're ready to try a flight. The right hand controls the forward jet, the left the backward one. Does the way look clear?''

''Yes.''

''Give it a forward burst, then—very gently! Not too much! Remember, the dragonfly weighs only a few ounces.''

Gingerly, she pressed her right thumb down for a moment. She felt herself glide forward and saw the edge of the table shoot toward her. The next instant, she was in the air.

Everything was very real, so that she forgot she was merely looking into screens inside the helmet, or hearing sounds through amplifiers, or experiencing the touch of things through sensory devices. She seemed to be actually soaring and she could even feel the rush of the air past her body. The far wall of the laboratory loomed closer and closer, and in sudden fright she pulled back one of the levers, forgetting which was which.

She felt herself leaning to the right, and skimmed away from the wall. She had a wild image of windows shooting past, and a glimpse of Joe, open-mouthed, below her. The Professor was shouting something, which at first she was too scared to understand. Then she made herself calm down.

"Touch the backward jet—the left one," he was saying. "It will slow you down."

She remembered, then, and pressed her left thumb down just for a second, and felt her movement slowing. She could feel an upward push of air, and as she slid into it, it lifted her lightly. Balancing as if she were on a tightrope, she let the air carry her on a wide spiral path toward the ceiling.

Now she was getting the knack of it. She found she could sense the different layers of air, some lighter and warmer, some heavier and colder, and feel the movement of their currents. She began to enjoy herself. It was like one of those wonderful dreams of flying. She turned easily in a half-circle, and glancing down, saw that she was above the Professor and the two boys. They were staring up with strained faces.

She saw something else—something that made the whole thing even more dreamlike. She saw *herself*, sitting

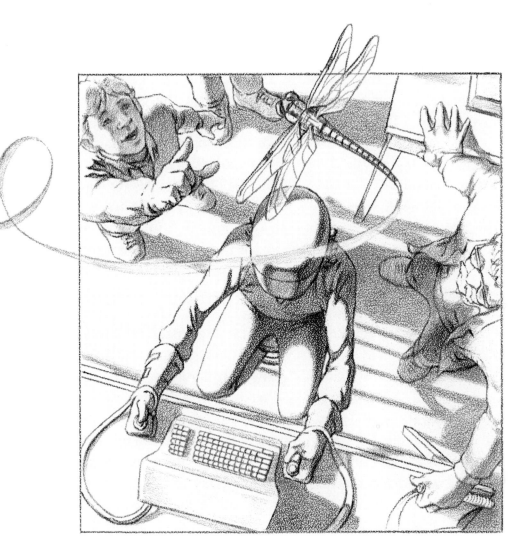

on the stool next to the Professor, her head covered by
the closed helmet, her hands inside the gauntlets, grasping
the levers on the box.

It was so eerie to look down at herself this way that
she almost lost control of the dragonfly, and only when
she felt herself beginning to wobble in the air did she set
herself, tight-lipped with concentration, back to flying.

"I'm okay," she called, forgetting again that she was
not really above them but right beside them.

She gave herself a little boost with the forward jet and
slipped sideways and forward out of the warm upward
current. On a long, even glide she skimmed right out of
one of the windows and into the open air.

"Don't take the dragonfly too far," the Professor said warningly. His voice seemed to come from the empty air next to her. "The microwave beam has a limited range."

She scarcely heard him, since she was so absorbed in seeing the lawn, the flowerbeds, and the trees from a position about twelve feet above the ground. Using her forward jet again, she sailed toward a row of thick bushes. The leaves came toward her swiftly, and just in time she slowed herself with the backward jet and landed on a twig. She felt its smooth bark under her hands and squeezed both fists so that the claws of the dragonfly closed around the twig and held her in place.

Leaves were all about her, and she could see little except their jagged edges and their glossy surfaces. She could count the tiny hairs on their undersides. One difficulty, she now found, was that she couldn't turn her head—or rather, the dragonfly's head. Its bulging lenses gave her a wide field of view, something like looking out of a curved window, but to see beyond that range meant that she would have to turn the whole body of the machine, which was something she didn't know how to do.

The branches around her suddenly dipped, and she was bounced sharply as if she were on a springy couch and someone else had jumped on it. There was a flutter nearby, and she realized that a bird had landed on the bush. It must be behind her somewhere, just out of sight.

"How do I turn this thing around?" she said aloud.

"Where are you—it, I mean?" said the Professor.

"I'm in a bush on the edge of the lawn. There's a bird here somewhere, and I want to look at it."

"You can't turn while you're perched. You'll have to take off, turn in the air and land again."

"Okay. Oh—Can the bird hear me talking?"

"Of course not, Irene. You're not out there—you're here!"

14

She felt the Professor tap her shoulder. "I keep forgetting," she grinned.

She opened the claws and shot out of the bush. She
banked and turned, more confidently this time, and as she
glided back to the bush, she saw a brown-and-white blur
flash past her. Slowing herself, she now noticed a nest
among the branches, and she was able to land just to one
side of it and facing it.

Irene had spent many hours watching birds through
her father's high-powered binoculars. But never before had
she had such a clear, close view of a nest with babies in
it. She saw how skillfully it was woven together of thin
twigs, bits of vine, and long grass stems to form a snug,
deep bowl in which lurked three nestlings. They were
snuggled close together, and she could see every damp-
looking quill of their sprouting feathers.

"Robin or thrush," she said to herself.

With the thought, a shadow fell over her, and a wood
thrush landed on the edge of the nest. He was so near
that she could feel the wind of his arrival and could clearly
see the way he dropped his tail to stall, raising his body
and cupping his wings to make a neat landing. He paid
no attention to her at all and with a thrill she told herself,
"Professor Bullfinch was right. It's the same as being
invisible!"

As the bird landed and the nest bounced, the young
ones raised their heads. They opened enormous mouths,
which looked much too big for their skinny necks. Irene
could look right down their red throats, just as the parent
thrush was doing.

She was no more than six inches away and she stared
at him in fascination. From her perch, he looked enormous.
She could see the smudged, dark, arrowhead markings on
his white front, his sleek reddish-brown back, and his bright
black, intelligent eye. She could even see the tiny pulse

throbbing in his breast, and she remembered that birds have a very high temperature and that their hearts beat as fast as ten times a second.

The thrush held a pale green caterpillar in his beak, and as she watched, he bent forward, thrust his beak far down into one of the gaping baby mouths and crammed it with food.

She watched for a moment or two longer, and then, when the thrush had finished and had flown off to look for more food, she decided to move on also. She was facing inward, so she gave a burst from the backward jet and whizzed into the open. It was not as easy to go backward as she had thought, and she found herself falling. The lawn spun up at her, and involuntarily she closed her eyes and gave a little scream. The dragonfly was too light to be harmed, however, and she felt only the soft rustle of grass as it touched the ground.

"What's the matter?" asked the Professor.

"I'm on the ground. Now what?"

She heard the noise of running feet and then Danny's voice shouting, "I see her. I mean it. A little shiny thing out there in the middle of the lawn."

The Professor said, "Now, Irene, make sure you're level. Then give yourself a good boost with the jet and slowly pull back both control levers just a little, so that the leading edges of the wings catch the air—"

"Oh—right! I know. Okay."

She was doing it as she spoke, and she found herself rushing along the tips of the grasses. Then, abruptly, she was in the air, swooping steeply, higher and higher, until she was above the tops of the tallest trees.

She heard Danny yell, "Watch it!" At the same time, she saw a swallow diving straight at her out of the blue.

She was too startled to move. She saw the sharp, stubby beak open as the bird flicked its wings to turn in mid-air. Then it was upon her. She felt a blow that rocked

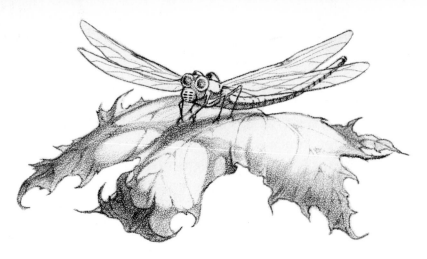

her as the bird snapped its beak on what it thought was a tasty dragonfly.

The sky whirled about her. Then everything went dark and silent.

"Where am I?" she cried. "Am I eaten?"

Professor Bullfinch had shut off the machine and was lifting the helmet off her head.

Danny, at the window, said, "I see where it fell. It's in that big old maple."

"That's going to be some climb," Joe said. "We'll have to have a ladder to get into the lower branches."

"I still don't understand what happened," Irene stammered. "That swallow got me, didn't it?"

"It got the dragonfly," said Danny. "I saw it—did you hear me yell to warn you? Then the minute it found out the thing was plastic instead of a real insect, it dropped it. You fell—I mean Isit fell—into that tree."

"The bird must have damaged one of the wings or broken a connection," said the Professor. "You lost power when you lost contact with the beam. We'll fix it, though, as soon as somebody climbs that maple and gets the dragonfly back."

Danny and Joe were staring at Irene.

"We'll go right away," said Danny. "But—what was it like, Irene?"

She drew a long breath and let it out in a sigh.

"I don't know the right words," she said. "It was wonderful!"

Think About It

1. Why did Professor Bullfinch invent Isit?
2. How would you describe Isit to someone who hadn't read the story?
3. What did Irene do, see, and feel after she put on the helmet and gauntlets?
4. Do you think Isit truly is a marvelous machine? Tell why or why not.
5. Do you think an invention like Isit will be developed someday? Why or why not?

Create and Share   Imagine that it is your turn to use Isit. Think about where you would like to go and what you would like to see, hear, and feel. Then imagine yourself feeling as if you were flying there. Describe what happens.

Explore   The author of this story wrote several books about Danny Dunn. *Danny Dunn and the Homework Machine* is one you might like. Or, for books about real machines, look in the library card catalog under INVENTIONS or INVENTORS. Learning how other people have invented machines might give you some ideas for an invention of your own.

Back to the Middle Ages

from MAX AND ME AND THE TIME MACHINE
by Gery Greer and Bob Ruddick

I guess I'm like everybody else. When I do something that's pretty terrific, I expect to get some credit for it. A little praise, a pat on the back, a bit of wild, thunderous applause—maybe even a chorus of "Bravo! Fantastic! Way to go!"

And that's just what I was expecting when I hauled that huge crate into our clubhouse and told my best friend, Max Zilinski, that it contained a time machine I had picked up at a garage sale down the street for $2.50.

But Max did not applaud. He snorted.

"Who're you trying to kid, Steve?" he said, barely glancing up from the electronics book he was reading. "There's no such thing as time travel *or* time machines."

I wiped the sweat off my forehead with the back of my sleeve and slouched against the crate. "When have I ever lied to you?" I asked, trying to look hurt and sincere at the same time.

"An interesting question," said Max, carefully laying his book aside on the rumpled cot and holding up his fingers to count on. "Now, let me see. I can recall the Rotten Toboggan Affair . . . "

Uh-oh, here we go. Max has all these code names for the various little misunderstandings we've had. The Rotten Toboggan Affair referred to that day last winter when I talked him into going down Quarter-Mile Hill on a beat-up old toboggan. "You're crazy," Max had said. "This hill is too steep and this toboggan is a mess. Look at it. It's even rotting out underneath."

It took a lot of doing, but I finally convinced him that the toboggan was as good as new and as sound as a rock. A couple of minutes later, as we were tearing down the hill at about eighty miles an hour, the toboggan began to come apart. Little pieces began breaking off, and we lost control, hit a tree stump, somersaulted through the air, and smashed into a snowbank. Max remembers things like that.

" . . . and let's not forget Operation Lousy Letter!"

See what happens when you try to help a friend? I mean, could I have known that Max, who is always trying to work up the nerve to talk to Dawn Sharington, would get upset when I broke the ice by writing her a love letter and signing his name to it?

"Okay, okay," I said, holding up my hands in surrender. "Let's not quibble over a few minor mistakes. After all, what do you care if Dawn knows you think she's the best-looking girl west of the Mississippi?"

Max made a choking sound.

"Besides, you should thank me. You wanted Dawn to notice you, and now she does. Whenever she sees you, she starts giggling like crazy."

"Agggggggggh," groaned Max, clutching his head with both hands.

"Look, Max," I said cheerfully, "forget about the letter. We've got something a lot more important to deal with. I mean, haven't we been wondering for the last two weeks what we were going to do all summer? Well, now we've got the answer."

I patted the time-machine crate meaningfully and read the black lettering stamped on the side:

MAINLY, ONE GENUINE, COMPLETELY AUTOMATED, EASILY ASSEMBLED, ONE-OF-A-KIND TIME MACHINE! FULLY GUARANTEED!

"Sure, sure," grumbled Max. "And you got it at a garage sale for two-fifty. You don't expect me to believe that, do you?"

"If you'll just listen a minute," I said, "I can explain the whole thing. Okay?"

Max grunted, but he was still suffering over Dawn. This sales pitch was going to have to be good.

"Okay. You know Mr. Cooper, right? The man who lives just around the corner in that great big old house? Well, he found this crate in his attic last night, and he's sure it was left there by the famous Professor Flybender."

Max's logical mind slowly clicked into gear. "Oh, yeah? If this professor guy is so famous, how come I've lived here in Flat Rock for five years and never heard of him? And why would he leave things in Mr. Cooper's attic?"

"Good points. I asked Mr. Cooper the same things. It turns out that Flybender used to live there and was some sort of crazy inventor."

"Okay, Sherlock, then why didn't Mr. Cooper find this marvelous invention before now?" Max smugly pushed his glasses back up on his nose.

"Because, Watson, there was so much junk in the attic when Mr. Cooper bought the house he never had time to go through it all."

"I still say you've been had," Max insisted stubbornly. "If Mr. Cooper actually believed this was a time machine, do you really think he would have sold it to you?"

"Of course not," I scoffed. I was ready for that one, too. "But just because Mr. Cooper is too short-sighted to recognize a great discovery like this doesn't mean we have to be, too. After all, you're the one who's always telling me that scientific geniuses are misunderstood in their own times."

"Well, just for the sake of argument," Max said, "let's *suppose* this Professor Flybender really was a brilliant inventor, and *suppose* he really did build this thing, and *suppose* he really did leave it in Mr. Cooper's attic . . . "

Max's voice trailed off as he mulled over his supposes.

"Max, my boy," I said, "this is Opportunity Knocking, THUMP! THUMP! Why, with this baby we could go anywhere we want—to any *time* we want. Just consider the possibilities!"

THUMP! "We could travel back three thousand years to ancient Egypt and catch the grave robbers as they jimmy their way into King Tut's tomb!"

Max's eyes glazed slightly as he considered that possibility.

"Yeah," whispered Max in an awed voice. "And if we stopped off in the seventeenth century, I could get Shakespeare's autograph."

He was hooked. Of course, I had no intention of chasing around through time trying to get some guy's autograph, but we could iron out that detail later.

I hopped up onto a stool. "We could drop in on the nineteenth century and solve the Jack the Ripper murders!"

"Wow!" said Max, joining in. "And attend the opening night of Beethoven's Fifth Symphony!"

I jabbed my finger at the ceiling and cried, "Babe Ruth, Billy the Kid, Blackbeard the Pirate!"

"Aristotle, Galileo, Einstein!" Max shouted.

I made a flying leap onto the table, threw back my head, and yelled, "The Gunfight at the O.K. Corral!"

Max was overcome. He snapped to attention and saluted up at me. "Say no more, chief," he said, his face glowing with enthusiasm. "Just tell me what you want me to do."

Putting the time machine together was a cinch. We just followed the step-by-step instructions in the professor's booklet on ASSEMBLING FLYBENDER'S FANTASTIC, FULLY GUARANTEED TIME MACHINE. Nobody bothered us either, which is one of the big advantages of having a clubhouse of our own. We'd built it ourselves out in my backyard, where it's almost completely hidden by trees. Even my nosy little sister usually leaves us alone.

By one o'clock, the time machine was finished. As we shook hands and stood back to admire our work, the weird seven-foot-tall contraption seemed to stare down at us.

"That's it," said Max, snapping the manual shut. "According to the professor, all we have to do now is select a time and place we want to visit. When our time is up, we'll be automatically returned to the present. And no matter how long we're gone, no time will have passed here, so no one will even know we've been away."

"You mean we'll come back exactly when we left?" I asked.

"That's what the manual says," said Max.

"Great!" I said, pacing the floor with excitement. "And of course since I found the time machine, I get to choose where we go on our first trip. I choose the Middle Ages."

"The Middle Ages?" said Max, with a puzzled frown. "What's so great about the Middle Ages?"

I slapped my forehead in disgust. "Haven't you ever heard of knights in shining armor? Haven't you heard of castles and dungeons and damsels in distress? Wouldn't you like a little Action, Adventure, and Excitement?"

"No," said Max.

Well, *I* figured it was now or never.

Almost without thinking, I reached out, grasped the huge ON-OFF lever, and by throwing my full weight against it, pulled it down to "ON." Max spun around, but there was nothing he could do. He was clear across the room, with his hand on the doorknob and one foot out the door. I barely had time to glimpse his startled expression before Professor Flybender's Fully Guaranteed Time Machine sprang to life.

Lights flashed, gauges gyrated, steam spewed out of loose joints with the force of a fire hose turned on full blast.

Flybender's machine was working, all right.

Then, from deep inside, came a weird, wild, wailing sound. It was low like a moan but rose steadily until it reached an eerie high pitch. And at that moment the giant fan on top of the machine began to spin, ghostly slow at first, but gaining speed . . . faster . . . faster . . .

The clubhouse began to vibrate . . . faster . . . I was thrown up hard against the shaking walls . . . faster . . . Max began to look fuzzy around the edges . . . faster . . . Now he was a blur . . . faster . . .

"*Max!*" I shouted and was immediately plunged into darkness.

The wind whistled by in furious whirlwinds, howling around my head and pulling at my hair. I felt as if I were on a vibrating conveyor belt, out of control and hurtling through a long ink-black tunnel.

A panicky feeling welled up inside me. I pushed it down and tried to call out to Max, but the wind caught his name and swept it away.

Where was Max? Why was this taking so long? Why weren't we in the Middle Ages? Why—

Without warning, the vibrating stopped, and I fell several feet, landing with a heavy thud.

It was all over, but where was I? There were no lights, no sounds.

Blinking into the blackness, I tried to look around, but for some reason I couldn't move my neck. I tried to stand up but discovered that I couldn't move my legs. I tried a dog-paddle, but it was no go. *I was pinned.*

Now what? I wondered grimly.

Suddenly, I was startled by a strange, clinky-jingling noise and the uncomfortable feeling that I was turning, like a chicken on a barbecue spit, slowl-l-l-l-ly in space.

A narrow slit of light appeared in front of my eyes.

Then, into that slit of light popped a face—round, eager, with brown bobbed hair. He examined me with concern for a few moments before asking anxiously, "Art thou all right, Sir Robert?"

Before I could answer, the round-faced stranger pulled me to a sitting position and lifted a massive, flat-topped helmet off my head. I gaped down at myself in amazement.

No wonder I made a clinking noise whenever I moved. My T-shirt, jeans, and tennis shoes were gone. In their place was a long chain-mail shirt that covered me from head to knee, and underneath that, a pair of chain-mail tights. Over the armor, I was sporting a sleeveless, emerald-green tunic with a coat of arms embroidered in gold across my chest. From my belt hung a long sword in a gold scabbard.

But even more amazing, I was wearing *someone else's body*! Someone tall and broad-shouldered, with plenty of muscles.

Not bad, I thought to myself, as I flexed my arm and felt the muscles ripple.

"Art thou all right, Sir Robert?" repeated the stranger. He was wearing a simple brown tunic over green tights, and soft leather boots with pointed toes.

"I sure art," I said cheerfully. As I spoke, I noticed that even my voice was different. It was deeper than my own, and stronger, too. "But if you don't mind my asking, who art you?"

"Why, I am Niles, Sir Robert. Thy squire. Dost thou not know me?" He shook his head and looked worried. "Thou hast taken a nasty tumble off thy horse, and me-thinks it hath rattled thy wits."

He was wrong there. My wits were in tip-top condition.
In fact, you might say that my wits were doing handsprings
for joy as I realized several things:

Flybender's machine had worked after all, and I
was in the Middle Ages as planned.

I had been transported into the body of a Sir Robert, a knight, and this guy, Niles, was his squire.

As I entered Sir Robert's body, I must have gotten
dizzy and fallen off my horse, which explained
why Niles thought my wits were rattled and why
I had arrived with my nose in the dirt.

Then it hit me. If I came back in someone else's body, Max could be here, too, and I'd never recognize him. I began to look around with serious interest.

I was on a grassy field, surrounded by a makeshift camp of large, brightly colored tents, each decorated with flags and pennants that fluttered in the breeze. Looming a short distance to the right were the gray stone walls and turrets of a medieval castle. And by my side stood a sleek white horse draped with yards and yards of green cloth trimmed in gold.

Here and there men and boys scurried, all dressed like Niles in tunics and tights. Max could be anywhere, even miles from here.

I realized that if I were ever going to find him, I'd need a lot more information. And as Niles helped me to my feet, I thought of a plan to get it.

I shook my head as if I were still dazed. "Niles," I said, hoping I looked lost and confused, "I can't seem to get my bearings. I'm afraid that falling off my horse has made me lose my memory. Maybe if you'd tell me where we are and what we're doing here, it will all come back to me."

It worked. Niles looked up at me anxiously, with loyal devotion written all over his face. "Why, Sir Robert, we are at the Great Hampshire Tournament, where we have camped these past three days in thy tent." He gestured to the yellow-gold tent with green banners that stood behind us. "We came at the invitation of Richard Lorraine, Earl of Hampshire, who heard tales of thy great strength and skill at jousting and would try thee against his own champion. 'Tis the last day of the tourney, and thou art undefeated as usual, sire. Eighteen knights have fallen already before thy lance. There remaineth only the joust with Sir Bevis, a minor feat for someone with thy mighty talents."

I nodded cautiously. "I see. And just when is this minor jousting match supposed to take place?"

"In but a few moments, Sir Robert," he said, busily dusting off my tunic and straightening my belt. "Then the tourney will be over, and thou wilt be the champion. The people await this last joust most eagerly."

"Hmmmm. And you think I can handle Sir Bevis, do you?"

Niles laughed merrily. "Oh, Sir Robert, thou art jesting, of course. 'Twill be a sad day for English knighthood when thou, the Green Falcon, canst not best the likes of Sir Bevis."

Bingo! Jackpot! Things were looking good. Not only was I in the Middle Ages, but I was in the body of a famous knight and was actually going to be in a jousting match on the field of honor! And it was my kind of contest—me against some harmless, lily-livered, mealy-mouthed twerp.

The only problem was that it all sounded a bit beneath my talents. Why then, I wondered, were the people so eager to see this particular match? I decided to fish for a few details.

"Tell me, Niles," I said, cracking my knuckles and flexing my muscles, "who is this Bevis turkey anyway?"

"Why, Sir Bevis Thorkell," replied Niles cheerfully, "the Earl's champion and a knight known throughout all England as the Hampshire Mauler."

"The Hampshire *Mauler?*" I didn't like the sound of that.

"Aye, Sir Robert, and a black-hearted varlet he is. Canst thou truly remember nothing? Dost thou not recall his vow to smash thy skull and feed thy guts to the castle dogs, the saucy fellow?"

I found myself wondering if Sir Bevis and I could talk this thing over. I mean, I didn't want to be a spoil-sport or anything, but let's face it, I don't perform well under pressure.

"Niles," I said, looking for an out, "give it to me straight. What has Sir Bevis got against me?"

" 'Tis no secret, sire. Sir Bevis is sore jealous that thou art a knight and art but eighteen years of age. And 'tis well known that the Earl hath taken a liking to thee during the tournament. Mayhap Sir Bevis feareth that thou wilt replace him as the Earl's champion."

Niles blushed slightly. "And, of course, there is the matter of Lady Elizabeth."

"Okay," I said, shifting my weight uneasily. "Let me get this straight. Sir Bevis is a little upset because he thinks I'm trying to steal his reputation, his job, and his girl. Right?"

"Aye. And thou art just the man to do it."

"But—"

Suddenly, there was a loud blast of trumpets from somewhere nearby.

"Make haste, sire!" gasped Niles. " 'Tis time!"

Before I could say another word, he clapped the iron helmet back onto my head. A page ran out of a nearby tent, carrying some portable stairs which he plunked down next to the white stallion. I was still confused and stunned as Niles hustled me up the stairs and onto the horse, thrusting a shield into my left hand and a ten-foot-long lance into my right.

With a hearty "Go to, Sir Robert!" he slapped the horse's backside, and off we trotted in the direction of the trumpets.

"Where is Max now that I need him?" I groaned.

"Right here," said a deep voice from under me. "And you have my full support!"

It was Max! He was my horse!

"I heard everything Niles said," he continued with a whinny, "and I think it's safe to say that we're about to experience a little Action, Adventure, and Excitement."

Lining one side of the large open field were long wooden bleachers crowded with cheering spectators. Women waved their scarves and handkerchiefs. Men stood and shouted. From the tops of tall poles, colored banners streamed and flapped in the breeze. On a raised platform behind the bleachers, twenty heralds snapped to attention, pressed golden trumpets to their lips, and blared out a rousing call to arms.

Little League was never like this.

Max tossed his head toward a lone figure mounted on a black steed at the opposite end of the field. "That must be Sir Bevis," he neighed.

It was the Hampshire Mauler, all right, and he looked ready to maul anything that got in his way. His chain mail, shield, sword, and helmet were coal black; and a blood-red tunic dripped from his massive shoulders. Even from a distance, he looked like a killer. I swallowed hard.

"Now what?" I hissed.

"No problem," whispered Max. "All you have to do is watch Sir Bevis and do whatever he does."

"Oh, sure," I said. "That's just great. And what if he runs me through with his lance?"

"In that case," said Max, "try not to land on your head. It'll only make matters worse."

I would have let him have it with my spurs, but I didn't have time. I caught some movement out of the corner of my eye, and I looked down the long field through the slits in my helmet. In the center were two narrow lanes separated by a low fence. And at the far end was Sir Bevis—evil, threatening, poised for the kill.

He lowered his lance until it was level and aimed steadily across the field straight at my heart.

What else could I do? I lowered my lance. It wobbled around like crazy.

Abruptly, the trumpets stopped, leaving the shock of silence. In that same instant, Sir Bevis spurred his black

stallion and charged forward, his red tunic flapping and the tip of his lance glinting in the sun.

Without a word, Max too leaped forward. We were on a collision course with the Hampshire Mauler.

The muffled thunder of hoofbeats filled the air. Hypnotized, I locked my eyes on the black figure bearing down on us. A cold fear gripped my spine, and I tried desperately to steady my lance.

He was almost upon us—so close that I thought I glimpsed his wild eyes gleaming evilly behind the slits in his black helmet. I braced myself for a terrible blow.

Suddenly, just before I was due to swallow the tip of Sir Bevis's lance, Max opened his mouth, curled back his lips, and at the top of his lungs bellowed:
"GERONIMO-O-O-O-O-O-O-O-O-O-O-O-O-O-O-O!!!!!"

Sir Bevis's horse gave an alarmed squeal, dug all four hooves into the ground, and skidded to an abrupt halt.

Sir Bevis catapulted out of the saddle, sailed through the air, and fell with a noisy CLANK! onto the field. He was knocked out cold.

Child's play, I thought to myself as Max slowed to a stop and turned around. *This jousting business is mere child's play.*

The crowd went wild. And so they should. It was a brilliant performance.

Of course, from the bleachers, no one heard Max yell or saw that I had never laid a lance on Sir Bevis. All they knew was that on the very first pass, the Hampshire Mauler had been easily unhorsed and lay in a dazed heap on the field. And I was not about to spoil their fun by setting the record straight.

After all, it was the least I could do for Sir Robert while I was occupying his body. Being a hero, I mean. Keeping up the old boy's image in his absence. I'd do the same for anyone.

Think About It

1. What was marvelous about Professor Flybender's machine?
2. How does Steve's experience satisfy his need for Action, Adventure, and Excitement?
3. How might the tournament have turned out if Max hadn't been around?
4. What do you think will happen to Max and Steve after the tournament? What clues did you use to make your prediction?
5. If you could use either Isit or Flybender's Fantastic Fully Guaranteed Time Machine, which would you choose? Why?

Create and Share   Travel back in time via Professor Flybender's Time Machine. Imagine an exciting adventure you would like to have during some part of the past or future. Then write a letter to someone at home. Tell how you happened to use the machine, and how it felt to travel in time. Then describe the surprises you found when you arrived.

Explore   This selection is from the book *Max and Me and the Time Machine*. You might want to read what else happens to Steve and Max. Another book about time travel is *Danny Dunn and the Time Traveler*. Or you might enjoy Madeline L'Engle's fantasy, *A Wrinkle in Time*. Look under SCIENCE FICTION in the library card catalog for more books.

Sizing It Up

The giant is great,
The giant is tall,
But the dwarf on his back
Sees farthest of all.

Wallace Tripp

HUFFER AND CUFFER

Huffer, a giant ungainly and gruff,
encountered a giant called Cuffer.
Said Cuffer to Huffer, I'M ROUGH AND I'M TOUGH,
said Huffer to Cuffer, I'M TOUGHER.

They shouted such insults as BOOB and BUFFOON
and OVERBLOWN BLOWHARD and BLIMP
and BLUSTERING BLUBBER and BLOATED BALLOON
and SHATTERBRAIN, SHORTY and SHRIMP.

Then Huffer and Cuffer exchanged mighty blows,
they basted and battered and belted,
they chopped to the neck and they bopped in the nose
and they pounded and pummeled and pelted.

They pinched and they punched and they smacked
        and they whacked
and they rocked and they socked and they smashed,
and they rapped and they slapped and they
        throttled and thwacked
and they thumped and they bumped and they bashed.

They cudgeled each other on top of the head
with swipes of the awfulest sort,
and now they are no longer giants, instead
they both are exceedingly short.

—*Jack Prelutsky*

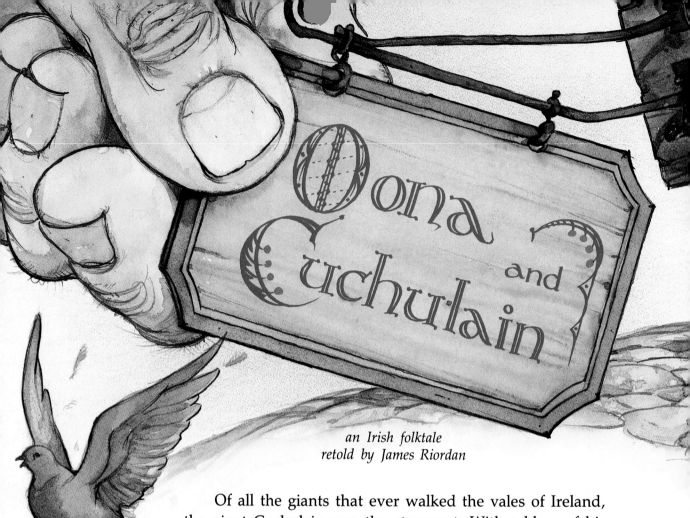

Oona and Cuchulain

*an Irish folktale
retold by James Riordan*

Of all the giants that ever walked the vales of Ireland, the giant Cuchulain was the strongest. With a blow of his mighty fist he could squash a mountain into a cowpat and he went about the land with one such cowpat in his pocket to scare the other giants.

He scared them all right. They tried to keep out of his way, but he hunted them down, one by one, and beat the living daylights out of them; then they scampered off into the mountains to lick their wounds.

There was one giant, though, that Cuchulain had not yet thrashed, and that was Finn Mac Cool. The reason was simple: Finn Mac Cool was so afraid of Cuchulain that he kept well out of his way. He even built his house atop a windy mountain to keep a lookout all about him; and whenever the mighty giant appeared in the distance, Finn was off like a shot from a cannon, hiding in bush or bog or barrow.

But Finn could not keep his foe at bay forever. And Cuchulain had vowed he would not rest until he had flattened the cowardly Finn. Finn knew the day must come. Do you know how? By sucking his thumb—that made all things clear to him.

So there he was, this Finn, sitting outside his house upon the windy mountain, sucking his great thumb. And, oh dear me! Rushing indoors shivering like a jelly, he cried to his wife Oona, "Cuchulain is coming this way. And this time there's no escape; my thumb tells me so!"

"What time is he due?" asks Oona.

Finn sucked his thumb again. "At three o'clock this afternoon. And do you know what he means to do? Squash me flat and carry me in his pocket."

"Now, now, Finn," says Oona, "just leave this to me. Haven't I pulled you from the mire many times before?"

"Indeed you have," said Finn. And he stopped his shivering.

41

In the meantime Oona went down to three friends at the foot of the mountain, and at each house she borrowed an iron griddle. Once home with her three griddles, she baked half a dozen cakes, each as big as a basket; and inside three she put an iron griddle while the dough was soft. Then she placed the cakes in a row upon two shelves, three above, three below, so that she would know which one was which.

At two o'clock she glanced out of the window and spied a speck on the horizon. She guessed it was Cuchulain coming. Straightaway she dressed Finn in nightgown and frilly nightcap, and tucked him into a big wicker cradle.

"Now, Finn," she says, "you'll be your own baby. Lie still and leave all to me. Suck your thumb so as you'll know what I want you to do."

Finn did as he was told.

"Oh, and by the way," she says, "where does that bully of a giant keep all his strength?"

Finn stuck his thumb in his mouth, then said, "His strength is in the middle finger of his right hand. Without that finger he'd be as weak as a baby."

With that they sat waiting for Cuchulain to come.
And it was not long before a giant fist pounded
on the door.

Finn screwed his eyes shut, drew the
blanket up around his nose, and tried to keep
his teeth from chattering. Boldly Oona flung
open the door—and there stood the mighty
Cuchulain.

"Is this the house of Finn Mac Cool?"
asks he.

"It is indeed," says Oona. "Come in and
sit you down."

Cuchulain took a seat and stared about him.

"That's a fine-looking baby you have there, Mrs. Mac
Cool," says he. "Would his father be at home, I wonder?"

"Faith, he's not," says she. "He went tearing down
the mountain a few hours ago, said he was out to catch
some pipsqueak called Cuchulain. Heaven help the poor
man when my Finn lays hands on him; there won't be a
hair or toenail of him left."

"I am Cuchulain himself, Mrs. Mac Cool," says the
visitor. "And I've been on your husband's track this past
year or more. Yet he's always hiding from me. For sure
he can't be so very big and strong?"

"*You* are Cuchulain!" says Oona, scornful-like. "Did
you ever see my Finn?"

"Well, no. How could I? He always gives me the slip."

"Gives you the slip, begorrah!" says she. "Gives you
the thrashing of your life, more likely. I mean you no ills,
Sir, but if you take my advice you'll steer clear of him.
He's as hard as rock and swift as the wind. Which reminds
me: would you do me a favor and turn the house around?
The wind is on the turn."

"*Turn the house around?*" stammered Cuchulain. "Did my ears hear right?"

"For sure," says Oona. "That's what Finn does when the wind's in the east."

Cuchulain stood up and went outside. He crooked the middle finger of his right hand three times, seized the house in his arms and turned it back to front.

When Finn felt the house turn, he pulled the blanket over his head and his teeth chattered all the more.

But Oona just nodded her thanks as if it was quite natural, then asked another favor.

"With all this dry weather we're having," says she, "I'm clean out of water. Can you fill this jug for me?"

"And where will I fill it?" asks Cuchulain.

"Do you see that big rock on top of yonder hill? When we need water Finn lifts that rock and takes water from the spring underneath. Just as soon as you fetch some water I'll put the kettle on and make you a nice cup of tea. You'll need a cup or two if you're to escape the clutches of the mighty Finn."

With a frown, Cuchulain took the jug and walked down the mountain and up yonder hill. When he arrived at the rock, he stood and scratched his head in wonder: it was at least as tall as himself, and twice as wide. He held up his right hand, crooked the middle finger nine times, then took the rock in both brawny arms and heaved. With a mighty effort, he tore the rock out of the ground, and four hundred feet of solid rock below as well. And out gushed a stream that gurgled and roared down the hillside so loudly it made Finn shut his ears with both hands.

"Dear wife," he cried, "if that giant lays his hands on me, he'll crush every bone in my body."

"Wisht, man!" says Oona, "he has to find you first."

And she greeted the jug-bearer with a smile of thanks as he came through the door.

"Thank you kindly," says she. "Now take a seat while I put the kettle on."

As soon as the kettle had boiled and the tea was poured, Oona set three cakes before Cuchulain—those with the iron griddles in.

All that work had made Cuchulain hungry. Smacking his lips, he picked up a cake and took a great bite of it. Oh musha! With a wild yell he spat out the cake and his two front teeth as well.

"What cake is this! It's hard as nails."

"That's Finn's favorite cake," says Oona. "He's mighty partial to it; so is the baby in the cradle. Perhaps it's too hard-baked for a weakling like you. Here, try this one, it's a mite softer than the first."

It certainly smelt appetizing. This time he took an even bigger bite. But, oh musha! Again he spat it out along with two more giant teeth.

"You can keep your cakes," he shouted, "or I'll have no teeth left."

"God bless us!" exclaims Oona. "There's no call to shout so loud and wake the baby up. It's not my fault your jaws are weak."

Now, just at that moment Finn sucked his thumb and guessed at once what Oona wanted him to do. Opening his mouth he let out the greatest, rip-roaring yell he'd ever made.

"Yoowwwlllllllllllllllllll . . . "

"Well, I be jiggered," spluttered Cuchulain, his hair standing on end. "What a pair of tonsils that baby's got! Does it take after its father?"

"When his father gives a shout," says Oona, "you can hear him from here to Timbuctoo!"

Cuchulain began to feel uneasy. Perhaps he was wrong to come in search of Finn Mac Cool. Glancing nervously towards the cradle, he saw the child was sucking his thumb again.

"He'll be crying for some cake any minute now," says Oona. "It's his feeding time."

Just then, Finn began to howl, "CAAA-AAKKE!"

"Put that in your mouth," says she. And she handed Finn a cake from the top shelf.

"How can a baby eat that?" said Cuchulain scornfully.

But in the twinkling of an eye, Finn had eaten every crumb, then roared out again, "CAAA-AAKKE!"

When the baby was well into his third cake, Cuchulain got up to go.

"I'm off now, Mrs. Mac Cool," he says. "If that baby's anything like its dad, Finn'll be more than a match for me. 'Tis a bonnie baby you have, ma'am."

"If you're so fond of babies, come and have a closer look at this one," says she.

And she took Cuchulain by the arm to guide him to the cradle, removing the blanket from Finn as she did so. Thereupon Finn kicked his legs in the air and yelled at the top of his voice.

"By golly, what a pair of legs he has on him!" gasped Cuchulain.

"You ought to have seen his father at that age," says Oona. "Why, he was out in the bogs wrestling with bulls at one year old."

"Is that a fact?" sighed Cuchulain, eager to get away from the house before Finn returned.

"The baby's teeth are coming through well, though," continues Oona. "Have a feel of them."

Thinking to please the woman before making his escape, Cuchulain put his fingers into the baby's mouth to feel its teeth.

And can you guess what happened?

When he pulled his fingers out, there were only four left: his middle finger had been bitten cleanly off.

You could have heard the yell from there to Venezuela!

Now that his strength was gone, the once mighty Cuchulain began to grow smaller and smaller, until he was no bigger than the cake he had bitten into. High above him Oona and Finn Mac Cool laughed and mocked the little man. The tiny figure tottered out of the house and down the mountain, fleeing for his life. And he was never seen again in Ireland.

As for Finn, he was ever grateful for the brains of his dear wife Oona.

Think About It

1. Who won the argument between Huffer and Cuffer?
2. What does Cuchulain have in common with Huffer and Cuffer?
3. If Cuchulain's strength was in the middle finger of his right hand, where was Oona's? How do you know?
4. Summarize Oona's plan to trick Cuchulain.
5. Which would you rather possess, enormous size and strength or clever thinking? Why?

Create and Share Pretend you have been asked to help settle things once and for all between Huffer and Cuffer or between Finn Mac Cool and Cuchulain. What would you say to them? Write a speech to persuade the giants to try your solution. Present your speech to the class.

Explore If you like silly giants, you'll find many more of them in fiction and folklore. Look under GIANTS, FOLKLORE, and TALL TALES in the card catalog to find some. Folktales are listed in alphabetical order, according to the countries they come from. Choose a tale from a part of the world that interests you.

LOOKING INTO THE INVISIBLE

by Tom Schiele

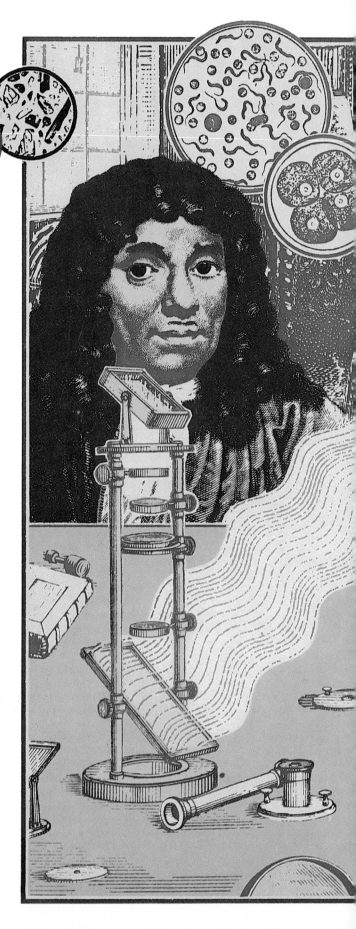

Anton van Leeuwenhoek was an amateur scientist who pioneered the use of the microscope. Although he did not invent the microscope, Leeuwenhoek used it to observe things that no one had ever seen before. Looking deep into the world of microscopic life, he was the first to describe the one-celled animals now known as protozoa, and bacteria, the tiny plants he called little animals.

Leeuwenhoek was born in Delft, Holland, in 1632. He was not a scientist by profession but a successful businessman. He owned a shop where he sold linens, woolens, and other kinds of cloth. Leeuwenhoek's business made him familiar with a simple kind of magnifying glass, called a linen counter, that was used to check the quality of cloth. But looking through a linen counter was just the beginning of Leeuwenhoek's fascination with the microscope.

50

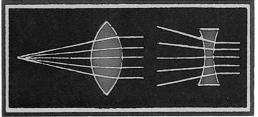

Magnifying lenses had been produced before the 1600s. People had found that a piece of glass curved in a special way would make things look bigger. Leeuwenhoek made his own lenses, over 250 of them during his lifetime, grinding and polishing them by hand. This was painstaking work, but Leeuwenhoek was very skillful. Some of his microscopes have been studied by modern scientists and are still considered excellent instruments, even 300 years after they were made.

Leeuwenhoek used his microscopes to look at everything he could find—parts of insects, hair, skin, muscle fibers, blood, and waters of every type—and continued his study right up to his death at the age of ninety-one. In addition, he made detailed records of his observations. His accurate descriptions and careful drawings set a standard for scientific study. Modern microbiology, the study of tiny plants and animals, owes much to this seventeenth-century Dutch businessman who opened the human eye to the invisible world.

51

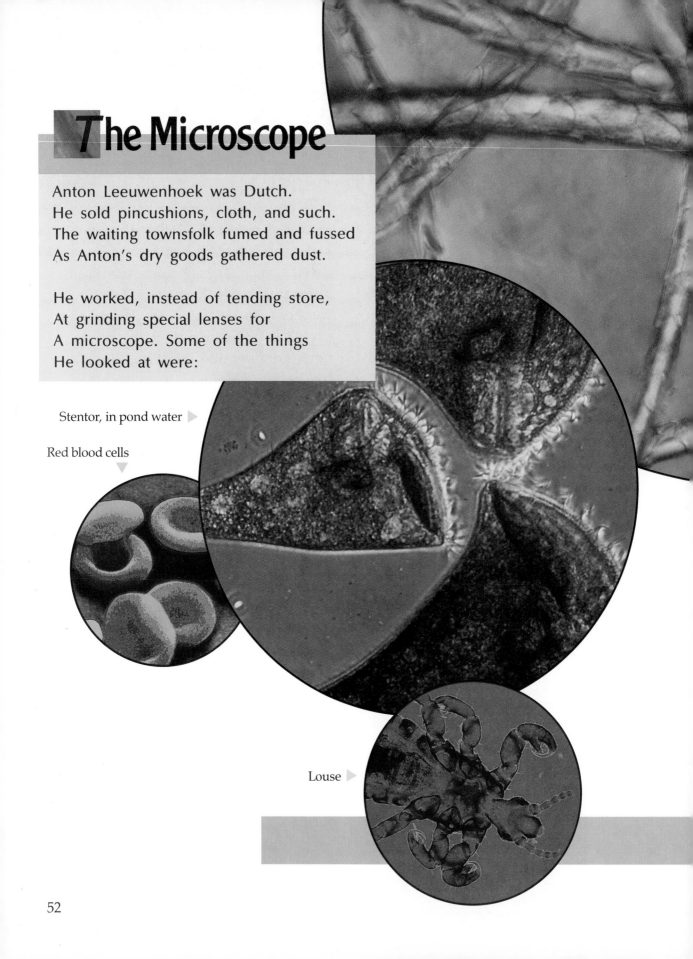

The Microscope

Anton Leeuwenhoek was Dutch.
He sold pincushions, cloth, and such.
The waiting townsfolk fumed and fussed
As Anton's dry goods gathered dust.

He worked, instead of tending store,
At grinding special lenses for
A microscope. Some of the things
He looked at were:

Stentor, in pond water ▷

Red blood cells
▽

Louse ▷

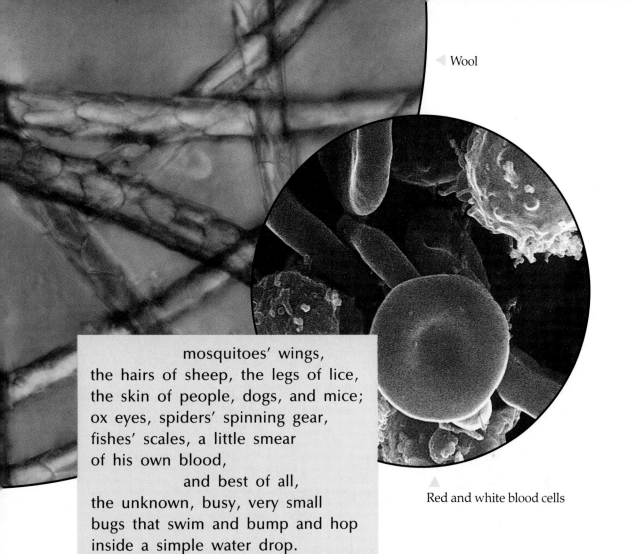

Wool

Red and white blood cells

                mosquitoes' wings,
the hairs of sheep, the legs of lice,
the skin of people, dogs, and mice;
ox eyes, spiders' spinning gear,
fishes' scales, a little smear
of his own blood,
                and best of all,
the unknown, busy, very small
bugs that swim and bump and hop
inside a simple water drop.

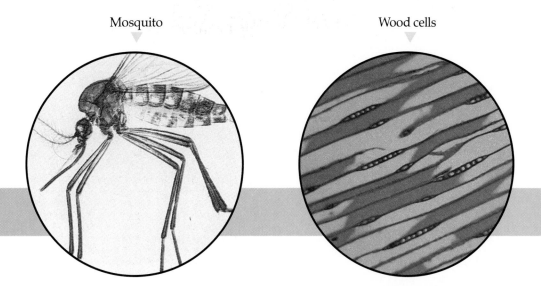

Mosquito

Wood cells

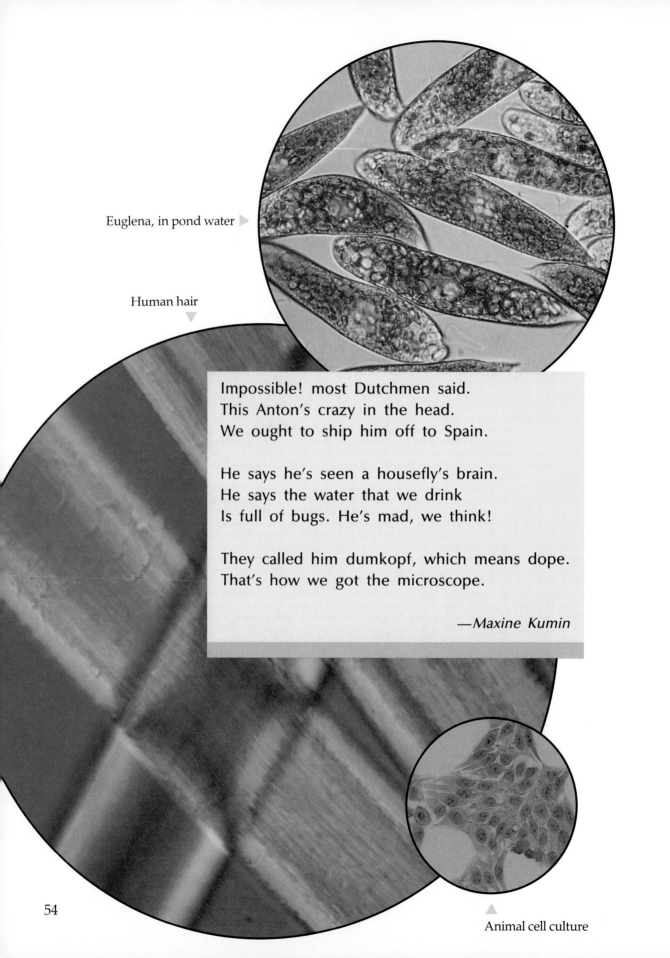

Euglena, in pond water ▶

Human hair ▼

Impossible! most Dutchmen said.
This Anton's crazy in the head.
We ought to ship him off to Spain.

He says he's seen a housefly's brain.
He says the water that we drink
Is full of bugs. He's mad, we think!

They called him dumkopf, which means dope.
That's how we got the microscope.

—*Maxine Kumin*

Animal cell culture ▲

Think About It

1. List four words that describe Anton van Leeuwenhoek's character. Use information from the biography and the poem to explain why each of your words is appropriate.
2. Summarize Van Leeuwenhoek's achievements.
3. Explain why "Looking Into the Invisible" is a good title for the article.
4. What makes the microscope a marvelous machine? Compare and contrast it with Isit and Professor Flybender's machine.

Create and Share   What do the "bugs" in a drop of water look like to you? Choose one of the photographs and study it. Then write a paragraph, describing it as carefully as you can.

Explore   You may want to find out more about Van Leeuwenhoek, or the history of microscopes. Or you may be interested in reading about the tiny living things in the environment. Look in the card catalog under LEEUWENHOEK, MICROSCOPES, and MICROBIOLOGY for books on the man and this topic.

Arrietty's Encounter

from THE BORROWERS
by Mary Norton

Borrowers are small creatures who live in old houses. They take their names from the places they inhabit; the Clocks—Homily, Pod, and their daughter Arrietty—live underneath a huge grandfather clock that stands in the hall. Borrowers live by "borrowing" from human beings; their food, clothing, and furniture is taken in secret from their "hosts." Borrowing is difficult, dangerous work, for a Borrower must never be seen by a human being.

As she followed her father down the passage Arrietty's heart began to beat faster. Now the moment had come at last she found it almost too much to bear. She felt light and trembly, and hollow with excitement.

Pod stood still. "Quietly, now," he warned her. "Yes, that's it: the hole under the clock. There are three steps up to it," he went on, "steep like, so mind how you go. When you're under the clock you just stay there; don't let your mind wander and keep your eyes on me: if all's clear, I'll give you the sign."

The steps were high and a little uneven but Arrietty took them more lightly than Pod. As she scrambled past the jagged edges of the hole she had a sudden blinding glimpse of molten gold: it was spring sunshine on the pale stones of the hall floor. Standing upright, she could no longer see this; she could only see the cave-like shadows in the great case above her and the dim outline of the hanging weights. So this, at last, was The Clock! Their clock . . . after which her family was named!

But Pod, she saw, stood crouched beneath the carved archway against the light: "Keep your eyes on me," he had said, so Arrietty crouched too. She saw the gleaming golden stone floor of the hall stretching away into distance; she saw the edges of rugs, like richly colored islands in a molten sea, and she saw, in a glory of sunlight—like a dreamed-of gateway to fairyland—the open front door. Beyond she saw grass and, against the clear, bright sky, a waving frond of green.

Pod's eyes slewed round. "Wait," he breathed, "and watch." And then in a flash he was gone.

A sudden movement near the shadowed lintel of the front door and there was Pod again, bag in hand, beside the mat; it rose knee deep before him like a field of chestnut corn. Arrietty saw him glance toward the clock and then she saw him raise his hand.

Oh, the warmth of the stone flags as she ran across them . . . the gladdening sunlight on her face and hands . . . the awful space above and around her! Pod caught her and held her at last, and patted her shoulder. "There, there . . . " he said, "get your breath—good girl!"

Panting a little, Arrietty gazed about her. She saw great chair legs rearing up into sunlight; she saw the shadowed undersides of their seats spread above her like canopies; she saw the nails and the strapping and odd tags of silk and string; she saw the terraced cliffs of the stairs, mounting up into the distance, up and up . . . she saw carved table legs and a cavern under the chest. And all the time, in the stillness, the clock spoke—measuring out the seconds, spreading its layers of calm.

And then, turning, Arrietty looked at the garden. She saw a graveled path, full of colored stones—the size of walnuts they were with, here and there, a blade of grass between them, transparent green against the light of the sun. Beyond the path she

saw a grassy bank rising steeply to a tangled hedge; and beyond the hedge she saw fruit trees, bright with blossom.

"Here's a bag," said Pod in a hoarse whisper; "better get down to work."

Obediently Arrietty started pulling fiber; stiff it was and full of dust. Pod worked swiftly and methodically, making small bundles, each of which he put immediately in the bag.

"See here," he exclaimed after a moment, "you leave it! It's your first time up like. You sit on the step there and take a peek out of doors."

"Oh, no—" Arrietty began ("If I don't help," she thought, "he won't want me again") but Pod insisted.

"I'm better on me own," he said. "I can choose me bits, if you see what I mean, seeing as it's me who's got to make the brush."

The step was warm but very steep. "If I got down on to the path," Arrietty thought, "I might not get up again," so for some moments she sat quietly. After a while she noticed the shoe-scraper.

"Arrietty," called Pod softly, "where have you got to?"

"I just climbed down the shoe-scraper," she called back.

He came along and looked down at her from the top of the step. "That's all right," he said after a moment's stare, "but never climb down anything that isn't fixed like. Supposing one of them came along and moved the shoe-scraper—where would you be then? How would you get up again?"

"It's heavy to move," said Arrietty.

"Maybe," said Pod, "but it's moveable. See what I mean? There's rules, my lass, and you got to learn."

"This path," Arrietty said, "goes round the house. And the bank does too."

"Well," said Pod, "what of it?"

"I was thinking," Arrietty went on. "Suppose I just went round the corner."

"Well," he said, "stay down a bit if you like. But stay close!"

Arrietty watched him move away from the step and then she looked about her. Oh, glory! Oh, joy! Oh, freedom! The sunlight, the grasses, the soft, moving air and halfway up the bank, where it curved round the corner, a flowering cherry tree! Below it on the path lay a stain of pinkish petals and, at the tree's foot, pale as butter, a nest of primroses.

Cautiously she moved toward the bank and climbed a little nervously in amongst the green blades of grass. As she parted them gently with her bare hands, drops of water plopped on her skirt and she felt the red shoes become damp. But on she went, pulling herself up now and again by rooty stems into this jungle of moss and wood-violet and creeping leaves of clover. The bank was warm, almost too warm here within the shelter of the tall grass, and the sandy earth smelled dry. She lay back among the stalks of the primroses and they made a coolness between her and the sun, and then, sighing, she turned her head and looked sideways up the bank among the grass stems. Startled, she caught her breath. Something had moved above her on the bank. Something had glittered. Arrietty stared.

It was an eye. Or it looked like an eye. Clear and bright like the color of the sky. An eye like her own but enormous. A glaring eye. Breathless with fear, she sat up. And the eye blinked. A great fringe of lashes came curving down and flew up again out of sight. Cautiously, Arrietty moved her legs: she would slide noiselessly in among the grass stems and slither away down the bank.

"Don't move!" said a voice, and the voice, like the eye, was enormous but, somehow, hushed—and hoarse like a surge of wind through the grating on a stormy night in March.

Arrietty froze. "So this is it," she thought, "the worst and most terrible thing of all: I have been 'seen'!"

There was a pause and Arrietty, her heart pounding in her ears, heard the breath again drawn swiftly into the vast lungs. "Or," said the voice, whispering still, "I shall hit you with my ash stick."

Suddenly Arrietty became calm. "Why?" she asked. How strange her own voice sounded! Crystal thin and harebell clear, it tinkled on the air.

"In case," came the surprised whisper at last, "you ran toward me, quickly, through the grass . . . in case," it went on, trembling a little, "you came and scrabbled at me with your nasty little hands."

Arrietty stared at the eye; she held herself quite still.

"Did you come out of the house?"

"Yes," said Arrietty.

"From whereabouts in the house?"

Arrietty stared at the eye. "I'm not going to tell you," she said at last bravely.

"Then I'll hit you with my ash stick!"

"All right," said Arrietty, "hit me!"

"I'll pick you up and break you in half!"

Arrietty stood up. "All right," she said and took two paces forward.

There was a sharp gasp and an earthquake in the grass; he spun away from her and sat up, a great mountain in a green jersey. He had fair, straight hair and golden eyelashes. "Stay where you are!" he cried.

There was silence while Arrietty waited, trembling a little. The boy stood a moment, as though embarrassed, and then he said: "Can you fly?"

"No," said Arrietty, surprised; "can you?"

His face became even redder. "Of course not," he said angrily; "I'm not a fairy!"

"Well, nor am I," said Arrietty, "nor is anybody. I don't believe in them."

He looked at her strangely. "You don't believe in them?"

"No," said Arrietty; "do you?"

"Of course not!"

Really, she thought, he is a very angry kind of boy. "My mother believes in them," she said, trying to appease him.

"Oh," said the boy. "Are there many people like you?"

"No," said Arrietty. "None. We're all different."

"I mean as small as you?"

Arrietty laughed. "Don't be silly!" she said. "Surely you don't think there are many people in the world your size?"

"There are more my size than yours," he retorted.

"Honestly—" began Arrietty helplessly and laughed again. "Do you really think—I mean, whatever sort of a world would it be? Those great chairs . . . I've seen them. Fancy if you had to make chairs that size for everyone? And the stuff for their clothes . . . miles and miles of it . . . tents of it . . . and the sewing! And their great houses, reaching up so you can hardly see the ceilings . . . their great beds . . . the *food* they eat . . . great, smoking mountains of it, huge bogs of stew and soup and stuff."

"Don't you eat soup?" asked the boy.

"Of course we do," laughed Arrietty. "My father had an uncle who had a little boat which he rowed round in the stock-pot picking up flotsam and jetsam. Once he was nearly shipwrecked on a chunk of submerged shinbone. He lost his oars and the boat sprang a leak but he flung  a line over the pot handle and pulled himself alongside the rim. But all that stock— fathoms of it! And the size of the stock-pot! I mean, there wouldn't be enough stuff in the world to go round after a bit! That's why my father says it's a good thing they're dying out . . . just a few, he says, that's all we need—to keep us. Otherwise,

he says, the whole thing gets"—Arrietty hesitated, trying to remember the word—"exaggerated, he says—"

"What do you mean," asked the boy, " 'to keep us'?"

So Arrietty told him about borrowing—how difficult
it was and how dangerous. She told him about the store-
rooms under the floor; about Pod's early exploits, the skill
he had shown and the courage.

The boy sat thoughtfully on his haunches, chewing a
blade of grass. "Borrowing," he said after a while. "Is that
what you call it?"

"What else could you call it?" asked Arrietty.

"I'd call it stealing."

Arrietty burst out laughing; she laughed so much that
she had to hide her face in the primrose. "Oh dear," she
gasped with tears in her eyes, "you are funny!" She stared
upward at his puzzled face. "Human beans are *for* Borrowers—like bread's for butter!"

The boy was silent for a while. A sigh of wind rustled
the cherry tree and shivered among the blossoms.

"Well, I don't believe it," he said at last, watching the
falling petals. "I don't believe that's what we're for at all
and I don't believe we're dying out!"

"Oh, goodness!" exclaimed Arrietty impatiently, staring
up at his chin. "Just use your common sense: you're the
only real human bean I ever saw (although I do just know
of three more). But I know lots and lots of Borrowers."

He leaned forward, his fair head blocking out a great
piece of sky. "Well," he said deliberately after a moment,
and his eyes were cold, "I've only seen two Borrowers but
I've seen hundreds and hundreds and hundreds and
hundreds and hundreds—"

"Oh no—" whispered Arrietty.

"Of human beings." And he sat back.

Arrietty stood very still. She did not look at him. After
a while she said: "I don't believe you."

"All right," he said, "then I'll tell you—"

"I still won't believe you," murmured Arrietty.

"Listen!" he said. And he told her about railway stations and football matches and race courses and royal processions. "Not hundreds," he said, "but thousands and millions and billions and trillions of great, big, enormous people. Now do you believe me?"

Arrietty stared up at him with frightened eyes; it gave her a crick in the neck. "I don't know," she whispered.

"As for you," he went on, leaning closer again, "I don't believe that there are any more Borrowers anywhere in the world. I believe you're the last three," he said.

Arrietty dropped her face into the primrose. "We're not. There's Aunt Lupy and Uncle Hendreary and all the cousins."

"I bet they're dead," said the boy. "And what's more," he went on, "no one will ever believe I've seen *you*. And you'll be the very last because you're the youngest. One day," he told her, smiling triumphantly, "you'll be the only Borrower left in the world!"

He sat still, waiting, but she did not look up. "Now you're crying," he remarked after a moment.

"They're not dead," said Arrietty in a muffled voice; she was feeling in her little pocket for a handkerchief. "They live in a badger's set two fields away, beyond the spinney. We don't see them because it's too far. There are weasels and things and cows and foxes . . . and crows . . ."

"Which spinney?" he asked.

"I don't know!" Arrietty almost shouted. "It's along by the gas-pipe—a field called Parkin's Beck." She blew her nose. "I'm going home," she said.

"Don't go," he said, "not yet."

"Yes, I'm going," said Arrietty.

"Listen," he said, "I'll go to that field. I'll go and find Uncle Hendreary. And the cousins. And Aunt Whatever-she-is. And, if they're alive, I'll tell you. What about that?

You could write them a letter and I'd put it down the hole—"

Arrietty gazed up at him. "Would you?" she breathed.

"Yes, I would. Really I would."

"All right," said Arrietty absently. Her eyes were shining. "When can I give you the letter?"

"Any time," he said, standing above her. "Where in the house do you live?"

"Well—" began Arrietty and stopped. Why once again did she feel this chill? Could it only be his shadow . . . towering above her, blotting out the sun? "I'll put it somewhere," she said hurriedly. "I'll put it under the hall mat."

"Which one? The one by the front door?"

"Yes, that one."

He was gone. And she stood there alone in the sunshine, shoulder deep in grass. What had happened seemed too big for thought; she felt unable to believe it really had happened: not only had she been talked to but she had—

"Arrietty!" said a voice.

She stood up startled and spun round: there was Pod, moon-faced, on the path looking up at her. "Come on down!" he whispered.

She stared at him for a moment as though she did not recognize him; how round his face was, how kind, how familiar!

"Come on!" he said again, more urgently; and obediently because he sounded worried, she slithered quickly toward him off the bank, balancing her primrose. "Put that

thing down," he said sharply, when she stood at last beside him on the path. "You can't lug great flowers about—you got to carry a bag. What you want to go up there for?" he grumbled as they moved off across the stones. "I might never have seen you. Hurry up now. Your mother'll have tea waiting!"

Small, Smaller

I thought that I knew all there was to know
Of being small, until I saw once, black against the snow,
A shrew, trapped in my footprint, jump and fall
And jump again and fall, the hole too deep, the walls too tall.

—*Russell Hoban*

Think About It

1. Describe Arrietty's and the boy's reactions when they first saw each other.
2. What do Arrietty and the boy argue about? Summarize both sides of the argument.
3. What happens in the story to suggest that a friendship might develop between Arrietty and the boy? What problems might this friendship cause?
4. Summarize the sequence of events that must have led up to the encounter between the shrew and the narrator in "Small, Smaller."
5. Explain how size influences the characters and events in the selections in SIZING IT UP.

Create and Share   You have become as small as a Borrower! Think about what might happen. How would the people at home and at school react? What problems would you have? What advantages would there be to being so small? Write a story about a day in your life as a Borrower.

Explore   You may want to read more about the Borrowers. Mary Norton has written several books about them. Or see TROLLS—FICTION and FAIRIES—FICTION in the card catalog for books about other small imaginary creatures. To find books about real animals that are very small, look under the name of the animal that interests you, such as MICE, SHREWS, or VOLES.

Wind now commences to sing;
Wind now commences to sing.
The land stretches before me,
Before me stretches away.

Wind's house now is thundering.
Wind's house now is thundering,

I go roaring over the land,
The land covered with thunder.

The Black Snake Wind came to me,
The Black Snake Wind came to me,
Came and wrapped itself around me,
Came here running with its songs.

from a Pima poem

Storm Warning

The Storm Cellar

from THE PRICE OF FREE LAND
by *Treva Adams Strait*

One day, our neighbors stopped by to introduce themselves. They were Kenneth and Mary Patterson.

"I'm glad to meet you," Mamma said. "It makes me feel better to have close neighbors. I've lived most of my life in the city. I like to have people around."

"Kenneth thinks we should try to own some land," Mrs. Patterson said, "and this is practically free. But I really don't like the idea at all. I'd rather live in town. We'll be spending part of each week there."

"You'll be here only part of the time?" Mamma asked.

"We have to stay here four nights of each week, if we are to claim that we have established a home. I sure couldn't stay here all the time like you do."

"This is our home," Mamma said, as she pushed Dorothy's buggy back and forth. "I'm glad you stopped to say hello. It gets pretty lonely here."

From then on, the Pattersons stopped a few minutes to chat whenever they were going by.

A couple of evenings after we'd settled on the home-stead, Papa said, "I must get started on that cellar. We never know when there'll be a big storm."

He rose and swung Dorothy astride his shoulders. He strolled across the prairie a few yards with all of us following. "We'll put it over here. That will make it about twenty feet east of where we'll build our house."

"How big will it be?" Howard asked.

"It has to be deep enough for me to stand erect in, and big enough for all of us to get into in case of a tornado or a bad windstorm."

"And big enough for shelves to store a lot of things that are now piled in the kitchen," Mamma added.

"I'll make it about ten by twelve feet, and seven feet deep. If I make it too big I'll never get it dug."

Papa stepped off the outline of the cellar, and Howard laid two-by-fours along the outline to show its shape. "We'll put the opening toward the tent," Papa said, and marked the location of the steps with his shovel.

Howard helped Papa start removing the prairie grass and the top layer of soil from the area inside the two-by-fours. Papa cut the sod loose and Howard carried it away.

"That's enough for tonight," Papa said after a while. He patted Howard's shoulder. "That's a good beginning."

Each evening after supper, Papa and Howard worked on the cellar, and the hole grew deeper and wider. To be sure the sides would be straight up and down, they made a plumb line. One end of a six-foot length of string was fastened to a two-by-four at the edge of the cellar wall. Papa tied a screwdriver to the other end to make it taut. When the string hung from the two-by-four, it was plumb—straight up and down.

It took about a week to finish the digging. Then Papa covered the hole with planks and shoveled dirt over them. The dirt on top was piled into a dome shape, so that water would run off when it rained. Papa made a ventilation hole in the center and ran a short length of stovepipe through it. Finally, he nailed twelve-inch boards together to make the door that covered the entrance.

"We'll feel much safer now," Papa said as he sat in his rocker admiring the first permanent structure on the homestead. "We'll put a kerosene lantern and a box of matches on the top shelf so they will be there in case we need them. I'll try to get the shelves made before the week is over."

When the four shelves were finished, Mamma carried all the glass jars that were filled with fruit to the cellar. Papa had bought milk and butter from a nearby farmer, and Mamma put them in the cellar too. She said, "We'll keep the vegetables in one corner . . . I must remember to save enough room for all of us to get in here if necessary. I sure hope that never happens."

It was the last Friday in August when the tornado came. We were gathering cow chips on the prairie. As Mamma lifted the third sack of chips into the buggy, we saw a funnel-shaped cloud in the west. It was moving rapidly toward us, its tail on the ground.

"A tornado!" Mamma gasped. "Howard, Treva, run!" She pulled up her long skirt and began to run, carrying Dorothy.

The atmosphere was very still. It was eerie—we felt as though there was no air to breathe. As we ran for the tents, the wind began to blow. Soon it was so strong we were fighting for each step.

Mamma took Dorothy into the cellar. Then we three unrolled the sides of the tents and tied them down firmly as the dust whirled about us.

As I started toward the cellar, the wind swept me off my feet, but Howard helped me up. We climbed down into the cellar. The open door of the cellar lay flat on the ground, and when Mamma tried to lift it, it wouldn't budge. The wind held it firmly in place. "Give me strength," she prayed. Twice the wind jerked the door from her grasp, but the third time, with a mighty tug, she pulled it up. Quickly she stepped inside on the stairs and pulled the door down over the opening.

We all sat silently on the floor of the cellar, listening to the howl of the wind and the sound of loose objects rolling by outside. Through the ventilation hole we could see the clouds tumbling about.

"Mamma, will the wind take the tents?" I whispered.

"I don't know," she answered softy and slowly.

As suddenly as the storm had come, it was gone. We could hear nothing. The tiny spot of sky we could see through the hole was blue again.

"It's over," Mamma said as she rose to her feet. "Your father was right when he decided we needed a storm cellar." She went up the stairs and lifted the door. Howard followed, carrying Dorothy, and I came last.

"It's here! It's still here!" Mamma said as she looked at our home. Her eyes were filled with tears.

"And we've still got the backhouse," said Howard. "But where's my wagon? Mamma, look at the woodpile! It's scattered all over. And the boiler is way over there."

Four of the hens were sitting near the boiler. Two had broken legs. The other two were dead. We put all four into the boiler and carried them home.

Mamma stepped on the heads of the two dead hens one at a time. She gave a quick jerk and the blood flowed freely as the heads came off.

"As long as the blood hasn't set, they'll be all right to eat," she told us. "I'll start the fire and get some water hot right away so we can pluck them. Now let's see those other hens."

"Can you fix their legs like a doctor?" Howard asked.
"I'll try."

She fastened a little stick to each broken leg with a narrow strip of cloth. "We'll have to bring them their water and feed until their legs mend."

We were watching them try to move about when Howard exclaimed, "Mamma, look! The Pattersons' house is gone!"

Howard was right. The small frame house was gone. Its pieces were scattered over the prairie.

"And this is their day to come back from town," said Mamma. "What a terrible sight to come back to! And these tents stood, while a frame house was torn apart. I just can't understand it."

Everything in our tents was gray with dust. After Mamma started the fire, we took up the sacks that covered the floor and carried them outdoors. We shook each one and carefully relaid it. Mamma hung her big bedspread on the clothes line and beat it with the broom. I took a cloth and pushed the dust from the chairs and table into a bucket. Mamma removed the rest of the dust with a damp cloth.

"Tomorrow I'll have to take all the dishes from the china cupboard and wash them," she said. "All we can do today is get this place clean enough for us to sleep in."

About four o'clock the Pattersons' buggy stopped near our tents. Mamma told them about the storm.

"We lived here less than two weeks. Now we're wiped out," Kenneth Patterson said. He turned to his wife. "It looks as though your wish has come true."

"I didn't like it here, but I didn't want it to end like this," she said. "You worked so hard to build our little house."

"Thank goodness we weren't here today," he said. He put a comforting arm around her as they drove on toward the place where their house had been.

Later the Pattersons stopped at our tents again. They were on their way back to town. "For some unknown reason I've had a feeling this wasn't going to be our home," said Kenneth. "This settled it."

"Then you aren't going to rebuild?" Mamma asked.

"Nope. The homestead is all yours as far as we're concerned. We're going back to Lincoln, where Mary's parents live."

"Mrs. Adams, I hate to say good-bye to you. You're a wonderful person. I wish I had your optimism," Mary said as she reached over the side of the buggy to shake Mamma's hand.

"I'll miss you so much. You were wonderful neighbors," Mamma said, and wiped her eyes.

It was nearly six before we saw Papa and Betsy coming from work. Howard and I ran to meet him and tell him about the tornado.

"I hear it was quite a day," Papa said to Mamma when we all got home.

Mamma smiled at him as she said, "I've decided that if we can live through a tornado, we can live through anything."

"From what the children have told me, I've decided you're stronger than a tornado," said Papa.

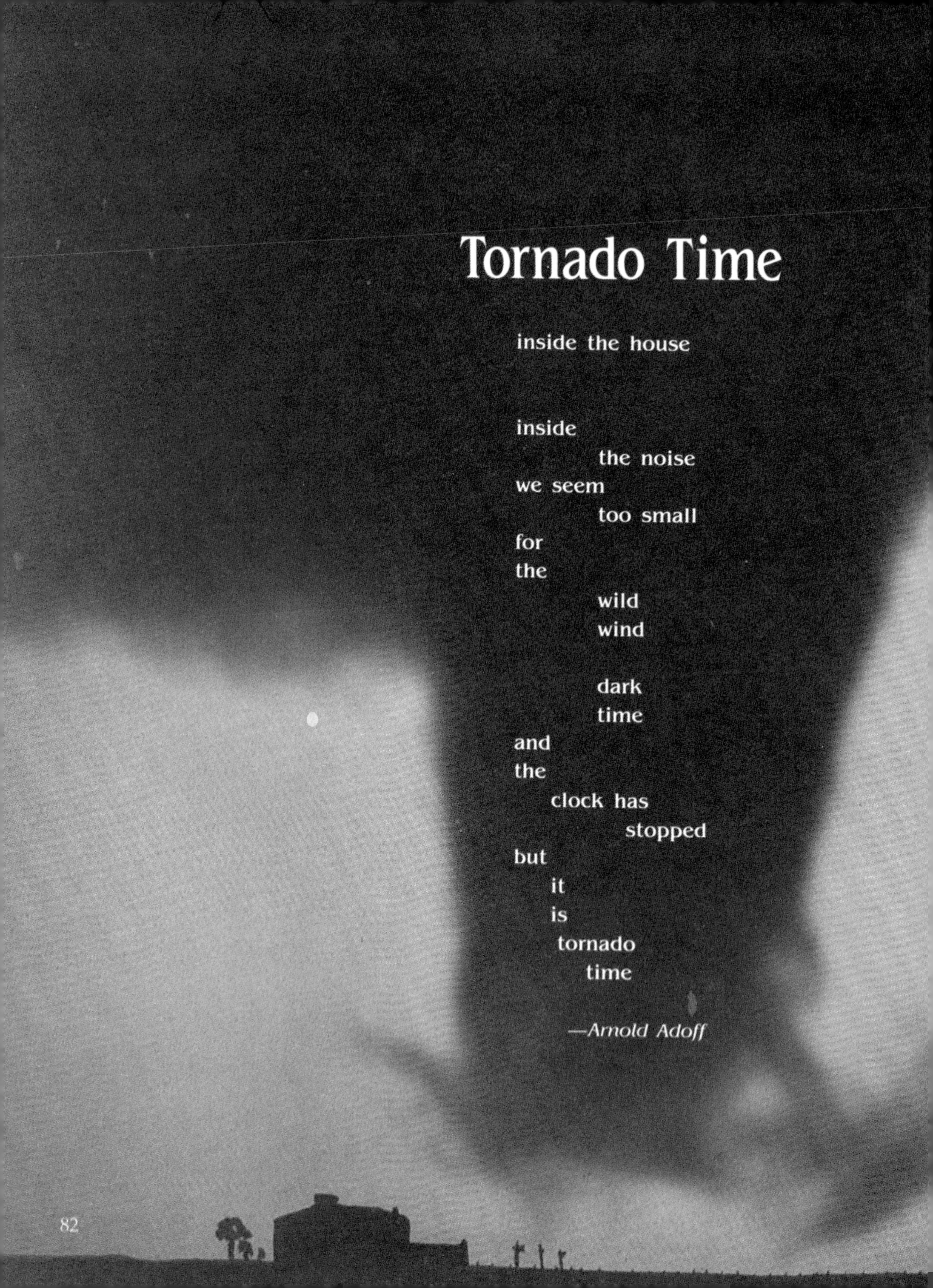

Tornado Time

inside the house

inside
       the noise
we seem
       too small
for
the
      wild
      wind

      dark
      time
and
the
     clock has
        stopped
but
   it
   is
   tornado
    time

—Arnold Adoff

Think About It

1. How could storms affect people's lives on the prairie?
2. How did Papa and Mamma prepare the family for an emergency and thus prevent a disaster?
3. In what ways would you say that Mamma showed herself to be "stronger than a tornado"?
4. What qualities do you think homesteaders needed in order to survive the struggles on the prairie?
5. Do you think the people in the story and the poem felt the same way during the tornado? Find details from each to support your opinion.

Create and Share   Have you ever been caught in a great storm or a tornado? Explain what happened or use your imagination to describe what might have happened. Write a paragraph that describes your feelings and actions.

Explore   Many good books tell about storms. Some are fictional and others are factual. Perhaps the most well-known fictional tornado occurs in *The Wizard of Oz*, by Frank Baum. You might also enjoy Arnold Adoff's book of poems, *Tornado!* Look in the card catalog under STORMS, TORNADOES, HURRICANES, and BLIZZARDS for other books on violent weather.

Each day millions of tons of water evaporate into the air. Lakes, streams, and oceans send up a steady stream of water vapor. A huge amount of water is given off by the leaves of green plants. As the moist air rises, it slowly cools and condenses, forming clouds.

WEATHER EYE

cirrocumulus

cirrostratus

altocumulus

stratocumulus

stratus

Clouds: The name of a cloud describes both its appearance and its height above the ground. There are two basic types: **cumulus,** which are piled up and puffy, and **stratus,** which form in sheets or layers.

cirrus

cumulonimbus

thunderhead

cumulus congestus

Storms: Storms are the most dramatic and dangerous of all weather events. Thunderstorms are caused by violent vertical movements of air. Lightning is caused by the attraction of unlike electrical charges within a thundercloud, or between it and the earth.

cumulonimbus cloud

vertical updraft

tornado funnel

Tornados: Tornados are violent whirlpools of air. The funnel dips down from cloud to ground, becoming visible as moist air is pulled into the area, and as the vortex of the storm sucks in debris from the ground.

86

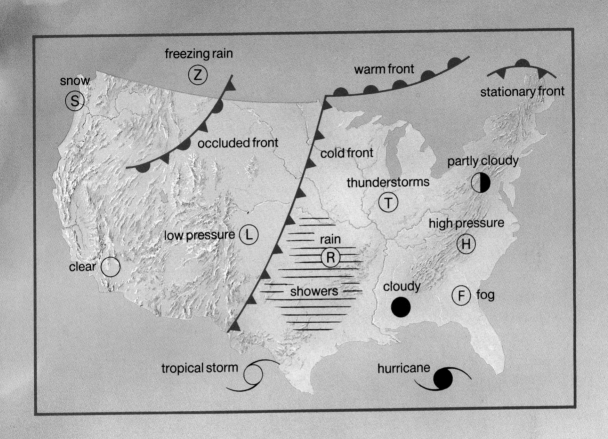

snow
(S)

freezing rain
(Z)

warm front

stationary front

occluded front

cold front

partly cloudy

thunderstorms
(T)

high pressure
(H)

low pressure (L)

rain
(R)

clear ( )

showers

cloudy

(F) fog

tropical storm

hurricane

Weather Map: This weather map displays conditions over a broad area. Charts like this are analyzed by the experts who prepare forecasts and weather bulletins.

Weather Lore

from A JANUARY FOG WILL FREEZE A HOG
compiled and edited by Hubert Davis

A long time ago, people didn't have radios, television sets, newspapers, or meteorologists to give them the weather forecast. When they wanted to find out about the weather, they looked carefully for signs that would show them how the weather was going to change. They noticed the color of the sky and the shapes of the clouds; they remembered when rainbows had appeared when the weather changed and how the sun and the moon looked before and after a thunderstorm or a snowfall. They also looked to see how animals behaved as the weather and the seasons changed. Then they made up simple little verses about what they observed. The verses they made were usually short and easy to remember. Some of them were just fun and nonsense, but many accurately gauged the environmental signs that help weather forecasters make their forecasts today.

Some of the people who came to the New World a long time ago settled in Canada, some in New England, and others scattered throughout the rest of the United States. They brought with them weather rhymes their grandparents had made up. But since the weather is different in different regions of the world, they made up new rhymes of their own and changed some of the older ones to fit the different climate, plant, and animal life that they encountered in America.

When sheep gather in a huddle,
Tomorrow we'll have a puddle.

Sheep are sensitive to small, telltale changes in the weather, because their wool traps air as insulation. Sheep huddle to keep warm, so may foretell the coming of cool air and rain. Found in the South and in New England; a good weather indicator.

When clouds look like black smoke,
A wise man will put on his cloak.

This describes several cloud patterns which may produce rain or snow. Flat, gray, altostratus clouds which form in one or more layers, may cause rain or snow. When altostratus clouds thicken and drift lower, they form the dark, heavy, ragged nimbostratus clouds from which continuous rain or snow falls. Cumulus clouds may build up to a towering cumulonimbus formation, bringing a thunderstorm. Found in Virginia, North Carolina, Kentucky, Scotland, and in parts of England; a very reliable weather forecaster.

When the cow scratches her ear
It means a shower is near;
But when she thumps her ribs with her tail
Expect thunder, lightning, and hail.

The hairs inside a cow's ear respond to the changes that come before rain (low atmospheric pressure and increased humidity) and may cause her to scratch. Before a violent thunderstorm, static charges of electricity can cause a cow's hair to stand out. To relieve this discomfort, a cow may continuously brush herself with her tail. Found generally in the South, Scotland, and England; a fair predictor of weather.

The owls hoot, peacocks toot,
The ducks quack, frogs yak—
'Twill rain.
The loons call, swallows fall,
Chickens hover, groundhogs take cover—
'Twill rain.

Most animals are more sensitive than we are to changes in the pressure, temperature, and humidity of the air. Some changes in the weather, such as the low pressure and increased humidity before a storm, may make animals uncomfortable, restless, and noisy. Their behavior tells us that the weather is soon to change. Found in Virginia, Kentucky, England, and Scotland; a reliable indicator that weather will change.

A circle around the moon,
'Twill rain soon.

The high, feathery, diffuse clouds that create haloes around the moon (and the sun) are cirrostratus clouds, made entirely of ice crystals. Ice crystals refract light differently from water droplets and thus give rise to the circles mentioned here, in some places also known as a "Cock's Eye." While these clouds themselves do not cause precipitation, they are frequently the first stages of an approaching storm and may themselves become more water-laden clouds at a lower altitude. Found in Virginia, North Carolina, throughout the U.S., and Scotland; a reliable indicator of stormy weather approaching.

Rainbow in the morning,
Shepherds take warning.
Rainbow at night,
Shepherds' delight.

When rain clouds filled with moisture are in the west and the morning sun shines on them from the east, a rainbow is created. The water droplets in the clouds scatter the sunlight, causing the colors of the spectrum to show. Although storms arise and travel in different patterns, many of our storms move from west to east, so a shepherd (or anyone observing such a rainbow) might expect rain when the clouds reached him. In the evening, when the setting sun shines on rain clouds in the east and makes a rainbow, this indicates that the clouds have already passed overhead and there will be no rain. Found generally throughout the United States; a reliable weather indicator.

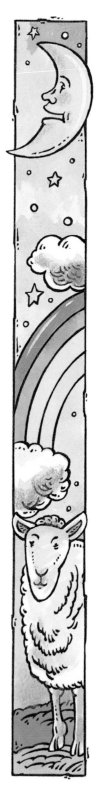

Think About It

1. How did the diagram of the tornado help you to understand what happened in "The Storm Cellar"?
2. Are the details in "Weather Lore" facts or opinions or a combination of the two? Give some examples, using information from the selection.
3. Why do people need to know what the weather is going to be or how weather conditions are changing?
4. Do you think scientific weather forecasting would have changed the way Treva's family prepared for a storm?
5. You have read a poem, a story, a scientific explanation, and folklore about weather. What special view does each type of writing offer you?

Create and Share   Make a chart showing how weather influences your own life. Think about seasonal changes as well as day-to-day changes. Show the effect weather has on your clothing and your activities.

Explore   You may want to find out more about meteorology and the instruments used to measure and predict weather. Look in the library card catalog under METEOROLOGY for books on the subject.

Twister

from DO BANANAS CHEW GUM?
by Jamie Gilson

Sam is planning a busy afternoon. First there's the dentist, and then his baby-sitting job. But a tornado tears into town and turns everything upside down.

Wednesday afternoon I ran all the way from school just to sit and wait in Dr. Reynolds' office. He was supposed to see me at three, but it was already three-ten on the tooth-shaped clock behind the receptionist. Alex and Chuck would be home soon. I had told their mother, Mrs. Glass, that I would join the kids at their house by 3:30 at the latest.

"Am I next?" I asked the receptionist.

"You are," she said brightly, "but 'next' isn't for a while."

I grabbed a *Seventeen*, sat down on the bench, took a pencil out of my pocket, and started erasing the eyes from the models in shampoo ads. It made them look like zombies. If you erase very, very carefully, it looks like the eyes are *supposed* to be blank. With totally white eyes, this glurpy girl looked like the walking dead. Turning the pencil around, I drew her eyeballs back in—black dots staring in opposite directions. It was a masterpiece. I felt wonderful. Best art I'd ever done. Holding the picture out, I smiled at it with pure pleasure.

I was still rubbing away, almost to the back of the magazine, when the hall door opened and a kid walked into the waiting room. He lifted the magazine out of my hand and sat down next to me, running his fingers through his curly red hair and showering me with water.

"Hey, Tinsel Teeth," he said, "I thought you sat on babies after school today." Wally's yellow slicker drooled water on the bench, the rug, the magazine, and me. "It's raining like crazy out there. Again!"

"What are you doing here?" I asked him, grabbing the wet magazine back.

Wally took the pencil from me and drew lines like wires across the crazy-eyed model's teeth. He stood up, hung his coat on a hook, and shook his head like a dog does to dry itself. "Listen," he whispered as he sat down on the wet puddle his coat had made. "I'm getting my dumb retainer today."

"Sam," the dental assistant called, and I jumped.

The minute I sat down in the green reclining chair I thought about calling Chuck and Alex. It was black as night outside and raining like mad. Maybe the kids were scared.

"I've got to get out of here fast," I told the dental assistant as she clamped the pink paper bib around my neck. She left just as Dr. Reynolds came in.

"Shall we just tighten these up a bit?" he asked, tilting the chair back and picking up the mirror. He flipped the light on and tipped it down from my eyes to my mouth. Moving in fast, he unfastened the wires, drew them out, snipped three new lengths of shiny wire from a big wooden spool, and then threaded them zip-zap through the holes. The ends of the wires stuck way out—about three inches—on both sides of my mouth. I felt like a wire-whiskered cat.

"Telephone, Doctor," the receptionist called. "Can you take it?"

"Sure," Dr. Reynolds said, patting me on the shoulders. "It's all right with you, isn't it, young man?"

"Og," I said, my mouth filling up with saliva.

I wondered what it would be like if Dr. Reynolds by mistake laced my top and bottom teeth together. I put my hands up to feel the edges of my antennas, and hissed like a black-eyebrowed panther.

The dental assistant breezed in and over to the window. "Well, would you look at that sky!" she said, and I looked. Even with the bright light in my eyes I could see it wasn't just plain dark anymore. It was weird dark—a yellow-green like split pea soup. "I don't like the way that looks at all," she said, hurrying out.

I could see into another office across the street where the lights were on and two women stood at the window pointing up at the strange sky. The linden trees that grew out of round holes in the sidewalk were whipping around in circles. Hailstones began to pelt the windows like BBs.

Alex and Chuck are scared, I thought, squirming around in the chair. I should have waited at school and brought them to the office with me.

"*Wowooooooowooooooowooooooowooooooo,*" the sirens outside began to howl over the wind.

"Oh, darn," the dental assistant sighed, coming in again to check the sky. "Tornado warning. Just when we're running so far behind. I always feel like such a fool," she said, "hiding in the hall when those things go off. It's one chance in a million a tornado would hit. Maybe a billion. Well, we better move it."

"*Wowooooooowooooooowooooooowooooooowooooooo,*" the siren blasted again. A dark cloud dipped down from the pea-green sky and a thin gray film broke away and swirled off toward the north. I leaned forward to see the trees across the street bend low. The window shivered like it was as scared as me. I leaped out of the chair, wires flapping, and ran like crazy for the hall.

"*Wowooooooowooooooowooooooowooooooo,*" the sound of the siren outside followed me.

The small gray sirens on the hall ceiling looked like toy horns, but they blasted like trumpets. "*Wahwahwah-wahwahwahwah!*" People rushed out of all the doctors' offices along the hall, holding their ears, not sure what to do or where to go.

"Sit on the floor," Wally yelled, but nobody listened.

"What's it about?" a little kid asked Wally.

"Tornado warning," he shouted back, pulling the kid down, "like at school."

I was huddled in a small knot across from them and I could see the little boy was scared. His face was the color of concrete. "It'll be all right," I shouted to him. He looked up to say something, but his eyes opened wide. He caught his breath and coughed back a laugh. Shaking his head, he grabbed Wally's arm and pointed at my mouth. My pink bib was tucked over my knees and my wires were bent up into a curly moustache. Wally laughed so hard he couldn't stop.

"Sam," he howled, cupping his hands around his mouth, "you look straight out of space."

"*Wahwowahwowahwow!*" the siren outside echoed the blasts from the ones in the hall. It did feel like we were in a spaceship, waiting for the bad guys to explode us. If we had been on TV, it would have been time for the commercial. I grabbed my knees tighter and made a face at the little kid.

Suddenly the lights went out. And the hall sirens stopped. The dark was all at once, but the sound wound down slowly to a thin shriek. Everyone sat quiet and scared, taking deep breaths of the medicine air that doctors' and dentists' offices always smell like. Outside we could hear the wind roar like a train rushing through a tunnel—and then, from Dr. Reynolds' office, we heard the crash of glass.

We sat quiet, just feeling our hearts beat for maybe five minutes. I imagined that my house had been blown away and that Alex and Chuck had gone running outside and been blasted away up into the sky because I wasn't there to hide them. My hands were sweating and my ears felt like they were going to explode. I had to yawn to make them stop vibrating.

It was still dark in the hall when the all-clear sounded outside. Everybody scrambled up, feeling their way down the rough stucco walls of the hall and back into offices where there were windows. I was afraid I'd knock somebody down if I ran, so I crawled to the end of the hall where the steps were and skidded down them like a seal at the zoo.

I guess everybody else wanted to be super safe because I was the first one outside. There weren't any buildings down, but the street was a bathtub of water and the windows of the travel agency next door had blown in.

I ran like a rocket toward the Glasses' house. Branches were scattered everywhere like pick-up sticks. The telephone in front of the grocery store was swinging back and forth off its hook. Up ahead a light pole tilted, though the wind

had died down and nothing was blowing it. I ran fast,
panicked about the kids.

"Hey, son, watch it," somebody shouted. I turned to
see the pole bending down closer to the ground, aiming
itself at me.

"Over here!" It was a policeman, his car up to its
hubcaps in water. As I dashed toward the squad car I could
hear a long low crack, and when I looked again I saw the
pole scrunch the top of a parked car, blocking the street.
A shower of sparks flew up like fireworks. I turned to run
again and tripped over the lid of a trash can that had blown
like a flying saucer into the middle of the sidewalk. It sent
me sailing, too. The concrete sandpapered the skin off my
hands. My pants and shirt were soaked.

"You OK?" the policeman in the squad car yelled. I
shrugged my shoulders.

"How bad is it?" I asked him.

"Dunno. Two funnels dropped down. Some damage
over on Euclid Avenue, I hear. More wires down over there,
too. Stay away from Euclid now, and go right home."

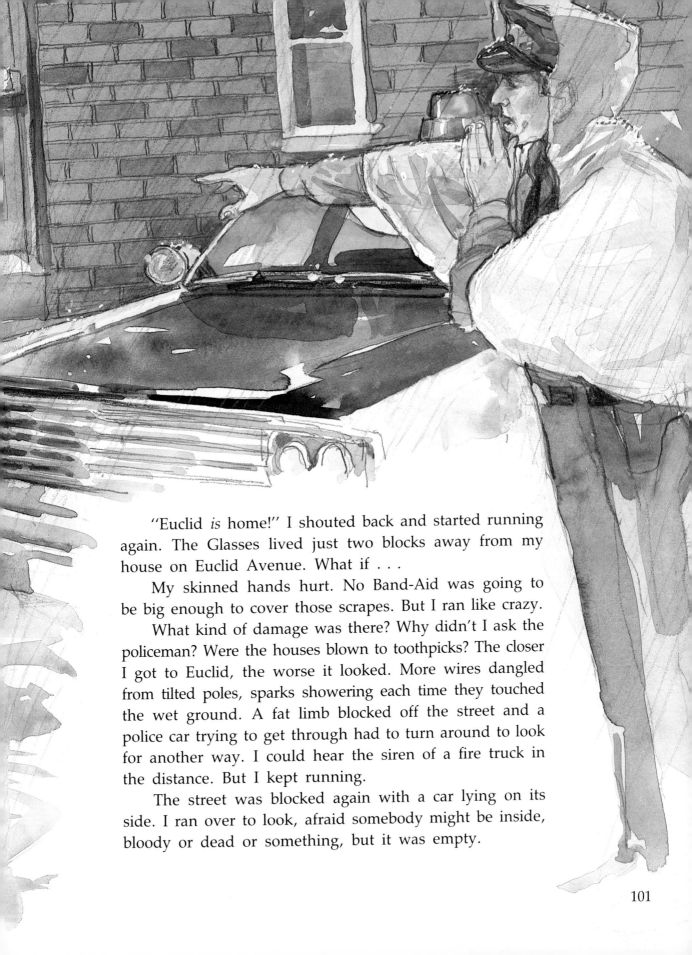

"Euclid *is* home!" I shouted back and started running again. The Glasses lived just two blocks away from my house on Euclid Avenue. What if . . .

My skinned hands hurt. No Band-Aid was going to be big enough to cover those scrapes. But I ran like crazy.

What kind of damage was there? Why didn't I ask the policeman? Were the houses blown to toothpicks? The closer I got to Euclid, the worse it looked. More wires dangled from tilted poles, sparks showering each time they touched the wet ground. A fat limb blocked off the street and a police car trying to get through had to turn around to look for another way. I could hear the siren of a fire truck in the distance. But I kept running.

The street was blocked again with a car lying on its side. I ran over to look, afraid somebody might be inside, bloody or dead or something, but it was empty.

101

An old guy with a cane came out on his front porch. "Is it safe now?" he shouted, waving his cane at me. I didn't have any breath to call back so I nodded my head yes. After I passed him, I thought, You stoop, that's a lie. All those wires down. It's not half safe. Stuff had been scattered around near Dr. Reynolds' office, but nothing like my street. It looked like it had been caught in a blender. A big pine tree was blown over, a smashed-up doll carriage in its branches like a Christmas tree decoration.

My house was still standing, but the chimney had fallen off. Bricks littered the yard. I didn't stop to check inside. Mom and Dad were both at work so nobody was home. I steamed ahead to look for Chuck and Alex.

I got there just when Mrs. Glass did. It's a good mile from her office, so she must have done some running, too. She came sailing down Ninth Street over to Euclid, splashing through puddles, her high-heeled shoes in her hand.

"Sam," she called to me. "Where are the boys?"

"I don't know," I admitted. "I just got here." I took the steps two at a time. The front windows were broken in. I flung open the door. Shattered glass lay scattered on the living room rug and all over the brown velvet sofa.

"Alex!" I yelled. "Chuck! You OK?"

Nothing. Zip. Silence.

"Chuckie!" Mrs. Glass screamed. "Alex!" I dashed around the house, searching. Something moved in the top bunk so I scrambled up the ladder, sure I'd found them. But just as I got to the top, Al the cat leaped down.

"Go find the boys," I yelled at him. He stared at me for a minute and then settled in the rocket-print chair to watch.

Mrs. Glass opened the basement door and shouted, "Boys! It's safe now." Only Rooster the dog scrambled up the steps. Dashing into the hall, I ran smack into Mrs. Glass, who was dashing someplace else. It almost knocked us both flat.

"Maybe somebody rescued them," she said. "I don't see any blood. The phone's dead. The electricity's off. The windows are blown in and the old maple tree in the backyard is roots up." She started biting her nails. "The place is a disaster area." She looked at me, glanced away, and then looked back again like she just couldn't believe her eyes. "And you," she said, "look like you're going to a costume party. Where were you all this time, anyway?"

"I was curled up in the hall outside Dr. Reynolds' office," I told her. "He was running late. I know I should have . . . " Then I looked down at my mud-spattered pink bib and put my skinned hands up to feel the curly metal whiskers. I'd forgotten all about them. "Dr. Reynolds had just put in my wires . . . " I started to explain.

Mrs. Glass frowned, closed her eyes, and shrieked. Her voice was as loud as all the sirens at full tornado force, *"Booooooooyyyyyyyyys!"*

From their bedroom I heard a faint whimper and an almost silent "shhhhhhhh." I ran in and threw open the closet door, but only shoes fell out.

So I got down on my belly, lifted the NFL bedspread, and looked under the bed. My old finding powers hadn't left me. There among the dirty socks and dust balls lay Alex and Chuck, scrunched up small against the wall, looking gray and scared.

"I found them, Mrs. Glass," I yelled. "They're alive!" I stuck my head under the bed again. "It's all over, you guys," I told them. "You can come out now."

"Alex turned it on!" Chuck yelled from deep under the bed.

"We didn't mean to do it," Alex whispered in a weak, dry voice.

"Come out here this minute!" their mother boomed.

Chuck poked his head from his hiding place. His bottom lip was quivering. "Alex did it," he cried. He slithered out, ran over, and clung to his mother's knees.

"Alex did what?" She tried to pry him loose so they could carry on some kind of conversation, but he hugged fast.

"Alex, come out!" I told the dark form pressed against the wall.

He inched toward me, peering at my face with interest. "What's wrong with your mouth?" he asked.

"It's a long story," I said, tearing off the pink bib and tossing it over toward the wastepaper basket.

"What's she gonna *do* to me?" Alex hissed.

I stuck my head under the bed. "She's going to be *so* glad to see you," I said, trying to grab him by the leg, "that she'll give you a big hug and a kiss."

"Yuck," he said. "No kidding, what's she gonna do, you think?"

"Alex," Mrs. Glass said in a low threatening voice. "You're going to die of dust inhalation if you don't get out of there." She shuffled toward the bed, Chuck clinging to her knees. Alex sneezed and shifted back toward the wall again.

"What is the matter with that crazy kid?" she asked nobody in particular.

"You've told him a billion times not to play with Daddy's stereo," Chuck said, sniffling, "but he did and . . . "

"I'm going to get you, Chuckie," Alex shouted from his cave. "Next time you beg me not to, I'm going to tell on you. You'll see." And he started to sob.

But Chuck kept going. "And he turned it up so loud the house started shaking, and it shook so much it exploded, and my ears hurt and the lights went out and there were noises outside . . . " He started to wail.

By then it was Tear City. Mrs. Glass was doing it, too. She burrowed under the bed, dragged Alex out by his foot, and they all three of them sat there and bawled. It was catching. I almost started in with them. I mean, really it was *my* fault as much as anybody's.

"*You* didn't do it, you funny nuts," Mrs. Glass said. "It was a tornado from the sky. You know, like that funnel cloud that picked Dorothy up in *The Wizard of Oz.*"

Geez, what a dumb thing to say, I thought. Next time they'll run out and try to catch a ride to the Emerald City.

"Well," she laughed, smoothing the dust balls out of Alex's hair, "I'll bet it's a couple of light years before you fool with Daddy's sound system again."

She bounced up, fluffed her hair, and smiled down at the two kids, who looked like they'd been personally responsible for losing the World Series. "Let me fix some popcorn to cheer you up. Sam, read to them, will you? That's the best soother I know."

"I'll stay longer if you really want me to," I told her, looking down at the holes in the toes of my gym shoes.

"No, Sam, I guess you do want to go home and check," she said. "Call me if you need help. You know our number?" She wrote it on a scrap of notepaper and handed it to me. "See you tomorrow. And don't be late."

Food for Thought

I never had a piece of toast
    Particularly long and wide
But fell upon the sanded floor
    And always on the buttered side.

James Payn

(Not Just) Loafing Around

from TOUGH-LUCK KAREN
by *Johanna Hurwitz*

Winter vacation was near but the deadline for the science project was also approaching, and Karen Sossi had no idea what to do. Everyone in her family had suggestions.

Her brother, Aldo, said, "Why don't you study the cats, Peabody and Poughkeepsie? You could write about what they eat, how much they sleep, and things like that."

"No," said Karen. "What could my class learn from that? Cats eat tuna fish and sleep a lot? Everyone already knows that."

All the following day Karen worried about a project for science. No one could be more miserable than she was, she decided. However, when she entered the house after school, Aldo was crying. Even when he was a baby, Aldo hardly ever cried. She wondered what could be bothering him.

"What's up?" she asked her mother and Aldo, who were sitting together in the kitchen.

"Peabody is a murderer," wailed Aldo through his tears.

"What are you talking about?" asked Karen.

"He just walked into the house with a dead bird in his mouth," said Mrs. Sossi. "I managed to get it away from him."

"Are you crying for the bird?" asked Karen.

"I don't know," said Aldo softly. "I feel bad about the bird, but I feel bad about Peabody too. Why would he do a thing like that? He never killed a bird before."

"Well, perhaps it won't happen again," Mrs. Sossi said.

She was wrong. That very evening, when Karen's sister, Elaine, was getting ready for bed, she let out a scream. Everyone came running into her room. "What's the matter?" asked her father anxiously.

"Look!" Elaine shouted, pointing to the floor of her closet.

Everyone crowded to look inside. There was a dead bird on the floor.

Two days later there was a third bird. This one was brought into the house by Poughkeepsie and was still alive. Mrs. Sossi let out a shriek of surprise, and Poughkeepsie dropped his prey. The stunned bird fluttered from the kitchen to the living room, leaving a trail of small feathers behind it.

Mrs. Sossi managed to rescue the bird before either of the cats was able to catch it again. That evening the family had a discussion on the subject as they were eating supper.

"I know I fed them enough," said Aldo. "I've been very careful and even have given them extra so they wouldn't go after the birds."

"Perhaps we shouldn't let them outside anymore," said Mrs. Sossi. "Soon there won't be any birds left in all of New Jersey with these two gangsters of ours on the loose."

"Don't be silly," said Mr. Sossi.

Mrs. Sossi changed the subject. "Karen, have you found a topic for your science project yet?" she asked.

Karen shook her head.

"I hope you're thinking about it," she said warningly.

"That's all I think about," Karen complained. "Soon I'll be having nightmares about it."

Early Friday morning, when everyone was rushing about getting ready for school, Peabody brought another bird into the house. Aldo still took the death of each small bird very hard.

Karen watched as he gingerly picked up the corpse of the dead bird and put it into the garbage. Suddenly she had an idea. Maybe she could write about cats and birds for science. She could keep track of the number of birds that the cats had caught and study the birds and make graphs and charts about her findings.

"That's a terrible project," said Aldo, when Karen told him about it.

"Well, maybe the cats won't kill anything anymore,"

said Karen. "But I want to keep score of the birds in the area and the number of cats. And besides, you were the one who suggested that I write about Peabody and Poughkeepsie in the first place."

"That's not what I meant," said Aldo. "What you want to do is disgusting."

"Well, it's disgusting to have to do a science project," said Karen, gathering her books together to go off to school.

"If you do that for your project, I won't ever speak to you again," threatened Aldo.

"OK, OK," said Karen, looking at the clock. She was afraid she would miss the bus to school in addition to all her other troubles. "I don't care. I won't do it. Just find me another science project."

She ran out the door.

Karen was not taking much pleasure in thinking about the approaching holidays. Her project was due on the Friday before school broke for the ten-day vacation, and she had been forbidden to do any cooking until she had completed it.

"No cooking!" she had screamed. "I wanted to make fruitcakes for gifts."

"No cakes, no bread, no experimenting in the kitchen until you get an experiment for school first," said Mrs. Sossi firmly.

"It's not fair! You eat all of whatever I make. You all like everything. So why shouldn't I bake or cook just because I haven't done my project?"

"Your mind should be on one thing and one thing only," said Mrs. Sossi. "If you haven't handed in a science project, you are going to have to spend the entire vacation working on one. Schoolwork comes first!"

So, even though vacation was approaching, Karen was feeling miserable. One evening more than two weeks later, she was looking through some science books she had borrowed from the public library, searching for an idea.

Mrs. Sossi sat down next to Karen and looked through the books with her. "Couldn't you do this?" She was pointing to an experiment.

Karen read the description of it. "Too late. You need three or four weeks for this project." Karen sighed. "That's what I like about cooking," she said. "You make something, and an hour or so later you eat it. Not this business of working for three weeks to get results."

"Well, you're not getting anything done by moping about and just turning pages in these books," said Mrs. Sossi. "Why don't you bake some fresh bread for us?"

"Do you really mean it?" Karen asked in amazement. The thought of being in the kitchen and quietly kneading some bread dough filled her with pleasure. She always felt a sense of peace and well-being when she cooked, but especially when she made bread.

Aldo came into the kitchen as Karen was kneading the dough. "It really is like magic how that glop turns into bread," he said, as he watched her. "It looks as though it should taste awful."

Karen laughed and kept on kneading.

While the dough was rising, Karen returned to her homework. She felt so relaxed that she didn't even mind doing her math problems.

Karen thought about the bread. What had Aldo said? Making bread is like magic. That was what Ms. Drangle had said about science. "Science is the answer to everything that we can't understand—all the things that seem like magic—such as why a bird can fly or a baby is born or a television set shows pictures or a calculator does math problems."

"I've got it! I've got it!" Karen screamed.

"Oh, no!" Aldo came running. "Not another bird," he cried out.

"Where is it?" called Mr. Sossi, jumping up from his chair.

"Here, I'll take it," Mrs. Sossi offered, coming with some paper towels in her hand.

"Boy, you make more noise than me," shouted Elaine, coming from her room.

They all stood in Karen's room looking about.

"Well, where is it?" asked Mr. Sossi.

"Where is what?" asked Karen, surprised to see her room full of her family.

"The bird!" said Aldo, Elaine, and Mr. and Mrs. Sossi in unison.

"What bird?" asked Karen.

"The one you're shouting about."

Karen looked confused. "I'm not shouting. There's no bird," she said.

"You said you've got it. We all heard you," said Mrs. Sossi.

"I've got something better than a bird," Karen laughed. "I just got an idea for a science project!"

"You're not going to report on Peabody and Poughkeepsie, are you?" asked Aldo.

"Nope!" Karen said, grinning.

"What is it then?" asked Aldo doubtfully.

Karen looked at her family. They were all waiting to hear her idea. Suddenly she looked at the clock. "Come on. I'll show you," she said.

She ran down the stairs with everyone following her. Even Peabody and Poughkeepsie had emerged from hidden nooks to join them.

Karen opened the oven door and showed them the bowl of dough rising inside. "This is going to be my science project," she said.

"Bread?" asked Aldo. "How can that be your project?"

"Silly," said Karen. "You're the one who gave me the idea. You said bread was like magic, and I'm going to explain how the magic works."

"That's a wonderful idea," said Mrs. Sossi. "You could even give everyone a taste of the finished loaf."

"You could do it the way the famous chefs do on TV and bring all the ingredients and show how each step is done," added Mr. Sossi.

Then everyone had suggestions. Elaine found a piece of poster board in her closet and offered it to Karen. "You could list the ingredients on this and draw pictures of each process," she said.

"You'll have to explain about yeast and how it functions to make the bread rise," said Mrs. Sossi.

"I'm sure glad that you're not writing about Peabody and Poughkeepsie!" said Aldo.

Karen spent the next afternoon working on her chart and gathering together all the ingredients that she would need to take to school. After supper, she didn't even ask to watch television. She just kept on working.

On Friday morning, Karen set her alarm clock for five thirty. She got up and dressed quietly. She tiptoed down to the kitchen so as not to wake any of the rest of her family. As she set out the ingredients for school, she almost tripped. Looking down, she saw that both Peabody and Poughkeepsie were underfoot. Despite the small bell that each of them wore on his collar, she had not heard them. "You're so quiet, I didn't know you were here," she complained aloud to the two cats. "Is that how you sneak up on those poor defenseless birds?"

She mixed the yeast with warm water and let it dissolve. She measured out the flour, butter, and milk that she would need for her bread. Karen's plan was to take a bowl of bread dough into the class and show them what it looked like at that stage. "The glop stage," Aldo called it. Then she would explain the scientific reasons that the dough increased in size and why the yeast worked the way it did.

The rest of the family began to waken. Mrs. Sossi came down to the kitchen. "I'll drive you to school this morning," she offered to Karen. "I don't think you'll ever make it on the bus with all your paraphernalia."

"What's paraphernalia?" asked Aldo. "Is it a kind of bread, like pumpernickle?"

"It's all that stuff," said Mrs. Sossi, pointing to the two loaves neatly wrapped in aluminum foil, the large bowl of dough, and the other ingredients that Karen was also planning to take to school.

"Oh, great," said Karen. "In that case, I'm going to take a jar of jam too."

"Why jam?" asked Mrs. Sossi.

"Since the bread is rescuing her from a jam, she is bringing jam with the bread," quipped Mr. Sossi, entering the kitchen.

Everyone laughed. The solution of Karen's science crisis was a relief felt not only by Karen but by the entire family.

One other classmate was giving his report this morning too. Karen sat only half listening. She was beginning to feel nervous. She didn't like to get up in front of the class. She fidgeted in her seat and looked at Ms. Drangle. Whenever her science teacher moved, she made a jingling sound today. She was wearing a necklace that seemed to be made out of coins, which hit against one another as she walked about the classroom.

Karen waited while Peter London told how astronauts could hear each other in space. He explained how sound could travel in gases, liquids, and solids. "Sound travels at about 750 miles per hour," he explained. "And the colder it is, the slower sound travels," he added.

Peter finished up his report. "All right, Peter, that was very interesting," said Ms. Drangle. Peter sighed with relief. He was finished. Now Karen's turn had come.

Karen stood up and cleared her throat. She had been practicing an opening sentence, since the beginning was always the hardest. "I have something in a little envelope for you to see," she said. She opened an envelope and poured the contents into a saucer. Then she began to walk slowly around the classroom so that everyone would have a chance to investigate the tan grains on the dish.

"Is it animal, vegetable, or mineral?" asked Roy Nevins.

"What do you think it is?" asked Karen. Of course, she knew the answer because she had read all about yeast in the encyclopedia.

"No fair," said Peter. "You should tell us what we're looking at."

Karen turned to look at Ms. Drangle.

"Tell them what it is," she said. "They probably have never seen that substance before."

"It's yeast," said Karen.

"Yeast is alive," said Peter knowingly. "So it must be animal."

"Nope," said Karen. "It's vegetable. This yeast that I bought at the supermarket contains a mass of tiny, one-celled plants. They are the simplest kind of plants and belong to a group known as fungi," she explained.

"Mushrooms are fungi," called out Peter.

"That's right," said Karen. "But we don't put mushrooms in bread. Instead, we use these little grains of yeast, which are actually made by mixing yeast cells and cornmeal."

"But how does it turn into bread?" someone called out.

Karen opened a bag of flour and began pouring some into a bowl. "Three cups of this mixed with just a couple of spoons of yeast, are the two main ingredients of bread," she explained. "Warm liquid starts the yeast growing, and the yeast makes the bread rise. When the bread is baked in the oven, the yeast plants are destroyed by the heat."

Then Karen lifted the cloth that had been covering the bowl of completed dough. "This is what dough looks like," she said, walking about the room once again to let everyone have a good look.

"It sure doesn't look or smell like bread," called out Roy.

"My brother says it's glop," said Karen, and everyone laughed. "But after it has finished rising and I put it into the oven and let it bake, it becomes bread. Yesterday I put two pans of the glop into the oven, and this is what happened." As she spoke, Karen removed the two loaves of bread that she had kept hidden in a shopping bag. She began unwrapping one of the loaves, and everyone gasped.

She turned to Ms. Drangle. "Would it be all right if I gave everyone a slice of bread?" she asked.

Ms. Drangle nodded her head and came toward the front of the room, jingling and jangling as she walked. Karen had a knife in her paraphernalia, and now she began slicing the bread. "It's even better with jam," she said, pointing to the jar of jam that she had with her.

"Why not?" said Ms. Drangle. "This is like a real holiday party we're having." She smiled at Karen.

Soon everyone was chewing on a slice of homemade bread. There were lots of questions. Karen was able to answer all of them.

Ms. Drangle helped distribute seconds to everyone. There was nothing left but a few crumbs. Her jingling added to the happy mood in the room. They really felt as though they were having a party.

Suddenly as she listened to Ms. Drangle's necklace, Karen thought of something. She stared hard at her teacher and wondered why such a simple idea hadn't occurred to her earlier.

Listening to the jingling sound, she realized that if the cats had *several* bells attached to their collars they probably wouldn't catch any more birds. Peter had said that the colder it is, the slower sound travels. No wonder Peabody and Poughkeepsie had suddenly succeeded in becoming murderers when the weather turned cold. She would buy them new collars as presents, she thought.

The bell rang. The science period was over, and the time had come to leave. Karen gathered her bowls and ingredients together. "That was an excellent report," said Ms. Drangle. "The idea was very creative," she said, smiling at her student.

Karen smiled too. It was going to be a wonderful vacation.

The Baker

wanted me to know

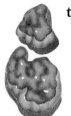that
underneath the cheese

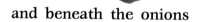and

sausage bits

and

pepperoni
slices 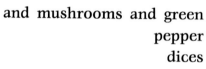 and beneath the onions

and mushrooms and green
pepper
dices

the only thing that counted

was

the
dough

—*Arnold Adoff*

120

Think About It

1. What two problems does Karen face?
2. Do you agree with Ms. Drangle that Karen is "creative"? Why or why not?
3. What idea for problem solving did you get from the story? Explain how you might use it.
4. Do you agree with the baker in the poem? Tell what part of the pizza you think is most important.
5. Describe an experience you have had with cooking or baking.

Create and Share   What hobby do you enjoy that you could demonstrate to your class? Make a list of the steps you would take and any materials you would need for a demonstration. Practice at home or with a friend before showing the class.

Explore   If you want to try baking bread or cooking other foods, you can find lots of books to help you. You might want to learn more about the history of bread and about the many different breads that are eaten all over the world. Look in the library card catalog under COOKERY for cookbooks and other books about food. Or you may already have a favorite recipe or cookbook at home to use.

It was 1492, and Christopher Columbus was lost.

The Queen of Spain thought he was on his way to India. The people who lent him money thought he was on his way to India. Even his crew thought he was on his way to India.

Instead, he stumbled onto a strange Atlantic island half a world away and came face-to-face with two of the most explosive forces ever found by a European: America and popcorn.

You know plenty about America. But what do you know about popcorn?

Do you know, for instance, that popcorn is a special corn? Do you know what makes it different from other corn? Or where it comes from? Or even what makes it pop?

Don't feel bad.

Even though Americans munch through seven and a quarter BILLION *quarts of it a year, most of them know less about popcorn than Columbus knew about finding India.*

America's Favorite Mystery Food
from WHAT MAKES POPCORN POP?
by David Woodside

Why Take Popcorn Seriously?

Even if you hate puppies and never laugh, you probably like popcorn. Popcorn is eaten at movies, carnivals, fairs, circuses, amusement parks, ball games—almost anywhere people get together to have a good time. And because it's such a good-time snack, no one takes it seriously. Who wants to

spoil a good time by studying it, or even reading about it?

Well, listen. We could learn a lot from popcorn. For one thing, we could learn something about ancient history.

Popcorn originated in Mexico. Yet in some parts of China, Sumatra, and India, people have grown popcorn since before Columbus came to America.

How did it get all the way to China? When? By what route? Did popcorn somehow float across the Pacific Ocean by itself? Did the Chinese come to America long, long ago and take popcorn back with them? Or did the Indians of America discover the rest of the world before the rest of the world discovered them?

No one knows the answers, yet. But popcorn raised these questions, so maybe popcorn will help answer them, too.

While it's fun to study history, there is a more important reason for studying popcorn—its ability to survive. Popcorn can grow in parts of the world other corns can't. When scientists find the secret of the popcorn plant's hardiness, they may be able to use it to improve other types of corn plants. Then other corns could grow in parts of the world in which they can't grow now and help solve the world's hunger problem.

That's why we take popcorn seriously.

The Thousand-Year-Old Popcorn That Still Pops

In Peru, archaeologists found that thousand-year-old tombs holding the bodies of Incan leaders also held gold, jewels—and popcorn kernels. The popcorn was probably stored in the tombs so the dead men would have a little something to snack on during their long stay.

This ceramic vessel from Peru is decorated with a corn design.

They weren't disappointed, because even after a thousand years, the popcorn still popped. The cool, dry environment that's perfect for preserving bodies was also perfect for preserving popcorn.

In Chile, some deserts haven't had rain for hundreds of years. Winds shifting these desert sands have uncovered popped kernels many centuries old, but still looking fresh and white.

In the Bat Caves of New Mexico, Indians left a six-foot-deep layer of household garbage on the floor over the course of three thousand years. Anthropologists like garbage. They dig through it to find things that tell them about the people who lived a long time ago. In the Bat Caves' garbage, they found 5,600-year-old popcorn ears, the oldest ever found.

Popcorn has been in the Americas much longer than man. Scientists think it originated in Mexico over eighty thousand years ago. They think it was the first corn, the granddaddy of all others. They also think it was the first corn eaten by Indians.

Now, without actually being there, how could scientists know that?

Scientists have found much more popcorn lying around pre-historic Indian ruins than other types of corn. But this corn had kernels as hard as glass, and it's a safe bet that the Indians did not like to chew glass. So they probably ignored the corn until one of them accidentally dropped a few glass-hard kernels into the fire. The heat of the fire caused the kernels to pop and fly out of the fire. The startled cook, wary at first, probably swallowed his fear, picked up the popcorn, sniffed it, licked it, and ate it. People have been eating popcorn ever since.

Indians—The World's Greatest Popcorn Experts

Indians were popcorn fanatics. By the time Columbus discovered America, they were growing over seven hundred types of popcorn. They were building fancy poppers, making ceremonial popcorn headdresses and necklaces, wearing popcorn in their hair, making popcorn beverages, even selling it. The Indians of San Salvador greeted Columbus and his crew by offering them popcorn corsages.

Popcorn meant so much to the Zapotecs of Mexico, they painted pictures of popcorn on the sides of funeral urns.

Because many native American civilizations depended on popcorn,

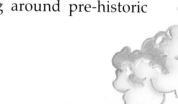

they were afraid of losing it. As insurance, the Aztecs would honor Tlaloc, their God of Maize, Rain and Fertility, by decorating statues of him with strands of popcorn. A happy Tlaloc would bring good crops and good fishing for the year. Even today in some Mexican villages, popcorn is still used to decorate religious statues.

The Wampanoag Indians who were invited to the first Thanksgiving at Plymouth knew that the Pilgrims didn't really have much of a feast. So they went into the woods and killed deer and gathered enough fruit and nuts to feed everyone.

One Indian, the chief's brother, Quadequina, brought a deer skin bag full of popcorn as his dinner gift. In this way, he helped establish the tradition of bringing popcorn as a token of good will during peace negotiations.

The History of Popcorn Popping

The Indian who discovered the pop in popcorn by accidentally dropping it into the fire discovered the simplest way to cook it. All that was needed was heat and popcorn.

But the Indians could see that when they tossed popcorn into the fire, they burned more than they

above: This ceramic figure of the god of maize dates from 500 A.D.
below: A coiled plaque made by the Hopi features a corn design.

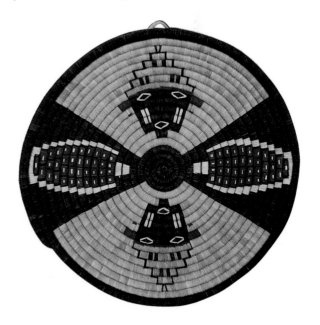

ate. So they brought up sand from the shore of a river or lake and heated it in the fire. When the sand was scorching hot, they spread it in front of the fire and stirred in the popcorn until it popped.

Other Indians were even more ingenious. They invented poppers that used the same basic elements as the poppers we use today: heat, oil and a pan of some sort. Some pans were merely hollowed out soapstone. Some, like the fifteen-hundred-year-old poppers found on the north coast of Peru, were made of clay and metal and had a lid with a hole in the top to let steam escape. These ancient poppers are very similar to the "ollas" the Papago Indians of Arizona and Mexico use to pop popcorn today.

Ollas, though, are a little larger— sometimes eight feet across.

What Makes Popcorn Pop?

There's a lot of hop in the pop; a whole lot. If you don't put a lid on your pan, some kernels will pop up to three feet into the air. That's higher than most of you can jump.

The Indians had no idea why popcorn popped, but that didn't stop them from making some guesses. Inside each kernel, they thought, there lived a tiny demon. The demon was comfortable and remained quiet and still as long as he wasn't disturbed. And nothing disturbed him, really, except one thing: heat. When the kernel got hot, the tiny demon got mad. The hotter the kernel, the madder the

demon. He'd shake his house, spinning it around. He'd struggle, pushing from inside, puffing out the walls of the kernel. When it was finally too hot, he'd blow his top. The popcorn exploded, and the tiny demon disappeared with the steam.

Scientists have found no demon, but they do think they've found the secret of what makes popcorn pop. And that secret is water inside the kernel. No water, no pop. So to know why popcorn pops, you need to know what happens to water when it's heated.

Water, like everything, is made up of millions of tiny particles called molecules. They move close together when they're cold and move farther apart when they're hot. As the water gets hotter, the molecules move farther and farther apart, turning to steam, taking up more room.

The water in the popcorn kernel is stored in a tiny glob of soft starch in the middle of the kernel. As the kernel heats up, the water in the glob of soft starch heats up, takes up more room, and builds up pressure. The hard, toenail-like

at left: Popcorn machines have been popular since the 19th century. This one on wheels was making the rounds in 1895.

starch surrounding the soft glob resists the pressure of the expanding water. When the kernel gets hot enough, the hard starch is no longer strong enough to hold in the expanding water.

The popcorn explodes.

And the soft starch pushes out, turning the popcorn inside out. The steam inside the kernel is released into the air.

Zea Mays Everta

The scientific name for popcorn is *Zea mays everta*. It's a very official name that probably tells scientists a lot. The trouble is, most popcorns have very little in common with each other except that they're corn and they pop. So even so official a name can't tell anybody anything about all the different kinds of popcorns.

Popcorn kernels can be almost any color, from off-white to light gold to deep gold to deep maroon to red to black to hundreds of shades in between. Yellow and white are the colors you'll find in stores. Of those, most people think yellow popcorn tastes best and that's why nine bags of yellow are sold for every one bag of white. In the early 1900s, however, it was exactly the opposite. Yellow popcorn was twice as expensive as

white popcorn because it was so scarce. Eventually, enough yellow popcorn was grown to make it as cheap as the white. And since the yellow pops larger than the white, vendors could sell an extra bag or two of popped popcorn per pound of raw popcorn. So, through the vendors' salesmanship, yellow became more popular.

However, no matter what color the kernels are, once they're popped, the popcorn is always white—although the yellow kernels may have a yellowish tinge. That's because popcorn turns inside out when it's popped, and popcorn is always white inside.

Most popcorn comes in two basic shapes when it's popped: snowflake and mushroom. Snowflake pops up big and is shaped like a cumulus cloud. Mushroom pops smaller, but pops into a round ball. Snowflake popcorn is used in theaters and at home because it looks bigger. Mushroom is used in making popcorn candy because it doesn't crumble in the candy factory.

There are thousands of popcorns, and you'll never see ninety-

Popcorn ears come in a variety of sizes and shapes, but they all have one thing in common—kernels that go off with a bang!

snowflake

mushroom

Don't believe them. There's no such thing as hull-less popcorn. Sometimes there's a little less hull, and sometimes the hull is a little thinner, but the hull is always there. Even though most of it will shatter into a thousand pieces, called bee wings, whenever you eat popcorn you'll always find a little hull caught in your teeth.

KABOOM POP CORN HULLESS

nine percent of them. Some have unusual shapes, like strawberry popcorn. The short, stubby ear is actually shaped like a strawberry and carries deep strawberry-red kernels.

Some are giants. Although most popcorn plants are smaller than regular corn, Dynamite popcorn has stalks six to eight feet tall and ears eight to nine inches long. And some are freaks. Just a few popped kernels of Snopuff popcorn will fill a bowl.

Be careful when you see the word "hull-less" in the name. People don't like popcorn hulls because the hulls get caught between teeth. So popcorn growers would like you to think their popcorn won't have any hulls once it's popped.

Why Corn Is Golden

a folktale from Mexico
adapted by Vivien Blackmore

Many years ago when your great-uncles and aunts and your grandparents were still young, there lived a man who wanted to know all about the Sun.

"Where do you think the Sun lives?" he asked his wife. "Where can his house be? What door does he come out of? Where does he sleep?"

In those days the Sun was a god and highly respected, and so the wife was afraid: "Don't ask such foolish questions," she answered. "The Sun might get angry and punish you."

However, the man's curiosity was so great that he ignored his wife's words. He turned himself into a sparrow so that he could fly, but the Sun was too far away and the sparrow couldn't reach it, and so the man returned to his house.

The next day he changed himself into an eagle and flew to the place where the Sun rises, but when he arrived the Sun wasn't there any longer, because he had gone off to warm the young seeds.

"Tomorrow I will wait for the Sun where he sleeps," resolved the man. "I will find the place where he hides." This time he found the end of the earth and the beginning of the sea. He hid behind a tree and watched how the Sun was spilling gold into the water, and how the sea was swallowing it up.

Now the man badly wanted that gold, but gold is heavy and he knew he couldn't lift it by himself. He set off to find someone to help him. After a while he met some dwarves and they said to him:

"Come with us and visit our cave!" And they went together through the door that leads to the center of the earth. The man did not know it, but these little men were really sun rays who warmed the roots of plants and fruit, helping them to grow. They led a good life; they had mice for messengers and ants for friends.

The man entertained the dwarves with stories about the world above. He explained about the gold and asked them if they would like to share it with him. They agreed to this, and they all went together to wait for the Sun, in the place where it sinks into the sea.

They waited on the beach and when at last the great god Sun lowered his golden body into the sea there was so much gold that half of it was swept onto the sand. They picked up all that they could carry and made their way to the man's house.

But the man was not only curious, he was very greedy as well. He really wanted all the gold for himself. When they had gone a little way, he started to cough on the dwarves and they all fell down. Then the man picked up all the gold and put it into an enormous sack and started to run away.

He hadn't got far when he felt the gold getting heavier and heavier—although really it was the man getting smaller and smaller. He shrank to the size of a dog, then a cat, then a bird! His body turned black and feathery, and he grew two big wings. The man's feet curled up and became ugly claws, and now the dwarves saw he was nothing but a buzzard, who looked very ashamed and soon flew away.

The dwarves collected the gold and gave half to the buzzard's wife. She was very happy because she was poor and had many children.

The dwarves carried the rest back to their cave in the center of the earth. They put it carefully into some roots that were growing there. It so happened that these roots were corn roots, and the gold flowed upward. This is the reason why the corn in our land is as golden as the Sun in the sky.

Think About It

1. Which reasons given by the author of "Popcorn: America's Favorite Mystery Food" convinced you that popcorn is worth studying?
2. What did you find out about popcorn that you didn't already know?
3. What part of the myth "Why Corn Is Golden" leaves the strongest impression in your mind?
4. What does the myth say about the importance of sun, corn, and gold to the people who told the story?
5. Why do you think people throughout history have told or written stories, poems, and articles about food and created art about it?

Create and Share   Choose a food that is important to you. Write a tale to explain how this food came to have its special quality. Read your folktale aloud to the class.

Explore   Read another Mexican myth about how something came to be. Look under FOLKLORE—MEXICO in the library card catalog. You might compare a myth that you read with a factual explanation in the encyclopedia. Which fictional details were based on fact?

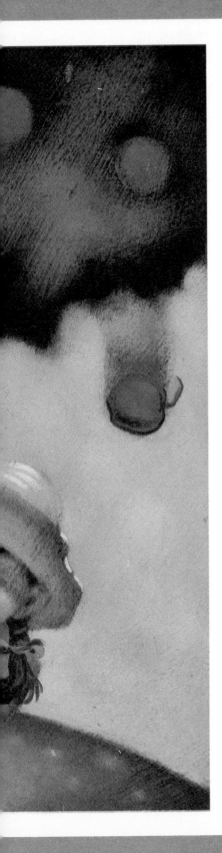

Help!

Help!
I need somebody,
Help!
Not just anybody,
Help!
You know I need someone,
Help!

from HELP!
words and music by
John Lennon and Paul McCartney

Help!

Words and Music
by John Lennon and Paul McCartney

Help!
I need somebody,
Help!
Not just anybody,
Help!
You know I need someone,
Help!

When I was younger, so much younger than today,
I never needed anybody's help in any way.
But now these days are gone, I'm not so self-assured.
Now I find I've changed my mind, I've opened up the doors.

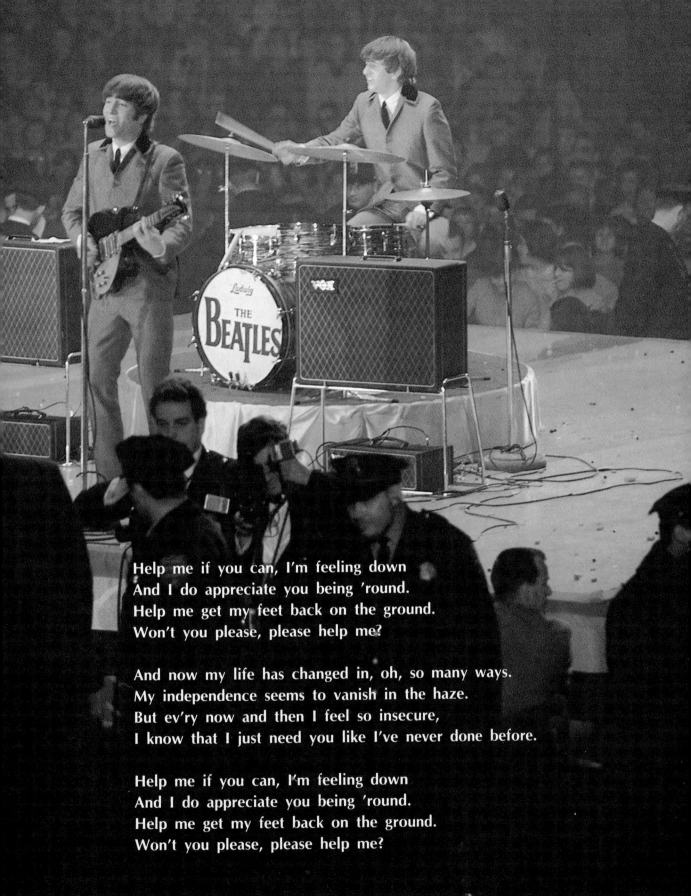

Help me if you can, I'm feeling down
And I do appreciate you being 'round.
Help me get my feet back on the ground.
Won't you please, please help me?

And now my life has changed in, oh, so many ways.
My independence seems to vanish in the haze.
But ev'ry now and then I feel so insecure,
I know that I just need you like I've never done before.

Help me if you can, I'm feeling down
And I do appreciate you being 'round.
Help me get my feet back on the ground.
Won't you please, please help me?

Like Jake and Me

by Mavis Jukes

The rain had stopped. The sun was setting. There were clouds in the sky the color of smoke. Alex was watching his stepfather, Jake, split wood at the edge of the cypress grove. Somewhere a toad was grunting.

"Jake!" called Alex.

Jake swung the axe, and wood flew into the air.

"Jake!" Alex called again. "Need me?" Alex had a loose tooth in front. He moved it in and out with his tongue.

Jake rested the axe head in the grass and leaned on the handle. "What?" he said. He took off his Stetson hat and wiped his forehead on his jacket sleeve.

Alex cupped his hands around his mouth. "Do . . . you . . . need . . . me . . . to . . . help?" he hollered. Then he tripped over a pumpkin, fell on it, and broke it. A toad flopped away.

Jake adjusted the raven feather behind his hatband. "Better stay there!" he called. He put his hat back on. With powerful arms, he sunk the axe blade into a log. It fell in half.

"Wow," thought Alex. "I'll never be able to do that."

Alex's mother was standing close by, under the pear tree. She was wearing fuzzy woolen leg warmers, a huge knitted coat with pictures of reindeer on the back, and a red scarf with the name *Virginia* on it. "I need you," she said.

Alex stood up, dumped the pumpkin over the fence for the sheep, and went to Virginia.

"I dropped two quarters and a dime in the grass. If I bend down, I may never be able to get up again," she said. Virginia was enormous. She was pregnant with twins,

and her belly blocked her view to the ground. "I can't even see where they fell."

"Here!" said Alex. He gave her two quarters. Then he found the dime. He tied her shoe while he was down there.

"Thanks," said Virginia.

Alex fiddled with his tooth. "Mom," he asked, "do you think the twins are brothers or sisters?"

"Maybe both," said Virginia.

"If there's a boy, do you think he'll be like Jake or like me?"

"Maybe like Jake *and* you," said Virginia.

"Like Jake *and* me?"

"Right," said Virginia.

"Well, anyway," said Alex, "would you like to see something I can do?"

"Of course," she said.

Alex straightened. Gracefully he lifted his arms and rose up on his toes. He looked like a bird about to take off. Then he lowered his arms and crouched. Suddenly he sprang up. He spun once around in midair and landed lightly.

Virginia clapped. "Great!"

Alex did it again, faster. Then again, and again. He whirled and danced around the tree for Virginia. He spun until he was pooped. Jake had put down the axe and was watching.

"Ballet class!" gasped Alex. "Dad signed me up for lessons, remember?"

"Of course I remember," said Virginia. "Go show Jake!"

"No," panted Alex. "Jake isn't the ballet type."

"He might like it," said Virginia. "Go see!"

"Maybe another time," said Alex. He raced across the field to where Jake was loading his arms with logs. "Jake, I'll carry the axe."

"Carry the axe?" Jake shook his head. "I just sharpened that axe."

Alex moved his tooth with his tongue and squinted up at Jake. "I'm careful," he said.

Jake looked over at the sheep nosing the pumpkin. "Maybe another time," he told Alex.

Alex walked beside him as they headed toward the house. The air was so cold Jake was breathing steam. The logs were stacked to his chin.

Virginia stood under the pear tree, watching the sunset. Alex ran past her to open the door.

Jake thundered up the stairs and onto the porch. His boots were covered with moss and dirt. Alex stood in the doorway.

"Watch it!" said Jake. He shoved the door open farther with his shoulder, and Alex backed up against the wall. Jake moved sideways through the door.

"Here, I'll help you stack the wood!" said Alex.

"Watch it!" Jake came down on one knee and set the wood by the side of the woodstove. Then he said kindly, "You've really got to watch it, Alex. I can't see where I'm going with so big a load."

Alex wiggled his tooth with his tongue. "I just wanted to help you," he said. He went to Jake and put his hand on Jake's shoulder. Then he leaned around and looked under his Stetson hat. There was bark in Jake's beard. "You look like a cowboy in the movies."

"I have news for you," said Jake. "I am a cowboy. A real one." He unsnapped his jacket. On his belt buckle was a silver longhorn steer. "Or was one." He looked over at Alex.

Alex shoved his tooth forward with his tongue.

"Why don't you just pull out that tooth?" Jake asked him.

"Too chicken," said Alex. He closed his mouth.

"Well, everybody's chicken of something," said Jake.

He opened his jacket pocket and took out a wooden match. He chewed on the end of it and looked out the windows behind the stove. He could see Virginia, still standing beneath the tree.

Jake balled up newspaper and broke some sticks. He had giant hands. He filled the woodstove with the wadded paper and the sticks and pushed in a couple of logs.

"Can I light the fire?" Alex asked.

"Maybe another time," said Jake. He struck the match on his rodeo belt buckle. He lit the paper and threw the match into the fire.

Just then Alex noticed that there was a wolf spider on the back of Jake's neck. There were fuzzy babies holding on to her body. "Did you know wolf spiders carry their babies around?" said Alex.

"Says who?" asked Jake.

"My dad," said Alex. He moved his tooth out as far as it would go. "He's an entomologist, remember?"

"I remember," said Jake.

"Dad says they only bite you if you bother them, or if you're squashing them," said Alex. "But still, I never mess with wolf spiders." He pulled his tooth back in with his tongue.

"Is that what he says, huh," said Jake. He jammed another log into the stove, then looked out again at Virginia. She was gazing at the landscape. The hills were fading. The farms were fading. The cypress trees were turning black.

"I think she's pretty," said Alex, looking at the spider.

"I do, too," said Jake, looking at Virginia.

"It's a nice design on her back," said Alex, examining the spider.

"Yep!" said Jake. He admired the reindeer coat, which he'd loaned to Virginia.

"She's got an awful lot of babies there," said Alex. Jake laughed.

"And boy! Are her legs woolly!" said Alex.

Jake looked at Virginia's leg warmers. "Itchy," said Jake. He rubbed his neck. The spider crawled over his collar.

"She's in your coat!" said Alex. He backed away a step.

"We can share it," said Jake. He liked to see Virginia bundled up. "It's big enough for both of us. She's got to stay warm." Jake stood up.

"You sure are brave," said Alex. "I like wolf spiders, but I wouldn't have let that one into my coat. That's the biggest, hairiest wolf spider I've ever seen."

Jake froze. "Wolf spider! Where?"

"In your coat getting warm," said Alex.

Jake stared at Alex. "What wolf spider?"

"The one we were talking about, with the babies!" said Alex. "And the furry legs."

"Wolf spider!" Jake moaned. "I thought we were talking about Virginia!" He was holding his shoulders up around his ears.

"You never told me you were scared of spiders," said Alex.

"You never asked me," said Jake in a high voice. "Help!"

"How?" asked Alex.

"Get my jacket off!"

Alex took hold of Jake's jacket sleeve as Jake eased his arm out. Cautiously, Alex took the jacket from Jake's shoulders. Alex looked in the coat.

"No spider, Jake," said Alex. "I think she went into your shirt."

"My shirt?" asked Jake. "You think?"

"Maybe," said Alex.

145

Jake gasped. "Inside? I hope not!"

"Feel anything furry crawling on you?" asked Alex.

"Anything *furry* crawling on me?" Jake shuddered. "No!"

"Try to get your shirt off without squashing her," said Alex. "Remember, we don't want to hurt her. She's a mama."

"With babies," added Jake. "*Eek!*"

"And," said Alex, "she'll bite!"

"Bite? Yes, I know!" said Jake. "Come out on the porch and help me! I don't want her to get loose in the house!"

Jake walked stiffly to the door. Alex opened it. They walked out onto the porch. The sky was thick gray and salmon colored, with blue windows through the clouds.

"Feel anything?" asked Alex.

"Something . . . " said Jake. He unsnapped the snaps on his sleeves, then the ones down the front. He let the shirt drop to the floor.

"No spider, back or front," reported Alex.

They shook out the shirt.

"Maybe your jeans," said Alex. "Maybe she got into your jeans!"

"Not my *jeans!*" said Jake. He quickly undid his rodeo belt.

"Your boots!" said Alex. "First you have to take off your boots!"

"Right!" said Jake. He sat down on the boards. Each boot had a yellow rose and the name *Jake* stitched on the side. "Could you help?" he asked.

"Okay," said Alex. He grappled with one boot and got it off. He checked it. He pulled off and checked the sock. No spider. He tugged on the other boot.

"You've got to pull harder," said Jake, as Alex pulled and struggled. "Harder!"

The boot came off and smacked Alex in the mouth. "Ouch!" Alex put his tongue in the gap. "Knocked my tooth out!" He looked in the boot. "It's in the boot!"

"Yikes!" said Jake.

"Not the spider," said Alex. "My tooth." He rolled it out of the boot and into his hand to examine it.

"Oh," said Jake. "Then hurry up." Alex dropped the tooth back into the boot. Jake climbed out of his jeans and looked down each leg. He hopped on one foot to get the other sock off.

"She won't be in your sock," said Alex. "But maybe—"

"Don't tell me," said Jake. "Not my shorts!"

Alex stared at Jake's shorts. There were pictures of mallard ducks on them. "Your shorts," said Alex.

"I'm afraid to look," said Jake. He thought he felt something creeping just below his belly button.

"Someone's coming!" said Alex. "Quick! Give me your hat! I'll hold it up and you can stand behind it."

"Help!" said Jake in a small voice. He gave Alex the hat. He brushed himself off in the front.

"Okay in the back," said Alex, peering over the brim of the hat.

Jake backed into his hat, and the raven feather poked him. He howled and jumped up and spun around in midair.

"I didn't know you could do ballet!" said Alex. "You dance like me!"

"I thought I felt the spider!" said Jake.

"What on *earth* are you doing?" huffed Virginia. She was standing at the top of the stairs.

"We're hunting for a spider," said Jake.

"Well!" said Virginia. "I like your hunting outfit. But aren't those *duck*-hunting shorts, and aren't you cold?"

"We're not hunting spiders," explained Jake. "We're hunting *for* a spider."

A big and hairy one that *bites!*" added Alex.

"A wolf spider!" said Jake, shivering. He had goose bumps.

"Really!" said Virginia. "Aha!" she cried, spying Alex's tooth inside Jake's boot. "Here's one of the spider's teeth!"

Alex grinned at his mother. He put his tongue where his tooth wasn't.

Jake took his hat from Alex and put it on.

"Hey!" said Virginia.

"What?" said Jake.

"The spider!" she said. "It's on your hat!"

"Help!" said Jake. "Somebody help me!"

Alex sprang up into the air and snatched the hat from Jake's head.

"Look!" said Alex.

"Well, I'll be!" said Jake.

There, hiding behind the black feather, was the spider.

Alex tapped the hat brim. The spider dropped to the floor. Then off she swaggered with her fuzzy babies, across the porch and into a crack.

Jake went over to Alex. He knelt down. "Thanks, Alex," said Jake. Jake pressed Alex against him. "May I have this dance?" Jake asked.

Ravens were lifting from the blackening fields and calling. The last light had settled in the clouds like pink dust.

Jake stood up holding Alex, and together they looked at Virginia. She was rubbing her belly. "Something is happening here," she told them. "It feels like the twins are beginning to dance."

"Like Jake and me," said Alex. And Jake whirled around the porch with Alex in his arms.

150

151

Think About It

1. Why do you think Alex wanted to help his stepfather? Why did Jake refuse his help?
2. What early details in the story helped you predict what would happen later?
3. What does the singer in "Help!" mean by "I've opened up the doors"?
4. What opened up the doors for Jake so that he could appreciate Alex?
5. Have you ever tried to help someone and been turned away? Describe what happened and tell how you felt.

Create and Share   Think about ways young people can help their families and the people in their community. Brainstorm for 15 minutes on your own. List as many ideas as you can. Share your most practical, most original, and most amusing ideas with your classmates.

Explore   If you enjoyed this story, you may want to read another book by Mavis Jukes. Or you might like to learn more about the Beatles. Look under BEATLES in the card catalog for one of the many biographies written about them. For books about children and their stepparents, look under STEPCHILDREN, STEPPARENTS, and STEPFATHERS.

GIVE YOURSELF SOME HELP

from THE OFFICIAL KIDS' SURVIVAL KIT
by Elaine Chaback and Pat Fortunato

ACCIDENT PREVENTION

Someone once described a sloppy character he knew as "an accident looking for a place to happen." It's often true. Sure, some accidents can't be prevented, but many accidents don't happen entirely "by accident"; they happen because people get careless. Nobody's perfect, and you can't do every little thing right, every single time. But you can be careful when it counts. Especially when you're alone, or when you're in charge of young children.

Accident prevention is mostly common sense. Anyone who goes around throwing banana peels on the floor, or running down the hall with a pair of long, sharp, pointed scissors, is headed for trouble. Be aware of what's going on around you, and watch out for dangerous situations. If you see that a fishbowl has been placed on top of the refrigerator, move it someplace safer before it moves itself—onto someone's head (maybe yours). You can't foresee every problem or prevent every accident, but you can use your head for better things than catching falling fishbowls.

Common Sense in the Kitchen

Certain areas in the house are more accident-prone than others. One such spot is the kitchen, and the worst danger is fire. Keep matches out of the hands of babes (this goes for *anywhere* in the house). And be careful when you're using them yourself. Never toss a match into the garbage unless you're sure it's out. When you light a gas broiler with a match, be sure that the gas has been on for only a few seconds. The combination of too much gas escaping and a lighted match can cause quite a blast, and not the kind you'd like to get caught in. For safety's sake, lean as far back as you can when lighting it, with your hair (if it's long) tied back and out of the way. And don't light it at all if you haven't been shown how.

When you're working at the stove, keep pot handles facing inward, toward the back of the stove. That way, pots are less likely to be knocked over by flying elbows. And dress in something that makes sense. You probably don't wear robes with long, flowing sleeves anyway. But in case you get the urge to, and you also want to do some serious cooking, choose one or the other—not both.

Don't leave anything made of paper or cloth—paper towels, bags, containers, napkins, pot holders—on the stove top (a good way to start a small fire), and never leave the house when anything is cooking (a good way to let a small fire get out of control). It's also best to keep young children away from the stove, and out of the kitchen altogether, if that's possible. (Sharp objects and cleaning materials, which can act as poisons, are often stored here.)

Another source of danger in the kitchen is sharp utensils, such as knives. Of course, you're careful when you're cutting something. But also be aware of where you've put down knives and other utensils when you're not using them. Knife holders are best, where you can't accidentally cut yourself, and if you have a silverware holder on your dish drainer, put knives and forks in upside down, so you won't get poked. There's also the danger of leaving a can hanging around after you've opened it. Those edges are rough, and can give nasty cuts. Get into the habit of cleaning as you go, and you'll not only have less mess, you'll have less danger.

Bathroom Baddies

The baddies of the bathroom world (accidentally speaking) are razors, scissors, and . . . soap. Right, soap. Sure, razors and scissors can cut, but soap, left on the floor or in the bathtub, can make you slip—a very common household accident. Put sharp or slippery things away even if someone else has left them around, and clean up after yourself. And remember, rubber duckies cause accidents too.

Watch That Medicine Cabinet

Medicines can also be a problem. Don't let any child near the medicine cabinet. Young children will put almost anything into their mouths. If you have to give them medicine, never call it "candy"—they might think all those pretty pills are candy, too. And before you take anything yourself, be sure to check the label. Many pills look alike, and it's easy to make a mistake.

Allover Safety

You can also avoid many accidents by following these tips:

- *Treat all electrical appliances with great respect.* If you have a question about a particular appliance, ask before you use it. If anything—a cord, plug, socket—looks suspicious, tell a parent about it right away.
- *Don't litter.* Pick up your belongings—clothes, games, equipment—rather than leaving them around where someone (even you) could trip over them.
- *Take it easy.* Don't play roughhouse games where things can easily be broken: the kitchen, bathroom, or anywhere where there's glass, china, or lamps.

ACCIDENTS

An accident can be anything from a broken glass to a broken bone. No matter what happens, *don't panic!* Think. Then do whatever you can yourself, and get help—quickly— if you need it.

EMERGENCIES

What They Are and What They Aren't

An emergency IS:
- A dangerous situation—such as a fire, flood, or leak
- A serious accident—such as a broken bone or heavy bleeding
- A life-threatening illness—such as an asthma attack or allergic reaction

An emergency ISN'T:
- Losing your homework assignment
- Spilling spaghetti on your clown costume just before the play
- Not having one ingredient for the cookies you're baking

These things may be important to you—but they're *not* emergencies. And it's a very bad idea to act as if they were. Every time you set up a cry of "Emergency!" you make people very, very concerned. That's fine when it's a real emergency: the people you alert will be grateful. But when it's not, they will be angry.

Unreal Emergencies: Two Senseless Scenes

Scene 1: Your mother is in the middle of an important meeting at work when she gets a frantic call from you. She's upset, she drops everything (including her hot cup of coffee on someone's lap), and runs to the phone. You tell her that your hamster, Alexandra, has escaped. *Uh-oh* . . .

Scene 2: You're in the middle of a great soccer game. Your coach comes running over to say that your father is on the phone and it's an emergency. You rush across the field and up the stairs and down the hall, and, finally, you get to the phone. Your father says he's run out of shaving cream and could you pick some up on the way home from school. *Moan* . . .

A Real Emergency

Okay. You've got a real genuine, actual, honest-to-Pete emergency on your hands. This is the time to be very aggressive. Try to reach the right people—immediately!—and don't be embarrassed about interrupting *anyone*, at any time of the day or night. Stay as calm as you can, but make it clear how important it is to get help.

Remember this, too: when it comes to emergencies, age is no object. If you're the one who knows what to do—even if you're the youngest person there—you're the one who can do the most good.

FIRST AID

In an Emergency

First aid is exactly what it says: the *first* thing you do to *aid* someone who's hurt. But it isn't usually meant to take the place of regular medical help—getting the person to a doctor or a hospital.

First aid can make a huge difference in how fast the person gets better, or whether or not there will be any permanent damage. It can even mean the difference between life and death!

Sounds scary. But luckily, there are some commonsense things you can learn *before* an accident or sudden illness happens. You don't have to be a Boy Scout to "be prepared," especially when it comes to first aid. Read this section carefully (maybe even twice) and pay special attention to the following:

- Don't panic.
- Get help.
- Get out of danger.
- Don't move the injured person unless absolutely necessary.
- Treat first for bleeding, then for other problems.

Don't Panic!

You've heard this so many times before, because it's really, really true. If you don't know anything else about a medical emergency, you can sometimes save the day by staying calm. That's easier said than done. So take a few deep breaths and tell yourself you're going to do the best you can. Besides helping you think more clearly, you'll make the injured person feel more confident. If that person thinks that everything is under control and things will be okay, he/she will relax more and have a better chance to recover.

Get Help!

Do whatever you have to do to make sure help is on the way. If you're alone, call for help as soon as you can safely leave the injured person. If there's no phone, get to the nearest person who can help. Of course, if there are other people with you, one can go for help while the others stay and give first aid. If the person is seriously injured, it's best to call for an ambulance with specially trained medical personnel called EMTs (Emergency Medical Technicians), who can give on-the-spot treatment and transport the injured person safely.

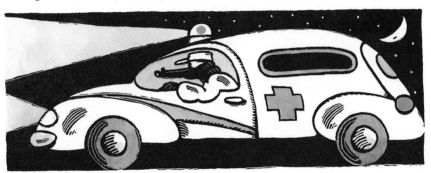

Get Out of Danger!

If the emergency is because of a fire, electrical shock, gas fumes, or other dangers, get the person—and yourself—away from the source of the danger *right away*.

WARNING: This is the *only* time you ever move an injured person. At all other times keep the person lying down until medical help arrives.

First Things First!

Breathing: If a person stops breathing, every second counts. Get help immediately.

Bleeding: If breathing is okay, but there's bleeding, then this is at the top of your list. The best way to stop bleeding is to apply direct pressure, holding a sterile gauze bandage over the wound and keeping your fingers flat.

Shock: If you've controlled the breathing and bleeding, and medical help still hasn't arrived, then treat for shock. In a first-aid situation, this means keeping the person warm and lying down.

Special Cases

There are some very special first-aid situations, such as epileptic, diabetic, or allergic attacks. The person may have information on the condition with him/her, or may be able to tell you about it. By the way, if you have any special medical problems of your own, be sure you have identification with you at all times stating the condition and telling what to do in an emergency. (Medic-Alert bracelets or necklaces are the best way to make sure you will be treated properly, if you have one of these problems.)

First Aid for Minor Injuries

Sometimes, the term "first aid" is used to mean taking care of small injuries, like cuts and scrapes. (As you may have noticed, life is full of these little lumps.) If the hurt is very small, it should really be called "first-and-last aid," because you can take care of the problem easily and quickly, without having to see a doctor. It depends on how serious the injury is.

FIRST-AID KITS

What and When

First-aid kits are really important for medical emergencies. But they also come in handy for "life's little lumps." You'll probably find many useful items for first aid in your home already—in the medicine cabinet or in the kitchen. But it's a good idea to have everything in one place, so that when something happens, you don't have to waste time wondering where you left the bandages or the iodine.

Safety experts say that every home should have at least one first-aid kit, and, if possible, two for the house and one for the car(s). First-aid kits should be in places that everyone in the family knows about. This is no time for hide-and-seek. Everything should be clean and organized so you can get to it quickly. It should *not* look like the bottom drawer of your friend's dresser or the back of your locker. If your family doesn't have a first-aid kit, perhaps you can make one for them.

A *basic* first-aid kit should include:
- *bandages*
- *sterile gauze pads and tape*
- *rubbing alcohol*
- *peroxide, Mercurochrome, or iodine*
- *an eyecup*

What the Well-Dressed Kit Will Wear (and Why)

If you want to put together a super-duper deluxe version of a first-aid kit, here's our suggestion:

Rx: Check the "health" of your first-aid kit from time to time to make sure everything is in working order. Watch for expiration dates.

Remember—being prepared takes a little thought and time, but it can make a *big* difference.

What	Why
Sterile bandages (4x4 gauze pads)	To dress cuts, stop bleeding
Adhesive tape (1 roll)	To hold bandages in place
Bandage adhesive strips (1 box)	To dress small cuts
Triangular bandages (4), safety pins	To make slings
Mild soap (1 bar)	To clean cuts, scrapes, burns
Peroxide or iodine (1 bottle)	To clean and disinfect cuts
Rubbing alcohol (1 bottle)	To sterilize tweezers
Tweezers (1 pair)	To remove splinters, bee stingers
Calamine lotion (1 small bottle)	To treat insect bites, poison ivy
Thermometer (1)	To check for fever
Cotton swabs (1 small package)	To clean cuts
Aspirin (1 small bottle)	To ease pain, reduce fever
Icebag or ice pack (1)	To prevent or limit swelling
Eyedropper and eyecup (1 of each)	To rinse eyes
Ipecac syrup (1 small bottle)	To treat poisoning

Think About It

1. Give examples of how sloppiness causes accidents.
2. It is important to remain calm in an emergency. How did Alex's ability to stay calm help Jake?
3. What helps you to predict the kinds of accidents that are likely to happen in a certain place?
4. What have you done lately at home and in school to prevent accidents?
5. What kind of first aid could you offer someone in an accident? Describe several ways in which you could be helpful.

Create and Share   Think about the accidents people might have in classrooms, in workshops and garages, at the beach or pool, on camping trips, traveling in the desert, or climbing mountains. Choose one situation and list as many mishaps and problems as you can that people might have there. Finally, write a paragraph to describe the supplies you would put in a special first-aid kit to have on hand. Explain how each item in it could be used.

Explore   You may want to find out more about first aid in a Boy Scout or Girl Scout handbook or Red Cross manual. Or you might want to learn what Emergency Medical Technicians and doctors do in emergencies. Look in the library card catalog under FIRST AID and HOSPITALS—EMERGENCY SERVICES.

Wiley, His Mama, and the Hairy Man

from THE PEOPLE COULD FLY
by Virginia Hamilton

Now, facts are facts. Wiley was a boy. He and his mama lived by themselves with just Wiley's dogs. Say Wiley's papa fell off the ferry boat one time. The river was quick there where he fell. They looked for Wiley's papa a long way down the river and in the pools of the sandbanks. And say they never found him. But they heard a great bad laughin' way off across the river. And everybody sayin' it, "That's the Hairy Man." Sayin' Wiley's papa never got across Jordan because the Hairy Man block his way.

"Wiley," his mama tell him, "the Hairy Man's got your papa and he's gone get you if you don't look out."

"Yes, Mama," Wiley said. "I'll look out. I'll take my hound dogs everywhere I go. You know, the Hairy Man can't stand some hound dogs."

Wiley knew this because his mama had told him. She knew because she was from the swamps near the Tombigbee River and she knew *conjure.* Knew how to lay tricks, put together charms, or take the tricks away. She could find a vein of water. She could see in front of her and behind her, and so was called a "two-head." So she knew.

One day Wiley taken up his axe and went in the swamp to cut him some poles for a hen roost. He took his hound dogs with him. The dogs went off, runnin' after a wild pig. That thing run so far off, Wiley couldn't hear his hounds atall.

"Well, I hope the Hairy Man is somewhere away and nowhere around here," Wiley said.

He picked up his axe to start work. But before he could begin, he spied the Hairy Man through the trees. Hairy Man just grinnin' at him. Hairy Man was ugly, even when he grinned. He was coarse-hairy all over. His eyes burned red as fire. He had great big teeth, with spit all in his mouth and runnin' down his chin. He was a terrible-lookin' Hairy Man.

"Don't you look at me like that," Wiley said. "Don't you come near me." But the Hairy Man kept on comin' and grinnin'.

Wiley threw down his axe and scrambled up a big laurel tree. He sees the Hairy Man hasn't any feet like a man. He has hooves like a cow's. And Wiley had never seen a cow way up a laurel tree. So he knew he was safe. He climbed almost to the top. He looked down. Then he did climb to the top.

"Why come you climbin' up that tree?" asked the Hairy Man.

"My mama tole me to stay away from you, Hairy Man. But what you got there in your croaker sack?"*

"Haven't got nothin', yet," said the Hairy Man.

"Go on away from here," said Wiley.

"Ha! I will not!" said the Hairy Man. He picked up Wiley's axe. He swung it like a strong man. And the wood chips flew out of that tree.

Wiley grabbed the tree as tight as he could. He rubbed his belly up against the tree trunk. And he hollered, "Fly, wood chips, fly! Go back in your same old place!" He meant for the wood chips to go back into the tree trunk.

And the chips flew back. And that Hairy Man fumed, stomped, and was fit to be tied. Then he swung the axe again. And Wiley knew he must holler faster. So the two of them went to it, tooth and toenail. Wiley was hollerin' and that Hairy Man was choppin'. Wiley hollered till he was hoarse; and pity, he saw that the Hairy Man was gainin' on him.

---

* A sack in which to keep animals that make croaking sounds, such as frogs.

"I'll come down partway if you'll make this tree twice as big around," Wiley said.

"I'm not studyin' you," said the Hairy Man. He swung the axe and swung the axe.

"I bet you can't do it," said Wiley. "I bet you can't make it bigger."

"I won't even try," said the Hairy Man.

So they went back to it again. With Wiley a-hollerin' and the Hairy Man just choppin' away. Wiley about yelled himself finished when he thought of somethin' his mama had told him. She had said, "Tell the Hairy Man you goin' to pray, and then call your dogs."

Wiley yelled to the Hairy Man, "Stop it now. I got to pray!"

"What's that mean?" asked the Hairy Man.

"Means I got to pray to the Man Above," said Wiley.

The Hairy Man knew what that meant, although he'd never heard prayer, and he stayed quiet a moment while Wiley chanced to pretend to pray.

"Heah-aaah, dogs! Heah-aah!" Wiley hollered. "Fly, wood chips, fly! Go back in your same old place!"

"You got no dogs," the Hairy Man said. "I sent that wild pig to draw them off."

"I'm just still prayin'," Wiley said, and hollered again, "Heah-aaah, dogs!" They both heard the hound dogs comin' on strong, yelpin' in a close pack.

The Hairy Man looked worried. "Come on down," he said, "and I'll teach you how to *conjure.*"

"I can learn all the *conjure* I need from my mama," said Wiley, and he could, too.

The Hairy Man fumed and muttered. But he threw down the axe and hightailed it off through the swamp.

Well, when Wiley got himself home, safe, he told his mama that the Hairy Man had almost got him that time. Hairy Man would have, too, but that he pretended to pray and called his hounds instead and the hounds run the Hairy Man off.

"Did he have his sack?" his mama asked Wiley.

"Yesum," Wiley said.

"Next time he come after you, don't you climb some tree," said his mama.

"I won't," said Wiley, "cause some tree not big enough around."

"Don't climb atall. Just stay on the ground and say, 'Hello, Hairy Man.' You hear me, Wiley?" asked his mama.

"Nosum."

"He won't hurt you, Wiley," his mama said. "You can put that Hairy Man down on the ground in the dirt, once I tell you how to do him."

"But if I put him in the dirt, he'll put me in the croaker sack," said Wiley.

"You just do what I say. You say, 'Hello, Hairy Man,' " his mama said. "And he says, 'Hello, Wiley.' And you say, 'Hairy Man, I heard you the best *conjure* doctor around here.' And he say, 'I reckon I am.' And you say, 'I bet you can't turn yourself into a giraffe.' You keep tellin' him he can't, Wiley," his mama told him, "and then he is sure to turn himself into a giraffe. Then you say, 'I bet you can't turn yourself into an alligator.' And he will, too. Then you say, 'Anybody can turn theyselves into somethin' big as a man. But I bet you can't turn yourself into a possum.' And the Hairy Man will, and you grab him and throw him in the croaker sack."

"Well," said Wiley, "it don't sound just right somehow, but I'll try it." So he tied up the dogs so they wouldn't scare away the Hairy Man. And he went down to the swamp again. Wiley hadn't been there long when he looked up, and here come the Hairy Man. Just grinnin' through the trees. Just as hairy all over and big teeth showin' so wet. He could tell Wiley was out there without his hound dogs. Wiley nearly climbed a tree when he saw that croaker sack. But he didn't. "Hello, Hairy Man," he said.

"Hello, Wiley," said the Hairy Man. He took the sack off his shoulder and started openin' it up.

"Hairy Man, I heard you were the best *conjure* doctor around these parts," Wiley said.

"I reckon that's true," said the Hairy Man.

"I bet you can't turn yourself into a giraffe," Wiley said.

"Shoot, that's no trouble atall," said the Hairy Man.

"I bet you can't do it," Wiley said.

So the Hairy Man twisted, made a long neck; and twisted around, made him long legs, and turned himself into a giraffe.

"Well, I bet you can't turn yourself into an alligator," Wiley said.

The giraffe twisted, got short legs and twisted around, got him thick skin, and turned into an alligator. He was watchin' Wiley to see he didn't try to run.

"Anybody can turn theyselves into somethin' big as a man," said Wiley, "but I bet you can't turn yourself into a possum."

The alligator twisted, got smaller and twisted around, long tail, and turned himself into a possum.

Just quick! Wiley grabbed it and threw it in the sack. He tied the sack up good and tight, and then he threw it in the river. Wiley went home through the swamp. He looked up, and there came the Hairy Man grinnin' through the trees.

"I turned myself into the wind and blew out of there," said the Hairy Man. "Wiley, I'm gone set right here till you get hungry and fall out of that tree you up in again. You want me to teach you some more *conjure?*"

Wiley thought awhile. He pondered over the Hairy Man and he worried about his hound dogs tied up a mile away.

"Well," Wiley said, "you sure lay some pretty good tricks. But I bet you can't make things disappear and go who knows where."

"Huh, that's what I'm good at," said the Hairy Man.

"Look at that old bird nest on the limb there. Now look again! It's gone for good and true."

"Now how I know it was there in the first place?" asked Wiley. "I didn't see it in the first place, either, let alone seein' it gone. But I bet you can't make somethin' I know is there disappear."

"Ha, ha," laughed the Hairy Man. "Look at your shirt."

Wiley looked down and his shirt was gone. But he didn't care. It was what he wanted the Hairy Man to do.

"That was just a plain old shirt," Wiley said. "But this rope I got tied round my pants has got my mama's *conjure* on it. I bet you can't make *it* disappear."

"Huh, I can make all the rope in this country disappear," the Hairy Man said.

"Ha ha ha," said Wiley.

The Hairy Man looked mad and threw his chest way out. He opened his mouth wide and hollered loud. "From now on, all the rope in this country has gone and disappeared!"

And truly, the belt that had held up Wiley's pants was gone. And quick! Wiley reared back holdin' his pants up with one hand and onto a tree limb with the other. "Heah-aaah, dogs!" he hollered, loud enough to be heard two miles away. The rope that had tied up his dogs was gone, too. And the dogs came and the Hairy Man lit out through the swamp one more time.

Well, then, when Wiley and his dogs got back to home, his mama asked him did he put the Hairy Man in the sack.

"Yesum, but he turned himself into the wind and blew right on out of that old croaker sack."

"That's too bad," said his mama. "But you fooled him twice. If you fool him again, he'll leave you alone. But he'll be mighty hard to fool the third time."

"We have to think hard on how to fool him," Wiley said.

"I'll work on it directly," said his mama. She sat down by the fire with her chin in her hands. Wiley was just there, worryin' about keepin' the Hairy Man away from him. He took his dogs out and tied one at the back door and one at the front door. He crossed a broom and an axe handle over the window. He built a fire in the fireplace. Wiley felt a lot safer. Then he sat down next to his mama to help her think hard. After a while, she said, "Wiley, go down to the pen and get that little baby pig away from the sow."

Wiley did as he was told. He took the squealin' pig out of the pen and back to his mama. She put the little pig in his bed.

"Now, Wiley," she said, "go clear up in the hayloft and hide."

So Wiley did as he was told again. And before long, he heard the wind howlin' and the trees blowin' and shakin'. The dogs started growlin'. He could see through a knothole. And the dog at the front door was starin' down at the swamps. Its hair standin' up and its lips drawn back in a snarl, too. Then an animal as big as a mule with horns on its head ran out of the swamp past the house. The dog jumped and jumped but he couldn't get loose.

A great big animal, like a giant dog with a long snout, came runnin' out of the swamp and snarled at the cabin. And this time one dog broke loose and took out after the big animal, and the animal headed back to the swamp.

Wiley looked out again in time to see his other dog break loose. The dog took out after another funny-lookin' animal.

"Oh, my goodness," Wiley moaned. "I just know the Hairy Man is comin' after me!"

And it was true, because in no time Wiley heard somethin' with big hooves clompin' like a cow up on the roof. He heard somethin' swear to heaven when it touched the hot chimney.

The Hairy Man saw that there was a fire in the fire-place. So he came off that roof and dared to come up and knock on the front door.

"Miz Mama," he hollered, "I've come to get your baby boy, Wiley."

"You won't get my baby," Wiley's mama hollered right back.

"Give him over. If you don't, I'll sure bite you and poison you."

"I'll bite you right back," Wiley's mama said.

"Give him here or I'll set your house afire with my lightnin'," the Hairy Man said.

"Well, I do have my sweet cream to put it out with," Wiley's mama said.

The Hairy Man heaved against the door and said, "Give him over to me if you don't want me to dry up your spring, make your cow come sick, and send a field of boll weevils out of the ground. They'll eat every cotton boll you've got."

"Hairy Man," said Wiley's mama, "you wouldn't do that. That's too mean, even for you."

"Oh, I'm mighty mean," said the Hairy Man. "I'm the meanest man I ever did see."

"Well, if I give over my baby, will you go on away and leave all else here alone?" asked Wiley's mama.

"That is just what I'll do," the Hairy Man said.

And with that, Wiley's mama opened the door and let in the Hairy Man.

"The baby's just there, in the bed," Wiley's mama said.

The Hairy Man came in, lookin' meaner than anythin'. He went over to the bed, pulled the covers off.

He hollered, "There's nothin' here but a sucklin' pig!"

"Well," said the mama, "I never said what *kind* of baby I was givin' up. And that little pig did belong to me before I gave it over to you, Mister Hairy Man."

"Shoot!" hollered the Hairy Man. He raged and he yelled. He stomped and yammered and bared his drippin' teeth. Finally, he took the pig and tore out to the swamp. He knocked down trees and let loose rocks and boulders all the way. In the mornin', say there was a big, wide path right through the swamp just like a cyclone cut along through it. Trees torn clear up, roots and all, and lyin' there on the ground.

After all that, when it was most safe, Wiley came down from the loft.

"Is that man gone, Mama?" he asked his good mama.

"Oh, yes, child," said his mama. "Old Hairy Man won't hurt you ever again. Because we did surely fool him three times."

And that was the end of that. But they say that Hairy Man is still deep in the swamps somewhere. Say he is waitin' on the right time.

Think About It

1. What is Wiley's problem and how does his mama help him?
2. What do you think Wiley would have done without his mama's help?
3. How is the final trick that Wiley and his mama played on the Hairy Man like the last trick that Oona and Finn Mac Cool played on Cuchulain?
4. Predict what the Hairy Man will do next. What clues help you predict?
5. What different kinds of help have the selections in HELP! shown?

Create and Share Choose a partner and make up a story about your narrow escape from an ugly and powerful character. Have your story tell how you get special help from another character in the story in outsmarting your foe. Prepare a dramatic reading of your story for your classmates.

Explore If you enjoyed this folktale, you may want to read other black American folktales from the book *The People Could Fly*. You might enjoy *Zeely*, another one of Virginia Hamilton's many books. Her work also includes nonfiction, like the biography *Paul Robeson: The Life and Times of a Free Black Man*.

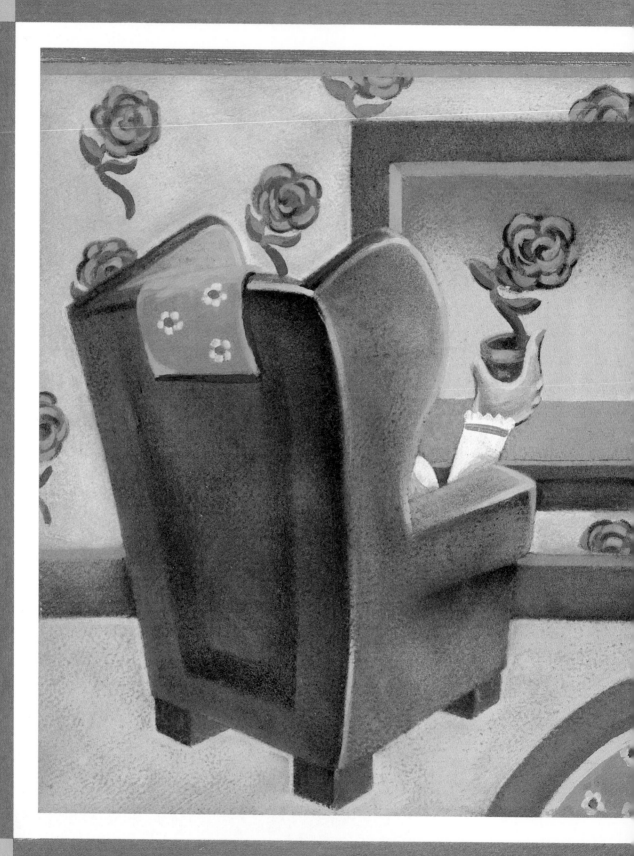

Plant People

There was a young farmer of Leeds,
Who swallowed six packets of seeds.
It soon came to pass
He was covered with grass,
And he couldn't sit down for the weeds.

Anonymous

THE PLANT

by Mary C. Lewis

The pinkish-yellow light of dawn peeked through the tall trees of the Missouri forest near George's home. George walked quietly down the path, stopping occasionally to examine a leaf or pick up a rock for his collection. As he approached his special spot, he smiled to himself. There wasn't anywhere else he'd rather be in the early morning. Surrounded by his favorite things, plants, he felt happiest.

DOCTOR

This was where George took care of sick plants. His special spot was like an open-air greenhouse to which he brought plants that needed special care and attention. George taught himself to nurse plants back to health. He never lost a plant.

Folks called him the plant doctor. The nickname was a clue to what would become his lifelong work. His real name was George Washington Carver.

Magnolia

George Washington Carver was born a slave at Diamond Grove, Missouri. The date of his birth isn't certain, but he was probably born in 1860 or 1864.

George's first year was a sad one. He never knew his father, who was accidentally killed while hauling logs. Then, less than a year after he was born, George and his mother were kidnapped. George was rescued, but his mother was never found.

By the time he was about ten years old, George knew that he wanted to go to school. This would not be easy because the nearest school that accepted black children was eight miles away, in Neosho. George had no idea where he would live, but he was determined to go to the one-room school. So off he headed by foot to Neosho.

George's determination paid off. The day after he got to Neosho, he found a black couple, Andy and Mariah Watkins, who let him live with them. School went well too: George learned quickly and got excellent grades.

Later, after studying music at Simpson College in Iowa, George Carver went to Iowa Agricultural College. At the end of his first year there he got a job as assistant botanist at Iowa's new agricultural experiment station. Carver was in charge of a large greenhouse; and like the plants that he grew there, he flourished in his job. He started a fungus collection that grew to 20,000 species and brought him fame in the field of botany.

Carver received his Bachelor of Science degree in 1894. Then he continued his studies and his work as a botanist in Iowa. During that time he bred new types of apples, pears, and plums—discoveries that helped fruit farmers vary the types of crops they could plant. More and more agriculture experts praised Carver's work.

In 1896, George Carver got his Master of Science degree. Then something important happened. He got a letter from Booker T. Washington, head of Tuskegee Institute in Alabama. Washington wanted Carver to become director of Tuskegee's department of agricultural science.

Carver saw the offer as the chance of a lifetime. In a letter to Washington he wrote:

Of course it has always been the one great ideal of my life to be of the greatest good to the greatest number of my people possible and to this end I have been preparing myself for these many years; feeling as I do that this line of education is the key to unlock the golden door of freedom to our people.

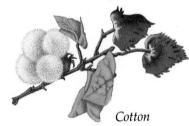

Cotton

Before Carver could do the greatest good for his people, there was much work to begin at Tuskegee. At first, only 13 students signed up to study agriculture, and the school lacked a laboratory and equipment. But Carver didn't let those problems stop him. His fascination with plants and his belief in a different kind of farming—using scientific, carefully planned methods— were his ways of holding his students' interest. Although Carver was really a shy person, when it came to agricultural science he forgot his shyness.

His message quickly got across to many students. Most of Tuskegee's students were from farm families, and they had come to college to get away from farming, not to study it. But by the end of Carver's first year there, the number of students enrolled in agricultural science jumped from 13 to 76! All over the campus students were talking excitedly about Professor Carver and his new ideas about *scientific* farming.

Carver wanted to do more than teach at Tuskegee. He wanted to continue conducting the experiments that he had begun in Iowa. Carver strongly believed that he could find ways to

improve southern farming methods. At that time, much of the South's land was sick from overwork. For too many years, farmers had been planting a single money crop, such as cotton or tobacco, that tired the land by draining the soil of nutrients. As a result, the topsoil was nearly all gone, and what remained contained dry, shifting sand. "Big Hungry" local folks called the land, because it was so undernourished.

Carver wanted to convince farmers to balance their usual money crops with different ones. He also wanted to show farmers how to make use of materials that were readily available to

Tobacco

them. Carver believed that if he could do this, farmers would be able to save the land from overwork and improve their lives as well. He persuaded Washington to let him start an agricultural experiment station like the one in which he had worked in Iowa.

Carver began increasing the amount of time he spent in the lab. He wanted to be completely undisturbed while he conducted his experiments, so six days a week he arose at four in the morning and went to work in his lab. No one asked Carver to drive himself so hard. In fact, the daily lab work pleased him greatly. It reminded him of the childhood mornings he spent in his forest greenhouse at Diamond Grove.

Some solutions came to Carver more quickly than others. He had little trouble discovering ways for farmers to use what was available to them. For instance, he found that vegetable scraps and leaves made excellent compost to fertilize the soil. He also found that acorns made good feed for hogs. Following Carver's advice, farmers began to take advantage of such little used yet freely available materials.

In addition, Carver used his lab time to answer some important questions. How could he find ways to get the most use from plants? What else could people do with plants besides eat them?

Carver was a patient, determined scientist. He believed that the answers were within reach, waiting for him. He thought about the process of photosynthesis, in which green plants trap and store the energy of sunlight. This process allowed plants to contain something extra, something valuable. What if he could find ways to use the something extra in plants to make other products? Carver began to see his work with new understanding. He could use the lab to make products from plants.

With Carver's new outlook came a burst of discoveries. The sweet potato was one of his first successes. Carver was sure that the sweet potato should be a money crop in the South, especially because it enriched the soil by putting badly needed nitrogen back into the ground. But most farmers weren't interested in the idea. Sweet potatoes spoiled rather quickly. Since they had to be sold faster than other crops, they were worth less money.

Carver's lab work showed farmers that they should grow sweet potatoes for uses other than food. He discovered 118 products—including flour, candy, and shoe polish—that could be made from this root. With that in mind, farmers could grow sweet potatoes, enrich their soil, and sell them to manufacturers as well as at the market. A new world of possibilities opened up for sweet potato farming.

With the peanut, Carver did perhaps his "greatest good." He discovered over 300 products that could be made from a plant that most farmers rarely thought of growing. Soap, ink, plastics, dyes, and an instant "coffee" mix were all peanut products that Carver discovered. In years past Carver had often advised farmers to grow peanuts because the plant was easy to raise and rich in nutrients, but most farmers had laughed off the idea. Now they saw that his idea made sense, and by 1919 the peanut was a full-blown money crop in the South.

Sweet Potato

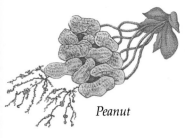

Peanut

Carver's discoveries helped save southern farming. No longer did southern farmers have to plant a single money crop and risk destroying the land.

Today we think nothing of using manufactured products in the home, office, or classroom. We cook with them, sit on them, play games with them, and wear them. Manufactured goods are everywhere. During Carver's time the field of manufacturing was brand-new. Carver was at the forefront of chemurgy, which involves the use of farm and forest products in making other products. Carver's work gave an important push to chemurgy's progress, and people are still reaping the benefits of his discoveries.

It is difficult to imagine life today without all the manufactured products that people enjoy using. It is also difficult to realize that an entire area of the United States almost had to give up farming completely because the land had been so misused. But George Washington Carver had no trouble imagining the future needs of people. His contributions brought science, farming, and manufacturing together in a way that will remain important for generations to come.

During Carver's lifetime, he received lots of awards and offers of money for his work. He accepted the awards, but he always refused the money. Three years before his death in 1943, he used his life savings—$33,000—to start the George Washington Carver Foundation for Agricultural Research. The foundation was his way of continuing the work that he had begun—doing the greatest good for the greatest number of his people possible.

Tiny Invaders

by D.M.Souza

Long ago, a shepherd boy was tending sheep on a hillside when his flock began to scatter. He put what was left of his lunch of bread and cheese in a nearby cave and hurried to round up his sheep. Weeks later, he returned to the cave and found a moldy piece of bread and a hunk of cheese with dark blue lines running through it. What had happened to his lunch?

One morning in Ireland, a farmer walked through his potato field and noticed that the leaves and stems of many of his plants were rotting. Quickly he dug up a few patches. Soon neighboring farmers made the same discovery in their fields. Something was destroying their most important crop! That was the beginning of the Irish potato famine in 1846.

During the American Revolution, the British were forced to sink several of their own battleships. But cannon fire wasn't to blame for these losses—a mysterious agent had been eating away the hulls of their ships!

Black bread mold, Rhizopus stolonifer

What caused these strange things to happen? Believe it or not, it was the work of a type of plant called fungus, or collectively, fungi. Fungi occur in over 250,000 varieties and have been around for millions of years. They are everywhere—in the air we breathe, the clothes we wear, the food we eat. They can destroy nearly anything—huge structures like bridges and railroad tracks, as well as small things like your stamp collection or your goldfish. Yet fungi have also helped save thousands of lives.

A fungus is invisible to the eye and can be seen only under the microscope or when it appears in groups as mold on bread, cheese, or fruit, or as slime on the surface of a pond. Fungi are made up of tiny threads that grow into a thick, tangled mass. After a rain some underground fungi may gather together so quickly that they swell and burst through the soil. We call them mushrooms.

Many fungi reproduce by making *spores*, or microscopic seedlike capsules. A single fungus can release millions of spores in a few days. These are scattered great distances by birds, insects, and the wind. But luckily, not all of them find suitable places to grow—otherwise the world might be overrun by these tiny invaders.

Fungi do not make their own food like most plants, but get it from others. Some attach themselves to the leaves

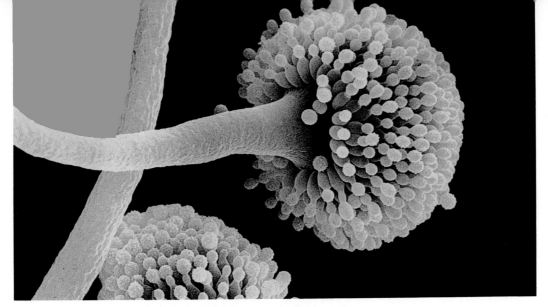

Close-up of bread mold, Rhizopus sparangia

and stems of other plants and live off their supply of food. Other fungi act as scavengers of dead plants and animals. They reproduce rapidly and speed up the decaying process, which helps release nutrients into the soil and air.

Some fungi find food on such things as shower curtains and cardboard boxes. They may live and grow on your raincoat, shoes, books, or lunch pail. They may find a meal under your fingernails, or decide they like the space between your toes (athlete's foot is the result).

But not all fungi are freeloaders. Those known as yeasts are useful in making bread and fermenting drinks such as wine. A type of fungus called mold is injected into ripening cheese to help give it the strong flavor of Roquefort or Limburger. Fungi are used to make candy, soft drinks, cloth material, and paper. Some even help produce useful chemicals and medicines.

Many years ago, in 1928, Alexander Fleming, a Scottish medical doctor, was studying some disease germs he had been growing in his laboratory. Quite by accident, he made a startling discovery. A small particle of mold had invaded one of the open dishes of germs. At first Fleming was angry, thinking he'd have to throw out the contaminated sample and start over. But then he took a closer look and was amazed to find that there were no longer any germs

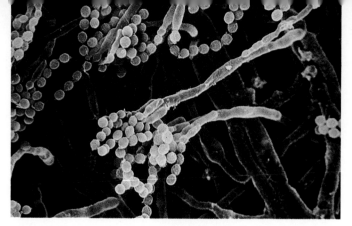

Penicillin

growing near the speck of mold. After many tests, he concluded that the mold must contain a substance that could weaken and gradually destroy germs. He called the substance penicillin.

It took years of work from scientists, agriculturalists, and technicians to produce the penicillin we know today. Dr. Fleming cultivated as much of the mold as he could, but it wasn't until 1941 that there was enough penicillin available to treat a human being. The first patient was a British policeman who was dying of blood poisoning. He began recovering very soon after penicillin treatments started and continued to improve every day. Unfortunately, the supply of penicillin ran out before the man had completely recovered, and the infection eventually killed him. But the medical world had seen what penicillin could do, and, with the help of mold specialists and technicians, a process was developed that made penicillin out of chemical substances. There were no shortages after penicillin could be manufactured, and it became a wonder drug for thousands of people.

Every year scientists are learning more about fungi. Because varieties of these plants have been found everywhere from the Arctic wastes to the Sahara desert, and because they seem to grow and prosper even in places with very little oxygen, many people believe that fungi may be able to live on other planets. Who knows? Someday astronauts may discover that some of these amazing plants have already invaded Mars.

Think About It

1. In what way are fungi different from green plants?
2. What were the writer's purposes in the two articles you just read? How do you know?
3. Explain why the titles for "The Plant Doctor" and "Tiny Invaders" are appropriate.
4. Think about Alexander Fleming, Anton van Leeuwenhoek, and George Washington Carver. Explain what qualities they have in common.
5. Do you agree or disagree with Carver's idea that education "unlocks the golden door of freedom"? Explain.

Create and Share   Create an amazing new plant that has unique characteristics and purposes. Name your plant and draw a picture of it. Describe the plant's uses and needs. Or begin a "Plant People Hall of Fame" and write recommendations explaining why George Washington Carver and Alexander Fleming should be members.

Explore   If you are interested in knowing more about the work of George Washington Carver or Alexander Fleming, you may want to read one of the many biographies written about them. Or you might want to find out more about molds and fungi. Look in the card catalog under MOLDS, FUNGI, and BOTANY.

Why Leaves Are Green

from CHILDCRAFT—THE HOW AND WHY LIBRARY

In the furry, finny, feathered world of the Animal Kingdom, there are many different colors. There are orange and brown giraffes, white polar bears, blue beetles, and red birds. But in the plant world—the Green Kingdom—the leaves of nearly all plants are just one color—green. Why?

The biggest difference between plants and animals is that animals eat and plants don't. Plants are able to make their own food. Leaves have a wonderful stuff inside them that makes food out of air and water, with the help of sunshine. This wonderful stuff is called chlorophyll. And chlorophyll is green.

So a leaf is green because it is filled with chlorophyll. And chlorophyll makes food for the plant.

Animals have no chlorophyll. They can't make food inside themselves as plants can. Neither can you. But wouldn't it be fun if you could? You would always be full and you'd never have to chew!

What Leaves Do

Leaves don't seem to do anything at all. But if you could become tiny enough to peek *inside* a leaf—you would have a surprise!

Sunlight comes into a leaf through the leaf's skin, which is clear like glass. Beneath the skin are millions of tiny "bags" called cells. These cells are like little balloons filled with water and living jelly. Inside the cells are small green packages called chloroplasts. The chloroplasts are green-colored because they are filled with a green stuff called chlorophyll. The chlorophyll catches some of the sunlight that falls on a leaf.

While the green packages are catching sunlight, other things are happening in the leaf. Air comes into the leaf through many tiny openings. Water, moving up from the roots far below, flows through the leaf. The air and water mix together and flow into the cells.

These cells are like little food factories. Here, the green chlorophyll works away. Using sunlight for energy, it changes water and a gas from the air (called carbon dioxide) into sugar. Some of this sugar is used as food for the plant. Some of it is mixed with minerals from the ground and is changed to other kinds of food.

So, all summer long, leaves are doing what leaves do best—making food.

sunlight

cells

carbon dioxide

oxygen

water

sugar

A PLANT PERSON

from TOP SECRET
by John Reynolds Gardiner

The process that plants use to make their own food is called photosynthesis. Allen Brewster is convinced that if plants can do it, people can too, and he plans to use his school science project to discover *human* photosynthesis.

I walked in the back door, careful not to let the screen door bang. The house smelled of fried chicken. Sure beats liver, I'll tell you. I put my books at the foot of the stairs, washed my hands in the downstairs bathroom, then went into the kitchen.

"How was school, honey?" my mom asked.

"Fine," I answered, getting the silverware out of the drawer. "Except for Miss Green's science class."

"Okay. What happened?"

"Nothing, really," I said. "It's just that I want to do one science project, and Miss Green wants me to do another."

"Better do as your teacher says," said my mom.

"But, Mom," I protested. "Miss Green wants me to do my project on lipstick."

"And what is wrong with that?"

"I don't want to do my project on *lipstick*," I said. "That's what's wrong with it."

I heard a car pull into the driveway. Dad was home. Good—at least he'd understand.

The door swung open and my dad walked in, carrying his briefcase. "How was your day?" my mom asked, as she always asked.

"The usual," my dad answered, as he always answered.

Dad gave me a big hug. "How was school?" he asked.

"The usual," I answered.

"That's not what I heard," said my mother, giving my father the eye.

"Tell me about it," said my father in his serious voice. He didn't like anything going wrong at school.

I told him the whole story, all about human photosynthesis, and the Science Fair, and the silver trophy, and Miss Green, and her stupid lipstick project.

"I'm sorry to say this," said my father when I had finished, "but your teacher's right."

"She's what?"

"Now hear me out," began my father, which was his usual beginning when he had something to tell me that he knew I didn't want to hear. "Nine-year-old boys just don't go around making discoveries. Especially like the mystery of human photosynthesis. You're not talking about an invention, like developing a new machine. You're talking about a discovery, which is unlocking a secret of nature. Very few major discoveries have been made since the beginning of time, and the people who made them are considered the most important people in history."

"So?"

"So none of them were nine years old."

"Then I'll be the first."

"Son, listen to me." My dad took hold of both my shoulders. "Do your project on lipstick as Miss Green wants you to. Do something you know you can do."

"Hogwash!" said a voice.

We all turned to see Grandpop standing in the doorway. "Let the boy find out for himself what he can and cannot do."

"But what Allen is talking about is impossible," insisted my father.

"It's not impossible," I said. "I don't care what anybody says. I'm going to do it. I'm going to solve the mystery of human photosynthesis."

The next day I rode my bike to the city library. With my notebook in hand, I ran up the wide stone steps to the entrance, pulled open one of the heavy glass doors and hurried inside.

"Good morning, Mrs. Snodgrass," I said to the elderly woman who sat at the reference desk. The kids called her "The Sergeant" because she was so strict.

Mrs. Snodgrass put one finger to her lips, reminding me to whisper. "What brings you here so early, Allen Brewster?"

"I'm going to make a discovery," I whispered. "It's for my science project at school."

"My goodness," said Mrs. Snodgrass, touching her hand to her face. "That sounds difficult."

"Yes, very difficult," I agreed. And then I pointed to my head. "You have to use this up here."

After I told Mrs. Snodgrass what my project was all about, she directed me over to a special part of the library.

"The books in this section are devoted to *biology*," she explained, "which is the study of living things." She smiled. "Good luck."

"Thank you, Mrs. Snodgrass."

Hours went by. I don't know how many.

"Human blood," I said to myself, chewing on the end of my pen. "That has to be it. Everything points to it. But does human blood contain all the necessary ingredients for photosynthesis to take place?"

I wrote the following down in my notebook:

	Necessary for Photosynthesis	Human Blood
○ ○		
○	1. Water	1. Blood is mostly water.
○	2. Carbon Dioxide	2. Blood carries carbon dioxide to
○		our lungs where it's exhaled.
○	3. Sunlight	3. Blood uses absorbed sunlight
○		through our skin to make Vitamin D.
○	4. Chlorophyll	4. Blood contains hemoglobin which
○		has a similar structure to Chlorophyll.
○		

What did Grandpop used to say? "Close is only good in horseshoes." Just because hemoglobin was close to chlorophyll didn't mean anything. They would have to be the same. Somehow there must be a way to make them the same.

As I reached for another book, I heard my name.

"Allen Brewster?"

I turned around quickly and saw the Sergeant.

"Are you still here?" said Mrs. Snodgrass. "I was just locking up. Am I ever glad I checked one more time or you would have had to spend the night."

"I'll spend the night," I said. "I don't mind. You see, I'm right on the verge of making my discovery. I can't go, Mrs. Snodgrass. Not now—please."

"Don't be foolish, young man. Now get your things together while I turn out the lights."

"But, Mrs. Snodgrass . . . "

"I'm sorry, Allen. Your discovery will just have to wait."

The next day I did not go back to the library. In fact, I did not go anyplace. I was not allowed to. It seems my parents were very upset that I had stayed so late at the library, especially when I let it slip that I had not been working on my lipstick project.

At first I was upset, too, but the way things turned out, I was sure glad I stayed home that day.

I spent the morning in my room reading over my notebook. In the afternoon, when my father was asleep on the couch and my mother was in the den playing the piano, I slipped out the back door to talk to Grandpop.

Grandpop was resting in a lounge chair on the back porch, listening to some old records on his old phonograph. I motioned for him to be quiet until I had shut the back door. He turned up the volume on the phonograph a little. We both nodded, agreeing that it was safe to talk.

"Tell me more about yesterday," he said.

"Let me show you my notebook," I said.

"No. Scientists work better alone. Just tell me what you found out."

"I think I've found all the pieces to the picture but one. I'm sure if I could have stayed at the library just a little longer . . . "

"Aren't you forgetting something, Allen?"

"What's that?"

"Just enough pieces, arranged in the proper order, so you can almost see the whole picture . . . Then you must use this." He pointed to his head.

"But I've tried, Grandpop. I've tried putting the pieces together. I just can't seem to see the picture."

"Have you tried thinking *crazy?*"

"Crazy?"

Grandpop smiled, and his eyes twinkled. "If I were to tell you," he said, "that you could whisper and someone halfway around the world in China could hear you, would you think I was crazy?"

"Sure." I laughed.

"What if I were whispering into a telephone?"

"That's different."

"Only because you see the whole picture."

"I see what you mean."

"And if I were to tell you that the sky was filled with waves that carry pictures . . . "

"Television."

"You're catching on. Learn to think crazy, Allen. Let your mind go. Don't be afraid to think of silly things, stupid things, things so ridiculous that you burst out laughing at the mere thought of them. That's the power of the brain, Allen. To think of things that no one else has ever thought of before."

"I understand."

With that Grandpop put on another record, leaned back in his lounge chair, and closed his eyes.

I opened my notebook to a clean page and wrote the words *THINK CRAZY*. Directly below it, I made the following two lists:

Plant Photosynthesis	Human Photosynthesis
1. Water	1. Water
2. Carbon Dioxide	2. Carbon Dioxide
3. Chlorophyll	3. Hemoglobin

The first list contained the necessary ingredients which in the presence of sunlight made photosynthesis possible in plants. The second list contained three substances found in our blood.

I ran head on into the same old problem. The missing piece. How to make the hemoglobin in our blood do what chlorophyll does in plants? But Grandpop said that I didn't need to find all the pieces. All I had to do was "think crazy."

Okay, Allen Brewster, you may begin now.

Go ahead. No one's looking.

Think.

I couldn't think.

Try.

I closed my eyes real tight.

Nothing.

Perhaps, I said to myself, it's a combination of different things—just the right things, just the right amounts.

But what things?

Think crazy.

Anything? Just try anything?

That's too many things to try.

And then it hit me.

I ran and got my notebook. I sat down at the kitchen table and began flipping through the pages. I had written something down. All I had to do was find it.

There it was!

In my notebook, I had written the following chemical formulas:

$$Chlorophyll—C_{55}H_{72}O_5N_4Mg$$
$$Hemoglobin—C_{34}H_{32}O_4N_4Fe$$

The biggest difference between these two substances was that chlorophyll contained Mg (magnesium), whereas hemoglobin contained Fe (iron).

Think crazy.

"I will only try those things that contain magnesium," I said, hitting my fist on the kitchen table.

I tiptoed into the living room past my father who was still asleep on the couch. I selected the M volume of the encyclopedia and returned to the kitchen. I looked up the word "magnesium" and found the following list of foods had it: beans, nuts, whole grain cereal, and *liver*.

I also read that salt water contained magnesium.

"Think crazy," I repeated the words.

I plugged in Mom's blender and started throwing things in, careful to write down in my notebook exactly how much of each thing.

The only beans we had were some leftover Mexican refried beans. Using the ice cream scooper, I put in one scoop. I found a can of mixed nuts in the cupboard but it was practically empty. I decided to use peanut butter instead (one scoop). We were all out of that natural cereal so I substituted Coco-Puffs (half a cup).

I found some raw liver in the refrigerator. I cut off the smallest piece I thought might work.

I was about to add some tap water to the blender when I remembered that the encyclopedia had mentioned salt water. Dad would kill me if he ever found out, but I went upstairs and took a half-cup of salt water from his aquarium, being careful not to scoop out any fish.

I turned on the blender and my concoction turned into a thick dark liquid.

I poured myself a glass.

I drank it.

That night I didn't eat any dinner. I wasn't hungry. Not one bit.

"I've done it," I told Grandpop before I went to bed. "I'll never have to eat again."

But I was wrong.

The next day when I woke up, I was starving. Beside my regular breakfast, I had an extra bowl of cereal and two extra glasses of milk.

A few days later, I repeated the experiment. Grandpop helped me measure out each ingredient. This time I added more liver.

Again, I went to bed without eating dinner. And the next morning I still wasn't hungry. I even gave away my lunch at school.

I had done it. I was sure of it.

Wrong.

By dinner-time I was so hungry I was the first one at the table.

"Stop chewing on your hand," my mother snapped at me as she served the food.

"Sorry," I responded, not aware of what I was doing.

I had three helpings of everything. Food never tasted so good.

But I didn't give up.

I performed my third experiment the following Sunday afternoon, after my parents had gone for a drive. They had asked Grandpop and me to go along, but we had declined—we had work to do.

"It seems the more liver I add," I told Grandpop, "the longer I can go without eating."

"You know," said Grandpop, his eyes widening, "I think you've got something there."

Mom had just gone to the store that morning, so there was plenty of liver in the refrigerator. I took out a huge, slimy piece and laid it on the countertop. I was about to cut some off when I stopped.

"In the name of science," I shrugged, and I threw the whole piece into the blender. I added the other ingredients.

I ran the blender for an extra couple of minutes, just to make sure all the liver got dissolved.

I poured myself a glass.

Did it ever look gross. I shut my eyes. I held my nose. I took a big gulp. It tasted just like *liquid liver*. I tried to take another sip, but I just couldn't.

That night I didn't eat dinner. My stomach felt funny. I also felt real light-headed. When I opened my eyes the room would start to spin around.

My mom was worried about me. She sat on the edge of my bed and rubbed my back until I fell asleep.

I woke up in the middle of the night.

Was I thirsty! I mean, I felt like I could drink the whole Atlantic Ocean, that is, if it weren't salt water.

I made my way down the hallway, past Grandpop's room, to the bathroom. I turned on the light, opened the medicine cabinet and took out my drinking glass. I filled it with water and drank. Water never tasted so good. I refilled my glass and drank again and again. And again.

When I was on my sixth glass, I noticed myself in the mirror.

I froze. I couldn't believe what I was looking at.

"I've done it," I said to myself, very faintly at first, then I said it louder. "I've done it! I've done it!" I began to jump around, shouting at the top of my lungs.

My mother was the first to arrive, appearing in the doorway to the bathroom. She took one look at me, then put her hands over her mouth.

Dad arrived next. "What have you done to yourself?"

"He's solved the mystery," said Grandpop, as he wedged himself in between them. "That's what he's done." Grandpop was smiling from ear to ear.

I looked at myself in the mirror again. I looked perfectly normal really, except for one small change. My skin had turned bright *green*, the color of a leaf on a tree.

HAVE YOU THANKED
A GREEN PLANT TODAY?

Thank you, thank you, lovely plant,
Eye-delighting oxidant.
You gratify the eye, and then,
To top it off, make oxygen.
You beautify, and then, to boot
(Oh lungs, rejoice) you depollute,
Thank you for this twofold bliss
Wrought by photosynthesis.
 (Now I hereby bequeath to you
 A life supply of CO_2.)

—*Don Anderson*

Think About It

1. What is the biggest difference between plants and animals?
2. Explain how plant cells are like "little food factories."
3. Tell why the author of "A Plant Person" had to do some research in biology before he wrote the story.
4. What purposes did each of the authors have in writing the three selections you just read? Compare and contrast them.
5. Name the plant people you have read about. Explain their relationship to plants.

Create and Share   Write your own thank-you poem to the plant of your choice. Have you thanked an apple tree? A tomato plant? A blueberry bush? Share the poem with your classmates. Or write the speech Allen must give when he presents his amazing findings at a conference of notable scientists. Read your work aloud to classmates.

Explore   Many poems have been written about plants. You can find them collected in anthologies, which contain poetry by more than one writer, and in books by individual poets. Both kinds of books are in the poetry section of the library.

Simple Solutions

I have no voice and yet I speak to you,
I tell of all things in the world that people do;
I have leaves, but I am not a tree,
I have pages, but I am not a bride or royalty;
I have a spine and hinges, but I am not
    a man or a door,
I have told you all,
I cannot tell more.
    What am I?

Answer: a book

E-R I M !

R-A-B-N G-N-E

PICTURE PUZZLES

from CDC?
by William Steig

In these riddles, letters and numbers form the captions for humorous cartoons. Can you solve them? Here's a hint: the pictures are clues to the puzzles.

B-U-T N D B-S

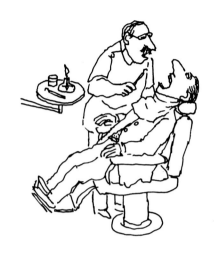

U F D-K N U-R K-9

D 2-2 S C-D

U F B-D I-S

V F E-10 D L-F-N

Stories to Solve

by George Shannon

Stories and mysteries have existed as long as there have been people to tell them and question why. The following folktales each involve a mystery or problem to be solved by the story's characters. This leaves a mystery for the reader—to figure out how the characters did it. Each story is different, but each can be solved with careful reading, and visualizing the story's events and images.

Fishing

One fine summer day two fathers and two sons went fishing at their favorite lake. They fished and talked all morning long and by noon everyone had caught one fish. As the two fathers and two sons walked back home, everyone was happy because each had a fish even though only three fish had been caught.

Two fathers and two sons. Only three fish and no fish were lost. How can this have happened?

Crossing the River

Once there was a man who had to take a wolf, a goat, and a cabbage across a river. But his boat was so small it could hold only himself and one other thing. The man didn't know what to do. How could he take the wolf, the goat, and the cabbage over one at a time, so that the wolf wouldn't eat the goat and the goat wouldn't eat the cabbage?

The Sticks of Truth

Long ago in India judges traveled from village to village.
One day a judge stopped at an inn to rest, but the inn-
keeper was very upset. Someone had just that day stolen
his daughter's gold ring. The judge told him not to worry
and had all the guests gather so that he could question
them. When he could not figure out from their answers
who the thief was, the judge decided to use some old
magic. He told them all he was going to have to use the
sticks of truth.

"These are magic sticks," he explained, "that will catch
the thief."

He gave each guest a stick to keep under his or her
bed during the night.

"The stick belonging to the thief will grow two inches during the night. At breakfast we will all compare sticks and the longest stick will be the thief's."

The next morning the judge had all the guests come by his table and hold their sticks up next to his to see if they had grown. But one after another all were the same. None of them had grown any longer. Then suddenly the judge called, "This is the thief! Her stick is shorter than all the rest."

Once caught, the woman confessed and the ring was returned. But all the guests were confused about the sticks of truth. The judge had said the longest stick would be the thief's, but instead it had been the shortest stick.

Why?

The Cleverest Son

Once there lived an old man who had three sons. When he grew old and ill and knew that he soon would die, he called all three sons into his room.

"There is no way I can divide the house and farm to support all three of you. The one who proves himself the cleverest will inherit the house and farm. There is a coin on the table for each of you. The one who can buy something that will fill this room will inherit all I own."

The eldest son took his coin, went straight to the marketplace, and filled his wagon full of straw. The second son thought a bit longer, then also went to the marketplace, where he bought sacks and sacks of feathers. The youngest son thought and then quietly went to a little shop. He bought two small things and tucked them into his pocket.

That night the father called them in to show what they had bought. The eldest son spread his straw about the floor, but it filled only one part of the room. The second son dumped out his sacks of feathers, but they filled only two corners of the room. Then the youngest son smiled, pulled the two small things out of his pocket, and soon filled the room.

"Yes," said the father, "you are indeed the cleverest and have filled my room when the others could not. You shall inherit my house and farm."

What had the youngest son bought and with what did he fill the room?

SOLUTIONS

Only three people went fishing. A boy, his father, and his grandfather: two sons and two fathers.

Solution 1: He could take the goat over and go back alone. Then take the wolf over and then bring the goat back. Then take the cabbage over and leave the goat behind. And finally make one last trip and take the goat over to join the wolf and cabbage.

Solution 2: He could take the goat over and go back alone. Then take the cabbage over and bring the goat back. Then take the wolf over and leave the goat behind. And finally go back and get the goat on the last trip.

None of the sticks were magical. The only one to worry about being caught, the thief had cut off two inches of her stick during the night in an effort to hide its growth. But since the sticks were not magical, her stick ended up the only short one.

A match and a candle that filled the room with light.

SCIENCE PUZZLES

from BET YOU CAN'T
by Vicki Cobb

The Sure Thing

Bet you can't read this without trying at least one trick. They look s-o-o-o easy, you won't be able to resist. But anyone who takes these bets is in for a truly humbling experience, for this is a collection of sucker bets. There is no way to win. Each challenge is designed to trick you into trying something impossible.

These really are impossible tricks. If at first you don't succeed . . . perhaps you never will. Not all things are possible.

The odds were stacked at the beginning of time by Mother Nature. It took some of the greatest minds in the history of the world to figure out what was happening. They reasoned and experimented and figured out why some things just won't work. Now you can cash in on their discoveries.

Take a chance. Even if the odds are insurmountable, you're bound to have a good time. *We'll* bet on that!

The Leak-Proof Hole

*Bet You Can't Make Water
Leak Out of a Hole in a Bottle!*

The Setup: Get a pair of scissors and a plastic bottle with a screw top. Make a small hole in

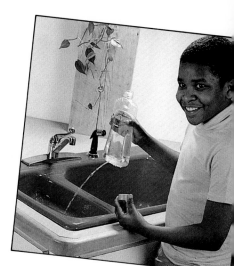

the side of the bottle near the bottom with the point of the scissors. Cover the hole with your finger while you fill the bottle with water to the brim. (Do this over the sink.) Screw on the top, making sure there is no air in the bottle. Take your finger away from the hole. Stand back and watch for the water to come pouring out!

The Fix: No water? That's because the odds were stacked against it. For water to leak out the hole, the air pressure pushing on the water has to be less than the force of gravity. Usually the pressure on top of a liquid is equal to the air pressure pushing on the hole. The two forces cancel each other out; gravity wins and the water rushes forth. (Open the top of the bottle and see this happen.) But as long as the surface of the water is protected from air pressure by the bottle cap, air pressure works to keep the water *in* the bottle. Air pressure then wins because it is stronger than the force of gravity!

You have something else working against you here, too. It's the surface tension of the water. It acts like a skin and holds the water together. It's a weak force, but it works for you when you have a small hole.

Blowing a Chance

Bet You Can't Blow Up a Balloon in a Bottle!

The Setup: Select a balloon that is easy to blow up. Put it in an empty soda bottle and stretch the neck of the balloon completely over the mouth of the bottle. Try to blow up the balloon so it fills the bottle.

The Fix: So you thought this one would be easy? It's not only difficult, it's downright impossible. To inflate the balloon, you would need to compress the air trapped between the balloon and the bottle. To compress air requires force. Human lungs are not strong enough to inflate the balloon *and* to compress the trapped air.

A Breathtaking Chance

Bet You Can't Blow a Wad of Paper into a Bottle!

The Setup: Place an empty soda bottle on its side. Put a small wad of paper in the neck. Try to blow the paper into the bottle.

The Fix: Not only won't the wad go in, it will fly out at you instead! When you blow into an enclosed space like a bottle, you increase the air pressure inside. Since pressure will equalize when it can, the air rushes out of the bottle, taking the wad of paper with it. Amazing, but that's the way it flows!

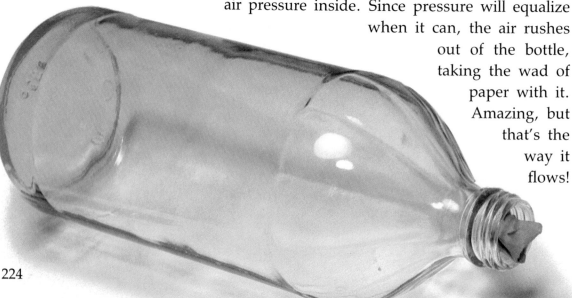

Floating Odds

*Bet You Can't Make a Cork Float
in the Center of a Glass of Water!*

The Setup: Fill a glass with water. Now overfill it by adding water slowly until the surface rises over the edge of the glass. Gently set a cork afloat in the center. Try to keep it there!

The Fix: That cork is going to move toward an edge no matter how many times you push it back toward the middle. Water molecules cling together. One evidence of this cohesive force is called surface tension. It's like an invisible skin. The cork must break the surface tension of the water and it does this where the force is weakest, usually the lowest point of the liquid. In this case, the lowest point of the water is the edge. If you view the glass at eye level, you can see that the water has a bulging shape that rises in the center.

Now as long as you're fooling around with that cork, try this one.

Bet You Can't Make a Cork Float
near the Edge of a Glass of Water!

The Setup: Empty some of the water from the overfull glass so that the surface of the water is well below the rim of the glass. Gently put the cork in the water. Guide it to an edge if you like. Try to get the cork to float near the edge.

The Fix: The cork is always going to end up in the center. Two forces work against you here. One is surface tension again. The other is a force of attraction between the water and the glass. The water sticks to the glass (wets it), pulling the surface up at the edges. The cork breaks the surface tension where it is weakest and, in this case, it is the center, the point where the water level is lowest.

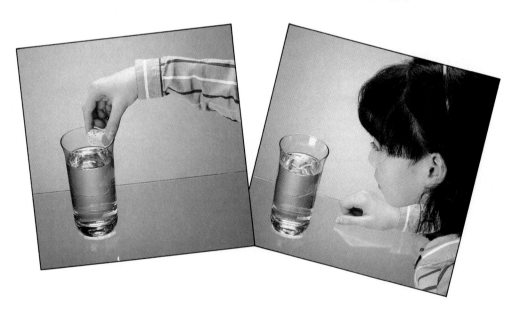

Think About It

1. What are the steps you use to solve puzzles?
2. What two kinds of clues did you find in the picture puzzles? How did you figure out what the puzzles meant?
3. Which stories did you find easy to solve? Explain what you knew or what you did that made them easy for you.
4. Which of the science puzzles were you able to figure out? What scientific facts did you have to know to do them?
5. What makes some of the picture puzzles, stories, and science puzzles *not* easy to solve?

Create and Share   Exercise your creative powers! Make up some picture puzzles, stories to solve, or science puzzles of your own. Share your puzzles by presenting them in a Marvelous Mystery Show or by displaying them in a special corner in your classroom.

Explore   There are books of all kinds of puzzles, secret codes, riddles, logical problems, or science puzzles to enjoy. You may find some under these headings in the card catalog: PUZZLES, CODES, and SCIENCE—EXPERIMENTS.

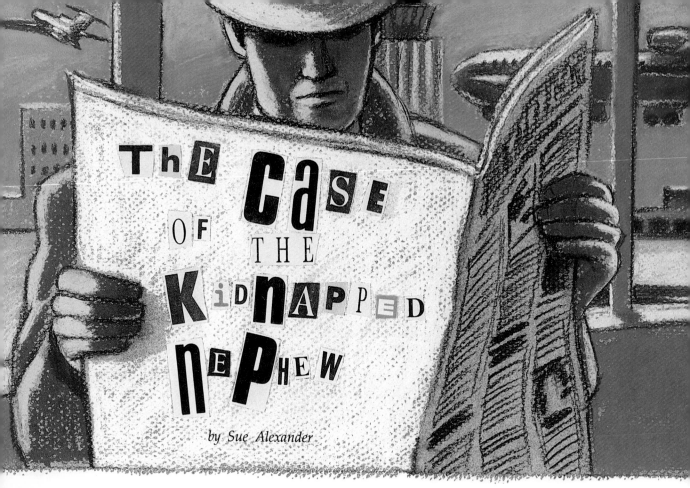

THE CASE OF THE KIDNAPPED NEPHEW

by Sue Alexander

Characters

COURT CLERK

JUDGE ALEXANDER FAIRMAN

TIMOTHY CRANE

MS. GARFIELD,
attorney for the accused

MR. BRADBURY,
prosecuting attorney

PAMELA MADISON

EDITH ALLWELL

JONATHAN SLOTE

BRIAN FARLEY

Setting, properties, production notes

The scene is a courtroom. There are three tables and ten chairs. A gavel is on the judge's table. PAMELA MADISON walks with the aid of a cane (or stick) and carries a purse containing a letter in an envelope and a folded piece of yellow paper. BRIAN is wearing one green sock and one red sock. Each attorney has a folder of papers.

The judge's chambers are to the audience's left; the doorway is to the audience's right. The COURT CLERK *and the* JUDGE *enter and exit from the judge's chambers. All others enter and exit on the doorway side.*

General note: The attorneys stand while they are questioning witnesses.

As the play begins everyone except the COURT CLERK *and the* JUDGE *enters.* GARFIELD *and* TIMOTHY *are talking to each other. The witnesses are talking among themselves. They sit down —* GARFIELD *and* TIMOTHY *are at the audience's left, and* BRADBURY *is at the audience's right.*

TIMOTHY: This whole thing is crazy! I can't believe it's happening. I'm on trial for something I didn't do!

GARFIELD: You know you didn't do it, Tim, and I know it. But the only way we're going to be able to prove it is to discover who did!

CLERK: (*The clerk enters and stands, facing the audience, in front of the judge's table.*) Hear ye, hear ye, court is now in session. Judge Alexander Fairman presiding. All rise.

(*Everyone stands up. The* JUDGE *comes in and sits down. Then everyone except the* CLERK *sits down.*)

CLERK: The People versus Timothy Crane! (*The clerk sits down.*)

JUDGE: Timothy Crane, you are charged with kidnapping and extortion. How do you plead?

TIMOTHY: (*He stands up.*) Not guilty, Your Honor. (*He sits down.*)

JUDGE: The clerk will enter the plea in the record. Ms. Garfield, as counsel for the defense, are you ready to proceed?

GARFIELD: (*She stands.*) Yes, Your Honor.

JUDGE: Mr. Bradbury, as prosecutor for the People, are you ready to proceed?

BRADBURY: (*He stands up.*) Yes, Your Honor.

JUDGE: Very well. Begin then, please, Mr. Bradbury.

(MS. GARFIELD *sits down.*)

BRADBURY: (*He walks back and forth while he is talking.*) Your Honor, the People will prove that Timothy Crane did, on the 22nd of May this year, kidnap Brian Farley and extort money for his release from Mr. Farley's aunt, Mrs. Pamela Madison. To begin testimony, I call my first witness, Pamela Madison.

(PAMELA *rises with difficulty and walks haltingly, leaning on her cane, to the witness chair and stands in front of it.*)

CLERK: (*The clerk stands.*) Do you swear to tell the truth, the whole truth, and nothing but the truth?

PAMELA: I do. (*She sits down. So does the* CLERK.)

BRADBURY: Mrs. Madison, you are a writer, is that correct? And Timothy Crane is your secretary?

PAMELA: Yes, that's correct. Tim is my secretary and research assistant. As you can see, I'm not able to get around easily—I have chronic arthritis. So Tim goes here and there on errands for me.

BRADBURY: I see. Now, Mrs. Madison, will you please tell us in your own words what occurred on the 22nd of May.

PAMELA: Well, Tim had gone out and I don't like to be alone in the house, so my friend Edith Allwell had come to stay with me. I was waiting for my nephew Brian to arrive from England. Earlier that day I'd received a telegram from him telling me not to meet him at the airport, that he would take a cab. Then, shortly before noon, the doorbell rang, and a messenger hand-delivered a letter. As soon as

he put the envelope in my hand, he left—even before I had time to open it. The letter stated that Brian had been kidnapped!

BRADBURY: Do you have that letter?

PAMELA: Yes. (*She opens her purse and pulls out the envelope.*) Here it is.

BRADBURY: Read it aloud, please.

PAMELA: (*She takes the letter out of the envelope and reads.*) "If you want to see your nephew Brian alive, put ten thousand dollars in a suitcase and wait for further instructions. Do not call the police."

BRADBURY: Your Honor, I would like to have the letter entered as the People's Exhibit A.

JUDGE: It is so ordered.

BRADBURY: (*He takes the letter from* PAMELA *and hands it to the* CLERK.) Go on, Mrs. Madison, what happened next?

PAMELA: For a while, I didn't know what to do. I was terribly frightened. And I was afraid to call the police for fear that something would happen to Brian. Then I remembered that I *had* enough money. I own several racehorses, and the day before I'd sold one to Admiral Denay. He'd paid me in cash. I got the money from my safe, and my friend Edith got one of my suitcases from the closet. I put the money inside and waited for further instructions. About an hour later the doorbell rang again. But this time there wasn't any messenger. There was just an envelope on the doorstep. It contained the instructions.

BRADBURY: What were you instructed to do?

PAMELA: To take the suitcase of money and put it in back of the newsstand at the corner. The letter said that if I did as I was told within ten minutes, Brian would be freed.

BRADBURY: And did you follow the instructions?

PAMELA: Yes, of course! Edith took the suitcase there for
    me since I'm unable to carry anything heavy while
    I'm walking.

BRADBURY: And was Brian freed?

PAMELA: Yes. He arrived at my home about an hour later.

BRADBURY: Mrs. Madison, where was your secretary,
    Timothy Crane, at this time?

PAMELA: I don't know. He had come to me quite early
    that morning and asked if he might have the day
    off. He seemed quite nervous about something. I
    told him he could, and he left immediately.

BRADBURY: I see. Now, Mrs. Madison, who besides
    yourself knew that your nephew Brian was due to
    arrive that day?

PAMELA: Only Tim and, of course, my friend Edith.

BRADBURY: Tell me, Mrs. Madison, did Timothy Crane know what your nephew looked like?

PAMELA: I would think so. When Brian wrote and said he was coming, he enclosed his picture so I'd recognize him. The picture had been on the mantel over the fireplace since I got it about two weeks before.

BRADBURY: Thank you. (*He turns toward* GARFIELD.) Your witness. (*He sits down.*)

GARFIELD: (*She walks toward* PAMELA *while she is talking.*) Mrs. Madison, could you describe the messenger who brought the ransom note?

PAMELA: Not really. I couldn't see his face at all. He was bundled up in a rain slicker and hat—you know, the kind that covers most of your face. And I really wasn't paying much attention to him. (*She stops and thinks for a moment.*) I did notice that he had on one red sock and one green sock. I remember thinking how peculiar that was.

GARFIELD: So the messenger could have been anybody at all?

PAMELA: Yes.

GARFIELD: You say that Timothy Crane was the only one besides your friend Ms. Allwell who knew that Brian was arriving from England. But a great many people—almost everyone—knew about the *money* you had, isn't that true?

PAMELA: Yes, I suppose so. It had been in the papers that morning. Admiral Denay is a bit eccentric in that he always pays cash for the racehorses he buys, and the newspaper reporters like that kind of story.

GARFIELD: Thank you, that's all. (*She goes back to her seat and sits down.*)

BRADBURY: (*He rises.*) One question on redirect, Your Honor.

JUDGE: Proceed, Mr. Bradbury.

BRADBURY: Mrs. Madison, could you say definitely that the messenger was *not* Timothy Crane? Think before you answer.

PAMELA: (*She thinks for a second.*) No, I couldn't say that.

JUDGE: You may step down, Mrs. Madison.

(PAMELA *gets up and goes back to her original seat.*)

BRADBURY: My next witness is Ms. Edith Allwell.

(EDITH *gets up and walks to the witness chair and stands in front of it.*)

CLERK: (*The clerk stands.*) Do you swear to tell the truth, the whole truth, and nothing but the truth?

EDITH: I do. (*She sits down. So does the* CLERK.)

BRADBURY: Ms. Allwell, are you acquainted with Timothy Crane?

EDITH: Yes, of course. He's been Mrs. Madison's secretary for a number of years. And I am a regular visitor at her home.

BRADBURY: Did you ever have occasion to see him elsewhere?

EDITH: Yes, as a matter of fact. Like Mrs. Madison, I own some racehorses. I go to the racetrack quite often. And I've seen Tim there—bumped into him, you might say.

BRADBURY: And did he win or lose?

GARFIELD: (*She rises.*) Objection! That's immaterial, Your Honor!

BRADBURY: (*He turns toward the* JUDGE.) Your Honor, I intend to show that it is not. In fact, it may be the *reason* for this crime.

JUDGE: Very well. Objection overruled. You may answer the question, Ms. Allwell.

EDITH: I've no idea whether Tim won or lost.

BRADBURY: Hmmm. All right. Now let's go back to the day of the kidnapping. What time had you arrived at Mrs. Madison's home?

EDITH: Oh, I'd say around 10 A.M. or so. She'd called me shortly after nine, and I got there as quickly as I could. I stayed with her until sometime after Brian arrived—about an hour or so.

BRADBURY: Were you there when Timothy Crane returned from wherever he'd been?

EDITH: Yes, I was.

BRADBURY: And when was that?

EDITH: About half an hour after Brian came in. We were listening to Brian tell what had happened to him when Tim came in.

BRADBURY: And how did he seem to you?

EDITH: He seemed to be agitated, nervous. But we were so taken up with Brian that I didn't pay too much attention to Tim.

BRADBURY: Thank you. Your witness, Ms. Garfield. (*He goes to his seat.*)

GARFIELD: Ms. Allwell, *you* say Timothy Crane seemed agitated. Yet, you admit you weren't paying too much attention to his mood.

EDITH: That's true.

GARFIELD: Weren't *you* agitated at that point, given the events of the day?

EDITH: Indeed I was! My heart was still jumping. I can't remember ever being so frightened or upset!

GARFIELD: Why, then, wouldn't Timothy Crane be agitated? After all, he had been in Mrs. Madison's employ for a long time. Certainly, you would credit him with caring about her.

BRADBURY: (*He rises.*) Objection! That's calling for an opinion!

JUDGE: Objection sustained. The witness will not answer the question.

GARFIELD: No further questions. (*She returns to her seat.*)

JUDGE: You may step down, Ms. Allwell. Mr. Bradbury, call your next witness.

(EDITH *goes back to her seat.*)

BRADBURY: (*He rises.*) I call Jonathan Slote.

(JONATHAN *gets up and walks to the witness chair.*)

CLERK: (*The clerk stands.*) Do you swear to tell the truth, the whole truth, and nothing but the truth?

JONATHAN: I do. (*He sits down. So does the* CLERK.)

BRADBURY: Mr. Slote, what is your occupation?

JONATHAN: I'm—I work for a literary agency. Mrs. Madison's agent is my employer.

BRADBURY: And do you know Mrs. Madison's secretary, Timothy Crane?

JONATHAN: Oh, yes. We come from the same town in Illinois. I've known him all my life. In fact, it was he who recommended me to my employer.

BRADBURY: And do you have occasion to see him often?

JONATHAN: Yes, sir. We have the same day off and generally spend it together.

BRADBURY: And what do you and Mr. Crane do on your days off?

JONATHAN: Usually, we go to the races. We both like to bet on the horses.

BRADBURY: Mr. Slote, do you know if Mr. Crane won or lost at the races?

JONATHAN: Well, lately he'd been losing.

BRADBURY: I see. Mr. Slote, do you know how much money he had lost?

JONATHAN: Not exactly. It has to be quite a lot, though. Because he's borrowed money from me—he owes me over a thousand dollars.

BRADBURY: And has he expressed an intention to repay you?

JONATHAN: Oh, yes. He told me that he'd have it for me very soon.

BRADBURY: When did he tell you that?

JONATHAN: Two days before Brian Farley was kidnapped.

BRADBURY: Thank you. Your witness. (*He returns to his seat.*)

GARFIELD: (*She rises.*) I have only one question for Mr. Slote. Tell me, Mr. Slote, since you have known the defendant so long, do you think him capable of committing this crime?

BRADBURY: (*He rises.*) Objection, Your Honor! Opinion!

JUDGE: Hmmm. I think I'll overrule your objection, Mr. Bradbury. The witness may answer.

GARFIELD: Mr. Slote?

JONATHAN: No, I don't *think* so.

GARFIELD: Thank you. No further questions. (*She sits down.*)

JUDGE: You may step down, Mr. Slote. Before you call your next witness, Mr. Bradbury, we will take a recess.

CLERK: (*The clerk stands up.*) All rise!

(*Everyone stands as the* JUDGE *goes out the chambers side, followed by the* CLERK. *Then everyone but* GARFIELD *and* TIMOTHY *go out the doorway side.* GARFIELD *and* TIMOTHY *sit down.*)

TIMOTHY: It doesn't look good for me, does it?

GARFIELD: No, Tim, I'm afraid it doesn't. (*She thinks for a second.*) The nephew will probably be the next witness. What's he like?

TIMOTHY: He seems nice enough. A bit down on his luck at the moment, I'd guess from his conversation. But he's got a good sense of humor. Takes after his father, according to Mrs. Madison. She says he has all the family traits.

GARFIELD: What do you mean, all?

TIMOTHY: Oh, just the odd things that occur in some families. You know, allergies and that sort of thing. Mrs. Madison says that all the men in her family are color-blind, hate squash, and are allergic to strawberries.

GARFIELD: Hmmmm. Color-blind. (*She thinks for a moment.*) I wonder . . .

(*Everyone except the* JUDGE *and the* CLERK *returns to the courtroom. They don't all come at once—they straggle in. When everyone is in his or her seat the* CLERK *comes in and faces them all.*)

CLERK: All rise!

(*Everyone stands up. The* JUDGE *comes in and takes his seat.*)

CLERK: Be seated.

(*Everyone, including the* CLERK, *sits down.*)

JUDGE: Mr. Bradbury, call your witness.

BRADBURY: (*He rises.*) Mr. Brian Farley.

(BRIAN *comes to the witness chair and stands in front of it.*)

CLERK: (*The clerk stands.*) Do you swear to tell the truth, the whole truth, and nothing but the truth?

BRIAN: I do. (*He sits down. So does the* CLERK.)

BRADBURY: Mr. Farley, please tell the court what happened to you on May 22nd.

BRIAN: Yes, sir. Just before my plane landed, the airflight attendant told me that I'd got a message not to go to my aunt's house. I was to meet her at a different address. I took a cab there. No sooner had I rung the bell, when the door opened and somebody grabbed me. I never did see the man's face. Before I knew what was happening, I was bound, gagged, and blindfolded. Then I heard the man go out. He came back some time later, pushed me out the door, and into a car. We drove for quite some time. Then he stopped the car, untied my hands, and pushed me out. He drove away before I could get the blindfold off. When I finally managed to remove it, I found that I was back at the airport. I hailed a cab and went to my aunt's house.

BRADBURY: Thank you, Mr. Farley. Your witness, Ms. Garfield. (*He sits down.*)

GARFIELD: (*She is talking to herself in a loud whisper.*) Something isn't . . . but what is it? (*She rises.*) I would like to reserve my cross examination until later, Your Honor. (*She sits down.*)

JUDGE: Very well. Call another witness, Mr. Bradbury.

(BRIAN *returns to his seat.*)

BRADBURY: (*He rises.*) The prosecution has no other witnesses, Your Honor. (*He sits down.*)

JUDGE: Then we will hear from the defense. Ms. Garfield.

GARFIELD: (*She rises.*) The defense calls Timothy Crane.

(TIMOTHY *goes to the witness chair and stands in front of it.*)

CLERK: (*The clerk stands.*) Do you swear to tell the truth, the whole truth, and nothing but the truth?

TIMOTHY: I do. (*He sits down. So does the* CLERK.)

GARFIELD: Mr. Crane, please tell the court what you did on the day in question.

TIMOTHY: I left the house a little after nine in the morning and went to the racetrack. I was to meet a guy I know. He'd promised to give me a good solid tip on the sixth race. And I needed that tip. I'd lost a lot of money, including most of what I'd borrowed from my friend, Jon Slote. I figured that with a good tip, I could make back what I'd lost— and maybe more. But the guy never showed up. I hunted all over for him. Then the races started. I bet—and lost. I felt sick so I went home, back to Mrs. Madison's.

GARFIELD: Did you see anyone you knew at the racetrack?

TIMOTHY: No. If it had been my regular day off, I probably would have—the same people seem to be there all the time. But this was a different day. Besides, I was busy looking for the guy I was supposed to meet. I didn't pay any attention to who was there.

GARFIELD: Were you aware that it was the day that Mrs. Madison's nephew was to arrive?

TIMOTHY: Yes. His telegram had come just before I left the house.

GARFIELD: (*She walks back and forth for a moment, thinking. Then she stops.*) Mr. Crane, did you read the telegram?

TIMOTHY: Yes. I open all the mail. As soon as I read it, I gave it to Mrs. Madison.

GARFIELD: Do you happen to know what she did with it?

TIMOTHY: Hmmm. I think she put it in her purse.

GARFIELD: (*She turns toward the* JUDGE.) Your Honor, if Mrs. Madison still has the telegram in her purse, perhaps we might see it?

JUDGE: (*He nods, then turns and looks at* PAMELA.) Mrs. Madison, do you have that telegram?

PAMELA: I'll see, Your Honor. (*She opens her purse and searches through it. After a second or two she pulls out a folded piece of yellow paper.*) Yes. Here it is.

JUDGE: Give it to the clerk, please.

(*The* CLERK *takes the telegram and brings it to* MS. GARFIELD.)

GARFIELD: Thank you. (*She takes it from the* CLERK *and reads aloud*.) It says: "Arriving 1:30 P.M. Do not meet me. Will take a cab." And it's signed Brian. (*She hands it to* TIMOTHY.) Is this the telegram you saw?

TIMOTHY (*He looks at it*.): Yes, it is. (*He hands it back to* GARFIELD.)

GARFIELD: Thank you, Mr. Crane. I have no further questions. Your witness, Mr. Bradbury. (*She returns to her seat and puts the telegram on the table*.)

BRADBURY: Your testimony was very interesting, Mr. Crane. But do you really expect us to believe that you saw no one you knew at the racetrack? After all, it is a place you go often.

TIMOTHY: Yes, but I didn't see anyone I knew that day.

BRADBURY: Of course, you didn't. Because you weren't there! You never went to the racetrack. Instead, you were holding Brian Farley prisoner! You knew your employer had a great deal of cash on hand and that she would gladly exchange it for the safe return of her nephew.

TIMOTHY: No! That's not true! I didn't do it! I didn't!

BRADBURY: I submit that you did, Mr. Crane. No further questions. (*He returns to his seat*.)

JUDGE: You may step down, Mr. Crane. Ms. Garfield, call your next witness.

(CRANE *returns to his seat*.)

GARFIELD: (*She rises*.) I have no other witnesses, Your Honor. But at this time I'd like to have Brian Farley recalled to the stand for cross-examination.

JUDGE: Very well. Brian Farley, take the stand.

(BRIAN *goes to the witness chair and sits down*.)

JUDGE: Remember, Mr. Farley, you are still under oath.

BRIAN: Yes, Your Honor.

GARFIELD: Mr. Farley, before you left England, you sent a telegram to your aunt not to meet your plane. Why was that?

BRIAN: I wanted to save her a trip to the airport.

GARFIELD: That was very considerate of you. By the way, what time did your plane arrive?

BRIAN: One-thirty in the afternoon.

GARFIELD: And it was a direct, non-stop flight from England?

BRIAN: Yes.

GARFIELD: (*She walks over to the table and picks up the telegram.*) Can you tell me then, Mr. Farley, how your aunt received this *telegram* from you and not a cablegram? Telegrams are *land* wires, not overseas wires.

BRIAN: Why—uhhh . . .

GARFIELD: Mr. Farley, how long have you been out of work?

BRIAN: About six months. But I don't see what that has to do with anything.

GARFIELD: Let's let the court decide that. Tell me, if you've not worked in six months, where did you get the money for the trip?

BRIAN: I—I—borrowed it. I'm to pay it back within a month.

GARFIELD: I see. Mr. Farley, what would you say if I contended that you were never kidnapped at all? That you, in fact, landed in the United States in the morning, saw the newspaper report of your aunt's sale of a racehorse to Admiral Denay, guessed that she had a lot of cash on hand—and cooked up this scheme to rob her?

BRIAN: That's ridiculous!

GARFIELD: Is it? Tell me, Mr. Farley, what color socks are you wearing?

BRIAN: What . . . ? (*He pulls up both legs of his pants so that his socks show and looks down at them.*) They're green. But I don't see . . .

GARFIELD: No, *you* don't. But perhaps the court will. You are not wearing two green socks, Mr. Farley. Only one is green. The other is red. You can't tell the difference because you are color-blind.

BRIAN: So what?

GARFIELD: Isn't it strange that the messenger who brought the ransom note also wore one red sock and one green one? Perhaps he, too, is color-blind. Or perhaps, Mr. Farley, *you* were the messenger!

BRIAN: I—I—oh, what's the use! Yes, I did it. Just the way you said. I thought no one would find out! (*He covers his face with his hands.*) I'll give the money back!

JUDGE: (*He pounds the gavel.*) Mr. Bradbury, I think a motion to dismiss the case against Mr. Crane is in order.

BRADBURY: (*He rises.*) I so move, Your Honor.

JUDGE: Motion granted. Case dismissed! (*He pounds the gavel once.*) The clerk will escort Mr. Farley to the bailiff where he will be advised of his rights and then removed to the jail.

(*The* CLERK *goes over to the witness stand and takes* BRIAN's *arm and escorts him out the doorway side.*)

JUDGE: Court is adjourned. (*He gets up and goes out.*)

(*Everyone, except* TIMOTHY *and* GARFIELD, *rises and heads for the doorway, talking among themselves.*)

TIMOTHY: (*He turns to* GARFIELD.) I don't know how to thank you . . .

(*On her way to the door,* PAMELA *has stopped next to* TIMOTHY's *chair. She puts her hand on his shoulder and faces* GARFIELD.)

PAMELA: Let me add my thanks, too. Though it hurts to know that my own nephew tried to rob me, it makes me feel better to know that my trust in Tim all these years hasn't been misplaced.

GARFIELD: No thanks are necessary. Tim's telling me that Brian is color-blind was what gave me the answer. The path to truth, in this case, was marked in red and green.

(GARFIELD *and* TIMOTHY *rise.* TIMOTHY *takes* PAMELA's *arm and all three go out together.*)

Think About It

1. Why is Timothy Crane in court?
2. At what point in the trial did you discover a clue that would prove Timothy Crane did not commit a crime?
3. Explain why this play belongs in a group of selections about puzzles.
4. If "The Case of the Kidnapped Nephew" were told as a story and not a play, how would it be different?
5. What do you think causes people to enjoy puzzles, riddles, mazes, mysteries, and other things to solve? Give as many reasons as you can.

Create and Share
Describe to your classmates the events surrounding an imaginary mystery in your school: "The Case of the Missing _____." Provide clues so that your classmates can try to solve your mystery. Give the solution if no one can figure it out. Remember that part of the fun of a mystery is in being able to solve it without being told the answer, so don't make your mystery *too* difficult!

Explore
If you would like to read other mystery stories, look in the card catalog under MYSTERY AND DETECTIVE STORIES. Your choices are many! Or look for Donald J. Sobol's books about Encyclopedia Brown, a boy detective who knows a lot and uses his knowledge to solve many puzzling cases.

Winning is seventy-five percent attitude. The other twenty-five percent is knowing how to lose gracefully.

Sheila Thomas

Winners All

THE CALF-RAISING CONTEST

from PHILIP HALL LIKES ME. I RECKON MAYBE.
by Bette Greene

Philip Hall struck the table with his gavel, which is pretty much the way the 4-H Club of Pocahontas, Arkansas, is always called to order. He asked everybody—one at a time—to tell how their project was coming along and if it was going to be ready for next Saturday's county fair.

Although my hand was the first raised, Philip was nodding toward Bonnie Blake, which was just as well, seeing as she had already begun talking. She told about the special problem of making a dress with a printed pattern, and then she explained with detail piled on top of boring detail how she overcame every single obstacle before concluding with: "But it's all finished now and I'm ready for the judging."

Waving my hand as hard as I could didn't help none 'cause our president had begun motioning toward Ginny, who got to her feet so slowly that you'd think she was the only one waiting to speak her piece. Then she did a powerful lot of explaining about all the trouble she went through getting a few garden vegetables into sealed jars before she finally said, "But my carrots, stewed tomatoes, and lima beans can't hardly wait for the canning contest."

I thought for sure I was going to be next, but Gordon was being asked to report on what he was doing to get himself prepared for the tractor maintenance contest. "Through the mail I got me this little booklet called *Maintaining Your John Deere Tractor* and I read it, top to bottom."

For a long time now Gordon's been working on Saturdays at the Randolph County Tractor Center and all us 4-H members think that if any one of us comes home with a blue ribbon (or even a red one) it is going to be him.

Next thing I knew, the Jones boys—Jordan and Joshua—were standing up explaining their pig's progress by weight and inches. Just when I got to thinking that that little pig is going to grow into a full-size hog before Jordan and Joshua finish up their explaining, the double Js did something truly amazing—they finished up their explaining.

Philip Hall smiled like folks do when they have been saving the best for last. He was fixing to call upon me. Ain't he a sweet thing? This time I didn't wave my hands. 'Cause when he tells the club about all the good work I'm

doing with my calf Madeline, well, I'm going to act surprised and a little embarrassed.

But he began: "I named my female calf Leonard because Leonard doesn't act like no girl. Leonard's as brave as any bull and smart—Ooooooeeeeee!"

I couldn't hardly believe what I was hearing from that low-down polecat! I told him, "When Leonard gets grown he's going to be giving milk, more like a Leonora than a Leonard."

Everybody laughed except our president, who didn't find my remarks the least bit amusing. He didn't even wait for the laughing to end before going on with his talk. "Up to the time Leonard was ten days old, he wouldn't put nothing in his mouth but mother's milk. So before feedings, I got to rubbing a little milk-soaked grain on his nose. Naturally enough, he'd lick it right off and that's how I tricked Leonard into liking grain."

I wasn't listening. I was thinking back, remembering how he never ever let me say one word about my Madeline.

Part of the problem with Philip is that he doesn't like the idea that our cow, Old Maude with the sagging back, could give birth to a calf good enough to compete with the very best from the Hall Dairy Farm. And another part of the problem has to do with boys and how they hate losing . . . especially how they hate losing to girls.

When Philip paused, I jumped to my feet. "Mr. 4-H President," I called out. "Reckon you is going to get around to calling upon me?"

"Speak your piece," said Philip, "if you have to."

"Well, Madeline is a Jersey cow and according to the United States Department of Agriculture, it's real good if a three-month-old Jersey calf weighs one hundred and thirty-eight pounds, but do you know how much my Madeline weighs?"

"Nope!" answered Philip as though he didn't know and didn't care to know.

"My Madeline's weight is now"—I paused to let the suspense build—"one hundred and fifty pounds."

Ginny clapped and Bonnie said, "Twelve pounds to the good."

Philip waved everybody quiet. "Don't go counting your blue ribbons before you win any, Miss Beth!"

Did I have me a thing or two to tell him! "You've been acting plumb miserable ever since my Madeline is trying for the same prize that your Leonard is."

"You saying that Leonard and me is scared of Madeline and you?" Philip tried laughing. "Ha ha ha ha!" But it wasn't what you'd call a real laugh.

I stood tall in front of him and the rest of the 4-H members saying, "I thinks you is at least half-right," before moving on toward the door. Our president's face showed that he needed a mite more explaining so I gave it to him. "I don't think your Leonard is one bit scared, but I think you, Mr. Philip Hall, is downright terrified."

After sundown I carried the kerosene lamp quietly through the barn toward Madeline's stall. For a while I stood stroking her head and thinking of another head I'd like to smack. The dumb bum! Where is it written that a girl's calf can't be in the same contest with a boy's calf? Well, Mister Philip Hall, for too long I've worried that you wouldn't like me if I became the number-one best student, ran faster in the relay race, or took the blue ribbon for calf-raising.

Well, I reckon I'm still worried, but with a difference. Now I'm worried that I might not win and that would give you entirely too much satisfaction.

By eight o'clock Saturday morning, all of us Lamberts, especially including Madeline the calf, got aboard Pa's

pickup truck and headed for Mountain Village and the annual Randolph County Fair.

Inside the early morning fairgrounds everybody was busy rushing to set up their egg, vegetable, poultry, flower, or clothing exhibits. Folks with livestock were leading them toward the barn, so Madeline and I followed.

A big man who wore the sign WM. PAULSEN, CATTLE JUDGE pointed to a long shed behind a circle of temporary fencing. "Take your calf in there and start preparing for the judging."

I gave the rough old rope harness a pull, and Madeline followed me into the barn past stalls filled with boys and their calves. At the first empty one, Madeline and I entered and then she looked at me with earth-colored eyes as if to ask, what's next?

"I'm going to make you beautiful for the judges," I explained as I rubbed brown shoe polish across her hooves. "You really are beautiful, sure enough."

After I buffed her hooves with a piece of an old flannel shirt, I got out Madeline's hairbrush. Brushing is what really puts the shine on.

I heard the voice of the judge in the distance saying, "Nice animal you got there, son." Walking with Mr. Paulsen was Philip Hall holding onto the polished leather bridle of a prettily spotted Holstein.

I said, "Leonard!"

Philip looked up.

"Philip," I said.

And Leonard looked up.

"Well, Philip," I said, trying for another start, "your Leonard looks real good. You sure did fatten him up."

Philip smiled wide enough to show the world how proud he was. "You know this here Leonard wouldn't eat a thing the first ten days of his life that wasn't mother's

milk. Bet you wouldn't know what to do with an animal like that."

He's all the time forgetting that he told folks what he already told them. "Well . . . ," I said, pretending to be thinking. "Well . . . reckon I might try soaking some grain with milk and rubbing it across the animal's nose."

He looked at me as though I had taken something very important away from him. "How did you know?"

I laughed at him. " 'Cause you told that to everybody at the 4-H Club, you old forgetful head."

He punched the air. "Calf-raising is for boys and Leonard's going to beat the pants off Madeline."

"Says who?" I asked, which was a silly thing to ask since nothing could be plainer.

He threw out his chest. "Says me!"

At ten o'clock all the exhibits from the dairy animals to the flowers, foods, and crafts were ready. Around about noontime the entire fairgrounds was packed with what looked like every living soul in Randolph County.

Mr. Paulsen walked through the long barn calling, "The judging is about to commence."

I gave Madeline one last brush across her backside before unwrapping the secret weapon. A package of peppermint Lifesavers. A sweet breath can't hurt none. Right away she took it and right away she spit it out, but not before it freshened up her mouth a mite.

The line began moving. I counted seven boys and me. And wouldn't you know who was out there leading the parade? Out there wearing his new leather harness and holding his head high as any clothesline. Funny, but I ain't liking Leonard any better than I'm liking Philip Hall.

All of us exhibitors walked backward so we could face our animals, seeing to it that they kept their heads high and mighty, leastways while the judge is a-looking. I looked into the eyes of my beautiful calf and made this sucking-in sound with my mouth, a sound that Madeline understands as friendly. Once around the ring as bits and pieces of applause broke out from the spectators. Judge Paulsen motions for us all to go around again while he stays center-ring and watches. Once more he motions for us all to round-the-rosie, and this time the clapping is louder and longer. I thought about how a piece of the clapping had to belong to me, and I felt proud.

The judge slapped one calf across the rump and pointed with his thumb toward the open stalls. The calf's boy looked hurt beyond belief, as he led his animal from the ring. Then the judge passed by Leonard to give the following calf the old rump slap and the hitchhiker's thumb. The very next one, poor thing, came in for the same treatment.

When Madeline came before the judge's eyes, I breathed in and kept my mind and eyes on her, praying that the judge was going to let us pass on by. The judge's head made a very definite nod which I took to mean that Madeline was still in the contest.

After more walks around the ring a Guernsey and one Jersey, but not my Jersey, were sent from the ring. Who was left? A cherry-red-and-white Ayrshire, Leonard, and Madeline.

Mr. Paulsen was studying the Ayrshire, pressing his hands against the ribs, feeling its udder and then its chest. Suddenly he shook his head no and pointed the direction toward the barn. Farewell fancy Ayrshire!

As Philip led his animal around the opposite turn, he gave me one of his squinty looks that I read good as print. It said: Now there is only you and me, but soon it's going to be only me.

I didn't squint him back any special look because just now I had better things to do. I made the whistle-through-my-teeth sound and Madeline's head rose, ever so slightly, as though searching for the wind. I did it again. That's it. Keep your head up there, girl. Makes you look like the sweet-breath winner that you is.

For the second time Leonard and then Madeline was carefully examined. Through the corner of my eye I saw Judge Paulsen's hand go to his chin as though thought was deep upon him. For a while he stared at Leonard and then he stared at Madeline, and all the while I kept the wind whistling softly, so softly that it only existed for Madeline.

The judge motioned Philip and me to bring our calves to the center ring. "Ladies and gentlemen . . . ladies and gentlemen. We have a winner." I struck my chest so as my heart wouldn't stop beating. "The blue ribbon for dairy-calf-fitting goes to the exhibitor who has best taken care of *and* shown to best advantage their calf. It is now my very great honor to present the blue ribbon and five dollars to Miss Elizabeth Lorraine Lambert for her three-month-old calf, Madeline."

Folks flooded into the show ring. Ma was the first one to reach me, not really hugging me but holding me at a distance as though to get a better look at what a blue-ribbon exhibitor really looks like. "Never knowed where you got all your smartness from, Little Beth, but I couldn't hardly be no prouder than I am right now."

"Awww, Mama," I said, dropping my head to her shoulder so that she couldn't see the tear or two that had

begun irritating my eyes. I had made her happy. I had done just what I had set out to do. So why was I fretting?

She pulled me away from her and took another long look before saying, "Phil ain't gonna be mad forever."

"You don't think so?" I asked, already beginning to believe.

When I saw Philip Hall, I tried to ease across the crowd to where he was, but when I got to where he was, he wasn't. Don't go thinking I care!

At the start of evening the lights strung about the grounds flashed on. A huge flatbed of a truck decorated to look like a stage wore a long banner sign: WELCOME SKINNY BAKER, KING OF THE SQUARE DANCE CALLERS.

I reminded the girls what nobody on the whole fairgrounds needed to be reminded of. "Square dancing oughta be starting up soon." As we wandered off to the side to "pretty ourselves up," Bonnie told us a secret. Gordon was going to be her partner. Then Ginny, Susan, and Esther admitted that they had been keeping the same secret, only with different partners.

Fact is, there was only one girl who didn't have a secret to tell 'cause not even a blue-ribbon winner can swing a partner she hasn't got.

When Skinny Baker struck up his do-si-do band, the girls jumped to their feet as though scared silly that they might miss a single square dancing step. As they ran off toward the lights and the music, I sat in the darkness and wondered, what now?

When Skinny Baker finished up his third song and got a ways into the fourth, I came out of the darkness toward the lights and the music and looked among the faces for his face. The jerk. I hope I never see him again.

Over there dancing up a storm was my ma and pa. I didn't know they could still do that. It seemed as though the whole world was dancing, with the exception of one girl and one boy who was nowhere to be seen.

"Well, Madeline," I said, heading back toward the barn, "now that you is the champ, reckon you have time to listen to my troubles?"

I put my arms around her neck and spoke directly into her spoon-shaped ear, "I like winning the blue ribbon, sure do, but I don't like losing my best friend."

Suddenly there was a lot of hoofing around a couple of stalls down. I looked up in time to see the face of Philip Hall rise above Leonard's slatted gate. Reckon I was too surprised to do anything, excepting stare. He wasn't smiling, speaking, or looking in any way pleasant, but then he wasn't exactly looking altogether unpleasant either. Then he said something. It was "Hi."

I answered with a "Hi" of my own. And neither of us seemed to be able to go on from there. Philip was looking down inspecting the floor while I was looking up counting the beams. It felt as though talking was something that neither of us had yet learned to do.

Suddenly I couldn't take another moment like the last one. "Sorry!" I heard myself saying. "I should've let you win."

Philip fastened his hands to his hips. "And you think that's what I want!" He was doing more telling than asking. "Think I'm some baby other folks have to *let* win?"

"No, Philip. I only thought—"

"Truth is," he continued, "all you been doing lately is winning, and that ain't hard to live with. Hard thing is losing."

"Reckon so," I said.

"No, you done forgotten about losing," he said, " 'cause if you'd remembered you'd know full well that it takes getting used to."

"And are you getting used to it?" I asked. "I mean, a little?"

Philip nodded his head. "I ain't no baby."

"Reckon I know that," I told him, " 'cause I can see you growing." When I saw on his face the makings of a smile, I said, "Come on, we still have time to enter the square dancing contest."

He stopped short. "I'm not about to enter no more contests with you, least ways not today."

"You don't understand, Philip. This contest is for partners. Win together or lose together."

"Sometimes I reckon I likes you, Beth Lambert," he said as we touched hands and together ran toward the lights, the music, and the microphone-amplified voice of Skinny Baker.

Think About It

1. What kind of a person is Beth Lambert? List three character traits. Give a detail from the story that illustrates each trait.
2. Explain how changing the narrator from Beth to Philip would change the story.
3. Why is the setting for the first part of the story so important?
4. What does the ending of the story show about Beth and Philip?
5. What is the theme of this story, or what is the author's message to readers about winning?

Create and Share   What would you tell a friend who had just lost a competition? Share your own experiences in a letter you might write to cheer up your friend.

Explore   If you enjoyed this story, you may want to read more about Beth Lambert and Philip Hall in *Philip Hall Likes Me. I Reckon Maybe*, or its sequel, *Get On Out of Here, Philip Hall*. For nonfiction books about life on a farm, look under FARM LIFE in the library card catalog.

Bonnie St. John

This article first appeared in PEOPLE MAGAZINE.

Bonnie Saint John has fond memories of the four years from 1980 to 1984, when she competed in the national championships for handicapped skiers. "Seeing 300 people together at one time was extraordinary," says Saint John, who, as a result of a birth defect, has only one leg. "People would just toss their artificial leg to one side as they got on the chair lift. There would be this huge pile of crutches and legs, as if people had suddenly been healed." The sense of newfound camaraderie, she adds, spilled over into displays of pleasantly warped humor. "I remember a couple of us felt so free we started telling these terrible jokes. Like someone would walk by and stare at us and one of us would say in a low voice, 'Gee, she's got two legs . . . I wonder if she was born that way?' "

Saint John, 21, was born with a right leg that wouldn't grow. For medical reasons, it was amputated just below the knee when she was 5. She says she has never regarded her handicap as a great limitation, and her accomplishments support that belief. In 1984 she finished second overall at the world championship for handicapped skiers in Innsbruck. More recently, and in a completely different field of competition, she was named one of the 32 U.S. winners of a Rhodes Scholarship. That June she got her B.A. in government from Harvard; then in the fall, she headed to Oxford University to study political philosophy.

Saint John grew up in San Diego, and credits much of her success to her mother, Ruby, a junior high school principal. (Bonnie's father, an engineer, died when she was 12.) "She never raised me as if I were handicapped—no special schools, no excuses," says Saint John, who off the slopes gets around on a prosthetic leg. "It was just so apparent that Mother loved books and loved learning. She influenced me more by example than by admonishment." Saint John became such an avid reader as a child that, she says, "I felt different not because I was handicapped, but because I was an egghead." She first tried skiing at 14 and fell frequently. ("On one leg, you can't even snowplow.") But she became so addicted to the speed and freedom that she began to take jobs after school to save money for lessons and lift tickets.

"My philosophy, if I have one, is that nothing is sure, nothing is guaranteed," says Saint John. "But the more work you do, the more the odds are in your favor."

What if you couldn't...?

from the book by Janet Kamien

Being a winner can demand strength of character. If you were physically challenged in any way, you would probably have a lot to contend with.

What if your legs didn't work right?

You have probably seen people who move around with the help of a wheelchair, braces, walkers, or crutches all the time. Able-bodied people who aren't used to seeing these aids being used are sometimes frightened by them. They may also be frightened by the people using the aid because they look different from other people. That's a pretty natural response, but it doesn't help the person using the aid much. Probably the two biggest problems for people who are physically challenged are trying to get around in a world that was not made for wheelchairs and braces, and dealing with the attitudes of able-bodied people toward non-able-bodied people.

Have you ever tried a wheelchair? They're lots of fun, especially if you don't have to use one all the time. If you ever have the chance to use one, you will probably find that it takes some practice and some strength to maneuver, and that you can't get to a number of places very easily or, maybe, not at all.

The next time you walk to school or to the store, think about what it would be like if you were traveling by wheelchair. Would you be able to get out of the house without help? How would you get up and down curbs to cross streets? Would there be a railroad or trolley tracks to cross? Could you get over them? Could you get into the building you were going to?

Think about your own house. Think about the width of a wheelchair, and how tall you are when sitting down. Could you get through doorways? Could you get into the bathroom? Could you reach things you need in the kitchen? Is the kitchen big enough so that you could be in front of the refrigerator in a wheelchair, and still get the door open?

I've ridden in wheelchairs a number of times, but the time that made the biggest impression on me was when I went to a simulation workshop at a university. Students from the university who were physically challenged got some wheelchairs and other equipment together to give able-bodied people a chance to try them and see what they felt like. Once we wheeled ourselves out of the room, the people whom we passed didn't know that we were only pretending. They thought we were physically challenged and treated us differently. Some stared at us, some avoided us, some went out of their way to smile and say hello. By the end of my trip, I was furious. I am the same person sitting down as I am standing up, but people treated me as though I were strange, breakable, or a baby. So even though I could get around the building easily and get from floor to floor by elevator, moving around in a wheelchair was an uncomfortable experience because of the way other people made me feel.

People need to use wheelchairs for a lot of different reasons. Usually, their legs are very, very weak or paralyzed, or they are unable to control their leg movements.

Extreme weakness or paralysis can be the result of a disease like polio. This disease can attack the nervous system, which carries messages from your brain to your muscles. If the nervous system is damaged, messages from the brain can't get through, and the muscles can't move.

Some problems are the result of a genetic mistake. Something goes wrong while the baby is growing inside his or her mother. Muscular dystrophy is one of these problems. You can't catch it; you are born with it. It causes your muscles to be very weak, so that even if messages from the brain are getting through, the muscles are not strong enough to respond.

Some paralysis is the result of an injury. The

most important part of the nervous system is called the spinal cord. If the spinal cord is badly damaged in a car accident, a war, or a sporting accident, messages from the brain will not be able to get through to the muscles. Depending on the severity of the accident, a person's whole body, including arms and hands, could be paralyzed.

Uncontrollable muscles can be the result of an injury to a baby just before or during birth. If the brain or nervous system is damaged, messages from the brain to the muscles might come through in an incomplete or garbled fashion. This kind of problem is usually called cerebral palsy. This is a very general term that can refer to very slight movement problems, which require no special equipment to help you get around, or to very severe problems, which can badly impair a person's ability to control any or all of the muscles. Besides movement, cerebral

palsy in its very severe state can affect other abilities such as seeing, hearing, and thinking. Even when it is not this severe, it may affect the mouth muscles so that a person whose thinking is perfectly clear may have difficulty speaking and being understood.

Little can be done to cure these problems. Unlike skin or bone, the brain, spinal cord, and nervous system cannot repair themselves or be repaired by doctors, although in certain cases surgery may improve a person's ability to move around. Physical therapy may sometimes also help to strengthen weak muscles or prevent unused muscles from wasting away.

What if you were missing an arm or a leg?

If you had been born without an arm or leg or lost a limb through an accident or because of a disease, you would probably get an artificial limb called a prosthesis. Prostheses are custom-made for individuals to replace lost or missing arms, hands, legs, and feet.

Prosthetic legs and feet look pretty much like real legs and feet. They are made by taking an impression of the stump to ensure that the fit will be secure and comfortable. Before you put the prosthesis on in the morning, you put a clean white cloth called a stockinette over the stump, so that there won't be any irritation to the skin. If the leg loss is above the knee, the prosthesis will have a hinge at the knee joint.

People who have had a lot of practice wearing a leg prosthetic can do almost anything that people with two real legs can do. They can ski, swim, go horseback riding, dance, and—to a more limited extent—run and climb. At first, these things take a lot of hard work and practice.

A prosthetic arm is slightly different, since it must be able to reproduce the abilities of the missing hand. This is usually done with a double hook at the end of the prosthesis. The hooks are hinged to each other, and the wearer can open and close them by means of a wire attached to a shoulder strap. When you move your shoulder, you apply tension on the wire that opens the hooks for grasping and holding things. Learning how to do this well takes a lot of practice too. People who learn to use this device well can achieve very fine control of the hooks.

Although this kind of mechanical device is most widely used, people have been experimenting with all kinds of other ideas for improving arm prostheses. Some of these include

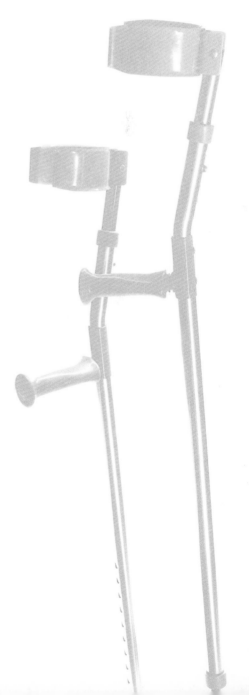

attaching the prosthesis to the nerves in the stump, so that the wearer could feel hot and cold and pressure through it and maybe even be able to partially control the device with his or her own nerves and muscles.

If you were physically challenged in any way, you would probably have a lot of things to contend with. People would certainly be curious about what was different about your body. They would stare sometimes and maybe ask you questions. Some people might also underestimate the things you could do, and that might be very frustrating. There would be things that you couldn't do and, if you use a wheelchair, places that you couldn't go. You would have to work very hard to get your body to do the things you wanted it to do, and that would probably take up a lot of time and energy that you would rather be spending on other things.

Many people who are physically challenged have become very politically active over the past few years. They have been lobbying for new laws that will guarantee equal education and employment opportunities for people who are physically challenged and that will require the designers and builders of housing, public buildings, streets, sidewalks, and parking lots to make these areas accessible by wheelchair. Many of these efforts have been successful, so you will be able to see curb cuts, ramps, and accessible bathrooms and parking spaces in more and more public places. As it becomes easier for people who are physically challenged to get out into the world, perhaps it will become easier for able-bodied people to become more accepting and not to feel awkward or afraid.

Think About It

1. What makes Bonnie St. John a winner?
2. What are two big problems facing physically challenged people?
3. Why do you think able-bodied people treat people in wheelchairs differently? What can be done about this?
4. What did you learn about the character traits a physically challenged person needs to lead an active life?
5. What did you learn from the winners in WINNERS ALL that you can use in your own life?

Create and Share   Spend part of a day without using one arm or hand. Try to do everything you usually do. Then describe the problems you faced. Tell what you could not do and what you learned about being physically challenged. Describe the feelings you had.

Explore   You may want to read more about physically challenged people. One good book is *Wheels for Walking,* by Sandra Richmond. Look for it in your library.

Persephone

a Greek myth
retold by Alice Low

Who wins and who loses is not always clear. Decide for yourself who comes out ahead in this story.

Persephone was a high-spirited, sunny girl who loved springtime and flowers and running outdoors with her friends. She was the daughter of Demeter, goddess of the harvest, and she and her mother spent more time on earth than in their home on Mount Olympus.

One bright day on earth Persephone was picking lilies and violets with her friends. She could not gather enough of them, though her basket was overflowing.

"Persephone, it is time to go home," called her friends.

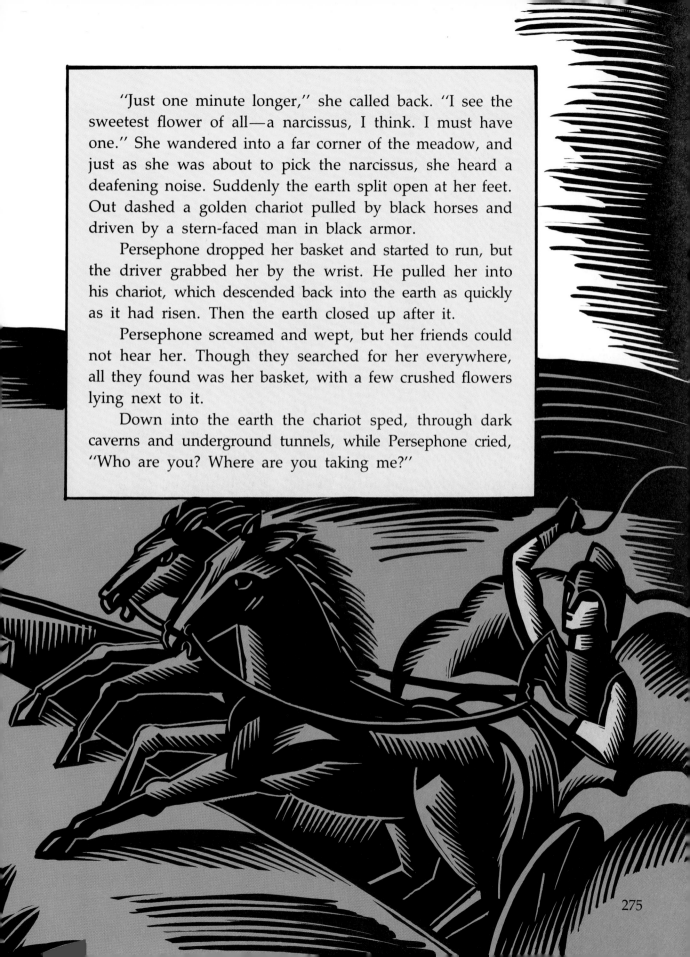

"Just one minute longer," she called back. "I see the sweetest flower of all—a narcissus, I think. I must have one." She wandered into a far corner of the meadow, and just as she was about to pick the narcissus, she heard a deafening noise. Suddenly the earth split open at her feet. Out dashed a golden chariot pulled by black horses and driven by a stern-faced man in black armor.

Persephone dropped her basket and started to run, but the driver grabbed her by the wrist. He pulled her into his chariot, which descended back into the earth as quickly as it had risen. Then the earth closed up after it.

Persephone screamed and wept, but her friends could not hear her. Though they searched for her everywhere, all they found was her basket, with a few crushed flowers lying next to it.

Down into the earth the chariot sped, through dark caverns and underground tunnels, while Persephone cried, "Who are you? Where are you taking me?"

"I am Hades, king of the underworld, and I am taking you there to be my bride."

"Take me back to my mother," screamed Persephone. "Take me back."

"Never!" said Hades. "For I have fallen in love with you. Your sunny face and golden hair will light up my dark palace."

The chariot flew over the River Styx where Charon, the boatman, was ferrying ghostly souls across the water. "Now we are at the gate to my kingdom," said Hades, as they landed next to the huge three-headed dog who guarded it.

Persephone shivered, and Hades said, "Oh, that is Cerberus. He guards the gate so that no live mortals enter and no souls of the dead escape. Nobody escapes from the underworld."

Persephone became speechless. Never escape from this terrible place full of pale, shadowy ghosts, wandering through stony fields full of pale, ghostly flowers!

Beautiful Persephone, who loved sunshine, became Hades' queen and sat on a cold throne in his cold palace. Hades gave her a gold crown and bright jewels, but her heart was like ice and she neither talked nor ate nor drank.

Persephone's mother, Demeter, knew that something terrible had happened to her daughter. She alone had heard Persephone's screams, which had echoed through the mountains and over the sea.

Demeter left Olympus disguised as an old woman, and wandered the earth for nine days and nine nights, searching for her daughter. She called to the mountains and rivers and sea, "Persephone, where are you? Come back. Come back." But there was never an answer. She did not weep, for goddesses do not cry, but her heart was heavy. She could not eat or drink or rest, so deep was her grief.

Finally she reached a place called Eleusis, not far from the spot where Persephone had disappeared. There a prince named Triptolemus recognized her and told her this story: "Over a week ago, my brother was taking care of the royal pigs. He heard a thundering noise, and the earth opened up. Out rushed a chariot, driven by a grim-faced man. He grabbed a beautiful young girl, and down into the earth they went. They were swallowed up, along with the pigs."

"That man must have been Hades," cried Demeter. "I fear that he has kidnapped my daughter."

Demeter hurried to the sun, Helios, who sees everything. And the sun confirmed Demeter's fears. Demeter cried, "Persephone, my gay, lovely daughter, is imprisoned in the underworld, never again to see the light of day or the flowers of spring."

Then Demeter became stony and angry, and she caused the earth to suffer with her. The earth became cold and barren. Trees did not bear fruit, the grass withered and did not grow again, and the cattle died from hunger. A few men succeeded in plowing the hard earth and sowing seeds, but no shoots sprouted from them. It was a cruel year for mankind. If Demeter continued to withhold her blessings from the earth, people would perish from hunger.

Zeus begged Demeter to let the earth bear fruit again, but Demeter said, "The earth will never be green again. Not unless my daughter returns!"

Then Zeus knew that he must take action to save people from starvation. "I will see that Persephone returns," he told Demeter, "but only on one condition. She must not have eaten any of the food of the dead."

Zeus sent Hermes, messenger of the gods, down to the underworld to ask Hades for Persephone's release. When Persephone saw that Hermes had come to take her home, she became lively and smiled and talked for the first time that year.

To her delight, Hades did not protest but said, "Go, my child. Although I love you, I cannot keep you here against Zeus's will. But you must eat a little something

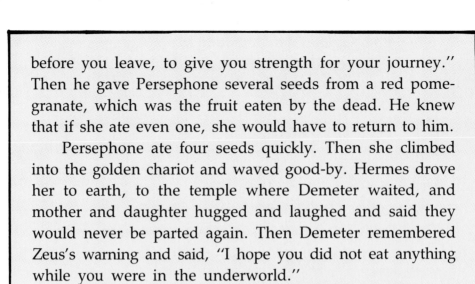

before you leave, to give you strength for your journey." Then he gave Persephone several seeds from a red pomegranate, which was the fruit eaten by the dead. He knew that if she ate even one, she would have to return to him.

Persephone ate four seeds quickly. Then she climbed into the golden chariot and waved good-by. Hermes drove her to earth, to the temple where Demeter waited, and mother and daughter hugged and laughed and said they would never be parted again. Then Demeter remembered Zeus's warning and said, "I hope you did not eat anything while you were in the underworld."

"I was too sad to eat," said Persephone. "I didn't eat or drink all year."

"Not anything at all?" said Demeter.

"Oh, just a few little pomegranate seeds before I left," said Persephone. "Why do you ask?"

"Because, my dearest," cried Demeter, "if you have eaten any of the food of the dead, you must return to Hades."

Zeus heard the loud wails of Demeter and her daughter, and he decided to compromise. Persephone must spend just four months of each year in the underworld, one for each of the seeds she had eaten. The rest of the year she could be with her mother on earth.

That is why every year, for four months, the earth becomes cold and barren. Persephone is in the dark underworld and Demeter is overcome with grief.

And every year, when Persephone returns to earth, she brings spring with her. The earth is filled with flowers and fruits and grasses. And summer and fall, the seasons of growth and harvest, follow in their natural order. Every year Demeter and the whole earth rejoice that Persephone has returned.

Land of the Brave

This land is your land, this land is my land,
From California to the New York island,
From the redwood forest, to the gulf
    stream waters,
This land was made for you and me.

from THIS LAND IS YOUR LAND
words and music by Woody Guthrie

Reading the Signs

from THE SIGN OF THE BEAVER
by Elizabeth George Speare

It was June in the year 1768. Matt was left alone to guard the log house in the Maine woods while his father returned to Quincy for the rest of the family. That was seven weeks ago. In that time, twelve-year-old Matt learned a lot about himself and his new wilderness home. Much of this was taught to him by Attean, the Indian boy, in return for reading lessons. But Matt knew that the Indians had little reason to love white settlers, and his relationship with Attean was never an easy one.

It was well into August. The silk tassels were glistening on the cornstalks. The hard green pumpkins nestling underneath the stalks were rounding out and taking on a coating of orange. It was time for his father to be coming. At any moment he might look out and see him walking into the clearing, bringing his mother and Sarah and the new baby. It was strange to think there was a member of the family he had never seen. Was it a boy or a girl? It would be a fine thing to have them sitting around the table again.

He hoped his mother would take over Attean's reading lessons, which were going badly. Matt couldn't make out why the Indian kept coming since he made it so plain he disliked the lessons. So often Attean made him feel uncomfortable and ridiculous. But he had to admit that on the days when Attean did not come the hours went by slowly.

Often Attean seemed in no hurry to leave when the morning's lesson was over. "Look see if catch rabbit," he might suggest, and together they would go out to check the snares. Or they would tramp along the creek to a good spot for fishing. Attean seemed to have plenty of time on his hands. Sometimes he would just hang around and watch Matt do the chores. He would stand at the edge of the corn patch and look on while Matt pulled up weeds.

"Squaw work," he commented once.

Matt flushed. "We think it's a man's work," he retorted.

Attean said nothing. He did not offer to help. After a time he just wandered off without saying goodbye. It must be mighty pleasant, Matt thought to himself, to just hunt and fish all day long and not have any work to do. That wasn't his father's way, and it wouldn't ever be his. The work was always waiting to be done, but if he got the corn patch cleared and the wood chopped today, he could go fishing with Attean tomorrow—if Attean invited him.

Sometimes Attean brought an old dog with him. It was about the sorriest-looking hound Matt had ever seen, with a coat of coarse brown hair, a mangy tail, and whitish patches on its face that gave it a clownish look. Its long pointed nose was misshapen with bumps and bristles. By the look of its ears, it had survived many battles. The instant it spied Matt, a ridge of hair went straight up on its back and it let out a mean growl. Attean cuffed it sharply, and after that it was quiet, but it watched the white stranger with wary eyes and kept its distance.

Matt tried not to show his own distrust. "What's his name?" he asked politely.

Attean shrugged. "No name. *Aremus*—dog."

"If he doesn't have a name, how can he come when you call?"

"Him my dog. Him come."

As though he knew what Attean had said, the scruffy tail began to weave back and forth.

"*Piz wat*," Attean said. "Good for nothing. No good for hunt. No sense. Him fight anything—bear, moose." There was no mistaking the pride in Attean's voice.

"What's wrong with his nose?"

Attean grinned. "Him fight anything. Chase *kogw*— what white man call? Needles all over."

"Oh—a porcupine. Golly, that must have hurt."

"Pull out many needle. Some very deep, not come out. Dog not feel them now."

Maybe not, Matt thought, but he doubted those quills had improved the dog's disposition. He didn't fancy this dog of Attean's.

During the lesson the dog prowled about outside the cabin and finally thumped down on the path to bite and scratch at fleas. When Attean came out, the dog leaped up, prancing and yapping as though Attean had been gone for days. Matt thought a little better of him for that. It minded him how his father's dog had made a fuss every time his father came home. That old hound must have just about wagged its tail off when his father came back from Maine. The fact was, Matt was a little jealous of Attean. A dog would be mighty fine company here in the woods, no matter how scrawny it looked.

But not this one. No matter how often the dog came with Attean, he never let Matt touch him. Nor did Matt like him any better. He was certainly no good at hunting. When the two boys walked through the woods the dog zigzagged ahead, sending squirrels racing up trees and jays chattering, and ruining any chance of a catch. Matt wondered why Attean wanted him along. Attean didn't pay him any mind except to shout at him and cuff him when he was too noisy. But for all his show of indifference, it was plain to Matt that Attean thought a sight of that dog.

Attean had not brought the dog with him the day that he led Matt a long distance into a part of the forest that Matt had never seen. Following after him, Matt began to feel uneasy. If Attean should take himself off suddenly, as he had a way of doing, Matt was not sure he could find his way back to the cabin. It occurred to him that Attean knew this, that perhaps Attean had brought him so far just to show him how helpless he really was, how all the words in a white man's book were of no use to him in the woods.

Yet he did not think this would happen. For some reason he could not explain to himself, he trusted Attean. He didn't really like him. When the Indian got that disdainful look in his eyes, Matt hated him. But somehow, as they had sat side by side, day after day, doing the lessons that neither of them wanted to do, something had changed. Perhaps it had been reading *Robinson Crusoe*, or the tramping through the woods together. They didn't like each other, but they were no longer enemies.

When they came upon a row of short tree stumps, birch and aspen cut off close to the ground, Matt's heart gave a leap. Were there settlers nearby? Or Indians? There was no proper clearing. Then he noticed that whoever had cut the trees had left jagged points on each one. No axe would cut a tree in that way. He could see marks where the trees had been dragged along the ground.

In a few steps the boys came out on the bank of an unfamiliar creek. There Matt saw what had happened to those trees. They had been piled in a mound right over the water, from one bank to the other. Water trickled through them in tiny cascades. Behind the piled-up branches, a small pond stretched smooth and still.

"It's a beaver dam!" he exclaimed. "The first one I've ever seen."

"*Qwa bit,*" said Attean. "Have red tail. There beaver wigwam." He pointed to a heap of branches at one side, some of them new with green leaves still clinging. Matt stepped closer to look. Instantly there was the crack of a rifle. A ring of water rippled the surface of the pond. Near its edge a black head appeared for just a flash and vanished again in a splutter of bubbles.

Attean laughed at the way Matt had started. "Beaver make big noise with tail," he explained.

"I thought someone had shot a gun," Matt said. "I wish I had my rifle now."

Attean scowled. "Not shoot," he warned. "Not white man, not Indian. Young beaver not ready."

He pointed to a tree nearby. "Sign of beaver," he said. "Belong to my family."

Carved on the bark, Matt could make out the crude figure of an animal that could, with some imagination, be a beaver.

"Sign show beaver house belong to people of beaver," Attean explained. "By and by, when young beaver all grown, people of beaver hunt here. No one hunt but people of beaver."

"You mean, just from that mark on the tree, another hunter would not shoot here?"

"That our way," Attean said gravely. "All Indian understand."

Would a white man understand? Matt wondered.

Wherever he went now, Matt watched for Indian signs. Sometimes he could not be sure whether a branch had broken in the wind or whether an animal had scratched a queer-shaped mark on a tree trunk. Once or twice he was certain he had discovered the sign of the beaver. It was a game he played with himself. That it was not a game to Attean he was still to learn. They were following a narrow trail one morning, this time to the east, when Attean halted abruptly.

"Hsst!" he warned.

Off in the brush Matt heard a low, rasping breathing and a frantic scratching in the leaves. The noise stopped the moment they stood still. Moving warily, the boys came upon a fox crouched low on the ground. It did not run, but lay snarling at them, and as he came nearer, Matt saw that its foreleg was caught fast. With a long stick Attean pushed aside the leaves and Matt caught the glint of metal.

"White man's trap," said Attean.

"How do you know?" Matt demanded.

"Indians not use iron trap. Iron trap bad."

"You mean a white man set this trap?"

"No. Some white man pay for bad Indian to hunt for him. White man not know how to hide trap so good." Attean showed Matt how cleverly the trap had been hidden, the leaves and earth mounded up like an animal burrow with two half-eaten fish heads concealed inside.

The fox watched them, its teeth bared. The angry eyes made Matt uncomfortable. "We're in luck to find it first," he said, to cover his uneasiness.

Attean shook his head. "Not beaver hunting ground," he said. "Turtle clan hunt here." He pointed to a nearby tree. On the bark Matt could just make out a crude scar that had a shape somewhat like a turtle. He was indignant.

"We found it," he said. "You mean you're just going to leave it here because of a mark on a tree?"

"Beaver people not take animal on turtle land," Attean repeated.

"We can't just let it suffer," Matt protested. "Suppose no one comes here for days?"

"Then fox get away."

"How can he get away?"

"Bite off foot."

Indeed, Matt could see now that the creature had already gnawed its own flesh down to the bone.

"Leg mend soon," Attean added, noting Matt's troubled face. "Fox have three leg beside."

"I don't like it," Matt insisted. He wondered why he minded so much. He had long ago got used to clubbing the small animals caught in his own snares. There was something about this fox that was different. Those defiant eyes showed no trace of fear. He was struck by the bravery that could inflict such pain on itself to gain freedom. Reluctantly he followed Attean back to the trail, leaving the miserable animal behind.

"It's a cruel way to trap an animal," he muttered. "Worse than our snares."

"*Ehe*," Attean agreed. "My grandfather not allow beaver people to buy iron trap. Some Indian hunt like white man now. One time many moose and beaver. Plenty for all Indians and for white man too. But white man not hunt to eat, only for skin. Him pay Indian to get skin. So Indian use white man's trap."

Matt could not find an answer. Tramping beside Attean he was confused and angry as well. He couldn't understand the Indian code that left an animal to suffer just because of a mark on a tree. And he was fed up with Attean's scorn for white men. It was ridiculous to think that he and Attean could ever really be friends. Sometimes he wished he could never see Attean again.

Even at the same moment, he realized that this was really not true. Even though Attean annoyed him, Matt was constantly goaded to keep trying to win his respect. He would lie awake in the night, staring up at the chinks of starlight in the cabin roof, and make up stories in which he himself, not Attean, was the hero. Sometimes he imagined how Attean would be in some terrible danger, and he, Matt, would be brave and calm and come swiftly to the rescue. He would kill a bear unaided, or a panther, or fend off a rattlesnake about to strike. Or he would learn about an enemy band of Indians sneaking through the forest to attack the place where Attean was sleeping, and he would run through the woods and give the alarm in time.

In the morning he laughed at himself for this childish daydreaming. There was little chance he would ever be a hero, and little chance too that Attean would ever need his help. Matt knew that the Indian boy came day after day only because Saknis, his grandfather, sent him. For some reason the old man had taken pity on this helpless white boy, and at the same time he had shrewdly grasped at the chance for his grandson to learn to read. If he suspected that Attean had become the teacher instead, he would doubtless put a stop to the visits altogether.

Fall was approaching, and the autumn weather seemed to bring about a restlessness in Attean. There were days now when the Indian boy did not come. He never offered a word of explanation. After a day or two he would simply walk into the cabin and sit down at the table. He rarely suggested that they hunt or fish together. Day after day Matt tramped the woods alone.

As he walked, Matt was careful to cut blazes in the bark of trees. They gave him courage to walk farther into the forest than he had ever dared before, since he was sure of finding his way back to the cabin. He also watched for Indian signs, and sometimes he was sure he had detected one. One day, looking up, he saw on a nearby tree the sign of the turtle. Time to turn back, he told himself. He felt secure now in the territory of the beaver, but he wasn't so certain that a strange people would welcome a white trespasser.

As he started to retrace his steps, he heard, some distance away, the sharp, high-pitched yelp of a dog. It didn't sound threatening but neither did it sound like the happy, excited bark of a hound that had scented a rabbit. It sounded almost like the scream of a child. When it came again, it died away into a low whining, and he remembered the trapped fox.

Attean had warned him to have nothing to do with a turtle trap. But he hesitated, and the sound came again. No matter what Attean had told him, he could not bring himself to walk away from that sound. Warily, he made his way through the brush.

It was a dog, a scrawny Indian dog, dirt-caked and bloody. As Matt moved closer he saw, through the blood, the white streak down the side of its face, then the chewed ear and the stubby porcupine quills. Only one dog in the world looked like that. It was caught by its foreleg, just as the fox had been, and it was frantic with pain and fear. Its eyes were glazed, and white foam dripped from its open jaws. Matt felt his own muscles tense with anger. His mind was made up in an instant. It had been bad enough to leave a fox to suffer. Turtle tribe or no, he was not going to walk away from Attean's dog. Somehow he had to get that dog out of the trap.

But how? As he bent down, the dog snapped at him so ferociously that he jumped back. Even if it recognized him, Attean's dog had never learned to trust him. Now it was too crazed to understand that Matt meant to help. Matt set his teeth and stooped again. This time he got his hands on the steel bands of the trap and gave it a tug. With a deep growl, the dog snapped at him again. Matt started, scraping his hand against the steel teeth. He leaped to his feet and stared at the red gash that ran from his knuckles to his wrist. It was no use, he realized. There was no way he could get that trap open with the dog in this maddened state. Somehow he would have to find Attean.

He began to run through the forest, back over the way he had come, back along the trails he knew, searching his memory for the signs he remembered that led to the Indian village. Luck was with him. There was the sign of the beaver cut into a tree and here were the fallen logs. He was never absolutely sure, but he knew he walked in the right direction, and after nearly an hour, to his great relief, he came out on the shore of the river across from the village. There was no canoe waiting, as there had been when Attean had led him there. But the river was narrow, and placid. Thank goodness he had grown up near the ocean, and his father had taken him swimming from the time he could walk. He left his moccasins hidden under a bush and plunged in. In a few moments he came out, dripping, within sight of the stockade.

He was greeted by a frenzied barking of dogs. They burst through the stockade and rushed toward him, halting only a few feet away, menacing him so furiously that he dared not take another step. Behind them came a group of girls who quieted the dogs with shrill cries and blows.

"I have come for Attean," Matt said, when he could make himself heard.

The girls stared at him. Tired, wet, and ashamed of showing his fear of the dogs, Matt could not summon up any politeness or dignity. "Attean," he repeated impatiently.

One girl, bolder than the others, answered him, flaunting her knowledge of the white man's language. "Attean not here," she told him.

"Then Saknis."

"Saknis not here. All gone hunt."

Desperately Matt seized his only remaining chance. "Attean's grandmother," he demanded. "I must see her."

The girls looked at each other uneasily. Matt pulled back his shoulders and tried to put into his voice the stern authority that belonged to Saknis. "It is important," he said. "Please show me where to find her."

Amazingly, his blustering had an effect. After some whispering, the girls moved back out of his way.

"Come," the leading girl ordered, and he followed her through the gate.

He was not surprised that she led him straight to the most substantial cabin in the clearing. He had recognized before that Saknis was a chief. Now facing him in the doorway was a figure even more impressive than the old man. She was an aging woman, gaunt and wrinkled, but still handsome. Her black braids were edged with white. She stood erect, her lips set in a forbidding line, her eyes brilliant, with no hint of welcome. Could he make her understand? Matt wondered in confusion.

"I'm sorry, ma'am," he began. "I know you don't want me to come here. I need help. Attean's dog is caught in a trap, a steel trap. I tried to open it, but the dog won't let me near it."

The woman stared at him. He could not tell whether she had understood a word. He started to speak again, when the deerskin curtain was pushed aside and a second figure stood in the doorway. It was a girl, with long black braids hanging over her shoulders. She was dressed in blue,

with broad bands of red and white beading. Strange, Matt thought, how much alike they looked, the old woman and the girl, standing side by side so straight and proud.

"Me Marie, sister of Attean," the girl said in a soft, low voice. "Grandmother not understand. I tell what you say."

Matt repeated what he had said and then waited impatiently while she spoke to her grandmother. The woman listened. Finally her grim lips parted in a single scornful phrase.

"*Aremus piz wat,*" she said. Good-for-nothing dog.

Matt's awe vanished in anger. "Tell her maybe it is good for nothing," he said to the girl. "Attean is fond of it. And it's hurt, hurt bad. We've got to get it out of that trap."

There was distress in the girl's eyes as she turned again to her grandmother. He could see that she was pleading, and that in spite of herself the old woman was relenting. After a few short words, the girl went into the cabin and came back in a moment holding in her hand a large chunk of meat, a small blanket folded over her arm.

"Me go with you," she said. "Dog know me."

In his relief, Matt forgot the torn hand he had been holding behind him. Instantly the old woman moved forward and snatched at it. Her eyes questioned him.

"It's nothing," he said hastily. "I almost got the trap open."

She gave his arm a tug, commanding him to follow her.

"There isn't time," he protested.

She silenced him with a string of words of which he understood only the scornful *piz wat.*

"She say dog not go away," the girl explained. "Better you come. Trap maybe make poison."

Having no choice, Matt followed them into the cabin. He saw now that the woman's straight posture had been a matter of pride. She was really very lame, and stooped as she walked ahead of him. While she busied herself over the fire, he sat obediently on a low platform and looked about him. He was astonished that the little room, strange, and so unlike his mother's kitchen, seemed beautiful. It was very clean. The walls were lined with birchbark and hung with woven mats and baskets of intricate design. The air was sweet with fresh grasses spread on the earth floor.

Without speaking, the woman tended him, washing his hand with clean warm water. From a painted gourd she scooped a pungent-smelling paste and spread it over the wound, then bound his hand with a length of clean blue cotton.

"Thank you," Matt said when she had finished. "It feels better."

She dismissed him with a shrug. The girl, who had been watching, moved swiftly to the door. As Matt rose to follow her, the grandmother held out to him a slab of corn bread. He had not realized how hungry he was, and he accepted it gratefully.

The girl took the lead, brushing aside the curious children and the still-suspicious dogs. At the river's edge she untied a small canoe, and Matt stepped into it, thankful that his half-dried clothes would not have to be drenched again. Once on the forest trail, she set the pace, and he did not find it easy to keep up with her swift, silent stride. She was so like Attean, though lighter and more graceful.

After a time, Matt ventured to break the silence. "You speak good English," he said.

"Attean tell me about you," she answered. "You tell him good story."

"Attean didn't tell me he had a sister."

The girl laughed. "Attean think squaw girl not good for much," she said. "Attean only like to hunt."

"I have a sister too," he told her. "She is coming soon."

"What she name?"

"Sarah. She's younger than you. But Marie isn't an Indian name, is it?" Matt asked.

"Is Christian name. Me baptized by father."

Attean had never mentioned a priest either, but Matt knew that the French Jesuits had lived with the Indians here in Maine long before the English settlers came.

"When my sister comes, will you come with Attean to see her?" he asked.

"It might be so," she answered politely. She sounded as though it never would be.

At last they heard the yelping just ahead of them and they both began to run. Even in his terror, the dog recognized the girl, and greeted her with a frantic beating of his tail. He gulped at the meat she held out to him. But he still would not let either of them touch the trap. The girl had come prepared for this, and she unfolded the blanket she had carried, threw it over the dog's head, and gathered the folds behind him. With surprising strength, she held the struggling bundle tightly in her arms while Matt took the trap in both hands and slowly forced the jaws open. In a moment the dog was free, escaping the blanket, bounding away from them on three legs, the fourth paw dangling at an odd angle.

"I'm afraid it's broken," Matt said. He was still breathing hard from that last run and from the effort of tugging those steel jaws apart.

"Attean mend," the girl said, folding up the blanket as calmly as though she were simply tidying up a cabin.

The dog hobbled slowly after them along the trail, lying down now and then to lick at the bleeding paw. They made slow progress, and now that the worry was over Matt was aware how tired he was. It seemed as though he had been walking back and forth over that trail all day, and the way to the village seemed endless. He was thankful when, halfway to the river, he saw Attean approaching swiftly along the trail.

"My grandmother send me," he explained. "You get dog out?"

"I couldn't do it alone," Matt admitted.

Attean stood watching as the dog came limping toward him. "Dog very stupid," he said. "No good for hunt. No good for smell turtle smell. What for I take back such foolish dog?"

His harsh words did not fool Matt for a moment. Nor did they fool the dog. The scruffy tail thumped joyfully against the earth. The brown eyes looked up at the Indian boy with adoration. Attean reached into his pouch and brought out a strip of dried meat. Then he bent and very gently took the broken paw into his hands.

Think About It

1. What kept Matt and Attean from becoming close friends?
2. What do you think kept Matt and Attean together despite their differences?
3. Do you think Matt's saving Attean's dog changed anything between them? Explain your answer.
4. What does the story tell you about life for the first European settlers?
5. What does the story tell you about American Indians?

Create and Share   Would you enjoy life in Maine at the time of the story? How would your life be different than it is today? What challenges would you face? What would you have to learn? Write a paragraph or two explaining why you would or would not like to be living in that time.

Explore   You might like to read the book from which this story was taken, *The Sign of the Beaver*. The author, Elizabeth George Speare, has written both fiction and nonfiction. To find other books on Colonial times, look in the library card catalog under INDIANS OF NORTH AMERICA (listed by their region and state), PILGRIMS, and UNITED STATES—HISTORY—COLONIAL PERIOD.

First Day on the Trail

from THE PRAIRIE SCHOONERS
by Glen Rounds

Until 1803, the Mississippi River marked the western boundary of the United States. Then, in 1803, President Thomas Jefferson bought the Louisiana Territory from France. This purchase moved the nation's western borders to the Rocky Mountains. The border remained there for over 40 years.

Then Americans began to open new frontiers in the 1840s. The trails to the West were clogged with wagons heading for Oregon, California, Texas, and even the dry deserts of Utah. As Americans moved farther and farther west, the nation's borders moved west as well. By 1848, the United States stretched across North America from the Atlantic Ocean to the Pacific Ocean.

The trip across the Rockies was too long and too dangerous to make alone. So each spring pioneers gathered in Independence, Missouri. There they formed wagon trains.

Getting a wagon train lined up and ready to start the first day's travel was not the simple matter one might think. The emigrants would have been up and stirring their cookfires at the first light, all with the best intentions of making an early start. But almost as soon as breakfast was over, things would begin to go wrong.

Someone was almost sure to discover that an ox—if not more than one—had wandered off, and hitching would have to be delayed until the creature was found and brought back. Elsewhere a half-trained animal, resenting the feel of the unfamiliar yoke on his neck, would break loose and create a great confusion among the wagons, scattering women and children and upsetting cookpots and grub boxes until he was finally cornered.

Cattle tend to be somewhat conservative, and an ox finding himself being yoked to a complete stranger might set up a diversion of his own—tangling chains and threatening to overturn the wagon during his violent objections.

Yokes and other gear were misplaced or discovered to be missing some essential pin or ring. And all through the camp cattle bawled and men shouted and waved their arms, while boys and barking dogs were underfoot everywhere.

What with one thing and another, it was usually well into the forenoon before the teams were finally hitched and ready to begin pulling the wagons into line. Even then the delays were not yet over. At the last minute some family was sure to have lost a dog, or have a child who had wandered away.

But sooner or later everybody would at last be ready, with the wagons roughly pointed in the direction of the Trail. But the picture of the white-hatted wagon boss standing in his stirrups to give the Cavalry "Forward" signal while crying "Wagons, Ho!" was seldom, if ever, seen in real life. As a general thing the lead driver waited until everybody down the line seemed to be ready, then whacked the nearest ox with his whip and hollered "Git!" or something like it. The next driver waited a proper interval and did the same—and so it went down the line until every wagon was moving.

Once under way such a wagon train made a handsome sight. The long line of white-topped prairie schooners strung out for a mile or two across the plain, rocking slowly over the rough ground while on either side of the trail were small bunches of loose stock—oxen, milk cows, horses, mules, and even sheep—herded by boys and older girls, or men working their way to the new country.

From their starting place to the first night's camp was a matter of only a few miles, but almost before they were off the old campground they began to encounter samples of the mishaps and delays that would plague them for the next few months.

The first trouble usually came to the herders of the loose stock. A headstrong old cow, not liking the looks of the trail ahead, might suddenly curl her tail and break back with the idea of rejoining the herds she could still hear

bawling on the old campground. And by the time she had been herded off and brought back, a dozen others might be lumbering across country in as many different directions.

While the herders ran here and there, dealing with these emergencies, the teamsters were having their own difficulties. Most of the wagons were drawn by two to four pairs of oxen, the yokes of all but the last pair being hooked at intervals along a chain. The teamster walked to the left and a little behind the lead team, guiding it to right or

left by shouts of "Gee!" and "Haw!" accompanied by appropriate whacks from his bullwhip. But the sharpness of the turn depended not only on the ideas of the oxen concerned, but on the loudness and authority of the command, so there was room for considerable misunderstanding. Inexperienced teamsters—as many of these folk were—could get into difficulty even with well-trained animals, and many of the teams were anything but reliable. So almost at once the orderly line of wagons began to show lengthening gaps between clusters where trouble had developed.

Confused drivers shouted "Haw!" when they meant "Gee!" cramping the wheels the wrong way while going down a slope, tangling their teams in their chains, and even upsetting their wagons. A command given too soon or too late or too loud or not loud enough could mean the difference between a wagon staying on firm ground or slipping into a gulley.

A driver unused to the plains might decide to take a short cut across a smooth, firm-appearing flat only to suddenly see his oxen floundering helplessly and his wagon mired to the hubs in a boggy spot. Outfits behind him would have to unhitch while the unfortunate greenhorn waded waist deep in the stinking mire, unhitching his own teams and attaching chains to the rear end of his wagon for his neighbors to hitch to. And when his wagon had at last been pulled back to firm ground, often as not his oxen were still trapped. That meant more wading to attach ropes to their horns so they could be pulled out one at a time.

Somewhere else along the line a clumsily lashed water barrel would be jolted loose from its moorings, meaning another delay while it was hoisted back and someone found to show how it should be done.

All these and dozens of similar mishaps dogged all but the most careful emigrants on the first shakedown leg of their trip. However, since they were still a long distance from dangerous country only the nearest wagons stayed behind to help the unfortunates in trouble, while the rest went on. So hour by hour the line of wagons lengthened as stragglers fell farther and farther behind.

Under those circumstances it is not surprising that the first night's camp was often a pretty disorganized ... The first arrivals, after picking a site, unhitched the teams and took them to water before herding them out to graze. Then they began the unfamiliar job of getting out their supply boxes and starting cookfires, while the children carried water or scoured the neighborhood for firewood.

Supper was a hurriedly eaten meal, with constant interruption, for the stock had not yet learned road habits and there were frequent alarms as the creatures scattered in this direction and that.

And all the while the outfits that had been delayed on the trail straggled onto the campground in twos and threes, adding to the confusion. Travelers trying to make camp in the dark drove their wagons over ox yokes and other gear or stumbled into the tent ropes and picket lines of earlier arrivals. Cattle blundered over cookpots and grub boxes and were almost stampeded by the shrill cries and armwaving of sleepy people in long white nightgowns.

The unexpertly arranged loads of many of the late-comers had been hopelessly jumbled by the day's jolting. Travelers rooted hopelessly inside the dark wagons for lost food boxes or tried to arrange bedding while the crying of their hungry and overtired children shortened their already ragged tempers. It could be long past midnight before the last wagon was in place, the last team turned out to graze, and the last pair of muddy boots scraped and set to dry.

It is small wonder that many families changed their minds about making the trip and turned back after the second or third day.

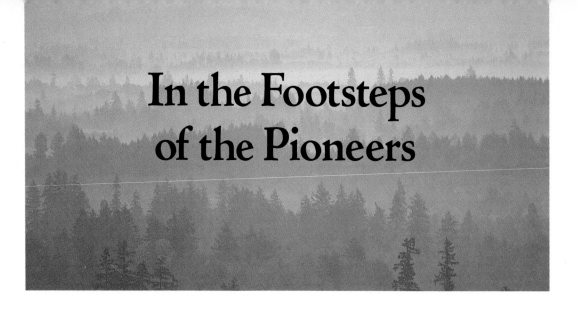

In the Footsteps
of the Pioneers

by Mary Emma Allen
This article first appeared in THE BOSTON GLOBE.

The Oregon Trail stretched from the Mississippi River across the Rocky Mountains. For many settlers moving west it was a road of opportunity—and hardship.

Now times have changed, but a modern adventurer traveling along the Oregon Trail will gain a real understanding and appreciation of what the settlers endured. Following in the footsteps of the pioneers can bring history alive for people today.

A Trail of History

The Oregon Trail comes alive for the modern adventurer who wants to follow in the footsteps of the pioneers and discover the exciting history of the Old West along US Route 26 through Nebraska and Wyoming.

Portions of the trail still are visible wending across the vast plains west of the Mississippi River, and many of the landmarks described in the early travelers' diaries remain intact despite the ravages of time and weather.

The present-day traveler can walk—as my husband, daughter and I have—along the deeply etched ruts made by thousands of covered wagons, gaze at the cliffs where the emigrants carved their names, and step back in time more than 100 years at Windlass Hill, Ash Hollow, Chimney Rock, Fort Laramie and other historic sites.

Starting at Independence, Missouri, the Oregon Trail crossed the present-day states of Kansas, Nebraska, Wyoming, Idaho and Oregon. Throughout the mid-1800s, a procession of emigrants in covered wagons, on horseback and on foot struggled westward every year, braving weather, Indians, illness and physical hardships.

Although you can buy guide books to assist you in finding the route from beginning to end, you may not have time to tour the entire length. My family and I have discovered that portion along US Route 26 from Ogallala, Nebraska, to eastern Wyoming provides the traveler with numerous opportu-nities to explore the trail and get the feel of the land. Journeying over this highway of legend by auto, as we have a number of times, enables you to stop and take short hikes and visit places that tell the story of this era of the West. Yet you can do it in a day or two if you're pressed for time.

Starting Out

The westward-bound travelers reached the Ogallala area about mid-June. They would have left

Independence in the middle of April, thus avoiding winter storms and hopefully finding grass for their cattle and horses as they journeyed westward. If they stayed on schedule without mishap, they generally would cross the Rocky

above: The Platte River in Nebraska.
below: Settlers crossing the prairie were familiar with scenes like this.

Mountains before the snows of early winter set in.

From Ogallala, located a short distance north of Interstate 80 in western Nebraska, follow Route 26 over the undulating Nebraskan plains and past Lake McConaughy. This lake did not exist in the 1800s, but it was created with the damming of the North Platte River in the 20th century. It has become a popular recreation area in western Nebraska, with a hundred miles of sandy beaches, fishing and boating. A turn-off beside the highway gives you a glimpse of the vast prairie over which the pioneers passed. Then, it was uncultivated; today, it is a patchwork design of planted fields and grazing land.

The first significant historical sites along Route 26 are Windlass Hill and Ash Hollow State Historical Park. After traveling over relatively level plains from Indepen-

dence, the emigrants encountered the challenge of the treacherous descent down Windlass Hill as they approached Ash Hollow and the North Platte River Valley.

The hill was described by one pioneer: ". . . the word 'steep' does not begin to describe the final descent into the hollow. We had to rough-lock the wheels for the first time and several times I felt sure that the wagon would tip over the tongue yoke of cattle."

At Windlass Hill today is an interpretive shelter with plaques describing the emigrants' adventures at this site. The deep ruts that thousands upon thousands of wagons gouged into the hillside have been deepened by erosion over the years. Nevertheless, you get an idea of the steepness of the incline they had to descend.

Gazing in Awe

You can descend a walkway to the crest of the hill, and gaze in awe—as Jim, Beth and I did—across the North Platte River Valley to see wagon tracks that more than a century has not obliterated. We stood there with the wind on our faces and imagined the emigrants' voices and creak of wagons as we stepped back in time to the era of the adventuresome pioneers.

The Oregon Trail is still clearly visible as it descends Windlass Hill.

Ash Hollow, with its tree-covered slopes and spring water, provided a welcome respite from the endless plains for the travelers. Sometimes the emigrants would spend a few days resting and repairing wagons before crossing the North Platte and continuing their arduous journey.

We stopped our journey for a few hours and visited the state historical park here. We wandered through the exhibits at the visitors' center and saw a short informational film, viewed an Indian cave and learned about the earliest inhabitants, and walked to the spring where the emigrants found fresh water at this "oasis" on the plains.

This area was known as Ash Hollow long before the emigrants passed through, and probably was on the route of the beaver trappers. A trading post once was located here, and an abandoned trapper's cabin became an unofficial post office at one time. There the pioneers left letters for friends and family back East, with the hope that a returning traveler would carry them homeward.

Nearby is a pioneer cemetery containing the graves of westward-bound pioneers who made it no farther. This area of Ash Hollow and Windlass Hill also is where the Mormon Trail joined the Oregon Trail, and some of those buried at the cemetery were Mormon emigrants.

above: "Barlow's Cut-Off", painted by William Henry Jackson.
below: Memorial at Register Cliff, Wyoming.

As we crossed the North Platte River by bridge, we tried to imagine the different situations the pioneers encountered as they forded this broad stream. Sometimes it was high and swift-running, causing much difficulty for the wagons and livestock.

Landmarks

Court House Rock and Jail Rock, near present-day Bridgeport, in the North Platte River Valley, were landmarks for the travelers as they made their way westward. Today, the modern traveler can explore these areas, as well as Chimney Rock a few miles farther on. The needlelike spire of this natural structure is visible for miles and lures the modern traveler westward as it did the pioneers.

Chimney Rock is a national historical site, with a mobile interpretive center and nature trails leading up to its base. Also, a wagon train re-creating the aura of Oregon Trail days operates from nearby Bayard and provides one- to three-day trips along the trail and around the base of Chimney Rock.

At Scotts Bluff National Monument beside Mitchell Pass, travelers have an opportunity to visit the museum with its paintings by pio-

Modern "pioneers" pass Chimney Rock as they recreate the journey West.

neer artist Henry Jackson and see other historical artifacts of this era.

A climb to the summit of Scotts Bluff by auto or on foot is a "must." My family and I have both driven and hiked to the top. We found we enjoyed taking the foot trail as the most scenic and adventuresome route. This trail winds in and out along the cliffs and at one place tunnels through the bluff. (The auto road also passes through tunnels.) There is a spectacular view of the surrounding countryside from the top, including Laramie Peak, 120 miles westward in Wyoming.

Fort Laramie

Fort Laramie, Wyoming, is the next major stop on the trail, and also requires a few hours' stay to be fully appreciated. Re-creations of life at this military post in the latter 1800s are performed for visitors. We also wandered through many of the restored buildings, and got the feel of the fort as it was when a large outpost existed on the plains. Some of the buildings date to 1849.

Now a national historic site, Fort Laramie was established in 1834 as a fur-trading outpost. Then the fort became a major military post until 1890. Thousands of weary pioneers stopped here to rest, repair wagons and take on supplies for the remainder of their long, grueling journey.

Register Cliff and the Trail Ruts at Guernsey are the final sites along Route 26. Don't miss them for an exciting glimpse of Oregon Trail history. This cliff rising one hundred feet above the prairie contains the names and home towns of thousands of emigrants who passed by and left their mark. We browsed along the cliff, reading the names and imagining what it was like when these pioneers were here.

The deep trail ruts not far away are equally impressive. Ruts five and six feet deep remain as evidence that the wagon trains passed here. And you can thrill to the aura of history as you walk along them and realize that you're walking in the footsteps of the pioneers.

A recreation of pioneer life at Fort Laramie, enables travellers to experience the past.

The Last Frontier, Gone Forever

from NATIVE AMERICAN TESTIMONY
edited by Peter Nabokov

Thousands of Americans on their way to Oregon or California crossed the Great Plains in the 1840s. Few thought of settling there. Most saw the plains as a dry, treeless, windswept land. They called it the last frontier.

The Indians, on the other hand, saw the plains as home. They hunted the great herds of buffalo that thundered across the grasslands. It was a way of life the Plains Indians valued greatly.

Then, in the late 1800s, the Indians' way of life suddenly ended. Over 5 million newcomers had moved on to the plains. They turned the plains into ranches, farms, cities, and towns. By 1890, the last frontier was gone.

In the mid-nineteenth century, when she was a child, Buffalo Bird Woman of the Hidatsa tribe lived along a bend of the Missouri River named "Like a Fishhook." As an old woman she looks back on those faraway times.

I am an old woman now. The buffaloes and black-tail deer are gone, and our Indian ways are almost gone. Sometimes I find it hard to believe that I ever lived them.

My little son grew up in the white man's school. He can read books, and he owns cattle and has a farm. He is a leader among our Hidatsa people, helping teach them to follow the white man's road.

He is kind to me. We no longer live in an earth lodge, but in a house with chimneys; and my son's wife cooks by a stove.

But for me, I cannot forget our old ways.

Often in summer I rise at daybreak and steal out to the cornfields; and as I hoe the corn I sing to it, as we did when I was young. No one cares for our corn songs now.

Sometimes at evening I sit, looking out on the big Missouri. The sun sets, and dusk steals over the water. In the shadows I seem again to see our Indian village, with smoke curling upward from the earth lodges; and in the river's roar I hear the yells of the warriors, the laughter of little children as of old. It is but an old woman's dream. Again I see but shadows and hear only the roar of the river; and tears come into my eyes. Our Indian life, I know, is gone forever.

—Buffalo Bird Woman, Hidatsa

These are the words of an old Omaha tribesman remembering the landscape as he and his people had once known it along the western bank of the Missouri River, between the Platte and Niobrara rivers, in present-day Nebraska.

When I was a youth, the country was very beautiful. Along the rivers were belts of timberland, where grew cottonwood, maple, elm, ash, hickory, and walnut trees, and many other kinds. Also there were many kinds of vines and shrubs. And under these grew many good herbs and beautiful flowering plants.

In both the woodland and the prairie I could see the trails of many kinds of animals and could hear the cheerful songs of many kinds of birds. When I walked abroad, I could see many forms of life, beautiful living creatures which *Wakanda* [the Great Spirit] had placed here; and these

were, after their manner, walking, flying, leaping, running, playing all about.

But now the face of all the land is changed and sad. The living creatures are gone. I see the land desolate and I suffer an unspeakable sadness. Sometimes I wake in the night, and I feel as though I should suffocate from the pressure of this awful feeling of loneliness.

—Anonymous, Omaha

Think About It

1. Why were pioneers eager to travel west?
2. Why would someone want to retrace the footsteps of the pioneers?
3. If you had been in charge of organizing a group for a wagon train, what skills would you have wanted group members to have? Explain why each skill would have been useful.
4. Describe how the taming of the wilderness by the pioneers affected the lives of the American Indians in "The Last Frontier." Does progress always mean a better life for everyone?
5. How have the selections in LAND OF THE BRAVE helped you understand what life was like on the early frontier?

Create and Share   Imagine you are part of a pioneer family headed for California. Write a letter to a friend back home, describing your trip. Tell what you like about the journey and what bothers you.

Explore   Many books have been written about frontier life. To read more about the pioneers, or the American Indians, look in the library card catalog under FRONTIER AND PIONEER LIFE and INDIANS OF NORTH AMERICA (listed by region and state).

Older, but Wiser

What of olden times,
shall I tell you of olden times?
What of olden times
my grandchildren?

from a Kwakiutl poem

THE
WISE
OLD WOMAN

a Japanese folktale retold by Yoshiko Uchida

Many long years ago, there lived an arrogant and cruel young lord who ruled over a small village in the western hills of Japan.

"I have no use for old people in my village," he said haughtily. "They are neither useful nor able to work for a living. I therefore decree that anyone over seventy-one must be banished from the village and left in the mountains to die."

"What a dreadful decree! What a cruel and unreasonable lord we have," the people of the village murmured. But the lord fearfully punished anyone who disobeyed him, and so villagers who turned seventy-one were tearfully carried into the mountains, never to return.

Gradually there were fewer and fewer old people in the village and soon they disappeared altogether. Then the young lord was pleased.

"What a fine village of young, healthy and hard-working people I have," he bragged. "Soon it will be the finest village in all of Japan."

Now there lived in this village a kind young farmer and his aged mother. They were poor, but the farmer was good to his mother, and the two of them lived happily together. However, as the years went by, the mother grew older, and before long she reached the terrible age of seventy-one.

"If only I could somehow deceive the cruel lord," the farmer thought. But there were records in the village books and everyone knew that his mother had turned seventy-one.

Each day the son put off telling his mother that he must take her into the mountains to die, but the people of the village began to talk. The farmer knew that if he did not take his mother away soon, the lord would send his soldiers and throw them both into a dark dungeon to die a terrible death.

"Mother—" he would begin, as he tried to tell her what he must do, but he could not go on.

Then one day the mother herself spoke of the lord's dread decree. "Well, my son," she said, "the time has come for you to take me to the mountains. We must hurry before the lord sends his soldiers for you." And she did not seem worried at all that she must go to the mountains to die.

"Forgive me, dear mother, for what I must do," the farmer said sadly, and the next morning he lifted his mother to his shoulders and set off on the steep path toward the mountains. Up and up he climbed, until the trees clustered close and the path was gone. There was no longer even the sound of birds, and they heard only the soft wail of the wind in the trees. The son walked slowly, for he could not bear to think of leaving his old mother in the mountains. On and on he climbed, not wanting to stop and leave her behind. Soon, he heard his mother breaking off small twigs from the trees that they passed.

"Mother, what are you doing?" he asked.

"Do not worry, my son," she answered gently. "I am just marking the way so you will not get lost returning to the village."

The son stopped. "Even now you are thinking of me?" he asked, wonderingly.

The mother nodded. "Of course, my son," she replied. "You will always be in my thoughts. How could it be otherwise?"

At that, the young farmer could bear it no longer. "Mother, I cannot leave you in the mountains to die all alone," he said. "We are going home, and no matter what the lord does to punish me, I will never desert you again."

So they waited until the sun had set and a lone star crept into the silent sky. Then in the dark shadows of night, the farmer carried his mother down the hill and they returned quietly to their little house. The farmer dug a deep hole in the floor of his kitchen and made a small room where he could hide his mother. From that day, she spent all her time in the secret room and the farmer carried meals to her there. The rest of the time, he was careful to work in the fields and act as though he lived alone. In this way, for almost two years, he kept his mother safely hidden and no one in the village knew that she was there.

Then one day there was a terrible commotion among the villagers, for Lord Higa of the town beyond the hills threatened to conquer their village and make it his own.

"Only one thing can spare you," Lord Higa announced. "Bring me a box containing one thousand ropes of ash, and I will spare your village."

The cruel young lord quickly gathered together all the wise men of his village. "You are men of wisdom," he said. "Surely you can tell me how to meet Lord Higa's demands so our village can be spared."

But the wise men shook their heads. "It is impossible to make even one rope of ash, sire," they answered. "How can we ever make one thousand?"

"Fools!" the lord cried angrily. "What good is your wisdom if you cannot help me now?"

And he posted a notice in the village square offering a great reward of gold to any villager who could help him save their village.

But all the people in the village whispered, "Surely, it is an impossible thing, for ash crumbles at the touch of the finger. How could anyone ever make a rope of ash?" They shook their heads and sighed, "Alas, alas, we must be conquered by yet another cruel lord."

The young farmer, too, supposed that this must be, and he wondered what would happen to his mother if a new lord even more terrible than their own came to rule over them.

When his mother saw the troubled look on his face, she asked, "Why are you so worried, my son?"

So the farmer told her of the impossible demand made by Lord Higa if the village was to be spared, but his mother did not seem troubled at all. Instead she laughed softly and said, "Why, that is not such an impossible task. All one has to do is soak ordinary rope in salt water and dry it well. When it is burned, it will hold its shape and there is your rope of ash! Tell the villagers to hurry and find one thousand pieces of rope."

The farmer shook his head in amazement. "Mother, you are wonderfully wise," he said, and he rushed to tell the young lord what he must do.

"You are wiser than all the wise men of the village," the lord said when he heard the farmer's solution, and he rewarded him with many pieces of gold. The thousand ropes of ash were quickly made and the village was spared.

In a few days, however, there was another great commotion in the village as Lord Higa sent another threat. This time he sent a log with a small hole that curved and bent seven times through its length, and he demanded that a single piece of silk thread be threaded through the hole. "If you cannot perform this task," the lord threatened, "I shall come to conquer your village."

The young lord hurried once more to his wise men, but they all shook their heads in bewilderment. "A needle cannot bend its way through such curves," they moaned. "Again we are faced with an impossible demand."

"And again you are stupid fools!" the lord said, stamping his foot impatiently. He then posted a second notice in the village square asking the villagers for their help.

Once more the young farmer hurried with the problem to his mother in her secret room.

"Why, that is not so difficult," his mother said with a quick smile. "Put some sugar at one end of the hole. Then, tie an ant to a piece of silk thread and put it in at the other end. He will weave his way in and out of the curves to get to the sugar and he will take the silk thread with him."

"Mother, you are remarkable!" the son cried, and he hurried off to the lord with the solution to the second problem.

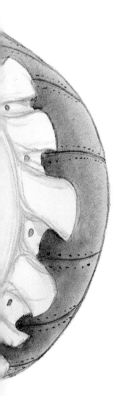

Once more the lord commended the young farmer and rewarded him with many pieces of gold. "You are a brilliant man and you have saved our village again," he said gratefully.

But the lord's troubles were not over even then, for a few days later Lord Higa sent still another demand. "This time you will undoubtedly fail and then I shall conquer your village," he threatened. "Bring me a drum that sounds without being beaten."

"But that is not possible," sighed the people of the village. "How can anyone make a drum sound without beating it?"

This time the wise men held their heads in their hands and moaned, "It is hopeless. It is hopeless. This time Lord Higa will conquer us all."

The young farmer hurried home breathlessly. "Mother, Mother, we must solve another terrible problem or Lord Higa will conquer our village!" And he quickly told his mother about the impossible drum.

His mother, however, smiled and answered, "Why, this is the easiest of them all. Make a drum with sides of paper and put a bumblebee inside. As it tries to escape, it will buzz and beat itself against the paper and you will have a drum that sounds without being beaten."

The young farmer was amazed at his mother's wisdom. "You are far wiser than any of the wise men in the village," he said, and he hurried to tell the young lord how to meet Lord Higa's third demand.

When the lord heard the answer, he was greatly impressed. "Surely a young man like you cannot be wiser than all my wise men," he said. "Tell me honestly, who has helped you solve all these difficult problems?"

The young farmer could not lie. "My lord," he began slowly, "for the past two years I have broken the law of the land. I have kept my aged mother hidden beneath the floor of my house, and it is she who solved each of your problems and saved the village from Lord Higa."

He trembled as he spoke, for he feared the lord's displeasure and rage. Surely now the soldiers would be summoned to throw him into the dark dungeon. But when he glanced fearfully at the lord, he saw that the young ruler was not angry at all. Instead he was silent and thoughtful, for at last he realized how much wisdom and knowledge old people possess.

"I have been very wrong," he said finally. "And I must ask the forgiveness of your mother and of all my people. Never again will I demand that the old people of our village be sent to the mountains to die. Rather, they will be treated with the respect and honor they deserve and share with us the wisdom of their years."

And so it was. From that day, the villagers were no longer forced to abandon their parents in the mountains, and the village became once more a happy, cheerful place in which to live. The terrible Lord Higa stopped sending his impossible demands and no longer threatened to conquer them, for he too was impressed. "Even in such a small village there is much wisdom," he declared, "and its people should be allowed to live in peace."

And that is exactly what the farmer and his mother and all the people of the village did for all the years thereafter.

Think About It

1. Compare and contrast the young lord and the young farmer.
2. How was the young farmer's problem solved?
3. How do you think the old woman knew how to meet Lord Higa's demands?
4. What lessons did the young lord learn from the farmer and his old mother?
5. In what ways is the farmer like his mother?

Create and Share   You are the young lord. Design a plaque to present to the old woman at a ceremony honoring her for saving the village. Then write a speech apologizing for your decree and explaining why you have changed your mind about the value of older people.

Explore   Through the centuries, the Japanese have always respected their elders for their wisdom and knowledge. To read more about Japanese culture, look under JAPAN—FICTION, JAPAN—HISTORY, and FOLKLORE—JAPAN. You might also enjoy reading a particularly beautiful form of Japanese poetry called haiku.

Fixing It Up

from THE WAR WITH GRANDPA
by Robert Kimmel Smith

*Sometimes living with
a grandparent can seem
like war.*

When I came out on the porch after lunch, Grandpa was waiting. "Let's meander," he said to me. "I figure we have some talking to do."

"What about your leg?"

"Well," Grandpa said, "it's still attached to my body."

"I mean, doesn't it hurt when you walk a lot?"

"Petey," he said, "it hurts when I walk and also when I don't walk. So maybe I ought to get some exercise and the heck with my leg."

We began to walk toward Beverly Road, the shopping street a few blocks away. "Is this a flag of truce?" I asked.

"There you go with that war business again," Grandpa said. "Forget that."

"I'm not forgetting," I said. "I declared war on you and I mean it."

"Pish-tosh," Grandpa said. I didn't know what that meant, exactly, but I kind of got the idea. "This isn't a war," he said. "It's a disagreement. Maybe even a dispute. And what you're doing is starting a family feud."

"It is too a war," I insisted. "You moved in and took over my territory, didn't you? Isn't that what wars are about?"

"No," said Grandpa. "Wars are about power and greed."

"And getting back what's yours," I said.

Grandpa stopped walking and I stopped too. His eyes seemed hard and cold when they looked at me. "So you think war is perfectly okay," he said. "Is that about it?"

"Sometimes," I said.

"Like when?"

"When you have to stick up for your rights," I said.

Grandpa's mouth made a thin line as he shook his head. "That's wrong, Petey. There are lots of ways of settling arguments without going to war. Peaceful ways."

"I tried that with my parents. It didn't work. That's why I had to go to war with you."

"Wrong," Grandpa said.

"Not wrong," I said back to him. "You took my room."

"Listen, Pete," Grandpa said slowly. "The only time you have to fight a war is when someone attacks you. Then, and only then, you have a right to defend yourself. You got that?"

I thought about that for no more than a second. "Wasn't I attacked?" I said. "Didn't they yank me out of my room and shove me away upstairs like I was some old chair or something?"

Grandpa sighed and looked away for a minute. I could see he was upset.

"It's just like Risk," I said. "Someone invades your territory, you zap them."

I felt Grandpa's bony hand on my arm. "War is no game, Petey," he said. "Only kids and fools and generals think that."

"You're my enemy," I said in a loud voice, "and I want what's mine."

I shook his hand off my arm. "You marched in here like an army and kicked me out of—"

WHACK!

Grandpa's right hand came whipping out of nowhere and slapped me hard across my cheek. I was so shocked and surprised, I couldn't say anything. My cheek felt hot and burning. It hurt.

"Why'd you hit me?" I said. I had tears in my eyes, but I didn't cry.

"War hurts," Grandpa said. "War wounds and kills and causes misery. Only a fool wants war."

I stared into Grandpa's brown eyes that looked so mean to me now. "I won't forget this," I said.

"That's the idea."

"And I won't forgive it either. From now on we're *really* at war." I turned away and started back to the house, walking as fast as I could. I left Grandpa on the street, calling my name.

Well, now we had a real war going and I didn't like it one little bit. I'm really not too good at being mad at someone. I really wanted to hate Grandpa for slapping me but I couldn't. I mean, he was my grandfather, for heaven's sake. He was old and alone and his leg hurt him. I was confused.

I think I was finally getting a little smarter about my war with Grandpa. Perhaps I had been following the advice of friends too much. And maybe I had been telling them too much about what was going on. Blabbing my head off would be more like it. So when Steve and Billy came by to play Monopoly at my house, I didn't tell them anything about the slap in the face from Grandpa.

Let me tell the truth about it. I was also a little ashamed.

We were all upstairs in my room. My new horrible and totally gross room, not my old wonderful and beautiful room.

"So this is where they put you," Steve said, looking around. "It's not an improvement."

"It stinks," Billy said.

"I'm getting used to it," I said.

"Any action?" Billy asked.

I shook my head.

"The war is over," Steve said, "just as I predicted."

"You're a loser," Billy said. He was sitting on the floor on the little braided rug in front of my bed. "I liked your old room better. It was roomier. And it had more light. And it didn't have a smell."

"Smell?" I said. "What smell?"

"Don't you smell it?" Billy asked. He wrinkled his nose like a rabbit and sniffed.

"It smells okay," I said. "Steve, you don't smell anything, do you?"

Steve took a breath through his nose. "Yes," he said.

We waited for a moment, looking at Steve, but he didn't say anything more. "Yes, you do, or yes, you don't?" Billy asked.

"I smell something, of course," Steve said.

"Let's play Monopoly," I said before it went any further.

I went to my toy cabinet and took out the Monopoly game. Steve sat down on the floor next to Billy.

I sat down on the floor with the guys and set the game down in front of me. Then I took off the cover. Then I saw something so unbelievable, I couldn't believe it.

The Monopoly board was in the box all right, but nothing else was.

There was no money, no playing pieces, no properties, no rules. All there was was a folded piece of paper. I unfolded it. It was a note, printed with a ball-point pen. This is what it said:

I will not put down here the actual words that Billy and Steve said. I know I set out to tell this story like it happened, but I don't want to put those words down on paper. Especially in a story for my teacher to read.

So I will make up some words to use instead of the real ones.

"I can't believe this," Billy said. "What a *gribetz mcplank* thing to do!"

"Exactly," Steve said, "it's *rorvish!*"

"Only a *macnishtop* would pull a *furrzy* trick like this!" Billy said.

"Wait a minute," I said. "And don't say that about my grandpa."

"I'll say what I like," Billy said. He was really mad. "He's a *macnishtop.* How can you deny it?"

"He is not a *macnishtop!*" I said in a loud voice. "My grandpa is a great guy."

"And he pulls *furrzy* tricks," Steve said.

Steve had me there. It was pretty *furrzy* all right. "Maybe," I said. "But I sure have given him a couple of reasons for it. I started this war, don't forget."

Well, the guys went on and on for a while, saying some more *rorvish* things about Grandpa. And I defended him. It took some time for all of us to simmer down. Then Steve got that funny look on his face and shut up while Billy ran down at the mouth.

"It may be terrific," Steve said then.

"What's so terrific about it?" Billy asked.

"He has risen to the bait, don't you see?" said Steve. "I mean, he's in the game now, he wants to play. And that's good."

"We can't play Monopoly now and you say it's good," said Billy.

"You've got your grandpa involved now," Steve said, ignoring Billy. "He's feeling the pressure. Now you've got to keep it up."

"How?" I said.

"Attack, attack, attack," Steve said.

"Yeah," Billy said, "hit him again."

"I'm not so sure," I said. I really wasn't sure either.

"Burn his underwear!" Billy said.

"What?" I didn't think I heard Billy right.

"Sneak in, grab all his underwear, and burn it. A man can't go anywhere without his underwear."

"And how do you burn underwear?" I asked sarcastically.

"Throw it in the furnace," Billy said.

"Don't be stupid," I said. I wouldn't go anywhere near our furnace for anything, much less throw underwear into it.

"Rip it up then," Billy said. "Just throw it in the trash. But do it."

"Not on your life," I said.

"You're not a Secret Warrior," Billy said. "You're a chicken."

"I'm a grandson," I said. "There are some things I'm not going to do, no matter how much my friends egg me on."

"Chicken!" Billy said.

"It's not your war," I said.

"*Gribetz Mcplank!*" Billy called me, which he knows I don't like. I didn't say anything back.

"You've got to do something," Steve said.

"I will," I said.

"What?" Steve asked.

"I don't know."

"When?"

"Sometime, someplace," I said.

Steve and Billy both laughed at me then. And in a little bit they left, both of them mad at me and me annoyed with them.

So Grandpa's first attack really worked after all. It took three good friends and made them *rorvish* with each other.

You can bet your life I went looking for Grandpa right after the boys left. But he was too clever for me. He hung around in the kitchen where Mom was preparing dinner. Then he played a few hands of casino with Jenny. By that time Dad was home from the office.

I didn't get to speak to him alone and in private until after school the next day. And he was up in my room when I got home. He had his big toolbox up there and he was sitting on my bed, carving a little piece of wood with his knife. "Hello, Pete," he said in a friendly way, "how was school today?"

I put my knapsack down. "A lot you care," I said.

"I care, I care," Grandpa said.

"How did you know we were going to play Monopoly?" I asked him.

"Ah-ah." He grinned. "A military secret."

"I suppose you think it was funny."

Grandpa chuckled. "Wasn't it? Here you guys get together to play a game and *surprise!*" Grandpa took the little piece of wood and knelt down next to my rocking chair. Then he tried to fit it into the hole in the back of the chair where the arm kept coming loose. "Just a touch too big," he said.

"You're fixing my rocker," I said.

"Trying to," Grandpa said. He had a piece of sandpaper and was rubbing that little piece of wood like crazy.

"Are you going to glue it again?" I asked.

"Nope," said Grandpa. "Glue won't do it. I'm repegging it, Pete. You see this hole in the back of the arm? I took the old peg out. It used to fit in this other hole here in the back of the rocker." Grandpa tried to put the little piece of wood into place, but it wouldn't fit. "Just a little more sanding now," he said.

"What about all the stuff from my Monopoly game? Can I have it back now?"

"Not until," he said.

"Until what?"

"Until our little disagreement, or whatever you want to call it, is over."

I looked at Grandpa, but he was busy sanding. "I don't think that's fair," I said.

"It's not," he said. "Let's just say your Monopoly pieces are prisoners of war. As soon as we make peace, back they come."

"I'll never do that. Not until you give up my room."

"Then they'll stay prisoners a long time," Grandpa said.

He took a pair of pliers and gripped them around the middle of the wooden peg. Then he stuck it into the arm hole and kind of twisted it while pushing all the time. It took a lot of effort, but Grandpa had big hands and big muscles and it finally went into the hole about halfway. "Got it," Grandpa said, "solid as the Rock of Gibraltar."

"I gave you back your slippers," I said.

"It seems to me that I had to come up here and find those slippers myself," he said. "I didn't see you hand them over, Pete."

I thought about that while Grandpa put the pliers away and got out a hammer from the toolbox. The hammer had a rubber tip on the hitting part.

"I'm going to have to get you back for this," I said. "The Secret Warrior will strike again."

"I know that," Grandpa said, grinning. "That's the fun of it."

I couldn't believe he'd said that. "You think it's fun?"

"Sure is," he answered. "Oh, it took me a while to see it. And then I realized something. I had darn near lost my whole sense of humor. Hadn't had a good time for ages and ages. Not the last year anyway. Imagine me slapping you like that. What a fool thing to do." He lined up the hole in the back of the rocker with the peg that was stuck in the arm. "Now, watch this, Pete old boy."

Tap-tap-tap! That's all it took, three good taps with Grandpa's hammer and the arm of the rocker was attached to the back. I sat right down in the rocker and tried it out. It was solid, just like Grandpa said.

"You're a good fixer," I said. "Thanks." I kissed his forehead.

"I'm the best," Grandpa said. "You know, Pete, I used to build whole *houses* from the bottom up. Still would, if it wasn't for this bum leg. But I'm starting to feel good again. Got my old pizzazz back, I think. There's lots of things in this house that need fixing. And I'm the man for the job, kiddo."

He gave me a hug then, and it felt good. But when he let me go I looked at him and said, "I'm going to get you for that Monopoly trick, you know."

"Sure you will," he said, then he laughed. "I can hardly wait."

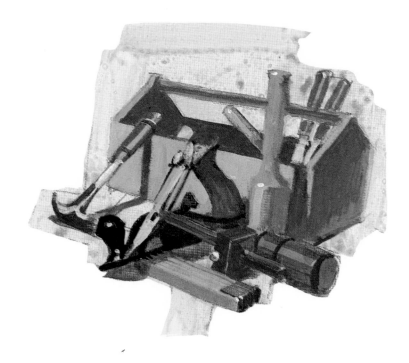

Think About It

1. Why was Pete angry at his grandfather? What did he do about it?
2. If you were Pete, how would you have handled the situation?
3. Compare and contrast how Grandpa acted at the beginning of the story with the way he acted at the end. What do you think caused this change?
4. Do you agree or disagree with the way Grandpa feels about war? Explain your point of view.
5. What did Pete and Grandpa learn from each other?

Create and Share   What do you think will happen next in this story? Imagine the next events and describe them in a page or two. Continue telling the story from Pete's point of view. Write some of your conversations with Grandpa.

Explore   If you liked this story, you might like to read the rest of *The War With Grandpa*. There are other good books of fiction about relationships between young and old people. Check the library card catalog under GRANDPARENTS—FICTION and OLD AGE—FICTION.

When Grandparents Were Growing Up

This soda truck driver paused on his delivery route in Columbia, South Carolina, in the mid-1920s.

from GRANDPARENTS
by Eda LeShan

When I was a little girl, there were so few automobiles that nobody ever had trouble parking a car on any street in New York City. If my granddaughter wonders why I get a little crazy driving on a big highway, surrounded by gigantic trucks, that's probably the reason. If she doesn't understand why I hate crowds, and why I don't want to play video games and can't stand loud rock 'n' roll music, it's probably because so many things were different when I was a little girl.

Stamps were three cents each and mail was delivered twice a day; a hot dog was five cents and a hamburger was ten cents. There were so few people that nobody ever stood on line at the post office or at the bank. A ride on a subway was five cents and we had streetcars instead of buses, except for one bus that was a double-decker, and if you climbed up a flight of stairs, you could sit on the top. In the summertime, some of the buses were open on top, and that was a wonderful ride. Nobody was allowed to stand up on the bus. There was a conductor as well as a driver, and he never let more people on the bus than could find a seat.

The streets were quiet; I never saw big crowds of people. An iceman came every other day with a big block of ice over his shoulder for our icebox because there were no refrigerators then. My family boiled dirty clothes in a big tub on the stove and then scrubbed them on something called a washboard, which was a piece of metal with ridges in it, in a wooden frame; there were no washing machines.

There was no television. There were no computers. Nobody I knew had ever flown on an airplane; and if you wanted to go to Europe you went by boat, unless you were Charles Lindbergh. I remember the parade when Lindbergh came home after flying to Paris. It seemed the biggest miracle that ever could happen. If anyone had told me people would go to the moon, I would have thought they were crazy. There were no frozen foods and no supermarkets and only two really tall buildings in New York: the Empire State Building and the Chrysler

below left: Listening to a radio set in 1927.
below: View of 5th Avenue and 34th Street, New York City, in the 1930s.

Building. If my granddaughter doesn't understand why I hate going downtown in New York because of all the hundreds of skyscrapers, that's probably why.

The way things are in the world that you live in right now will always seem to you to be the way things ought to be. All your life you will be more comfortable with the things that were familiar to you during your childhood. When you are old enough to have children and grandchildren, you will probably think that the world they live in is pretty strange. You won't like a lot of the changes that have taken place.

That's how it is for your grandparents. There have been more important changes in the way people live and work and travel during your grandparents' lifetimes than in hundreds of years before they were born! It's very hard for people to get used to so many changes in such a short time. You will understand your grandparents much better if you ask them to tell you about how the world has changed and what life was like when they were children.

below: Setting off for school in Kansas, in 1938.
below right: Boarding a plane for Florida at the East Boston Airport in 1931.

If you have a great-grandparent, he or she was probably alive when there were few telephones, when very few people had electricity, when there were no radios and the car had just been invented. Most people still traveled in horse-drawn carriages and wagons. Just think about how strange the world must seem to great-grandparents now! All the things that seem so natural and not at all unusual to you sometimes still seem surprising to them.

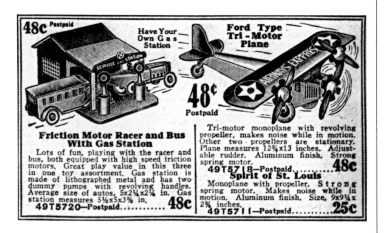

above and left: These toys were popular items in the Sears catalog of 1929.

The best way to understand more about the time when your grandparents were growing up is to ask them questions. Jonathan got a tape recorder for his twelfth birthday, and one of the first things he did was to ask all four of his grandparents to tell him stories about when they were young. His grandparents were delighted. One of Jonathan's grandfathers said, "You save this tape for your children and grandchildren, Jonny, and with what you will add to it, you'll have a story that will cover about a hundred and fifty years!" It makes grandparents feel very good to know that they are leaving a family history behind for future generations.

Your grandparents probably would love to tell you about train trips or boat trips they took. Trains and boats were the two means of transportation most people used for going long distances. I remember taking an overnight boat up the Hudson River to Albany. Now I can fly there in less than an hour—and it still seems surprising! Most grandparents wish there were more railroads still around. Did your grandfather wave to the train engineer when he was a child? Did he have a set of electric trains?

below: A Girl Scout prepares for a parade in Massachusetts in 1921. right: A streetcar in Topeka, Kansas, in 1936.

You might want to ask your grandparents why they get very worried if you have a high fever. When we were young, there were no antibiotics to help make us well. Most of us knew children who got polio, and that was very scary. People got sick and sometimes died from measles and scarlet fever and smallpox and diphtheria. When I was a little girl, there was little anyone could do when we were very sick except give us aspirin or cough medicine and keep us in bed. Parents got much more frightened when their children were sick than they do today.

When your grandparents were young, there was much less entertainment. There were fewer restaurants. People did go to the movies, but they stayed home most of the time. Grown-ups read stories and whole families played games. Sports were very, very different than they are today. Baseball and football were games people played just for fun; they weren't big businesses.

If you enjoy sports, your grandfathers probably have some good stories about what it was like to play or watch a game forty or fifty years ago. I say "your grandfathers" because not too many of your grandmothers were allowed to play in team sports. It wasn't considered ladylike.

You might ask your grandmothers how they felt about being taught that their only real goal in life was to get married and have children. Women were not supposed to think about being

above: A clubhouse in Gloucester, Massachusetts, in 1925.
left: Football! Notre Dame vs. Southern California, 1928.

351

below: This family portrait was taken in Columbia, South Carolina, in the 1930s.
opposite page, clockwise from left: First grade at a country school in Kansas, 1940. A modern convenience from the Sears catalog of 1929. Telephone operators at the switchboard in 1927.

doctors or lawyers or business executives. It was all right to be a nurse or a teacher, but usually that was considered a job that a woman would give up once she had a family.

Ask your grandparents about what it meant to be a boy or a girl fifty or more years ago. See if your grandfathers ever washed the dishes or cooked a meal or did the laundry. Ask your grandmothers if they ever took "shop" in school; ask your grandfathers if they ever took cooking or sewing. What you probably will find out is that they were raised to think that men and women each had separate jobs—and women didn't have very many choices.

Martha's grandmother started college when she was forty-five years old and now she's a lawyer. "I'm making up for lost time," she told Martha. "My father sent my three brothers to college, but he wouldn't send me because I was a girl. I'm glad I lived long enough to do what I always wanted to do."

Sam's grandfather, on the other hand, gets very angry at Sam's mother because she works in an office even though she has three children and her husband is able to support her. Sam heard his grandfather say, "They'll all grow up to be bums because you're not home to take care of them after school!" Sam asked his mother why Grandpa felt this way and his mother said, "Grandpa can't help it. That's what he was taught when he was young."

Some grandparents change; some find that too hard to do. By asking questions, you can begin to understand which grandparents feel comfortable with most of the changes that have taken place in their lifetime and which ones have

a hard time. When you ask questions about that, you will find that there are no right or wrong answers for everyone. Peter asked his grandmother why she still stayed home and did all the cooking and cleaning and shopping now that women are supposed to be liberated. Grandma said, "I thought about it and I decided that I'm doing what I like best. I don't have to change just because other people aren't happy doing what I do."

Sometimes it's a good idea to ask questions at a time when grandparents seem most upset with you. Very often this happens when you forget to say "please" or "thank you," and a grandparent starts to give you a long lecture on politeness that begins with, "When I was a boy" or, "When I was a girl." That's a good time to ask how boys and girls were expected to act fifty years ago, and maybe your questions can lead

to a most interesting discussion about how people treat other people. Together you might come to agree that it's harder to be polite today, when there are so many people and everything happens so fast, and there's so much noise and so many crowds—but you might also end up agreeing that even if it's hard, it's important for people to show they care about each other.

When your grandparents start yelling about how loud you play your records and how terrible the music is, ask them what *they* like. Jean's grandmother has records of all the Big Bands of the 1930s and the Broadway musicals of the 1940s and '50s; and Jean has discovered she likes them, too, although some songs are too slow and too sugary for her taste. Jean said, "Grandma, those songs are nice, but I'm going to play you some country music that doesn't sound too different. Just listen to the words."

By asking questions, you can start important conversations that help you and your grandparents understand each other's worlds—and when that happens, everybody gains.

The Care and Feeding of Your Family Tree

by Susan Schoon Eberly

Could your family be distantly related to royalty? Was your great-grandmother's uncle a drummer boy in the Civil War? What does it mean when someone tells you that she is Swahili and Armenian, and you reply that you're Portuguese and Welsh? A study of your family tree—your own personal genealogy—can help you discover the answers to these and other questions.

Begin your study right at home—in fact, begin with yourself! What is your full name? Were you named after a relative? Where were you born? What is the most interesting thing about you? Remember that some day your great-grandchildren will be curious about just what sort of person *you* were.

When you start out on your ancestor hunt, tell your family what you're up to—they may be eager to join the search. Then gather together your supplies: lined paper, a ring-bound notebook, and pencils (so you can erase, correct, and rearrange information without making a mess of your notes).

Record keeping is easiest if you make one work sheet for each married couple, like this:

WORKSHEET 23

WIFE		HUSBAND
Catherine Anne (Kitty) Pendleton	NAME	James Lewis
Date? Virginia	BORN	7-11-1859 Essex Co., Virginia
Dec. 19, 1882	MARRIED	Culpepper Co., VA
VA?	DIED	1914 KY?
KY	BURIAL	Virginia
?	FATHER	William Lewis
?	MOTHER	Mary (Polly) Brown
Josiah Capps (2nd Husband)	OTHER	None

NOTES (Important Events)

Kitty married Josiah Capps on May 19, 1924 in KY. James may have died in KY, but is buried in VA. Perhaps he died on a visit to his parents' home in VA? The family must have migrated to KY between 1886 and 1891.

CHILDREN NAME	BORN	BIRTHPLACE	MARRIED TO	DATE	DIED
Mary Jane	2-13-1886	Culpepper Co., VA	Stephen Berry	?	?
John A	?	?	Nancy Berry	?	?
Catherine Anne (Kitty)	3-1-1891	Meade Co., KY	Wm. T. Berry	?	2-14-1988
Elizabeth C.	?	?	Wm. Nelson	?	?
William Henry	?	?	?	?	?

SOURCES OF INFORMATION:

Letter from Annie Chesher, Wm. T. Berry's daughter.
Meade County, KY marriage records, book A, B, and C.

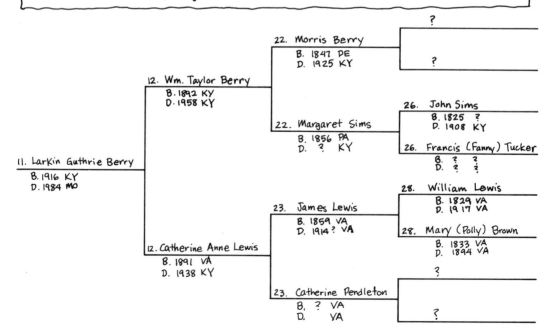

First, fill out work sheets about yourself and your brothers and sisters. (Leave blank spaces for information you don't have.) Next, fill out one about your parents—remember to use full names, including your mother's maiden name. Ask your parents about their occupations, about where they've lived, about their schooling and military experience. Ask them to tell you what is most important in their lives. When you've completed their work sheet, you'll have four new names to work on, those of your grandparents.

It's nice to have your family helping with a genealogy, because with each step—each generation—the number of your ancestors doubles, from one of you to two parents, to four grandparents, to eight great-grandparents, to—well, if you were to trace back about nine generations and count all of your direct ancestors living in 1776, you'd find yourself working with 512 great-great-great-great-great-great-great-grandparents! Knowing this, you might want to parcel out the detective work: You and your mother might research her mother and father (your *maternal* grandparents), while your sister and father study his parents (your *paternal* grandparents).

How do you keep all these names straight? With lineage charts! They serve as maps, showing you at a glance where you've been and where you're headed. Take a look at the lineage chart at the left. If stood on end, it would look like a family tree.

Each name on the chart has a number on it—the number of the sheet about that relative. Looking at this chart, you can see where more information is needed: The facts are fairly complete for the Simses and the Lewises, but more work is needed on the Berry and Pendleton lines. Part of the excitement in family-tree climbing comes when you're finally able to fill in blanks like these on your charts.

Once you and your helpers are armed with lineage charts, work sheets, pencils, and perhaps a tape recorder, the next step is to talk to grandparents, aunts, uncles, cousins, and other relatives. Sooner or later, someone will say, "Why, Aunt Tillie has a whole boxful of this family-tree stuff."

Go to see Aunt Tillie! She'll be thrilled to find someone else who shares her interest in the family, and you'll learn a lot about your family history that might otherwise have been forgotten forever.

Many older people are wonderful storytellers and may have fascinating histories just waiting for a good listener like you. But write down or tape-record everything you hear—names, places, and dates are easy to confuse. Ask to see old family Bibles, for they often contain carefully recorded information about births, marriages, and deaths. Go through old photographs, find out who's who, and ask for permission to write the information on the back.

If your relatives live too far away for a personal visit, write letters to them—but ask only a few brief questions in each letter, so you don't overwhelm them. Sending a self-addressed, stamped envelope (SASE) with each of your letters may speed a reply.

After you've contacted all your living relatives, it's time to begin work on the older generations of your family. Consult your charts, choose one line to pursue, and carefully plan your attack. Using the sample chart as an example, you might decide to begin with your mother's grandparents, William and Kitty Berry. From talking to your mother and other relatives, you already know when and where William was born (6 June 1892 in Washington County, Kentucky) and when and where he died (1958 in Hardin County, Kentucky). Now find a map of Kentucky and locate the county seats for Washington and Hardin counties. Then write a letter like the one at the right to the clerk of court in each of those county seats. Be sure that you have your name and address on the letter, in case your SASE gets lost.

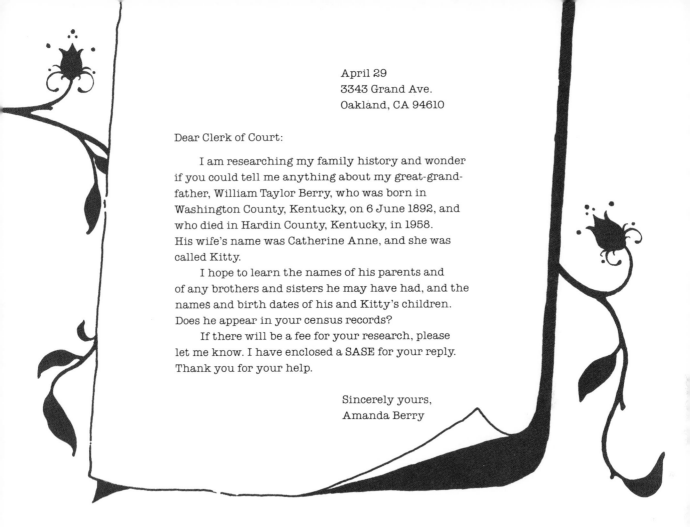

April 29
3343 Grand Ave.
Oakland, CA 94610

Dear Clerk of Court:

I am researching my family history and wonder if you could tell me anything about my great-grandfather, William Taylor Berry, who was born in Washington County, Kentucky, on 6 June 1892, and who died in Hardin County, Kentucky, in 1958. His wife's name was Catherine Anne, and she was called Kitty.

I hope to learn the names of his parents and of any brothers and sisters he may have had, and the names and birth dates of his and Kitty's children. Does he appear in your census records?

If there will be a fee for your research, please let me know. I have enclosed a SASE for your reply. Thank you for your help.

Sincerely yours,
Amanda Berry

A clerk of court may be able to send you birth and death certificates, marriage records, wills, and sometimes information from court proceedings. In the same courthouse, the registrar will have land records, which can tell you when your family arrived in a certain area and what land they owned.

Sometimes a letter to a county courthouse will bring you only a photocopied sheet: *Sorry, we don't do research like this.* In that case you might ask them to suggest the name of a local genealogist who will check the records for a reasonable fee.

Visit your local library and ask the librarian to recommend how-to books on genealogy—they're full of ideas for the ancestor-hunting family.

As you work your way up into the branches of your family tree, you might become curious about the world in which your ancestors lived. Did your great-great-grandfather flee Ireland in the late 1840s because of the potato famine? Why did your great-grandmother come alone to Montana as a girl—was she one of the many women who homesteaded their own land? Why did your great-great-great-grandfather live out his last days in Canada—was he fleeing slavery?

Where can you look for more information? Census records are often valuable, and some libraries have these on microfilm.

For research by mail, there are two important information sources: the National Archives in Washington, D.C., and the Genealogical Library of the Church of Jesus Christ of Latter-day Saints. At your library, look through the *Guide to Genealogical Research in the National Archives* to see what information is available—everything from ships' passenger lists to military records to homestead grants and more! The Church of Jesus Christ of Latter-day Saints (the Mormon Church) maintains an immense storehouse of genealogical material and will be happy to send you information on their services. (These records cover ancestors of many different faiths, not only Mormons.) Write to: The Church of Jesus Christ of Latter-day Saints, Genealogical Library, 35 North West Temple Street, Salt Lake City, Utah 84150.

Working on a family tree can become a long-term hobby, one that the whole family will want to share. You and your helpers will have to decide just how complete a genealogy you want to put together, and how much time you can devote to it. Whatever you decide, keep neat records—remember, you may be an "Aunt Tillie" someday, a link with the traditions that will shape the lives of your descendents.

Think About It

1. How is the world you are growing up in different from the one Eda LeShan grew up in?
2. What do you think you would have enjoyed if you were a child 50 years ago?
3. How do you think the world will be different when you have children? Give reasons to support your ideas.
4. What similar recommendations were made in "When Grandparents Were Growing Up" and "The Care and Feeding of Your Family Tree"? Explain why these recommendations were made.
5. Do you think older people are always wiser than young ones? Explain your answer.

Create and Share   You have been asked to write an article for a children's magazine about getting along with older people. What advice could you give? Write an article about the problems children might have with older relatives, neighbors, or friends of the family. Give your readers some tips about how to avoid or solve them.

Explore   You might want to read *What's Going to Happen to Me?* or the rest of *Grandparents: A Special Kind of Love*, by Eda LeShan. To explore your family tree further, look in the library card catalog under GENEALOGY. For information on the history of your neighborhood, look under the name of your town, city, county, or state.

What has eighteen legs and catches flies?

a baseball team

What's the biggest diamond in the world?

a baseball diamond

Baseball
Fever

Baseballs
and
Meatballs

from BASEBALL FEVER
by Johanna Hurwitz

Ezra Feldman's father knew six different languages. He had a doctorate in history, and he could do hard arithmetic problems in his head. His hobbies were reading history and sociology books. He had a photographic memory and could play a whole chess game without using a board. He just moved the pieces around inside his head. In short, he understood all sorts of long and complicated things. But there were two things he didn't understand at all. He didn't understand Ezra, and he didn't understand baseball.

Ezra was almost ten years old, and he liked baseball more than anything else in the world. He listened to baseball games on the radio, and he watched baseball games on television. When he read books, they were books about baseball. When he talked, he talked a lot about baseball. At night when he slept, he often dreamed about baseball.

"Ezra would eat and drink baseball if he could," his mother said laughingly.

A typical conversation between Ezra and his father went this way:

"Dad, watch out! You're blocking the TV screen. The bases are loaded, and there are two men out. The man at the plate has three balls and two strikes. This is the payoff pitch coming up."

"I can't understand a word you're saying," Mr. Feldman would grumble. "Why should a boy your age sit around watching grown men taking turns hitting a ball with a stick? It's ridiculous!"

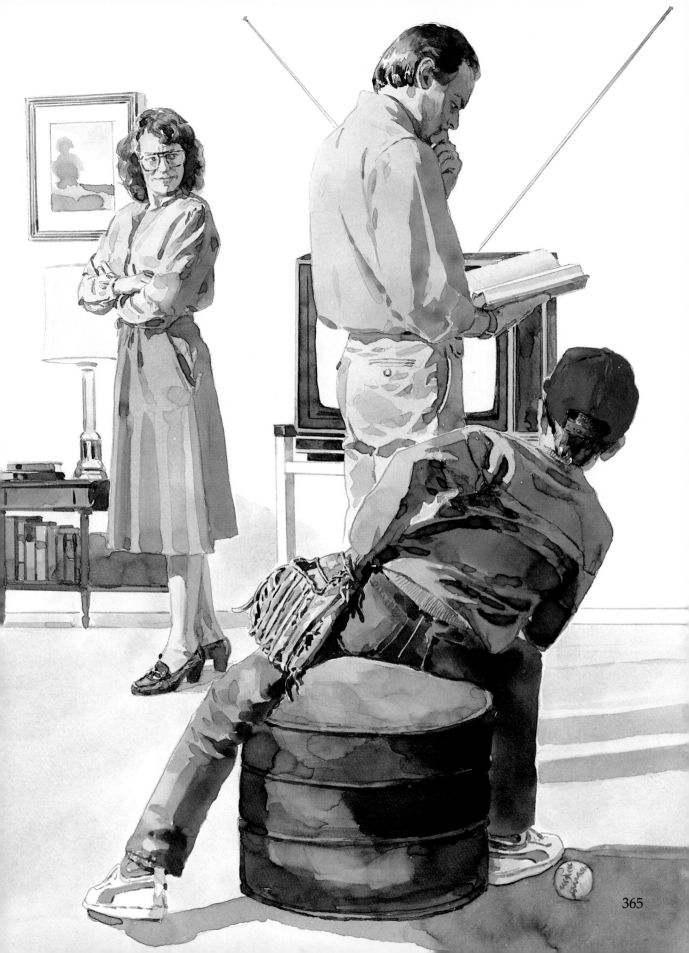

365

Ezra groaned, partly because his father continued to block the television screen and partly because the man at bat had struck out.

Even though he had explained them to him a hundred times, his father kept forgetting the rules of baseball. He still insisted that RBI meant "rubbish brought inside." He couldn't remember "runs batted in." And if Ezra told him that somebody hit a double, Mr. Feldman always asked, "Does that mean they got two points?" Ezra didn't know how a person who could read ancient Greek could be that dumb.

Mrs. Feldman said it was because Ezra's father had grown up in Europe, where baseball is not a popular sport. Mr. Feldman had been born in Germany and had been sent to England before the Second World War. After the war he came to the United States, but it was too late. Mr. Feldman didn't like pumpkin pie either, and both Ezra and his mother loved it.

Pumpkin pies came in the fall just when the baseball season was ending. They were a small compensation. Ezra's favorite month of the year was April when the baseball season opened and his birthday occurred. His birthday was April first, and the baseball season usually opened a few days later.

"April is when the income tax is due," Mr. Feldman would remember. He forgot the new baseball season, but at least he remembered the taxes and his son's birthday. Two and a half weeks before Ezra's tenth birthday, his father came home with an early gift, an electronic chess game for them to share. But sharing a chess game with his father wasn't like sharing a pumpkin pie with his mother. For one thing, Mr. Feldman played with the chess game much more than his son did. Ezra understood the basic rules of chess, but the game wasn't exciting like baseball. Besides, when he played chess with his father, he always knew the outcome of the game in advance. Mr. Feldman won every time.

April finished and May began, and Ezra's favorite team, the Mets, won a few and lost a few. That's the way the season went. Almost before Ezra knew it, Saturday morning, May seventh, had arrived, and he was about to go off to Albany with his father for the weekend. Mrs. Feldman sat at the kitchen table with a cup of coffee and the morning paper opened to the crossword puzzle. In a few minutes she would be leaving for the hospital where she worked as a doctor. Looking up at her son, she said, "Ezra, I think it's very good that you and your father are going to spend a little time together this weekend."

Ezra wasn't so sure. He went to his room to get his overnight bag. He opened a drawer to take out a sweat shirt. He had a huge collection of shirts, because every time his father went off on a trip to give a lecture or to attend a conference at a different college or university, he brought home a new shirt for him. The shirts were all different colors, which was nice. They were all different sizes, which was not nice. Mr. Feldman often got confused when he went shopping, and instead of buying a child's size, he sometimes brought home a man's. Ezra had made a game of giving new meanings to the words on the shirts. He looked through them:

YALE
(You Are Large Enough)

COLUMBIA
(Can Only Ladies' Umbrellas
Maim Big Intelligent Alligators)

DARTMOUTH
(Do All Red Tongued Mouths Open Up To Hiss)

"Ezra!" Mr. Feldman called from the next room. "What's keeping you?"

Ezra grabbed his red **OHIO STATE** (**O**h **H**eavens **I** **O**wn **S**even **T**hin **A**merican **T**urkey **E**ggs) and came running. He kissed his mother good-bye. Then he followed his father outside to the car.

"Here," said Mr. Feldman, handing Ezra the road map of New York State. "Study this. You may learn something this weekend." His father was always on the lookout for educational experiences. He didn't seem to believe in doing anything just for fun.

"Do you know how to spell Albany?" Mr. Feldman asked. Then he spelled it out before Ezra could show him that he knew: "*A-l-b-a-n-y.*"

Ezra thought of the new shirt he would probably bring home with him: **A**ll **L**ong **B**ooks **A**lways **N**ag **Y**ou. Carefully he opened the map. After a few minutes, he finally located Albany.

"Did you remember to bring your toothbrush?" asked Mr. Feldman.

Ezra thought for a moment. He realized that he had forgotten his comb, but he did have the toothbrush. "Yes," he said. His finger slipped and he lost Albany, so he tried to find it again. "Did you bring a book to read while I'm at my meeting?" asked Mr. Feldman.

This time Ezra didn't even have to think. He knew that he had packed his baseball encyclopedia. It took up more room than his underwear and clean T-shirt and pajamas. In fact, he had almost had to leave everything else at home in order to pack the huge book.

"I've got something to read," he said.

His finger slipped on the map again, and he couldn't find Albany. He looked at the names of the cities and towns on that side of the map. Then he made a fantastic discovery.

"Dad," Ezra said. "Did you know that Cooperstown is only an inch away from Albany?"

"What?" asked Mr. Feldman.

"An inch," repeated Ezra. "I've always wanted to go to Cooperstown. Couldn't we stop there?"

"The New York Historical Association is in Cooperstown," said Mr. Feldman. "Since when are you interested in history?"

"I'm interested in baseball history, and Cooperstown is the home of the Baseball Hall of Fame," said Ezra. "Please, Dad, let's go there," he begged.

"I should have known it had something to do with baseball!" Mr. Feldman sighed. "Anyhow, we won't have time to go off our route to other places."

Ezra bit his lip. If he had been clever, he would have said that he wanted to go to the New York Historical Association, whatever that was. Then, once they got to Cooperstown, he could have found a way to get to the baseball museum.

For the rest of the ride Ezra and his father hardly exchanged a word. Ezra wondered if his father was nervous about the meeting that he was going to. Mr. Feldman turned on the car radio and listened to the news and some music. Ezra stared out the window. He read the license plates on the cars on the highway. Some of them had messages or words like DIANE, I LUV YOU, MY CAR, and GEORGE I. When he got tired of looking at the license plates, Ezra studied the map. He added up the little red numbers showing the mileage. He discovered that the inch between Albany and Cooperstown came to sixty-five miles. If they drove fast, they could reach it in an hour. But Ezra knew that when his father had made up his mind about something, it was useless to nag. So he saved his breath and sat silent all the way to Albany.

By one o'clock Ezra and his father had checked into their room and had a sandwich in the motel coffee shop.

"All right," said Mr. Feldman. "You're on your own for the afternoon. You can read your book or watch TV in the room. I packed the chess computer in with my things in case you want to play with it."

The afternoon was going to be a long one. Ezra went upstairs to their room and turned on the TV. If he were lucky, there would be a baseball game to watch. Unfortunately, it was raining in New York City and the Yankee game had been called off. The Mets weren't scheduled to play until later in the day, in Houston. There was nothing to watch.

Ezra lay down on his bed with his baseball encyclopedia. He checked out all the statistics for Ty Cobb. Though Cobb had lived and played long before he was born, Ezra liked reading about the old-time baseball players. Ty Cobb had 4,191 base hits in his career. His lifetime batting average was .367, and he had 892 stolen bases. Ezra flipped the pages of the encyclopedia. It had over 2,000 of them. He would need a long time to learn everything listed there, and he read for a couple of hours until he got a little restless.

Ezra tried the television set again, but there was nothing that looked interesting. Finally, from boredom, he went to his father's overnight bag and took out the chess game. He plugged it in and set it for the simplest level.

Ezra lost the first two games he played with the machine. He was about to begin a third one when the phone rang. His father was checking up on him.

"I'll meet you in the lobby in twenty minutes," said Mr. Feldman. "Then we'll go off somewhere to dinner."

"OK," said Ezra. "How's the meeting going?"

"Not so good," admitted Mr. Feldman. "We've been covering the same ground all afternoon, and we seem to be getting nowhere. They can't decide whether or not to set up the lecture series that I'm proposing."

At 6:20, Ezra got ready to meet his father. He washed his face and hands, because he could imagine his father asking him if he had done so. Without a comb, he smoothed his hair with his fingers. He took out his Ohio State sweat shirt and put it on. It was a man's large, and so even with cuffs the sleeves hung below his wrists. Ezra went downstairs and found his father waiting for him.

"At least we'll have a good dinner," said Mr. Feldman. "I heard of an Italian restaurant a couple of miles from here. Imagine coming all this way just for a plate of Italian food."

Ezra wanted to suggest that if they went to Cooperstown on the way home, the trip wouldn't be wasted. But he knew better than to upset his father. Instead, he asked, "Why do you think they haven't made a decision about your lecture series?"

"It's very simple," Mr. Feldman explained. "It's a way of exercising power. Professor Strauss, who is the committee chairman, controls the money. The minute he makes a decision about this series, he is handing over money and power to someone else. So for the moment, he's enjoying himself. It's a capricious act on his part. Tomorrow he can just as easily change his mind."

Ezra felt proud to have his father speak so seriously with him. He didn't know the word *capricious*, but he thought he understood what his father was saying. "Sometimes baseball managers act like that," he said. "If a manager has a fight with a player, he might keep him out of a game, even though he might hit a home run or make a great catch. A good manager doesn't use his power that way."

"Exactly," said Mr. Feldman. "But that's why they say that power corrupts." Ezra smiled at his father. They didn't often agree on something, but when they did, it felt very good.

When they arrived at the restaurant, it was crowded with Saturday evening diners. They got the last empty table, close to the entrance door.

"Well, at least we got a place," said Ezra.

They studied the menus. Everything on the menu had a long and unfamiliar name.

"I just want spaghetti," said Ezra when the waitress came to take their orders.

Suddenly Mr. Feldman jumped up. "Strauss!" he called out.

Ezra saw an elderly man with a heavy white moustache and thick eyeglasses standing at the doorway of the restaurant.

"Hello, Feldman," said the old man. "No wonder I can't find a seat. If you knew to come here, then the whole place must be filled with out-of-towners."

"Please, join us," urged Mr. Feldman.

"I guess I have no choice if I don't want to starve," the old man answered. Ezra thought he didn't sound very polite, but he noticed that Professor Strauss was quick to sit at their table.

"Strauss, I'd like you to meet my son Ezra," said Mr. Feldman. "Ezra, this is Professor Laurence Strauss of the history department here. He's one of the men I spent the afternoon with."

Ezra tried to look friendly, even though the man had been giving his father such a hard time.

The two men began conversing, and Ezra let his mind wander. The waitress came with the food for Ezra and his father. The steam rising from it smelled delicious. No wonder there was now a line of people standing in the lobby waiting for seats.

Ezra was starved, and so he stabbed one of the little meatballs with his fork and lifted it to his mouth.

"Well, young man, what are your interests?" asked the professor.

Ezra was not expecting to be addressed, and he started at the question. His hand shook, and the meatball fell from his fork and slid down into the wide sleeve of his sweat shirt.

It was a terrible moment. The meatball burned his arm, and Ezra blushed as red as the tomato sauce on his plate. He wondered if his father and Professor Strauss had noticed the mishap. He wanted to cry out from the burn and slide under the table with embarrassment. Instead, he said and did nothing.

"He has baseball fever," said Mr. Feldman, answering for his son. "One of these days I hope he'll learn that there are a few other things in the world besides baseball."

Ezra always felt bad when his father spoke about him that way, as if he were an idiot or something. But now, with the burning meatball in his sleeve, he didn't care what he said. He was too busy trying to shake out the meatball

secretly. Holding his arm under the table, he moved it inside his shirt. Luckily the large sleeve that had caught the meatball now released it, and the meatball slid out onto the floor. Ezra felt as relieved as if he were safe at home plate.

"What team do you root for?" asked the professor.

"The Mets," said Ezra.

"You're crazy! You look too intelligent for that nonsense," said the professor. "You should use your time more constructively."

"That's what I always tell him. If I've told him once, I've told him a hundred times that baseball is just a waste of time," Mr. Feldman agreed.

"The Mets haven't a chance in the world," said the professor. "I would have thought you would root for the Yankees."

"You never can tell what will happen," said Ezra. "This is a new season. Did you know that one year the Yankees won three World Series games with scores of sixteen-three, twelve-nothing, and ten-nothing, and they still lost the series?"

The professor nodded his head. "That was in 1960, when Pittsburgh won," he said. "Still the odds are against the Mets. Do you realize how many times the Yankees have won the World Series?" he asked Ezra.

"Sure," said Ezra. "In 1923, '27, '28, '32, '36, '37, '39, '41, '43—"

"Enough, enough," said Professor Strauss.

Ezra wondered why he didn't want to hear about 1947, '49, '50, '51, '52, '53 . . .

"Do you know who won the series in 1924?" asked Professor Strauss, interrupting Ezra's thoughts.

"The Senators," said Ezra, grinning. He was having fun.

The waitress brought the professor his food. "Who managed the St. Louis Cardinals to their first pennant in 1926?" he asked Ezra.

"Rogers Hornsby," said Ezra with a smile. This was a game he often played with his friends. They asked one another baseball questions and tried to see who knew the most. Ezra almost always won.

"Your son is brilliant," said Professor Strauss, turning to Mr. Feldman. "His memory is phenomenal for a boy his age." He turned to Ezra. "How old are you? Twelve?"

"I'm ten. My birthday was last month," said Ezra. "I got *The Baseball Encyclopedia* for my birthday, and I've been doing a lot of reading in it," he said by way of explanation. He didn't want the professor to think that he always knew so much.

"Incredible! This boy will go far. He has an excellent mind. You must be very proud of him," said the professor.

"Of course I am," said Mr. Feldman, looking rather surprised at the professor's praise of his son. "But he doesn't seem to have any other interests besides baseball."

"That's a sign of intelligence. Concentration in one area is excellent. And someday he will surprise you by transferring his interest, his concentration, and his memory skills to some other totally different area of study."

"Really?" Mr. Feldman seemed stunned by the way the conversation was going. "I'm surprised that you are so knowledgeable about baseball," he said.

"There's nothing like baseball to take your mind off the problems of the world," said Professor Strauss. "Tell me," he asked, "have you been to Cooperstown?"

"No," said Ezra. "It's too far off our route."

"Nonsense," said the professor with authority. "It's only an hour and a half from here. I insist that you go," he said, turning to Mr. Feldman. "You'll be surprised at how interesting it is."

He paused a moment. "I'll tell you what. Let's cancel the meeting we scheduled for tomorrow morning. I want more time to think over some of the things you said today. You had some good ideas, but I'm not quite ready to make any decision. And you can use the time to take your son to Cooperstown."

Mr. Feldman looked surprised. He had anticipated a Yes or a No to the following morning. Instead, he found himself agreeing to take Ezra to Cooperstown, the home of the Baseball Hall of Fame. The development wasn't what he had expected.

Ezra was surprised too. "Great!" he said. "I measured the distance to Cooperstown with my knuckle. It's only an inch from Albany," he informed the professor.

Then he turned to tackle his remaining meatballs and spaghetti. After baseballs, he liked meatballs next best.

The Base Stealer

Poised between going on and back, pulled
Both ways taut like a tightrope-walker,
Fingertips pointing the opposites,
Now bouncing tiptoe like a dropped ball
Or a kid skipping rope, come on, come on,
Running a scattering of steps sidewise,
How he teeters, skitters, tingles, teases,
Taunts them, hovers like an ecstatic bird,
He's only flirting, crowd him, crowd him,
Delicate, delicate, delicate, delicate—now!

—Robert Francis

Think About It

1. How are Ezra Feldman's problem with his father and Mr. Feldman's problem with Professor Strauss alike? How are they different?
2. How do you think Mr. Feldman and Ezra's dinner with Professor Strauss will help resolve the problems?
3. Do you think poems like "The Base Stealer" appeal only to sports fans? Explain your answer.
4. What makes a person a fan of baseball or any other sport? How do fans think, feel, and act?
5. Tell about a special interest that you and other members of your family share. Tell about an interest of yours that they do not share.

Create and Share   Pick your favorite sport. Try to convince someone you know doesn't share your enthusiasm for the sport to attend a game with you. List reasons (as many as you can think of) to persuade your friend to go. Or write a poem about your favorite sport.

Explore   If you enjoyed "Baseballs and Meatballs," you may want to read the book the story was taken from, *Baseball Fever*. For other books on sports, look in the library card catalog under SPORTS or under the name of the sport that interests you—BASEBALL or SOCCER, for example.

Baseball Encyclopedia

from THE BASEBALL BOOK
edited by Zander Hollander

Half Swing. The action of a batter trying to stop his swing, but failing to do so. Even a half swing counts as a whole strike.

Hall of Fame. Baseball maintains a Hall of Fame in order to honor outstanding players, managers, umpires, and others connected with the game. Proposed by Ford Frick in 1935 soon after he became National League president, it was begun the next year with the election of Ty Cobb, Walter Johnson, Christy Mathewson, Babe Ruth, and Honus Wagner. There are now more than 150 members.

Members are chosen each year from two categories. Members of the Baseball Writers Association of America vote on players who have been out of the game for at least 5 but not more than 20 years. The Committee on Baseball Veterans votes on players of the more distant past and others who have distinguished themselves in various branches of the game, such as umpires, managers, sportswriters, and league and team officials.

The actual Hall of Fame, containing bronze statues of those elected, is a room in the Baseball Museum in Cooperstown, New

York, a site chosen in the now disputed belief that baseball was invented there by Abner Double-day. Ironically, Doubleday is not in the Hall of Fame.

In addition to the bronze statues of the members, there are other mementos in the Hall of Fame that help make it a favorite tourist attraction. Among them are the bench Connie Mack sat on in the Philadelphia Athletic dugout for many years; a ball used in 1866; Stan Musial's spikes; the baseball with which Cy Young won his five-hundredth game; the lockers of Honus Wagner, Babe Ruth, Lou Gehrig, and Joe DiMaggio; and the sliding pads used by Ty Cobb when he stole 96 bases in 1915.

Besides the players, managers, and umpires elected to the Hall of Fame, others honored include Henry Chadwick, an early baseball writer credited with inventing the box score; and Alexander Cart-wright, whom many historians recognize as the true founder of baseball rather than Doubleday.

Hit. A batted ball on which the batter reaches base without benefit of an error, fielder's choice, interference, or the retirement of a preceding runner. A one-base hit is a single, a two-base hit a double, a three-base hit a triple, and a four-base hit a home run.

Robinson, Jackie. Jackie Robinson became the first black player on a modern American major-league baseball team when he joined the Brooklyn Dodgers in 1947.

Robinson was carefully selected by Brooklyn Dodger owner Branch Rickey as the man who would shatter baseball's color line. "I'm looking for a ballplayer with guts enough not to fight back," Rickey told Robinson. To his credit Robinson, one of the game's fiercest competitors, kept his pledge to Rickey and turned the other cheek to the abuse that was heaped on him. His courage forced open the doors of the sport to blacks, who had been previously barred from the majors.

Robinson was born in Cairo, Georgia, on January 3l, 1919, and was a four-sport college star at

R

taunting pitchers with fake starts, then stealing a base—and clutch hitting made him the unquestioned leader of the Dodgers.

Robinson was elected to the Hall of Fame in 1962, his first year of eligibility. Ten years later, at age 53, he died of a heart attack.

Rookie. A first-year player. Outstanding rookies are candidates for the Rookie of the Year award given in each league. They are chosen by the Baseball Writers Association of America, whose votes are based on best all-around performance. The award was begun by the National League in 1947 and by the American League in 1949. Jackie Robinson of the Brooklyn Dodgers was the first Rookie of the Year.

Run. The score made by an offensive player who advances from the batter's box and touches first, second, third, and home in that order. The team with the most runs wins the game.

Runs Batted In. Also known as RBI's. Credit given to a batter for each run that scores when he makes a safe hit, is retired by an infield or outfield putout, or when a run is forced in because he becomes a base runner.

UCLA. Rickey chose him from baseball's black leagues in 1946 and changed the face of baseball forever.

In 10 seasons with the Brooklyn Dodgers, Robinson achieved a .311 batting average and hit over .300 six times. He played on six pennant winners and was the National League batting champion and MVP in 1949 when he batted .342. His base-path daring—

Although Davy was sixty years old and Sam was only twelve, they were best friends who shared a love of baseball. Summer weekends almost always found them together at Ebbets Field, home of the Brooklyn Dodgers and the great Jackie Robinson. But when Davy had a heart attack, Sam decided to set out on his own to find a special present for his friend.

A Ball for Davy

from THANK YOU, JACKIE ROBINSON
by Barbara Cohen

What really got me was when Davy's daughter, Henrietta, told me he was asking for me. I think she thought that would please me and make me feel better about not getting to see him, but it only made me feel worse. I had been hanging around that hospital for days, in the afternoon or evening—whenever there was no game on the radio— but they kept saying I was too young, and they wouldn't let me in. The news that he wanted to see me was the last straw. I'd had it. I was going to do something spectacular. I was going to make him better all by myself. It would be like magic.

Thursday afternoon I got on my bike and rode downtown. I went into Muldoon's Sporting Goods and bought a brand new regulation baseball. I couldn't count on catching one at the ball park. In all the time Davy and I had gone to the games that had never happened to us. It probably never would, if we went to a thousand million games. I would have to persuade the players to autograph the ball, even if I hadn't caught it.

I had gone into the kitchen real early Saturday morning, before anyone else was up, and made myself a couple of egg-salad sandwiches. I had them and my money and the baseball in its little cardboard box. I walked the mile and a half to the bus station because there'd be no place to leave my bike if I rode there. I took the bus into New York City and I took a subway to Ebbets Field.

You could see flags flying above the ball park when you climbed up out of the subway station. You had to walk three blocks and there you were. Inside it was as it always had been, as bright and green as ever. In the excitement of being there, I almost forgot about Davy for a moment. But then I remembered.

I thought maybe I'd better start trying right away. My chances were probably better during batting practice than they would be later. I took my ball out of its box and stashed the box underneath my bleacher seat. Then I walked around to the first-base side and climbed all the way down to the box seats right behind the dugout. I leaned over the rail. Billy Cox was trotting back to the dugout from home plate, where Erskine had been throwing to him.

I swallowed my heart, which seemed to be beating in my throat, and called out, "Billy, hey Billy," waving my ball as hard and high as I could. But I was scared, and my voice wasn't very loud, and I don't think Billy Cox heard me. He disappeared into the dugout.

Marv Rackley came out of the dugout and then Carl Furillo. I called to them too, but they didn't seem to hear me either.

This method was getting me nowhere. I had to try something else before the game began and I'd really lost my chance. I looked around to see if there were any ushers nearby, but none was in sight. It was kind of early and the place hadn't really started to fill up yet. I guess the ushers were loafing around the refreshment stands.

I climbed up on the railing and then hoisted myself onto the roof of the dugout. I could have stood up and walked across the dugout roof to the edge, but I figured if I did that an usher surely would see me. I sneaked across the roof on my belly until I came to the edge, and then I leaned over.

Only trouble was, there were just a couple of guys in there—Eddie Miksis, and Billy Cox whom I'd seen out on the field a few minutes before. I was disappointed. I had certainly hoped for Campy's signature, and Gil Hodges', and Pee Wee Reese's, and, of course, Jackie Robinson's. But I figured Davy would be thrilled with Miksis and Billy Cox, since their names on a ball would be more than he'd ever expected. And anyway a few more guys might come meandering in before I was through.

But no matter how hard I swallowed, my heart was still stuck in my throat. "Eddie," I called. "Eddie, Billy." Hardly any sound came out of my mouth at all.

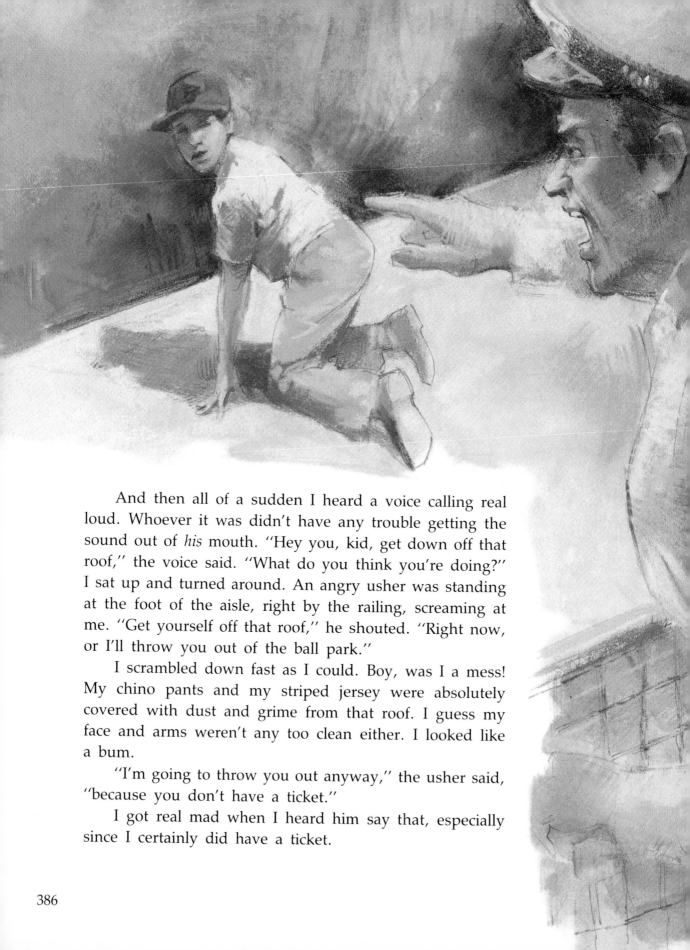

And then all of a sudden I heard a voice calling real loud. Whoever it was didn't have any trouble getting the sound out of *his* mouth. "Hey you, kid, get down off that roof," the voice said. "What do you think you're doing?" I sat up and turned around. An angry usher was standing at the foot of the aisle, right by the railing, screaming at me. "Get yourself off that roof," he shouted. "Right now, or I'll throw you out of the ball park."

I scrambled down fast as I could. Boy, was I a mess! My chino pants and my striped jersey were absolutely covered with dust and grime from that roof. I guess my face and arms weren't any too clean either. I looked like a bum.

"I'm going to throw you out anyway," the usher said, "because you don't have a ticket."

I got real mad when I heard him say that, especially since I certainly did have a ticket.

"You can't throw me out," I shouted back at him. "I've got as much right to be here as you have." I had suddenly found my voice. I was scared of the ball players, but this usher didn't frighten me one bit. I pulled my ticket stub out of my pocket. "See?" I said, thrusting it into his face. "I certainly do have a ticket."

He made as if to take it out of my hand. I guess he wanted to look at it close, to make sure it was a stub from that day and not an old one I carried around in my pocket for emergencies. But I pulled my hand back.

"Oh, no, you don't," I said. "You can't take this ticket away from me. You won't give it back to me and then you'll throw me out because I don't have a ticket!"

"I better not see you on that roof again," the usher said. "I'll have my eye out for you—and so will all the other ushers."

"Don't worry," I said.

Then I felt his hand on my shoulder. "As a matter of fact, kid," he said, "I think I'll escort you to your seat where you belong. Up in the bleachers where you can't make any trouble!"

Well, right then and there the whole enterprise would have gone up in smoke if Jackie Robinson himself had not come trotting out onto the field from the dugout that very second. "Hey, Jackie," I called, "Hey, Jackie," in a voice as loud as a thunderbolt. I mean there were two airplanes flying overhead right that minute and Jackie Robinson heard me anyway.

He glanced over in the direction he could tell my voice was coming from, and I began to wave frantically, still calling, "Jackie, hey, Jackie."

He lifted up his hand, gave one wide wave, and smiled. "Hey, kid," he called and continued on his way to the batting cage. In another instant he'd have been too busy with batting practice to pay any attention to me.

"Sign my ball," I screamed. "Sign my ball."

He seemed to hesitate briefly. I took this as a good omen. "You gotta," I went on frantically. "Please, please, you gotta."

"He don't gotta do nothing," the usher said. "That's Jackie Robinson and everyone knows that he don't gotta do nothing."

I went right on screaming.

"Come on, kid," the usher said, "we're getting out of here." He was a big hulking usher who must have weighed about eight hundred pounds, and he began pulling on me. Even though I gripped the cement with my sneakers and held onto the rail with my hand, he managed to pull me loose. But he couldn't shut me up.

"Please, Jackie, please," I went right on screaming.

It worked. Or something worked. If not my screaming, then maybe the sight of that monster usher trying to pull me up the aisle and scrungy old me pulling against him for dear life.

"Let the kid go," Jackie Robinson said when he got to the railing. "All he wants is an autograph."

"He's a fresh kid," the usher said, but he let me go.

"Kids are supposed to be fresh," Jackie Robinson said.

I thrust my ball into Jackie Robinson's face. "Gee, thanks, Mr. Robinson," I said. "Sign it, please."

"You got a pen?" he asked.

"A pen?" I could have kicked myself. "A pen?" I'd forgotten a pen! I turned to the usher. "You got a pen?"

"If I had," the usher said triumphantly, "I certainly wouldn't lend it to you!"

"Oh, come on," Jackie Robinson said, "don't be so vindictive. What harm did the kid do, after all?"

"Well, as it happens, I don't have one," the usher replied smugly.

"Wait here," I said. "Wait right here, Mr. Robinson. I'll go find one."

Jackie Robinson laughed. "Sorry, kid, but I've got work to do. Another time, maybe."

"Please, Mr. Robinson," I said. "It's for my friend. My friend, Davy."

"Well, let Davy come and get his own autographs," he said. "Why should you do his dirty work for him?"

"He can't come," I said. The words came rushing out of me, tumbling one on top of the other. I had to tell Jackie Robinson all about it, before he went away. "Davy can't come because he's sick. He had a heart attack."

"A heart attack?" Jackie Robinson asked. "A kid had a heart attack?"

"He's not a kid," I explained. "He's sixty years old. He's my best friend. He's a black man, like you."

"How did this Davy get to be your best friend?" he asked.

So I told him. I told him everything, or as near to everything as I could tell in five minutes. I told him how Davy worked for my mother, and how I had no father, so it was Davy who took me to my first ball game. I told him how they wouldn't let me into the hospital to see Davy, and how we had always talked about catching a ball that was hit into the stands and getting it autographed.

Jackie listened silently, nodding every once in a while. When I was done at last, he said, "Well, now, kid, I'll tell you what. You keep this ball you brought with you. Keep it to play with. And borrow a pen from someone. Come back to the dugout the minute, the very second, the game is over, and I'll get you a real ball, one we played with, and I'll get all the guys to autograph it for you."

"Make sure it's one you hit," I said.

What nerve. I should have fainted dead away just because Jackie Robinson had deigned to speak to me. But here he was, making me an offer beyond my wildest dreams, and for me it wasn't enough. I had to have more. However, he didn't seem to care.

"O.K." he said, "*if* I hit one." He had been in a little slump lately.

"You will," I said, "you will."

And he did. He broke the ball game wide open in the sixth inning when he hit a double to left field. The Dodgers scored six runs, and they scored them all in the sixth inning. They beat the Cubs, 6–1. They were hot, really hot, that day and that year.

But I really didn't watch the game as closely as I had all the others I'd been to see. I couldn't. My mind was on too many other things—on Jackie Robinson, on what was going to happen after the game was over, on that monster usher who I feared would yet find some way of spoiling things for me, but above all on Davy and the fact that he was missing all of the excitement.

And then I had to worry about getting hold of a pen. You could buy little pencils at the ball park for keeping box scores, but no pens. It was the first—and last—time in my life I walked into a ball park without something to write with. And I didn't see how I could borrow one from someone, since in all that mess of humanity, I'd never find the person after the game to return it to him. Unless I took the guy's name and address and mailed it back to him later.

It didn't look to me like the guys in the bleachers where I was sitting had pens with them anyway. Most of them had on tee shirts, and tee shirts don't have pockets in them for pens. I decided to walk over to the seats along the first-base line to see if any of the fans looked more like pen owners. I had to go in that direction anyway to make sure I was at the dugout the second the ball game ended. I took with me my ball in its box.

On my way over I ran into this guy hawking drinks and I decided to buy one in order to wash down the two egg-salad sandwiches I had eaten during the third inning.

This guy had a pen in his pocket. As a matter of fact he had two of them. "Look," I said to him, as I paid him for my soda, "could I borrow one of those pens?"

"Sure," he said, handing it to me after he had put my money into his change machine. He stood there, waiting, like he expected me to hand it back to him after I was done with it.

"Look," I said again, "maybe I could sort of buy it from you."

"Buy it from me? You mean the pen?"

"Yeah."

"What do you want my pen for?"

"I need it because Jackie Robinson promised me that after the game he and all the other guys would autograph a ball for me." Getting involved in all these explanations was really a pain in the neck.

"You don't say," the hawker remarked. I could tell he didn't believe me.

"It's true," I said. "Anyway, are you going to sell me your pen?"

"Sure. For a dollar."

I didn't have a dollar. Not any more. I'd have to try something else. I started to walk away.

"Oh, don't be silly, kid," he called to me. "Here, take the darn pen. Keep it." It was a nice pen. It was shaped like a bat, and on it, it said, "Ebbets Field, Home of the Brooklyn Dodgers."

"Hey, mister, thanks," I said. "That's real nice of you." It seemed to me I ought to do something for him, so I added, "I think I'd like another soda." He sold me another soda, and between sipping first from one and then from the other and trying to watch the game, I made very slow progress. I got down to the dugout just before the game ended in the top of the ninth. The Dodgers didn't have to come up to bat at all in that final inning, and I was only afraid that they'd all have disappeared into the clubhouse by the time I got there. I should have come down at the end of the eighth. But Jackie Robinson had said the end of the game. Although my nerve had grown by about seven thousand per cent that day, I still didn't have enough to interrupt Jackie Robinson during a game.

I stood at the railing near the dugout, waiting, and sure enough, Jackie Robinson appeared around the corner of the building only a minute or two after Preacher Roe, who was pitching, threw that final out. All around me people were getting up to leave the ball park, but a lot of them stopped when they saw Jackie Robinson come to the rail to talk to me. Roy Campanella, Pee Wee Reese, and Gil Hodges were with him.

"Hi, kid," Jackie Robinson said. He was carrying a ball. It was covered with signatures. "Pee Wee here had a pen."

"And a good thing, too," Pee Wee said, "because most of the other guys left the field already."

"But these guys wanted to meet Davy's friend," Jackie Robinson said.

By that time, Preacher Roe had joined us at the railing. Jackie handed him the ball. "Hey, Preacher," he said, "got enough strength left in that arm to sign this ball for Davy's friend here?"

"Got a pen?" Preacher Roe asked.

I handed him the pen the hawker had given me. I was glad I hadn't gone through all the trouble of getting it for nothing.

"Not much room left on this ball," Roe said. He squirmed his signature into a little empty space beneath Duke Snider's and then he handed me both the pen and the ball. Everybody was waving programs and pens in the faces of the ball players who stood by the railing. But before they signed any of them they all shook my hand. So did Jackie Robinson. I stood there, clutching Davy's ball and watching while those guys signed the programs of the other fans. Finally, though, they'd had enough. They smiled and waved their hands and walked away, five big men in white uniforms, etched sharply against the bright green grass. Jackie Robinson was the last one into the dugout and before he disappeared around the corner, he turned and waved to me.

I waved back. "Thank you, Jackie Robinson," I called. "Thanks for everything." He nodded and smiled. I guess he heard me. I'm glad I remembered my manners before it was too late.

When everyone was gone, I looked down at the ball in my hands. Right between the rows of red seaming, Jackie Robinson had written, above his own signature, "For Davy. Get well soon." Then all the others had put their names around that.

I took the ball I had bought out of the box and put it in my pocket. I put the ball Jackie Robinson had given me in the box. Then I went home.

Think About It

1. Why do you think someone would write an encyclopedia about a sport?
2. What entries could you add to the *Baseball Encyclopedia?* Find some in "A Ball for Davy."
3. Who tells the story "A Ball for Davy"? How does the author show you what the narrator is like?
4. Why does Sam want an autographed baseball for Davy? What problems does he have to overcome to get it?
5. Compare and contrast Sam's situation with Ezra's. Who do you think is the happier baseball fan? Explain your answer.

Create and Share   What do you think will happen when Sam gives the baseball to Davy? Write that scene, telling how Sam presents the ball and how Davy reacts. You may want to use dialogue. If you do, be sure to put Sam's and Davy's words in quotes.

Explore   Jackie Robinson has figured in other books of historical fiction, including *In the Year of the Boar and Jackie Robinson*, by Bette Bao Lord, the story of a young Chinese girl who comes to Brooklyn in 1947. For stories about baseball with a modern setting, look for books by Alfred Slote and Matt Christopher.

At night, with the water glowing blue and Joshua moving serenely—reflections of yellow and gold and orange—above the pink gravel, it seemed to Emma she had never seen anything so pretty. She watched her aquarium the way astronomers watch stars.

from A PET *by Cynthia Rylant*

Fur, Fins, and Feathers

A Bad Road for Cats

by Cynthia Rylant

"Louie! Louis! Where are you?"

The woman called it out again and again as she walked along Route 6. A bad road for cats. She prayed he hadn't wandered this far. But it had been nearly two weeks, and still Louis hadn't come home.

She stopped at a Shell station, striding up to the young man at the register. Her eyes snapped black and fiery as she spit the question at him:

"Have you seen a *cat?*" The word *cat* came out hard as a rock.

The young man straightened up.

"No, ma'am. No cats around here. Somebody dropped a mutt off a couple nights ago, but a Mack truck got it yesterday about noon. Dog didn't have a chance."

The woman's eyes pinched his.

"I lost my cat. Orange and white. If you see him, you be more careful of him than that dog. This is a bad road for cats."

She marched toward the door.

"I'll be back," she said, like a threat, and the young man straightened up again as she went out.

"Louie! Louis! Where are you?"

She was a very tall woman, and skinny. Her black hair was long and shiny, like an Indian's. She might have been a Cherokee making her way alongside a river, alert and watchful. Tracking.

But Route 6 was no river. It was a truckers' road, lined with gas stations, motels, dairy bars, diners. A nasty road, smelling of diesel and rubber.

The woman's name was Magda. And she was of French blood, not Indian. Magda was not old, but she carried herself as a very old and strong person might, with no fear of death and with a clear sense of her right to the earth and a disdain for the ugliness of belching machines and concrete.

Magda lived in a small house about two miles off Route 6. There she worked at a loom, weaving wool gathered from the sheep she owned. Magda's husband was dead, and she had no children. Only a cat named Louis.

Dunh. Dunh. Duuunnh.

Magda's heart pounded as a tank truck roared by. *Duuunnh.* The horn hurt her ears, making her feel sick inside, stealing some of her strength.

Four years before, Magda had found Louis at one of the gas stations on Route 6. She had been on her way home from her weekly trip to the grocery and had pulled in for a fill-up. As she stood inside the station in front of the cigarette machine, dropping in quarters, she'd felt warm fur against her leg and had given a start. Looking down, she'd seen an orange-and-white kitten. It had purred and meowed and pushed its nose into Magda's shoes. Smiling, Magda had picked the kitten up. Then she had seen the horror.

Half of the kitten's tail was gone. What remained was bloody and scabbed, and the stump stuck straight out.

Magda had carried the animal to one of the station attendants.

"Whose kitten is this?" Her eyes drilled in the question.

The attendant had shrugged his shoulders.

"Nobody's. Just a drop-off."

Magda had moved closer to him.

"What happened to its *tail?*" she asked, the words slow and clear.

"Got caught in the door. Stupid cat was under everybody's feet—no wonder half its tail got whacked."

Magda could not believe such a thing.

"And you offer it no *help?*" she had asked.

"Not my cat," he answered.

Magda's face had blazed as she'd turned and stalked out the door with the kitten.

A veterinarian mended what was left of the kitten's tail. And Magda named it Louis for her grandfather.

"Louie! Louis! Where are you?"

Dunh. Duuunnh. Another horn at her back. Magda wondered about her decision to walk Route 6 rather than drive it. She had thought that on foot she might find Louis more easily—in a ditch, under some bushes, up a tree. They were even, she and Louis, if she were on foot, too. But the trucks were making her misery worse.

Magda saw a dairy bar up ahead. She thought she would stop and rest. She would have some coffee and a slice of quiet away from the road.

She walked across the wide gravel lot to the tiny walk-up window. Pictures of strawberry sundaes, spongy shakes, cones with curly peaks were plastered all over the building, drawing business from the road with big red words like CHILLY.

Magda barely glanced at the young girl working inside. All teenage girls looked alike to her.

"Coffee," she ordered.

"Black?"

"Yes."

Magda moved to one side and leaned against the building. The trucks were rolling out on the highway, but far enough away to give her time to regain her strength. No horns, no smoke, no dirt. A little peace.

She drank her coffee and thought about Louis when he was a kitten. Once, he had leaped from her attic window and she had found him, stunned and shivering, on the hard gravel below. The veterinarian said Louis had broken a leg and was lucky to be alive. The kitten had stomped around in a cast for a few weeks. Magda drew funny faces on it to cheer him up.

Louis loved white cheese, tall grass and the skeins of wool Magda left lying around her loom.

That's what she would miss most, she thought, if Louis never came back; an orange and white cat making the yarn fly under her loom.

Magda finished her coffee, then turned to throw the empty cup in the trash can. As she did, a little sign in the bottom corner of the window caught her eye. The words were surrounded by dirty smudges: 4 Sal. CAT

Magda caught her breath. She moved up to the window and this time looked squarely into the face of the girl.

"Are you selling a *cat?*" she said quietly, but hard on *cat.*

"Not me. This boy," the girl answered, brushing her stringy hair back from her face.

"Where is he?" Magda asked.

"That yellow house right off the road up there."

Magda headed across the lot.

She had to knock only once. The door opened and standing there was a boy about fifteen.

"I saw your sign," Magda said. "I am interested in your cat."

The boy did not answer. He looked at Magda's face with his wide blue eyes, and he grinned, showing a mouth of rotten and missing teeth.

Magda felt a chill move over her.

"The cat," she repeated. "You have one to sell? Is it orange and white?"

The boy stopped grinning. Without a word, he slammed the door in Magda's face.

She was stunned. A strong woman like her, to be so stunned by a boy. It shamed her. But again she knocked on the door—and very hard this time.

No answer.

What kind of boy is this? Magda asked herself. A strange one. And she feared he had Louis.

She had just raised her hand to knock a third time when the door opened. There the boy stood with Louis in his arms.

Again, Magda was stunned. Her cat was covered with oil and dirt. He was thin, and his head hung weakly. When he saw Magda, he seemed to use his last bit of strength to let go a pleading cry.

The boy no longer was grinning. He held Louis close against him, forcefully stroking the cat's ears again and again and again. The boy's eyes were full of tears, his mouth twisted into sad protest.

Magda wanted to leap for Louis, steal him and run for home. But she knew better. This was an unusual boy. She must be careful.

Magda put her hand into her pocket and pulled out a dollar bill.

"Enough?" she asked, holding it up.

The boy clutched the cat harder, his mouth puckering fiercely.

Magda pulled out two more dollar bills. She held the money up, the question in her eyes.

The boy relaxed his hold on Louis. He tilted his head to one side, as if considering Magda's offer.

In desperation, Magda pulled out a twenty-dollar bill.

"Enough?" she almost screamed.

The boy's head jerked upright, then he grabbed all the bills with one hand and shoved Louis at Magda with the other.

Magda cradled Louis in her arms, rubbing her cheek across his head. Before walking away, she looked once more at the boy. He stood stiffly with the money clenched in his hand, tears running from his eyes and dripping off his face like rainwater.

Magda took Louis home. She washed him and healed him. And for many days she was in a rage at the strange boy who had sold her her own cat, nearly dead.

When Louis was healthy, though, and his old fat self, playing games among the yarn beneath her loom, her rage grew smaller and smaller until finally she could forgive the strange boy.

She came to feel sympathy for him, remembering his tears. And she wove some orange and white wool into a pattern, stuffed it with cotton, sewed two green button eyes and a small pink mouth onto it, then attached a matching stub of a tail.

She put the gift in a paper bag, and, on her way to the grocery one day, she dropped the bag in front of the boy's yellow house.

Think About It

1. Why was Magda so anxious to find her cat?
2. How would you describe Magda to someone who had not read the story?
3. Explain why Magda described the boy as "unusual."
4. Tell what you think is going on in the boy's head when Magda is talking to him.
5. Why do you think Magda made the wool cat for the boy?

Create and Share   You are a reporter and are curious about how the characters in the story felt about their encounter with Magda. Create a Roving Reporter page as it might appear in a newspaper. Draw a small picture of each character and write two or three sentences that give each character's thoughts about Magda. Present your finished page to the class.

Explore   This story is taken from *Every Living Thing,* a book of short stories by Cynthia Rylant. Look in the card catalog under the author's last name for more of her books. For stories of people and animals by other authors, look under ANIMALS—FICTION.

PLANNING YOUR ZOO

from A ZOO IN YOUR ROOM
by Roger Caras

Two fish circled each other, keeping a "safe" distance between them, yet something was drawing them in toward the center of the deadly circle they were drawing with their flowing red and blue fins.

The message "danger, Danger, DANGER" was being mysteriously broadcast through the water. Other fish moved away and hid among plants or sought shelter in rocky caves. A freshwater clam clamped shut, and several snails slithered away on trails of slime. It was as if time had stopped and the whole underwater world was suspended, waiting for an explosion. A life-and-death struggle was unfolding in slow motion.

Suddenly the graceful movements of the fish erupted in a murderous assault. As if on a secret signal known only to them, the two bettas closed in on each other. The circle vanished, and in its place a tumbling mass of fins and tails rolled and rocked. Death soon relieved the loser's desperate struggle.

John and Pamela moved back from the aquarium tank, breathless. Obviously they had made a terrible mistake. They put two fish together that should never have been allowed in the same tank—two male Siamese fighting fish.

Across the street another drama was taking place. While one brother and sister stared at death, Joanne and Clay were witnessing a birth. "Come on!" shouted Joanne to her brother. "They're beginning to hatch."

Inside three eggs, young chicks had reached the full measure of growth possible without facing the dangers and the opportunities of the outside world. They were turning more often with each passing minute, and now they began pecking at their shells. Each bird in its own prison bobbed its head up and down, using its egg tooth to begin the cracks in the egg wall that would spell freedom and the beginning of its adult life. The egg tooth located near the tip of the bill would fall off shortly after the chick hatched.

Clay and Joanne could hear peeping sounds—the tiny, almost imperceptible squeaks that spelled life. They could see cracks developing in the shells and then small dark holes appearing. They sat for over an hour and watched as the crack in the first egg worked its way around. Finally, the shell fell apart revealing a tiny infant bird. It fell back exhausted and waited for its strength to return before

attempting the enormously difficult task of standing up for the first time in its life. By now the crack in the second egg had moved halfway around, and the children knew that this chick, too, would survive. In the third egg, however, the chick was too weak to break through the shell. After barely cracking it, the bird sank down and waited for death. Although the children tried to help by carefully opening the egg, nature had already made her decision.

Both of these exciting events were taking place not in a city zoo, but in the bedrooms of these playmates who had decided to have a zoo in their homes.

Sooner or later almost everyone gets the notion that it would be fun to have a zoo of his or her own. The idea often comes soon after a trip to a real zoo, or perhaps after visiting a natural history museum. It is not only a popular idea, but it can also be a good one if your zoo is a gentle, humane world where animals can live out their lives in comfort and security.

The kind of zoo you have depends on how good a zookeeper you can be. If you are equipped from the very beginning with the right information and some special tips, your zoo can be a source of pride that will offer hours of pleasure for you and your family. So, let's choose a zoo for *your* room.

Before you even begin planning your zoo, you must be sure your family likes the idea, too. You will need everyone's cooperation; so your first job is to sell your zoo not only to your parents, but also to anyone who shares your room with you and any other people whose lives will be affected by your becoming a zoo keeper.

right: Small animals like this Siberian hamster are ideal pets for the home zoo.
far right: An exercise wheel helps to keep this hamster happy and healthy.

Why is a private zoo a good idea? You and your parents may have your own answers. If not, consider the following:

1. Everyone should enjoy a hobby.
2. Pets teach respect for life and help children grow up to be humane adults.
3. A home zoo gives the zookeeper a chance to accept responsibility.
4. A home zoo can help in developing school projects and earning school credit.
5. Brothers and sisters can share in the project.

There are lots of other reasons to have a zoo in your room, of course; but if you agree with these few, you should be equipped to persuade your family by a very good job of salesmanship.

Once you have cleared the way for your zoo, you have to decide in advance who is coming to live with you so that you can arrange accommodations for them. Choosing the kind and number of animals you will care for is important and fun to do, but there are several criteria to use in making your selection:

1. Size is obviously important. You have to adjust your thinking to the actual room you have for your project.
2. Food requirements must be another consideration because an animal's diet must be easy to provide and also be inexpensive.

Cobras don't eat very much, they don't take much room, and they are quiet. How about a cobra? Definitely no. Cobras have a venomous bite, and they aren't intelligent enough to be able to tell their friends from their enemies. That means they are dangerous. A fifteen-year-old boy in Philadelphia recently did manage to buy a cobra for his home zoo, and it bit him. He almost died.

3. Safety, then, is a factor that must be taken into account as well. No dangerous animals should be kept in the home zoo.

4. A very important consideration is your love for animals. (We can assume that because you want a zoo in the first place.) A home zoo is an act of love, and you won't want to keep an animal that would suffer from confinement.

Keeping in mind these few points, let us suppose someone went for a walk in the woods and found a bear cub whose mother had been killed by a hunter. Would the bear cub belong in your zoo? Unfortunately not. He would grow to be too big. He would be difficult to feed properly, and he would one day be dangerous, no matter how sweet a cub he was. It is sad but true that all animals, like all people, have to grow up. And the cub would not be happy living in your house. Bears are active animals. They need large areas for proper exercising. They should have pools of water for hot days. So as you make your choice of animals, you must ask yourself if that animal will be happy in your small zoo.

5. You have heard a great deal about conservation, and it is very important to employ it. You must never keep an animal in a home zoo if that animal's species is becoming scarce in the wild.

An example of that kind of animal would be a macaw. You sometimes see these very large parrot-like birds in pet

above left: A clean cage is home to this blue parakeet.
above right: Perched on its owner's shoulder, this
parakeet knows it is well cared-for.

shops. They are brilliantly marked in red, green, blue, and gold. There are many different kinds, and they are quite expensive—as much as $400 each. Nobody has much luck at breeding these splendid birds in captivity, so all the ones you see for sale have been caught in the wild. Natives paddle along jungle rivers in South America and capture young specimens to sell to traders who ship them out to the United States. It is the way the natives capture these birds that is bad.

The macaws, like most birds of the parrot family, are *hole nesters.* They take over holes in trees because they can't dig them out themselves, and they lay their eggs on a bed of vegetable matter. It is the young birds in the tree holes that the traders want. So the natives collect them by chopping down the trees! They destroy a nesting tree every time they collect a young macaw. Nesting trees are becoming more and more scarce in South America, and pretty soon there won't be any place macaws can nest. That may mean no more macaws in the future.

The way baby gibbons are collected for pet shops is even worse. Natives in Asia find a troop of gibbons in the trees and shoot every mother they see carrying a baby. If the baby isn't killed in the fall, they take it. Most of them die anyway, but a few do make it to the pet shops.

It isn't easy to get people to change their ways if they receive money for what they are doing. It can be very difficult to explain conservation to a poor native in a dugout canoe in Brazil or in southern Asia. So what we have to do is stop buying animals that shouldn't be captured in the first place. Unfortunately, just because you see an animal for sale doesn't mean it should be sold. For example, nobody should ever buy a turtle, chicken, or duck that has been painted or dyed. Those chemicals are bad for the animals, and it is all wrong anyway. An animal is a product of nature, and we learn nothing if we dip it in vats of color or change its appearance. It is cruel and really quite silly if you think about it. People who think it is smart to treat living animals like Easter eggs might like to take a swim in the glop themselves.

below left: A painted turtle peers out at its zookeeper.
below right: This angel fish is one of a great variety of tropical fish suitable for the home zoo.

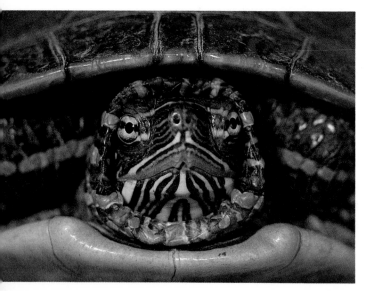

above: Caring for your pet includes proper grooming.
Here a guinea pig receives a bath.

There are, then, five considerations. Before accepting any animal for citizenship in your room zoo you must give it a test:

> Is it too big to keep?
>
> Will it be difficult to feed or require more food than you can afford to feed it?
>
> Is it or will it be dangerous someday?
>
> Will your pet be made unhappy and discontented by the life you can provide?
>
> Will your choice threaten a species or hurt the cause of conservation?

Every animal you keep should get a No answer to these five questions. If you get a single Yes, the animal does not belong in the zoo in your room.

But does that leave anything? It might seem that almost all the interesting animals would be banned from your zoo. That isn't the case at all. There are probably at least a million and a half species of animals in the world, and a great many of them are perfect for the home zoo.

Mother Doesn't Want a Dog

Mother doesn't want a dog.
Mother says they smell,
And never sit when you say sit,
Or even when you yell.
And when you come home late at night
And there is ice and snow,
You have to go back out because
The dumb dog has to go.

Mother doesn't want a dog.
Mother says they shed,
And always let the strangers in
And bark at friends instead,
And do disgraceful things on rugs,
And track mud on the floor,
And flop upon your bed at night
And snore their doggy snore.

Mother doesn't want a dog.
She's making a mistake.
Because, more than a dog, I think
She will not want this snake.

—Judith Viorst

Think About It

1. Tell what information you found important, surprising, or disturbing in "Planning Your Zoo."
2. What considerations not listed in the article might you have in choosing a pet or animal for a home zoo?
3. What information in the article would the mother in the poem use as a reason for not keeping a snake?
4. What do you think people learn by living in close contact with one or more animals?
5. What convincing arguments could you make for getting a pet you want?

Create and Share Working with a research team of four or five friends, find a variety of animals that pass the zoo test in the article. Write a paragraph describing each one and explaining why it would be a good choice for a home zoo. If possible, find pictures to show when you present your findings.

Explore Many good books have information about raising animals at home. There are also collections of poems about animals that you might enjoy. Look in the library card catalog under PETS and ANIMALS—POETRY.

Eeny, Meeny, Miney and... Moe

from CRANES IN MY CORRAL
by Dayton O. Hyde

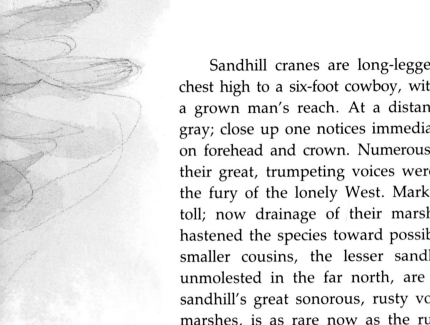

Sandhill cranes are long-legged marsh birds standing chest high to a six-foot cowboy, with wingspreads exceeding a grown man's reach. At a distance they are a soft pearl gray; close up one notices immediately the lovely rose skin on forehead and crown. Numerous in covered-wagon days, their great, trumpeting voices were part of the sound and the fury of the lonely West. Market hunters took the first toll; now drainage of their marshy nesting grounds has hastened the species toward possible extinction. Only their smaller cousins, the lesser sandhill cranes, which nest unmolested in the far north, are still in abundance. The sandhill's great sonorous, rusty voice, rolling out over the marshes, is as rare now as the rumble of moving buffalo herds or the squeal of wooden wagon wheels.

Four years before, I had hatched a sandhill crane from an egg rescued from a flooding, ice-choked stream. The crane, a female we named Sandy, had grown up as a member of our family and now, of breeding age at last, had found a mate somewhere in the marshes and laid two eggs in the calf pasture. When Sandy showed more interest in following me about the ranch than in incubating her eggs, we gathered them up and placed each egg under a broody bantam chicken. Sandy promptly laid two more, which she also ignored.

These eggs, too, went under chicken foster mothers. I had dreams of building a captive flock, of learning enough about raising sandhill cranes in captivity that I might rebuild the wild population, thus saving them from extinction. But since no books were available on how to raise sandhill cranes, I would have to learn as I went along.

For the moment my experiment seemed to be paying off. Wild sandhills hatch only two chicks; by the time they raise these two, tending them dutifully, it is too late in the season to raise another brood. Now under captive conditions, by gathering the eggs and relieving the parents of the tedious responsibility of raising the young, I had increased production. Never before in recorded history had four sandhill cranes been raised in one season from a single pair of parent birds.

"What on earth will you name them?" my wife asked a little nervously, as though she, too, found it strange that a cattle rancher could be interested in birds.

"Name them?" I asked. "Why not call one Choo Choo Crane, and another Ichabod Crane after the character in Washington Irving's *The Legend of Sleepy Hollow* and then—"

My wife groaned. "How about Eeny, Meeny, Miney, and Moe?"

"Preep!" called Eeny, largest of the chicks.

"Preep!" cried Meeny, who was almost as large.

"Preep!" said Miney, next in line.

But poor little Moe said nothing at all. Smaller than the rest, just as he was about to go "Preep!" he stubbed his toe and fell flat in the water dish.

Moe wasn't much to look at, but fortunately his adoptive mother thought him quite the handsomest baby "chicken" she had ever seen. But then maybe she was ready to accept anything. The previous summer, when a raven stole her eggs from a nest hidden on a shelf in the blacksmith shop, she had spent her days trying in vain to incubate three pebbles, four marbles, a piece of bubble gum and a golf ball autographed by the President. She clucked to Moe in deep contentment, and soon he was nestled deep in the soft warmth of her feathers, none the worse for his dunking.

As content as the chicks seemed, there was, nevertheless, the problem of getting them to accept food. For two days after hatching, as they absorbed the remnants of their yolk sacs, the soft, downy chicks seemed bound and determined to starve themselves to death. Then, one by one, they learned to take bits of crushed earthworm from my fingers. Soon they were not only eating by themselves from a dish but were growing fast.

Though Eeny, Meeny, and Miney quickly adjusted to pen life, Moe was soon in trouble again. On the floor of his pen he discovered what looked like the biggest, fattest, juiciest worm, right beneath his beak. He glanced around hastily, perhaps thinking that a bigger chick might come along and take it from him. Hardly believing his good luck, he cocked his head and regarded the worm with one big, brown eye. It seemed so tame, almost friendly.

"Preep!" Moe said proudly, seized it with his bill, and straightened up tall.

But alas! It wasn't a worm at all but his own middle toe. This time Moe landed flat on his back in the food trough.

For several days the four little cranes were content with their foster mothers, and the hens loved them as though they were their very own. Each crane was in a separate pen to keep him from fighting with his brothers and sisters, but in the afternoons they were let out for a stroll. They ate worms, gobbled bugs, chased dragonflies across the meadow, stared in wonder at butterflies, and grew and grew until, as was inevitable, they began to outgrow their mothers.

At night they flopped down, long legs folded beneath them, while the hens settled happily over them to ward off the chill of the night. But now and then, lured by some irresistibly fascinating noise, a little sandhill crane head would periscope up through the feathers of his mother's back. As the crane rose higher and higher on his stiltlike legs, the mother would rise up with him until, with an angry squawk, she fell on her ear in a pile of ruffled feathers.

Soon the rusty brown chicks traded their down for the pearl gray of the adult. Their blue-black wing quills were heavy now with blood as the great, new flight feathers pushed out from the quills, light but strong feathers which would one day take them safely over the pine ridges which screened the ranch from their future world. I was sad as I watched them, almost afraid that they were growing up too soon.

But I couldn't keep them from changing. Their beaks grew iron-hard, long, saber-like, able to probe deep into the soil for worms. No longer caged, the four took over the ranch as though they owned the place. They had a sixth sense for trouble, but promptly got into it anyway.

"Eeny!" I yelped as Eeny stole a button off my shirt. "Meeny!" I squalled as Meeny hammered away at the laces of my shoes. "Miney!" I warned as Miney stabbed hard at the rivets of my jeans. Smaller than the rest, little Moe always came last, even for a scolding. He stood apart to

enjoy the way the others were tormenting me, then, when my back was turned, stole my wallet and rushed off down the hill for a game of toss-the-wallet-into-the-spring.

"Moe!" I shouted, rushing after. But it was too late.

"Preeeeep!" Moe said happily as I fished my dripping wallet out of the drink.

The cranes on their black stilt-legs soon towered over their foster mothers who stared at them in dismay, not quite knowing how to mother such giants though desperately determined to try. Inevitably, Eeny, Meeny, Miney, and Moe soon tired of being followed about by nervous Nellies who fussed and scolded most of the day.

Now almost two months old, it was a simple matter for the cranes to solve. They merely waded out into the middle of the pond, ignoring the frantic cackling of the hens, who ventured out ankle-deep, then retreated to the safety of the shore. It was only when the cranes came out on the far side of the pond and wandered off that the hens returned to the regular life at the chicken house.

But a strange thing had happened. The cranes still had need of a parent symbol, someone who loomed taller than they. To my dismay they turned all their attentions to me.

"Now there's a sight," my wife said as the four cranes marched single file behind me across the ranch. "If you ask me, there go five goofy birds."

All day long they followed me about my work, leaving no job uninspected, no moment unsupervised. They were my shadows, as hard to shake as a guilty conscience. As each night fell I felt a sense of relief, yet felt neglected, too, when I saw them silhouetted against the crimson pool the setting sun made in the pond, standing knee-deep in the chill waters, each one's wavelets lapping those of another.

But my rest was generally short-lived, for as darkness came and pools of light flowed out from the living room over the front porch, I would hear them calling to me in their loneliness. Then I would hear tiny footsteps, soft whisperings of feather against feather, the same rustlings my aged grandmother made years back, taking off her dozen petticoats in the room next to mine. Sharp tappings of beaks against windowpanes. Click, bang, pling. Signals demanding that I look up from my book and notice them.

"It must be nice," my wife said once, "to be loved."

There was always much activity as they discovered the moths fluttering toward the lights. Jackhammer blows struck against the panes as they made a late-evening snack of moths, shredding the wings of those they didn't eat. "Preep, preep," insistent as a katydid in the grass. I refused to look up from my book as they called to me.

"You must be very talented," my wife remarked one evening. "You're reading that book upside down."

In the morning the first squeak of a door hinge usually brought them running. One day I tried to slip out the back, but they were coming at a run. I rushed to the front door, but they had guessed my plan. Eeny, Meeny, Miney, and— Wait! Where was Moe?

I rushed about the yard, expecting to find a pile of feathers where an eagle had dined on sandhill crane. Already I missed him. Why hadn't I been nicer to him? Poor Moe!

Suddenly I heard a rusty squawk from the basement of the ranch house. Moe had slid down the coal chute into the coalbin and now looked like a monstrous black raven. As I strode off I hid my head in my jacket, not wanting Moe to see me laughing. My four bosses came traipsing on behind to begin our day. Eeny, Meeny, Miney, in that order, with poor Moe always coming last.

It wasn't that he couldn't keep up. Mostly he was so curious that he just couldn't resist investigating the world as he passed through it. Often before he ever got to his destination, he would meet the others coming back. Now and then the three larger cranes would find a luscious feast of grasshoppers; but by the time Moe rambled up, the last of the hoppers was eaten and he poked around in vain to see what the excitement had been about.

But sometimes, just sometimes, he found his own bonanza in the grass; and since none of the others gave him credit for much sense, he was able to finish off his meal all by himself without ever having to share.

In all nature there are few sights more spectacular than the dance of the sandhill cranes. It is a happy thing, a group thing, done at all seasons of the year but especially in the spring when the joy of living seems just too riotous to be contained. It can be a part of courtship and pairing, or a meaningless release of nervous tension. Quick as a blink the dance begins when one bird bows, seizes a handy stick, and tosses it into the air. Then, as others join, the bird leaps high, flapping its wings, ducking, twirling, bowing, stabbing the air and leaping high again. The action is so infectious that quickly the whole group shares in it.

The dance of the sandhill crane is one of the few things in life I'm rather good at, sort of a specialty of mine, you might say. My wife first noticed the change in me when she discovered that I was actually getting up early on my own accord without the usual nagging on her part, and for a time she thought I was doing something awfully important on the ranch. I would come in for breakfast tired enough to go back to bed and find myself some sort of family hero for the hard work she thought I was doing.

In reality, once I had skipped out of the house, I dashed for the meadow outside the barn where my cranes were waiting for me, and once I had done the honors by tossing up the first stick, we would all get very excited and emotional, leaping high, flapping our wings, bowing and pirouetting, caught up in the ancient ritual.

There would be Eeny, Meeny, Miney, Moe, and Sandy as well as any wild sandhill cranes who happened to be visiting. While these wild cranes kept their distance, they watched the whole proceedings with such interest that I came to believe they had come a long way out of their way just to watch me perform their dance. I was really that good.

But I had to limit my performance to early in the morning because I had a reputation to maintain, and it isn't wise to be seen doing that sort of thing when you are supposed to be a rough, tough rancher running a rough, tough ranch in the heart of rough, tough cattle country.

Always one to do things right, I built some nice little dusters of moulted crane feathers tied into bundles with strips of inner tube, which I held in each hand when I flapped to help me fly a little better. I kept these hidden in the barn because they would have been a little hard to explain.

I also had one special little bunch which I stuck into the back pocket of my Levis to simulate a tail, but this I lost one day when I forgot and wore it into town.

If I was the best dancer in the bunch, Moe was the worst. Frequently it took Moe so long to get warmed up and into the mood of the dance that the rest of us were all through and Moe would have to dance all by himself. Although some of the cranes could flap their wings and jump clear over my back, Moe generally managed a wild leap that took him about one inch off the ground, but he was proud of it anyway. As a matter of fact, every time he took that wild leap, he just had to look around to make sure everyone was watching.

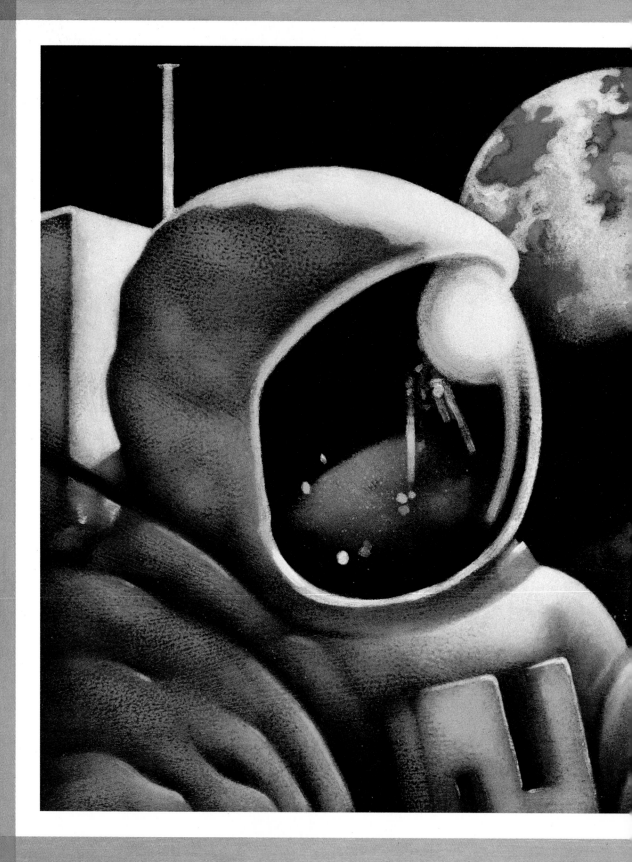

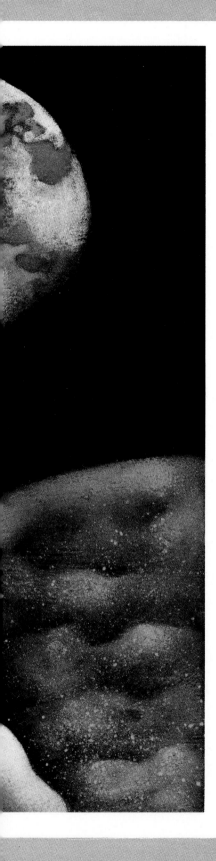

Against All Odds

It's all uphill, but the view from the top is worth it.

Pierre Lejuste

TEACHING
TUCK
TO SEE

from THE TROUBLE WITH TUCK
by Theodore Taylor

*N*o one can definitely say when Friar Tuck began to go blind, not even Dr. Douglas Tobin, who was undoubtedly one of the best veterinarians in California. But the light probably began to fail for big Tuck long before any of us suspected it, and of course, being a dog, he couldn't very well talk about it.

I suppose that exactly when the shadows began creeping in, or when he finally slid into total darkness, doesn't really matter.

Yet I can clearly recall that miserably hot summer day so long ago when we first thought something might be wrong with Tuck. It didn't seem possible. Young, beautiful, so free-spirited, he had a long life ahead.

But the August of Tuck's third year, on a Monday, about midmorning, some neighborhood cats got into a noisy brawl along our back fence, spitting and screeching.

To Friar Tuck, that was always an unpardonable sin. Not only were these cats intruding in *his* yard, a private and sacred kingdom, but, worse, they were creating an ear-splitting disturbance. His answer was immediate attack, as usual.

My mother was in the kitchen at the time and heard him scramble on the slick linoleum, trying to get traction with his paws, and as she turned, she saw him plunge bodily through the screen door, ripping a gaping hole in the wire mesh.

Up in my room, making my bed as I remember, I heard her yell, something she seldom did, and, thinking she'd hurt herself, I hurried downstairs and out to the kitchen.

Mother was standing by the back door, looking outside, puzzlement all over her face, which was usually a mirror of calmness. "Tuck just went through this door," she exclaimed, unable to believe it. "I declare."

I then saw the big hole in the wire, as if something had exploded there.

"Some cats were fighting, and he got up and ran right through the door." Mother was awed.

I was sure that Tuck was far too intelligent to do a stupid thing like that. He'd always put on skidding brakes and just barked loudly if there was something outside disturbing him.

I said, "Maybe he was dreaming?"

Mother scoffed, "Helen!"

All right, he wasn't dreaming. He'd done a very dumb thing.

I looked out at him, thinking about excuses.

Tuck was sitting innocently on his powerful haunches in the grass, that dignified lionlike head pointed skyward. He seemed to be sniffing the air as if to make certain the squabbling cats had departed. To be sure, he wasn't concerned about any whopping hole in the screen door.

My mother shook her head and went outside, quickly going down the short flight of back steps and crossing over to him, maybe to scold him properly. He deserved it.

I followed her.

As she approached Tuck, his thick tail began to wag, switching back and forth across the grass like a scythe. She said, "You silly dog, you just broke the door," leaning over to take his big yellow-haired head into her slender hands and examine his eyes. She bit her lip and frowned.

Wondering why she'd done that, I had the strangest feeling.

Mother straightened up, still frowning widely.

"Why did you do that?" I asked. "Look at him that way?"

"Well, he acted as though he didn't even see the door."

Now it was my time. "Mother," I scoffed.

Then I went over and peered down into his eyes. To me, they were the same as they had been for more than three years—liquid deep brown with dark pools in the center. They were so expressive, in laughter or sadness.

"Have you noticed anything different about Tuck lately?" Mother asked.

"What do you mean?" He hadn't been sick or anything, to my knowledge.

"Oh, just anything different."

Offhand, I said, "No."

But there was something, now that I thought about it. I glanced into the acacia trees at the back of our deep lot. Doves often roosted up there, cooing in the day hours, and then they'd drop down to the yard and peck around. Tuck had always chased them, in rousing good fun and fair game, never catching one. They'd fly up and scatter, terrified of the bounding dog with the deep-throated bark. He loved to do it.

However, a while back, maybe three months earlier, the doves had suddenly turned defiant, I'd noticed. They'd begun to parade brazenly across the backyard. And I'd also noticed that Tuck wasn't going after them anymore. Maybe he was just bored with them, I thought. Or maybe the doves knew something that we didn't. I didn't want to think about that.

I said, "He's quit chasing the doves."

My mother's laugh was hollow. "I don't know what that means."

"Neither do I," I said.

She sighed and went back to the door and stood there for a moment, staring at it, then shook her head and went on inside.

A little later she summoned me to the kitchen. "I want to try something," she said. "Bring Tuck in here."

He was by the garage door, sprawled out asleep on the concrete, which was in cooling shadows. I whistled for him, and he rose up, stretched lazily and luxuriously, then meandered into the house, probably thinking it was mealtime.

There was a round oak breakfast set in one corner of the large kitchen, and Mother placed one of the ladderback chairs about three feet away from the screen door.

Holding Tuck by the collar, she instructed, "Helen, go outside now."

I did so.

"Okay, make him come to you."

That was usually easy. All I had to say was, "Tuck, let's go." He was always ready to go. Anywhere.

This time, when I called, though, my handsome pedigreed dog headed for the back door and ran headlong into the tall chair, spilling it with a clatter.

It was obvious he did not see it.

I heard Mother's dismayed voice from the kitchen. "Oh, no."

By that time, I was opening the door, and Tuck was standing by the knocked-over chair, staring in my direction, quite confused.

I said to my mother, "Something must be wrong with his eyes." I now had to admit it. My stomach was suddenly cold and empty.

She nodded. "I think so too. I'll make an appointment with Dr. Tobin for Saturday morning."

All week I worried and kept looking into Tuck's pupils for answers that were not there.

When Dr. Tobin examined Tuck, he found that the dog was incurably blind. The only option seemed to be confining Tuck to a chain for his own safety. But Helen knew that a chain would break Tuck's spirit. Searching for another way to help her dog, she went to a guide dog agency. And so the blind Friar Tuck Golden Boy was introduced to Lady Daisy, his guide.

The arrival of Lady Daisy at our house was loudly, angrily announced by none other than Friar Tuck Golden Boy himself. He knew that a canine intruder was on his front porch, and he set up a din in the backyard, straining at the very end of his chain.

Daisy followed Mrs. Chaffey through the door as if she were two-footed and totally human, and then she sat down politely by Mrs. Chaffey's feet and looked around as though inspecting her new house.

My mother said, "That's the most sedate, serene dog I've ever seen in my entire life."

Soon, that most sedate, serene dog met the entire family, excepting Friar Tuck. He was unserenely making enough noise for a pack of barking wolfhounds.

I went out to shush him.

When I returned to the living room, my mother was saying, "I'm worried that Tuck might resent her. Plain jealousy. Listen to him now."

"That's a real worry," Mrs. Chaffey admitted.

I asked, "You mean Tuck might not let her stay here?"

"Yes, that's possible," Mrs. Chaffey said. "He might even hurt her. He's a very powerful dog."

"I wouldn't let that happen," I promised.

"You can't be around them twenty-four hours a day. And if Tuck really wanted to hurt her, I doubt you could stop it."

"I'll teach them to be friends," I said.

"That's a good start," she replied. "But there's no instruction for what you're about to do. Another thing, you and you alone should be the trainer. It's always best that way. One person doing it."

My father said, "Suppose Tuck and Daisy just don't get along."

"Well, the answer to that is simple," Mrs. Chaffey replied. "We'll place Daisy in another home or take her back to the school. We never abandon these dogs, under any circumstances."

My father said, "Okay, let's see how Mr. Tuck reacts."

We all went out to the backyard, and Tuck, fur standing in a ridge on his back, growled the moment the door swung open. Unable to see, he'd smelled Daisy, and even though she was female, she was intruding into his space nonetheless.

Mrs. Chaffey quickly said to me, "Talk to him, reassure him."

I commenced talking fast, telling him Daisy wanted to be his friend, but the low, throaty growling went on as Tuck circled her, tense and suspicious. Daisy stood absolutely still as he inspected her, sniffing and sizing her up.

The growling worried me, and I said sharply, "Behave, Tuck!" I'd seen some of his wild fights in the park, and they'd begun that way, growling and circling.

"How do I do it?" I asked.

Mrs. Chaffey looked at me. "You're the trainer, Helen. But I'd go slowly. Very slowly. You can't force friendship—humans or dogs."

She departed for San Carlos a few minutes later, extracting a promise from my parents to call her at the least sign of trouble.

I stayed out in the backyard a while longer, just watching the activity. Tuck soon seemed to lose interest in Daisy and clanked over to his favorite sleeping spot by the house. She then lowered herself to the walk by the back steps and closed her eyes too.

Deciding to take Mrs. Chaffey's advice to go slowly, I did nothing with Tuck and Daisy that night except feed them in separate bowls, well apart from each other.

By bedtime, when Mother came into my room, Tuck was in his usual place on the rug beside me, and Daisy had taken up a neutral position in the middle of the floor.

Sitting down on the edge of my bed, Mother said, "Well, tomorrow you start an adventure. A big one."

I said that so far Lady Daisy had been very careful. "Not drinking out of Tuck's bowl. Not taking Tuck's place here by the bed."

"She's obviously an extremely intelligent dog. Now, Helen, don't ask too much of her—nor of Tuck; nor of yourself, for that matter."

I said I wouldn't, though, of course, I really wasn't listening to that kind of instruction.

"We'll be rooting for you."

"And for Tuck?"

Mother smiled. "Daisy, too."

Most everyone I know who owns a dog talks to him or her occasionally, or even frequently, but aside from the few basic commands, I don't think the exact words count for too much. The tone of voice means much more, along with the movement of one's hands. The latter did not apply to Tuck now. Looking back, I see that I talked a lot to him over the next weeks. Pleaded might be a better word. Whether he understood or not, he began to display almost every bad trait there is. Selfishness, jealousy, anger, pettiness. I could go on for a page. He was an awful dog for quite a while.

As soon as I arrived home the next afternoon, I brought Daisy out of the house and unsnapped Tuck from his yard chain. He chose to ignore her, as if she didn't exist.

I then led Daisy up to his side, positioning her so that his big ears were about opposite her ample rump. I then said to him, "Tuck, put your head against her," and simultaneously pushed his skull her way.

A tremendous roar of anger and defiance rumbled from deep within him. His jaw was open, and his fangs were bared. Those sightless eyes were aimed in my direction, and there was a glare in them of a strange kind. There was no love in them.

I jumped back. He hadn't bared his teeth at me since he was a pup. This was another Tuck I was seeing and hearing—maybe a frightening one. I remembered Dr. Tobin saying that the worst bite he'd ever had was from a blind Labrador.

Go slowly, Helen, Mrs. Chaffey had said, and I told Tuck, "Okay, we'll just take a walk today."

I put leashes on both of them, and off we went. Again trying to ignore Daisy, Tuck growled only when she bumped him. But it was evident that he didn't at all like sharing his walk with Lady Daisy.

On the way home, I stopped at Ledbetter's to pick up a box of small dog biscuits, putting them on our charge account. They were to be rewards for accomplishments.

Mr. Ishihara wanted to know how the training was progressing, how "they" were doing. I said it hadn't started as yet, but "they" weren't likely to be any problem. It was "he," bullheaded F.T. Golden Boy, who might mess up the whole idea.

Day after frustrating day for almost two weeks, I attempted to train Tuck to put his head against Daisy's rump, the first step in teaching him to be guided by her. Day after day I failed. Aside from an occasional sniff, he refused to have anything to do with her. Force certainly did not work. Though he didn't bite her, he growled mightily and exposed those big ferocious teeth. She remained cool and passive and didn't even flinch.

Day after day, I also saw someone or another watching my failures through the kitchen window. Now, nothing can make you angrier than being spied upon when you are losing. And each night at the dinner table, I was asked how I was doing, and my answer was a tight-lipped "Fine," though it was evident I wasn't doing fine at all.

One Saturday I snapped a leash on Daisy and then took another leash and attached one end to Daisy, the other end to Tuck. Maybe if she towed him along, he'd get the idea of what it was all about. But when I attempted to lead her away, Tuck promptly backed up and sat down, donkey-style.

I went over to him and whacked him hard on the back, hurting my hand more than I'd hurt him. Yet I hadn't hit Tuck for years, for anything, and here I was, feeling terrible remorse. Kneeling down, I said, "I'm sorry, Tuck. I didn't mean to do that."

My father heard me. He came boiling down the steps and said, "Don't apologize! He's misbehaving even if he is blind. Don't feel sorry for him—belt him."

That was easier to say than to do.

Another week went by, and the following Saturday the family went to the beach. As soon as we arrived, I opened the back of the station wagon, and the dogs leaped out, free to go as fast and as far as they could. They began running and sniffing along the dune line of the deserted beach. Though each went freely on individual explorations, they stayed within a few feet of each other. They were a pretty sight, bounding along, the wind whipping at them.

The four of us—my parents, my brother Luke, and I—walked several miles south, watching the dogs and the diving sea birds and keeping a lookout for whale spouts.

Eventually we returned to where the station wagon was parked.

443

With no warning, my father said, "Helen, you saw how well Tuck and Daisy got along today. We think it's time to let the dogs just be friends. No more training."

"Give up?" I asked, in alarm. They couldn't ask me to do that. I wouldn't do it, anyway.

"Yes, give up," Mother said. "You've tried so hard for almost two months, and nothing is working. I talked to Mrs. Chaffey yesterday. She agreed with your father and myself. Just let them be companions now. No more training."

"But I—"

My father interrupted firmly. "Now listen to us, Helen. Your schoolwork and your mental health are more important. I'm sorry but that's true."

"Tuck will stay on the chain," I protested.

He nodded. "Probably. Yes. Forever, maybe."

"I have to—" I began, feeling panic.

He interrupted again. "For everybody's sake, you *have to stop*. You tried very hard."

Mother added, "And we're so proud of you."

Those words, or words like them, have been said to daughters and sons since the cave days, I suspect, but they don't take you off the hook of failure.

That night I whispered into Daisy's ear, "We won't stop."

In fact, I already had something else in mind. By now, however, I wouldn't discuss with anyone anything I was going to try. They were all defeatists, except Mr. Ishihara. But the previous week I'd seen an old circus picture on TV, and in it some elephants were walking along in their traditional parade way, trunk to tail entwined.

I went into Luke's room to ask casually, "Don't you have a book on elephants?"

Without even looking at me, he motioned to his shelf. "It's over there."

I pulled it out and went to my own room, where the two dogs were sleeping peacefully, and got into bed with *The Book of Elephants*.

To keep prying, snoopy eyes out of my dog business, I went to the very end of the park.

No one in my family would ever see me there, I thought, and I could continue to train Tuck in complete secrecy. How wrong I was.

As soon as I arrived, I took Tuck's seven-foot leash and attached it to Daisy's collar, then attempted to make Tuck grasp the looped end in his teeth. Sticking the leash end in, I pushed his jaws together and held them a few seconds. Of course, he dropped the leash as soon as I took my hands away.

Trying to be patient with him, I said, "All right, we'll start all over again."

We did the same routine a half dozen times daily for two or three days, and it turned out the same each time. Tuck stood there and opened his mouth, accepted the leash, and then dropped it right out. By Friday, I believe he thought it was a game we were playing, and much fun.

Put the leash in!

Drop the leash out!

Friday was also the day that Luke accidentally discovered my secret training place. Something was wrong with his bike, and he decided to walk it through the park and there I was, holding Tuck's jaws closed on the leash.

Pushing his bike up to me, my brother, having caught himself a criminal, said, "You're not supposed to be training those dogs."

I replied, "Luke, I'm only doing what I have to do, and don't you dare tell anyone." Now that I was thirteen, I didn't let him push me around so much.

"Aw, who cares?" he said and went on his way.

That night, just before dinner, when I was alone in the kitchen with my mother, she said, offhandedly, "I hear you're still training Tuck and Daisy."

Curse Luke anyway, I thought. I knew things about him that I hadn't told anyone. I knew things that could get him into so much trouble.

"Are you?" she asked.

What could I say? "Yep."

Eyeing me as if trying to make up her mind, she said, "I should be angry."

I just stood there, waiting for whatever was going to come—the firing squad or A for effort. It should have been the latter.

She laughed softly. "Any luck?"

I shook my head. "But I can't give up."

"Never be so definite about anything," she said. "Okay, I won't tell your father, and I've told Luke to quit spying on you. But I'm giving you a firm deadline, Helen. Two weeks more, and then no more."

That was fair enough, and then I told her about my elephant idea.

On a firm deadline now, with no time to waste, mid-morning of the next day I went over to see wise Mr. Ishihara at Ledbetter's. He was in the back storage room.

Bent over, using a small crowbar to open a wooden crate of lettuce from the Salinas Valley, Mr. Ishihara listened to Tuck's latest unwillingness to cooperate.

"He drops the leash out. He thinks it's a game," I said.

"Try rubbing some food on it."

I hadn't considered doing that.

Mr. Ishihara straightened up suddenly. "Don't, on second thought. It's a bad idea, very messy, and he might chew on the leash."

Knowing Tuck, I figured that was a distinct possibility.

Mr. Ishihara, pursing his expressive lips, wrinkling his

smooth walnut forehead, examined me for a moment longer, then said, "I've told you about my cat, Ichiban, haven't I?"

"Yes, you have."

"He likes to sleep on my dirty shirts. I think he likes to smell me."

Picking up the opened lettuce crate by its ends, Mr. Ishihara continued, "Ichiban gives me an idea for Tuck. Suppose you put something of your own on the leash. Tuck can't see what it is, but he'll definitely smell it."

I followed him out of the storage room. "Like what?"

"Like your shirttail, but don't wash it," he said, over his shoulder. "Leave it dirty and just tear it off." Moving quickly to the sidewalk stands, he dropped the crate by his lettuce bin and laughed loudly. "The way to Tuck's stubborn brain may be through his nose."

That made good sense. How much I appreciated Mr. Ishihara.

The next day I cut off the end of the shirt I'd worn
to school on Friday and went to Montclair Park, ready to
tell anyone that training a blind dog was a very long, difficult, and frustrating thing to do.

I tied the rag around the hand loop of the long leash,
snapped the leash on Daisy's collar, and then dropped the
wadded end to the ground right under Friar Tuck's pinkish
nose.

"Pick it up," I ordered.

Tuck stood there, as usual, motionless as a hairy
sphinx. Be positive, I thought.

Reaching down to guide his head, none too gently, I
repeated, "Pick it up, Tuck."

He sniffed the rag several times, then opened his jaws,
and, lo and behold, grasped the leash end firmly.

For a moment, I was so surprised I didn't react, but
then I finally woke up and said sharply, "Forward, Daisy."

She started off, with Tuck in tow, the leash end
between his shining rows of teeth.

After so many weeks of struggle, it had finally happened, like a snap of fingers. Tuck could come off the hated chain at last.

"Stop, Daisy," I yelled joyously, and she halted on the dime, so to speak, with a front paw almost in midair.

Tuck stopped in his tracks too, dropping the leash end and standing over it as if nothing had happened—the dumbo.

Running over, I hugged them both and gave them their due biscuit rewards. I felt giddy, like telling the whole world, but I said to them, "We'll not tell a soul until we're ready."

I wanted to see Daisy guide Tuck *without a leash*.

Tuck soon began to enjoy the fabulous new trick he'd learned—that of picking up a stinky, wadded rag between his teeth and trekking along behind Daisy.

But by twilight I noticed that Tuck had trouble locating the leash end if it was on the ground more than three or four feet away.

I went right back to Mr. Ishihara.

After a moment studying the dogs, he said vaguely, almost to himself, "Tuck can't see, but he can smell and he can hear."

I said, "Sound!"

He nodded. "Sound."

Up on the shelves in the back of the garage were large cartons containing holiday decorations, and in one of them, I knew, was a long, narrow piece of leather. Attached to it were eight small brass bells, for placing on the front door.

That night I rummaged through the boxes and found the bells. Next day, in the park, I wired one to Daisy's collar. I thought she might object, but she didn't even seem to notice the bright bell tinkle each time she moved.

I still had the shirttail, damp with Tuck's saliva, tied to the leash, and I ordered Tuck to pick it up. He nosed down, and then I said to Daisy, "Forward."

With Tuck moving along to about three feet behind Daisy, leash firmly in his mouth, the little bell rang as though it were on the harness of a sleigh horse. A jingle-bell sound. I walked behind them as we went the length of the park.

Each day that week I shortened the leash until Tuck's head was directly opposite Daisy's rump. He now seemed content to trot along with her, his left ear rubbing conveniently against her flank, listening to her bell as if it were a symphony.

Think About It

1. Tell how Tuck's temperament was a help as well as an obstacle in solving his problem.
2. Describe Daisy's character. Why is the temperament of a guide dog important?
3. What kind of person was Helen? Use details from the story to support your answer.
4. What good ideas did Mr. Ishihara have? Explain his thinking about training the blind dog.
5. Tell about a time you overcame an obstacle to achieve something.

Create and Share   You are a TV news reporter who heard about Helen's efforts to train Tuck. Choose a friend to work with and conduct a TV news show interview with Helen. Prepare your questions and answers in advance and practice the interview with your friend before you present it to the class.

Explore   Learn more about the use and training of guide dogs. Look under GUIDE DOGS for information. Share that information with your class.

HARRIET TUBMAN

Harriet Tubman was born into slavery in 1821. She worked as a field hand until 1849, when she escaped to free territory in the North. In the years that followed, Harriet Tubman guided more than three hundred slaves to freedom through a route known as the Underground Railroad. She died in 1913.

Harriet Tubman didn't take no stuff
Wasn't scared of nothing neither
Didn't come in this world to be no slave
And wasn't going to stay one either

"Farewell!" she sang to her friends one night
She was mighty sad to leave 'em
But she ran away that dark, hot night
Ran looking for her freedom

She ran to the woods and she ran through the woods
With the slave catchers right behind her
And she kept on going till she got to the North
Where those mean men couldn't find her

Nineteen times she went back South
To get three hundred others
She ran for her freedom nineteen times
To save Black sisters and brothers

Harriet Tubman didn't take no stuff
Wasn't scared of nothing neither
Didn't come in this world to be no slave
And didn't stay one either

And didn't stay one either

—*Eloise Greenfield*

I Will Become a Doctor

from DR. ELIZABETH: A BIOGRAPHY OF THE FIRST WOMAN DOCTOR
by *Patricia Clapp*

A little over one hundred years ago there were no women doctors
in the United States. To become the first one seemed impossible.

I have written a number of letters to doctors known by my family and me in various parts of the country, and there have been two points on which all my correspondents have agreed. First, that the entire prospect of a woman becoming a doctor is unsuitable, unfeminine, distasteful, and impossible. Second, that if I were foolhardy enough to pursue this course I would soon discover that no American school would accept me as a student. Oh dear, that is *not* the way to discourage Elizabeth Blackwell! The more I am told "no," the more I think "yes."

But if I cannot study in the United States, then where can I? I have asked this question of several physicians, and the guarded answer has come back—well, possibly Paris. I had an opportunity to talk with a well-known Cincinnati physician, Dr. Muzzey, and broached the possibility to him, knowing he had spent some time working in French hospitals. I thought his sparse hair would stand up straight on his shocked head!

"Miss Blackwell! You surely are not serious!"

"But I am," I assured him. "Why should I not be?"

"The very thought of a woman going into the Parisian schools horrifies me! It's impossible!"

"But *why?*" I persisted.

"It would be offensive to both of us for me to go into detail," he said firmly. "I will simply say that the method of instruction is such that no American or English lady could stay there for six weeks!"

And I could get no more information out of him.

I talk to everyone who will listen! One of my closest friends is a happy and clever woman named Harriet Beecher, who has married a very dull and stolid man named Stowe. When I mentioned my idea to Harriet she was stunned.

"Oh, Elizabeth! How could you ever do it? It's—it's so impracticable!"

"So I am constantly being told," I said. "But if I *could,* Harriet. What then?"

"If you could, I think it would be the very greatest boon to women!"

"I'm not sure what you mean."

"I mean women who are ill—or even just having babies, as I do—would feel so much more at ease with a female physician! And women who want to—to kick over the tight traces that tie them down would have an example to follow! But—how could you ever do it, Elizabeth?"

"I don't know," I confessed, "but I think I am going to try."

We have another family friend, an educated, intelligent man, James Perkins. When I mentioned the idea to him he neither gasped nor blushed, but simply asked me several succinct questions which I answered. When I had done, he said, with a very bright face, "I do wish you would take the matter up, if you have the courage—and you have courage, I know!"

At that moment I felt I could conquer the world! How far a little encouragement can go! He gave me a copy of Jackson's Memoirs which deals with medical training, especially in French schools. I am eager to read it!

A few days ago I did read it. What am I getting myself into? The immensity of the field before me is unbelievable! But someday some woman is going to do it. Why should I not be the one? I am gradually coming up to the resolution.

Enough of shilly-shallying! I have made the decision and my family is in accord. I Will Become A Doctor!

My first necessity is money for my studies, though where and when those will take place I have no idea. For this reason I have accepted the position of music teacher in a school in Asheville, North Carolina. Teaching again! Ugh! But it is the only way I know to raise enough money to carry on this plan I have committed myself to follow. My main reason for accepting this particular offer was that the Reverend John Dickson, who is the principal of the school, was formerly a doctor and will start me on a medical education.

Mother would not accept the idea of her undersized chick making the journey to Asheville alone, so Samuel and Henry are to drive me there. I must admit I am relieved! I hear the roads through Kentucky are little traveled, and there are rivers to ford and mountains to cross—rather like the course I have set myself!—and it will take a good eleven days to make the trip. Henry is twenty now, and Samuel a year older, and they are such good company I look forward to this interlude with them.

Everyone in the family has been gathering books and other small comforts for me to take, and the carriage has been packed and repacked. Tomorrow, June 16, 1845, we will leave! I have never been so far from home before, and now, even before we start, I can feel the throat-tightening pangs of homesickness. But I feel something more, too. A deep, strong, inevitable force that leads me on, a purpose I must accomplish.

I have arrived. There were times, as Sam and Henry and I jolted our way over the Alleghenies, or forded a frighteningly rapid river, when I doubted we would ever see the end of the journey. Yet what fun it was! We sang, and talked, and picnicked by the roadside (where there were roads), and I feel I know my two oldest brothers better than ever before. As we came down from the last stretch of mountain onto the beautiful plateau where Asheville lies, I wished devoutly that the shared journey

could go on, that Samuel and Henry would not have to leave me here—a forlorn little music teacher in a strange town, dedicated to a most dubious course.

I was very kindly welcomed by Reverend Dickson and his wife, and shown to my room, and for a while all was easy talk and hospitality. But then, that evening, no matter how I tried to hold it back, the moment came when I had to say good-bye to Sam and Henry, who were to start back at first light the next morning. Standing outside in the tranquil summer night I could find nothing to say that did not make the tears start in my voice, and at last I just kissed each of them and felt them hug me tightly for a minute, before I ran in the house and upstairs to my room.

I dropped to my knees before the open window. The surrounding mountains were dimly visible in the starlight, blurred by my tears, seeming to shut me away from all I knew or cared for, and suddenly I was terrified of what I was undertaking. I must have crouched there for several minutes, praying, weeping, holding my loneliness and doubts deep within myself, yet reaching out for help, and then, suddenly, I felt as though my whole soul were flooded with brilliance! I felt a—*something*—around me, an influence, a presence, that was so gentle, so joyful, yet so powerful that all doubt disappeared! I can't explain this. There was nothing to be seen—I opened my eyes, but the room, the dark night, the dim mountains had not changed. Only I had changed, for I knew then, quite positively, that however insignificant my individual effort might be, it was in a right direction, and there was no more need to hesitate.

It was a most marvelous occurrence! I went to bed and to sleep, and in the days that have passed since then, this new assurance has never left me.

Now that I dare to speak openly of my intention of becoming a doctor, it has resulted in benefits as well as teasing. Reverend Dickson has opened his medical library to me, and I read until my eyes are red with weariness, trying to remember the strange new terms and words—like a new language!—studying the charts and diagrams, and listening as this kind man patiently explains some of the myriad things I don't understand. I suppose it is an amusing contrast. During the day Miss Blackwell thumps away on the piano, guiding awkward young hands, asking for the same notes to be given over and over. During the evening Medical Student Blackwell mumbles her way through the muscular system, repeating the terminology over and over. I do not know which is more likely, that my students will learn to play well, or that I shall learn to be a doctor!

Just yesterday I came close to discarding the whole idea. Another young woman teacher, who knows of my "unbelievable" ambition, brought me a large beetle, thoroughly dead from having been smothered between her pocket handkerchiefs, and offered it to me as a first subject for dissection. Trying to look very businesslike, I placed the creature in a small shell and held it with a hairpin, while I poised my mother-of-pearl-handled penknife for the incision. It was impossible! The idea of penetrating that small carcass was so repugnant to me that I could feel my hair growing damp with perspiration, and see my hand shake. My friend stood gleefully waiting, and I was on the verge of giving up when I suddenly knew quite simply that, like it or not, I had to do it. So I did. The knife point went in gently but firmly, and all it revealed was a little yellowish dust. After a moment, faint with relief, I felt larger than the mountains that surround me here! One small "beetle battle" had been won, and by me.

But what in heaven's name will I do when it is something more than a beetle into which I must thrust my knife?

Life here in Asheville is quite pleasant, and people are very friendly. Last week I attended a party with Reverend

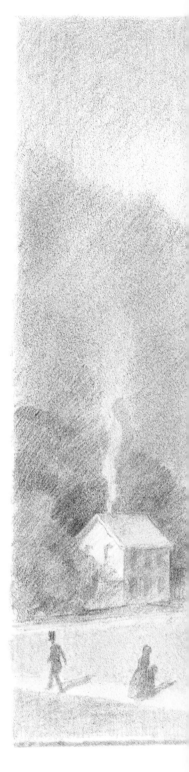

and Mrs. Dickson—rather reluctantly, I must admit, since parties have never been my particular forte—and to my amazement I found myself to be quite a social success! This was so unusual that it must have made me a little giddy, for I found myself chattering away vivaciously over the ice cream and whips and cakes and jellies; playing the piano with the top up and the bass pedal down; and even performing some tricks of logic, the sort of thing we do often at home, such as transporting the wolf, the goat, and the cabbage across the stream.

There was one young gentleman from New York, attractive enough, but full of the silly, twaddling conversation that has always irritated me. He seemed quite beguiled by all my goings on, and insisted on escorting me home.

"You come from Cincinnati?" he asked, as we walked through the soft southern night. I admitted I did. "If I had only known!" he said. "I should have made the trip from New York to Cincinnati, just to accompany you here!"

He was tall and I am short and fortunately my bonnet brim hid the smile on my face. I could think of nothing duller than having him for a traveling companion!

"And you are teaching piano?" he went on.

"For a while," I said, and then could not resist the temptation to add, "I am going to become a doctor."

He stopped dead on the path. "A *doctor*?" he repeated, and his voice sounded a trifle weak. "What—er—what sort of doctor?"

"A physician," I announced calmly. "A surgeon, I expect."

He started walking again, but he said nothing for several minutes. At last he murmured, "Well! That's—er—that's very unusual, isn't it? I don't recall ever having known a—lady doctor before."

"That's not surprising," I said with satisfaction. "There has never been one."

Think About It

1. Explain Harriet Tubman's achievements and the terrible obstacles she had to overcome.
2. What words would you use to describe Harriet Tubman to someone unfamiliar with her accomplishments?
3. What kind of person was Elizabeth Blackwell? Use details from the story to support your ideas.
4. Why do you think the author had Elizabeth Blackwell tell her own story? How did this affect what you learned and how you felt about her?
5. What do the main characters in the last three selections have in common? Compare and contrast the obstacles Helen, Harriet Tubman, and Elizabeth Blackwell faced and the traits that helped them succeed.

Create and Share   Imagine that you are one of the slaves Harriet Tubman led to freedom. Or imagine that you are a patient whose life has been saved by Dr. Elizabeth Blackwell. Write a letter expressing your gratitude to the woman whose courage has helped you.

Explore   You may want to read the rest of the book *Dr. Elizabeth*, or look in the library card catalog under TUBMAN, HARRIET, and BLACKWELL, ELIZABETH, for other biographies on these remarkable women. Also, you could browse through the library shelves of individual biographies, which are alphabetized by the last name of the person written about.

TV or Not TV?

In one day, Americans watch 1.5 billion hours of television. That's equal to 2,300 human lifetimes spent in front of the tube every day.

In one day, the average child watches more than 50 television commercials.

from IN ONE DAY *by Tom Parker*

Talking About TV

This article first appeared in PENNY POWER *magazine*

Tyrone is a young reader in Pennsylvania. He tells us he spends an average of six hours a day in front of his TV. So do his buddies Matt, Brian, and Mike. They know they're having fun and maybe even learning a thing or two as they watch. But scientists* have discovered that something else is happening to them—something important.

Answer the questions below, then read on to find out what may be happening to Tyrone—and perhaps to you!

TV and Me

YES NO

I usually watch four or more hours of TV every day.

I think the real world is a lot like the world I see on TV.

I wish I were like some of the stars on TV shows.

I watch action shows the most.

I often want to buy (or ask my parents to buy) things I've seen on TV.

I'd rather watch TV than do most other activities.

I usually eat snacks while watching TV.

My parents and I rarely talk about what I see on TV.

---

* Hundreds of scientists have studied the effects of TV on kids. Most of the studies in this article were described by the National Institute of Mental Health.

Do you watch TV four or more hours most days?

If you answered "yes," you're like most other American children. They watch an average of four to five hours a day. (Adults watch more!) Viewing four or more hours of television makes you a "heavy viewer," according to scientists. A "light viewer" watches just one hour or less each day.

Is that much TV a problem? "Not for me!" seems to be the opinion of most *Penny Power* readers. We asked Tyrone, his friends, and 450 other *Penny Power* readers about their TV habits. Just about everyone claimed to be happy with the amount of time spent in front of the television.

Our readers did admit TV might be a problem for some. They said too much might "hurt your eyes," "keep you from doing your homework," or "stop you from getting enough exercise." But 10 years of scientific study on the subject has turned up some new information. Television can affect you in ways you never thought of.

Scientists say the long hours Tyrone spends watching TV may actually change the way he *thinks and behaves*. Dawn, his classmate, watches two hours or less each day. She is less likely to be affected. Why? Because TV has proven to be a very powerful teacher. Its lessons are more likely to be learned by Tyrone than Dawn, because he watches more. What is TV teaching him and other heavy viewers?

FACT: People spend more than nine years of their lives watching TV.

Is the real world like the world you see on TV?

The many TV characters Tyrone watches each week probably aren't much like the folks who live in his Pennsylvania town. For one thing, there are three times as many men as women on TV. There are hardly any old people, especially old women. He'd have to search hard to find characters who are retarded or deaf or have other handicaps. Very few black, Oriental or Hispanic characters have important roles, except in comedy shows. In fact, there are more speaking parts on TV for animals and robots than for minorities like these!

Life on TV isn't very realistic. But TV is one of the main ways heavy viewers learn about the world. Maybe that's why studies show that kids who watch TV a lot have stereotyped (unreal and unchangeable) ideas about the way men, women and other races behave.

FACT: Little kids are more likely to recognize Ronald McDonald than Santa Claus.

469

Do you want to be like the stars on TV?

TV shows are crowded with adults who act in irresponsible ways. Are these characters a bad example for children who are learning how to behave like adults? Many educators and parents think so.

FACT: TV characters are ten times more likely to drink alcohol than water.

Do you watch action shows the most?

TV-land is a dangerous place to live. One out of every three characters is either a criminal or a crime fighter. Fights are everywhere. Bullets whiz overhead. Cars screech around corners.

On action shows, wild driving rarely ends in a bad accident. Gunshots hardly ever kill people. Fights break up with no one getting hurt. How realistic is this?

Studies in several countries found that children who watch a lot of TV are more likely to behave roughly. Maybe some kids get used to violence when they see a great deal of it on TV. It seems exciting instead of horrible. After a while, it might not seem so bad to act that way yourself.

Kids aren't the only ones affected by TV violence. In one study, adults who were heavy viewers saw the world as a violent and scary place, and were more suspicious of other people.

FACT: Crime occurs ten times more often on TV than in real life.

Do you want things you've seen on TV?

You may think TV shows exist mainly to make you laugh or think. But the people who pay for the shows have another reason—to sell you something. They hope you'll watch the programs. Then you'll see their ads and run out and buy their products. (This isn't true for TV channels that don't have ads.)

Little kids often have trouble knowing what is an ad and what isn't. They may see characters in commercials as their friends. Then they may believe those characters are telling them a product is good for them. Even older kids are affected by ads. Heavy viewers are more likely to want the products they see advertised.

But commercials aren't the only things on TV that tempt kids to want products. Many of the afternoon and Saturday morning children's *programs* sell toys, too. If you like the show, you'll want the action figures, dolls and robots in it. So programs like these are really like 30-minute commercials!

FACT: Kids see 20,000 TV commercials a year.

471

Would you rather watch TV than do most other activities?

Remember Tyrone, the six-hour kid? Even he is aware that TV takes a big chunk out of his life. "People shouldn't be dependent on TV," he says. "You should do other things with your time."

In our poll, most readers said they'd read or play more if they couldn't watch TV. One reader wrote, "I'd die." But lots more claimed they'd do interesting things with their extra time. Willy, in West Virginia, told us he'd "hike, draw, work around the neighborhood and do my homework instead of staying up late to do it."

Studies suggest kids might be more creative if they watched less TV. For instance, scientists studied a town in Canada when it didn't have any TV. After TV was introduced, they studied the town again. They found the children didn't speak as easily and creatively.

FACT: Kids who watch a lot of TV tend to do worse in school than kids who don't.

Do you snack while watching TV?

The time you spend in front of a TV can affect your weight. A recent study showed that kids who watch TV a lot are more likely to be overweight. TV takes up time they might have spent outside playing and exercising. Perhaps they also eat while watching. Maybe the many ads for fattening foods tempt their appetites.

FACT: The more TV kids watch, the more likely it is they'll be overweight.

Do you talk with your parents about the programs you watch?

Studies show that some of the problems with TV viewing are lessened when families watch and discuss shows together. Adults can help kids understand where a show is unrealistic or irresponsible. You may find watching as a family is more fun than watching alone.

FACT: Families spend half their free time at home watching TV.

MAKING CHANGES

Do you want to make changes in your TV-viewing habits? If so, here are three suggestions:

Find an activity you like better than watching TV.

Before TV arrived in 1948, families spent their spare time reading, playing games and doing crafts. Nowadays, we've lost the knack. Some communities have experimented with no-TV months. But people had trouble filling the extra time. It doesn't take any planning or effort to switch on the TV. But it *does* take some effort to take out a library book, get the wood for a carpentry project or gather the ingredients for baking granola bars.

You can replace your TV time with activities you'll enjoy even more. Join a sports team. Take up the piano. Build a dog house. Start a computer club. Sing with a band. You'd be amazed at how little you'll miss those long hours in front of the TV.

473

Put a limit on the amount of TV you watch.

A recent study says that watching TV for 10 hours a week or less may actually improve your schoolwork. Decide how many hours are best for you. See if your family and friends will set limits, too. Then you can help each other stick to them.

Plan ahead to watch only the best programs.

Some people watch TV. Some people watch TV *programs.* Try to become the second kind of person by being choosy about what you watch. (Don't just flip on the TV whenever you're in the room.) Sit down with the weekly program schedule and decide which shows you really *want* to catch. Then skip the rest. You can use the schedule below as a model.

T.V. SCHEDULE		
Day	Hours	Program
Monday	1½	
Tuesday		
Wednesday	1	
Thursday		
Friday		
Saturday		

Think About It

1. What is the author's opinion of TV? Use details from the article to support your answer.
2. What information does the writer use to try to convince you to believe what the article says?
3. Do you think TV does cause all of the problems mentioned in the article? Why or why not?
4. Describe your TV viewing habits and tell how they affect the time you have to do other things such as reading, studying, and participating in an activity.
5. If you took care of a six-year-old child, how would you decide how much TV and which programs the child should watch?

Create and Share Study *TV Guide*, or the television section of a newspaper or magazine to see what is offered. What kinds of information is given in a TV program listing? What kinds of programs seem to be aired at certain times of the day and certain days of the week? Record your findings on a chart and share them with your class.

Explore Keep a log of your TV viewing habits for one week. Record the amount of time you spend, the names of the programs you watch, and your responses to them. You may also want to keep track of the advertisements that appeal to you and any snacks you eat. At the end of the week, study your log and draw some conclusions about your habits. Write a summary of what you learned.

THE PROBLEM WITH
PULCIFER

by *Florence Parry Heide*

Pulcifer had a problem.

He knew he had a problem because he had heard his parents talking about it. About his p-r-o-b-l-e-m. Actually, that was how he had learned to spell his name. Listening to his parents.

"What on earth are we going to do about P-u-l-c-i-f-e-r?"

Pulcifer's problem was that he didn't watch television.

"You're not really trying, Pulcifer," said Pulcifer's mother.

"When I was your age," said Pulcifer's father, "you couldn't pry me away from the television set. First thing in the morning. Last thing at night." Pulcifer's father sighed and shook his head. "I'd always hoped that my own son would follow in my footsteps."

"It isn't because we haven't set a good example," said Pulcifer's mother. "We're always watching television. And we've always had the nicest television sets. We've tried to make it easy for him. Color, remote control, even TV dinners."

"I just can't understand it," said Pulcifer's father.

Pulcifer's teacher couldn't understand it, either.

His class at school was divided into groups: the Eaglets, the Bluebirds, and the Sparrows. Pulcifer was the only one in his group, the Sparrows.

"I know you could be a Bluebird if you really tried," said Pulcifer's teacher, Mrs. Pruce. "Not that there's anything wrong with being a Sparrow, of course. We all start out being Sparrows. But look at Ethel Gawp. She used to be a Sparrow. Now she's a Bluebird. And the Bluebirds are already watching situation comedies and crime dramas."

Pulcifer couldn't seem to get beyond the cartoons and the commercials. And most of the time he didn't really understand those. He didn't get the point, that was it.

"You're not trying, Pulcifer," said Mrs. Pruce. "No one can teach you to watch television unless you try."

After school Pulcifer stopped at the library. There weren't too many books, because the audio-visual equipment took up so much room, but finally he found a book about a boy and his dog that he'd been wanting to read.

When he went to the desk to check it out, the librarian said, "It's very disappointing to see you taking out a book, Pulcifer, when you could be watching television. Do your parents know you come here to get books?"

Pulcifer shook his head.

"I didn't think so. I don't think they would like to know that you were coming in here, getting books out, taking them home to read."

She frowned at Pulcifer.

"I remember one boy, Pulcifer, who started with just one book. Two months later he was checking out three books. Three, Pulcifer! The habit had formed. It was too late to help him. What do you think of that?"

Pulcifer scratched his ear. "It's very interesting," he said.

When Pulcifer got home, he went to his room and settled down on his bed to read the library book. He had just come to the best part when his mother walked in.

"Oh, Pulcifer," she said sadly. "You're reading again." She sat down on his bed. "I just don't know where all this is going to end, Pulcifer. How are you ever going to learn to watch television if you spend so much time reading?"

After dinner that night Pulcifer's father said, "Your mother tells me you've been reading again, Pulcifer. Do you realize that you could have spent those same hours watching television, my boy? Now those hours are gone, gone forever. All those programs. All those game shows and soap operas and situation comedies and talk shows, gone, never to return."

Pulcifer's leg was going to sleep.

479

"It must be the school's fault," said Pulcifer's mother. "I'll have to have another talk with his t-e-a-c-h-e-r."

She called Mrs. Pruce.

"He simply can't keep up with the rest of the class," said Mrs. Pruce. "The other children watch a great deal of television. Some of our better students watch night and day."

"There must be something the school can do to help," said Pulcifer's mother.

"We can always try, of course," said Mrs. Pruce. "We'll put him in a special corrective remedial class for non-watchers."

The next day Pulcifer started attending the special class. His teacher was Mr. Plim.

"You can read all you want to," said Mr. Plim kindly. "Abiding by certain rules, of course. If we have no rules, we have no system, right?"

Pulcifer nodded. Then he shook his head. He wasn't quite sure what the right answer was.

"You don't have to watch any television at all while you're with us," said Mr. Plim. "We don't even have television here, so you can relax."

He pointed to a chair. "This is where you will do all your reading. We can't carry our books around any more than we can carry our television sets with us wherever we go."

Mr. Plim rubbed his hands together. "Now the first thing we'll do is select a book. You have several choices at this hour."

Pulcifer chose a mystery book, *The Case of the Mummified Mask*.

Mr. Plim looked at the big clock on the wall. "You've missed the first twenty-seven pages, but just plunge in at page twenty-eight and see if you can make any sense out of it."

Pulcifer started to read. It took him a while to figure out the plot because he'd missed the first part, but it seemed pretty exciting:

Joe felt his scalp prickle.
He wheeled around.
There, in a corner of the dark garden,
a mysterious shape stood up.

Pulcifer turned the page. It was an advertisement. Mr. Plim looked over his shoulder. "We can't skip, you know. But there are only about ten pages of ads. Later, of course, as the book becomes more exciting, there will be more advertising pages."

Pulcifer started to read the advertisements:

Finally Pulcifer finished reading the advertisements and could start reading the mystery again. He'd sort of forgotten where he left off.

> The shape drew nearer. Joe saw with relief that it was kindly old Mr. McGregor who lived next door. But what was that that he was holding? Joe stared. It was a gun. And it was pointed at Joe.

Pulcifer was pretty thirsty. Maybe he'd just go out to the bubbler in the hall to get a drink of water.

When he came back he picked up the book again.

"You missed the exciting part," said Mr. Plim. "I'm afraid you're just in time for more advertisements. And the ending. But we have other books scheduled for our next session."

When Pulcifer went to the special class the next time, Mr. Plim told him he could choose between two books. One was called *Mystery at Silver Creek* and the other was called *The Facts about Facts.*

Pulcifer chose *Mystery at Silver Creek.* After he had read a few pages, he found that it was a series of articles about the different kinds of vegetation that grew in and around Silver Creek, Nebraska.

He decided to read *The Facts about Facts* instead.

"I'm afraid you've already missed the first two chapters," said Mr. Plim.

Pulcifer started to read it anyway. It turned out to be a very exciting story about a time warp. It took him a while to understand it because he'd missed the first of it. Now he was just getting into the best part.

"Lunch time," announced Mr. Plim.

By the time Pulcifer had finished lunch it was too late to read *The Facts about Facts.* The other books that were available after lunch were very boring.

Pulcifer went to the special classes every day. At the end of a month, Mr. Plim had a conference with Pulcifer's mother.

"We've done everything in our power to turn Pulcifer against books," said Mr. Plim. "I'm afraid there's nothing more we can do."

Pulcifer's mother sighed. "Maybe I should take him to a p-y-s—a p-s-y: a psychiatrist," she said.

"A psychiatrist," said Pulcifer's father that evening. "Well, the best is none too good."

The next day Pulcifer's mother took him to a psychiatrist.

When they got to the office, the receptionist gave Pulcifer's mother a questionnaire to fill out.

Pulcifer looked over his mother's shoulder as she filled in the questionnaire.

Has the patient ever eaten nothing but raisins for more than three consecutive days?

Has the patient ever exhibited unusual interest in any of the following:

_ the color green   _ lamp shades   _ even numbers

Pulcifer stopped reading.

When his mother had finished filling in the questionnaire, the receptionist said to Pulcifer, "Dr. Tawke will see you now."

Pulcifer followed her into the doctor's office.

The receptionist put Pulcifer's questionnaire on Dr. Tawke's desk and left the room. Dr. Tawke shuffled some papers around on his desk. Then he looked up at Pulcifer.

"Now, young man, we have to establish some rules, eh? Number one, you and I are friends. Don't think of me as your doctor; think of me as your pal."

Dr. Tawke reached over and shook Pulcifer's hand. Pulcifer wasn't absolutely positive but he thought that maybe two of his fingers were broken. He rubbed his hand. Maybe they were just sprained.

Dr. Tawke leaned back in his chair. "Mind if I call you Herbie?"

Pulcifer shook his head.

"Or perhaps you feel that Herbie is a baby name. Maybe you'd feel more comfortable with Herb."

Dr. Tawke pointed his finger at Pulcifer. "I want to make something absolutely clear, Herb. What we talk about will stay right in this office. You can tell me just what's bothering you and it won't go any further."

The only thing that Pulcifer could think of that was bothering him was that his fingers still hurt a lot.

Dr. Tawke leaned back and clasped his hands behind his head. "Would you be surprised, Herb, if I told you that yours is not an unusual problem? Let me tell you, Herb, there is nothing to be ashamed of. It is perfectly natural to be jealous of a new baby in the house. Perfectly natural."

He leaned forward. "I'm going to tell you something very, very interesting, Herb. I had problems adjusting to *my* baby brother when he was born! What do you think of that?"

"I'm sorry to hear it," said Pulcifer. "I mean, I'm glad you told me, and it's very, very interesting, just the way you said it would be."

"Now, Herb, admitting our problems, facing up to them, is the first step in conquering them. You can tell me right out that you're jealous of the new baby and I'll understand."

"There isn't a new baby," said Pulcifer. "There's only me."

Dr. Tawke leafed through the papers on his desk once more. "Herbert Fishley," he said. "You're Herbert Fishley."

Pulcifer sighed. Maybe he *was* Herbert Fishley. It was sort of like trying to understand a program on television.

Dr. Tawke picked up another paper. "You're Pulcifer," he said. "Mind if I call you—um—Pulcifer?"

Pulcifer shook his head.

"Well, Pulcifer, I understand that you have a little problem. And the problem is that you haven't learned to watch television."

Dr. Tawke smiled. "I'm going to tell you something that will surprise you. I had exactly the same problem! Yes, Pulcifer, hard as it may seem to believe, I didn't know how to watch television. And yet I overcame my handicap, just as you can overcome yours."

He leaned forward. "You must strive, Pulcifer, you must struggle. You must buckle down and watch television as you have never watched before. Remember, there's no such word as 'can't.'"

That night Pulcifer's mother said, "I'm sure Dr. Tawke will get to the b-o-t-t-o-m of Pulcifer's p-r-o-b-l-e-m."

"It's our last hope," said Pulcifer's father.

Pulcifer went to Dr. Tawke's office many times. Every visit seemed very much like the visit before.

After a few weeks Dr. Tawke called Pulcifer's mother into his office. "I can sum up this lad's problem with one word. One word! And that word is *motivation*. It's as simple as that. Once he understands the reason to watch television, he'll be watching just like everyone else."

"Motivation," said Pulcifer's mother. "We never thought of that."

"My boy," said Pulcifer's father that evening, "we've solved your problem. Apparently you haven't understood the *reason* for watching television."

"Well, what is the reason?" asked Pulcifer.

"Everyone watches. There's your reason, son: everyone watches."

"I don't think it's a very good reason," said Pulcifer.

"But it's the only reason there *is*, dear," said Pulcifer's mother.

"I still don't think it's a very good reason," said Pulcifer.

Pulcifer's mother sighed.

"We've done all we can," she said. "No one can say we haven't tried."

Pulcifer's father put his arm around Pulcifer's shoulder.

"We want you to know that we love you anyway," he said. "After all, a son is a son. We stand behind you, son."

"Yes, dear, even if you are d-i-f-f-e-r-e-n-t," said Pulcifer's mother, turning on the television set.

Pulcifer settled down comfortably with his new stack of library books.

Think About It

1. Who has a problem in the story and what is it?
2. Explain how the other characters in the story tried to make Pulcifer feel.
3. What is the final argument Pulcifer's parents use to try to convince him to watch television?
4. Which parts of the story seemed realistic to you? Which parts seemed unrealistic?
5. Tell what you think is the author's purpose in writing this story. How do you think the author feels about television and books?

Create and Share You are Pulcifer, and you are being interviewed for the six o'clock news because of your "unusual" behavior. What reasons will you give for preferring books to television? List your reasons. Share and compare your list with a friend's.

Explore If you enjoyed *The Problem With Pulcifer* you may want to read another book by Florence Parry Heide. Or you might want to find another book about children and TV. Check the library card catalog under TELEVISION—FICTION to see what is available.

GETTING IT ON THE AIR

from A DAY IN THE LIFE OF A TELEVISION NEWS REPORTER
by William Jaspersohn

Television reporters lead exciting lives. On any day they may find themselves assigned to interview famous people, or to travel to distant news sites, or to report on major fires and other disasters. Since news stories can break at any time, TV reporters lead suspenseful lives, too, never knowing when or where their next assignment will be.

Dan Rea loves the reporting life. He's a news reporter for a TV station in Boston, and his regular assignment, or *beat*, as it's called, is the city itself.

You don't necessarily have to go to college to become a television news reporter, but for those who do, there are schools with courses in broadcast journalism throughout the United States.

Dan Rea didn't study broadcast journalism in college. Instead, he majored in English and then earned a law degree. While he studied law, Dan wrote a regular political column for a newspaper and later he hosted a call-in talk show on current events for a radio station. Dan discovered

he liked broadcasting and not long after graduating from law school, he began television reporting. Now his news stories are seen five nights a week by hundreds of thousands of viewers.

Usually Dan works from 3:30 to 11:00 P.M., but sometimes his day starts earlier.

At ten o'clock on a warm August morning, Dan is awakened by a phone call from the assignment desk at the station. Dan gropes for the ringing phone; he is tired. Two nights ago he worked twenty-four hours without sleep, and he still hasn't caught up on his rest.

Could he come in early? asks the assignment editor. A reporter is out sick today, and the news department could use some extra help. Could Dan maybe come in at noon? "Sure," Dan replies, and hangs up the phone.

As always, the newsroom is a hive of activity when Dan arrives. Typewriters clackety-clack, phones ring, people mill and shout—to an outsider it might seem bewildering. But in fact, everybody here has a special job, and somehow five times a day it all works. Their energy works. The news is gathered and aired.

Two men oversee all this bustle: the *assistant news director*, and his boss, the *news director*. The news director hires workers for the newsroom, oversees its budget, and controls the general style and makeup of the news shows. The assistant news director makes more of the day-to-day decisions about what news stories get aired.

The person who organizes the news stories into a complete news show is known as a *producer*. Since time is limited during a news show—each show lasts only a

half hour or an hour—one of the producers' main jobs is making sure the time in each show is properly used.

While Dan checks his mail, several reporters who work earlier shifts have already gone out and come back with their day's news stories. One types a story about a bank robbery that occurred early this morning, while another reads a piece she has written about noise pollution near the airport. Meanwhile, a third reporter uses a stopwatch and a machine called a *video playback* to time some videotape footage he will use for a story about nuclear power plants.

ssignment Desk

Dan is pouring himself a glass of soda when the assignment editor, Jerry, calls him over to the assignment desk.

"I just heard a call over the police radio," says Jerry. "The police have just raided a warehouse in Jamaica Plain, and it sounds as if they found some stolen goods."

"Any arrests?" asks Dan.

"Haven't heard," says Jerry. "But I think we should check it out."

"Could make a good story," Dan agrees. "Do we want something for the six o'clock news?"

Jerry nods. Dan pockets the slip of paper, grabs his jacket off his desk, and off he goes to cover a story about a police raid in Jamaica Plain.

He picks up a fresh reporter's note pad from the stockroom, then steps into his cab, which is waiting by the back door. Reporters travel by taxi to many story locations. Dan finds cabs good places to think about stories and take notes; and luckily, the station pays the fare.

Fifteen minutes later the cab cruises up to the Jamaica Plain address, and Dan finds himself alone in front of a three-story warehouse. It is quiet. Dan's footsteps click on the pavement as he walks to the warehouse door, rattles it, and finds it locked.

Undiscouraged, he follows an alley along the side of the building and makes his way around back.

Soon, other reporters, for radio, newspapers, and television, begin arriving at the warehouse. Their assignment desks, too, are equipped with shortwave radios, and that is how they first got word of the police raid.

At first, the police detectives, who are inside the warehouse, ask Dan and the others to wait outside for a few minutes. Then Deputy Police Inspector Anthony DiNatale, who is in charge of the case, steps out to brief the press. He tells them the raid occurred at approximately 11:00 A.M. this morning, and that stolen goods worth more than $250,000 were discovered. He will answer questions later, he says. For now, he asks everyone to promise not to touch anything because the crime lab is still dusting the stolen goods for fingerprints. Everyone promises.

Deputy DiNatale then says, "You're welcome to step inside."

Everyone enters the warehouse, eager to see the thieves' hideout.

Sure enough, just as the deputy said, there are the stolen goods. "That sports car alone is worth forty-five thousand dollars!" someone whispers. Elsewhere, there are skis, ski boots, a boat, a camp trailer, radios, power tools— all allegedly stolen from stores and homes and hidden here. Even to an untrained eye it looks like the work of professionals—people in the business of stealing things and selling them for profit. But when you're a reporter you must withhold quick judgments. Dan draws no conclusions until he can talk with Deputy DiNatale.

Before they can write their stories, good reporters must have answers to five basic questions: Who? What? When?

Where? and Why? Now, Dan knows the *what* of this story: the stolen goods. He knows *when*: the police raided the building at 11:00 A.M. this morning. And he knows *why* the raid happened: because Deputy DiNatale says the building has been under surveillance for a long while. Now Dan asks the deputy if the police know *who* stole the goods, and the deputy replies that he's not at liberty to say. But he can say that the work is that of professionals, and arrests are expected soon.

Meanwhile, from the careful notes he took at the warehouse, Dan writes his story of the police raid. Good reporters must know how to write fast and clearly, and Dan says that for him the hardest part of writing is finding an opening, or *lead line*. Once he has that, he says, the rest of the writing comes quickly.

Now he curls his fingers over the typewriter keys and writes: BOSTON POLICE RECOVERED A QUARTER MILLION DOLLARS IN STOLEN GOODS TODAY AT A JAMAICA PLAIN WAREHOUSE.

And *that* will be his lead line! He begins typing his story.

Twenty minutes later, Dan finishes his script, which he hands to the producer of six o'clock news, Pat. She in turn will discuss the stolen-goods story with the assistant news director, who will agree it should appear in the beginning, or *A-section*, of the show.

Crime stories aren't the only kind of reporting TV reporters do. At any time, day or night, they may be called on to cover a fire or other catastrophe.

Once Dan was awakened at 5:00 A.M. to cover a fire that had broken out on a pier in the Charlestown area of Boston. Amid the blare of the fireboats' horns and the pall of smoke, he interviewed Fire Captain John Collins, who, unlike some people Dan interviews, is always cooperative, and answered all of Dan's questions. Luckily, the blaze injured no one.

The news events most frequently covered by TV reporters are meetings of one kind or another. At least once a week Dan can expect to be present at some meeting hall in Boston, taking notes, listening, and watching. Since reporters can't possibly describe *everything* that happens in a meeting, they try to capture its main ideas, or *essence.* Before entering a hall Dan always asks himself, "What is this meeting for?" then tries to answer his own question.

Another common source of news for any reporter is a press conference. These special meetings for reporters are designed to give them information and answer questions about particular newsworthy topics.

There are always news-making people to interview. Dan's favorite times are presidential election years, because then he gets to interview all the candidates. Sometimes these interviews can be difficult. Candidates usually don't have much time, so you must ask your questions as quickly and clearly as possible. Dan says that doing interviews has taught him that even famous people are human beings. "I'm not in awe of them," he says. "As a reporter, I can't be. In journalism, there's no place for hero worship."

Think About It

1. What problems do television reporters face? Use information from the article and your own ideas.
2. Make a list of questions that you would like to ask a TV news reporter about his or her job.
3. Describe the steps between the time an event takes place and the time it is broadcast.
4. In what ways is writing a TV news story like writing a research report?
5. What did the selections in TV OR NOT TV? tell you about television?

Create and Share Work with a partner to compare the evening news on two channels. Choose channels and look at the news every evening for several days. Use a stopwatch or clock to help you find out how much time is given to each story. Take notes on how each story is handled. Decide whether you feel the story is important, and the reporting objective and informative. Compare your findings.

Explore You may want to read a book about the TV news business or find out more about how TV stations operate. Look in the library card catalog under TELEVISION BROADCASTING.

All happy families resemble one another.

Tolstoy

Family Ties

A New Song

from SARAH, PLAIN AND TALL
by Patricia MacLachlan

$\mathcal{D}$id Mama sing every day?" asked Caleb. "Every-single-day?" He sat close to the fire, his chin in his hand. It was dusk, and the dogs lay beside him on the warm hearthstones.

"Every-single-day," I told him for the second time this week. For the twentieth time this month. The hundredth time this year? And the past few years?

"And did Papa sing, too?"

"Yes, Papa sang, too. Don't get so close, Caleb. You'll heat up."

He pushed his chair back. It made a hollow scraping sound on the hearthstones, and the dogs stirred. Lottie, small and black, wagged her tail and lifted her head. Nick slept on.

I turned the bread dough over and over on the marble slab on the kitchen table.

"Well, Papa doesn't sing anymore," said Caleb very softly. A log broke apart and crackled in the fireplace. He looked up at me. "What did I look like when I was born?"

"You didn't have any clothes on," I told him.

"I know that," he said.

"You looked like this." I held the bread dough up in a round pale ball.

"I had hair," said Caleb seriously.

"Not enough to talk about," I said.

"And she named me Caleb," he went on, filling in the old familiar story.

"I would have named you Troublesome," I said, making Caleb smile.

"And Mama handed me to you in the yellow blanket and said . . . " He waited for me to finish the story. "And said . . . ?"

I sighed. "And Mama said, 'Isn't he beautiful, Anna?' "

"And I was," Caleb finished.

Caleb thought the story was over, and I didn't tell him what I had really thought. He was homely and plain, and he had a terrible holler and a horrid smell. But these were not the worst of him. Mama died the next morning. That was the worst thing about Caleb.

"Isn't he beautiful, Anna?" Her last words to me. I had gone to bed thinking how wretched he looked. And I forgot to say good night.

I wiped my hands on my apron and went to the window. Outside, the prairie reached out and touched the places where the sky came down. Though winter was nearly over, there were patches of snow and ice everywhere. I looked at the long dirt road that crawled across the plains, remembering the morning that Mama had died, cruel and sunny. They had come for her in a wagon and taken her away to be buried. And then the cousins and aunts and uncles had come and tried to fill up the house. But they couldn't.

Slowly, one by one, they left. And then the days seemed long and dark like winter days, even though it wasn't winter. And Papa didn't sing.

Isn't he beautiful, Anna?

No, Mama.

It was hard to think of Caleb as beautiful. It took three whole days for me to love him, sitting in the chair by the fire, Papa washing up the supper dishes, Caleb's tiny hand brushing my cheek. And a smile. It was the smile, I know.

"Can you remember her songs?" asked Caleb. "Mama's songs?"

I turned from the window. "No. Only that she sang about flowers and birds. Sometimes about the moon at nighttime."

Caleb reached down and touched Lottie's head.

"Maybe," he said, his voice low, "if you remember the songs, then I might remember her, too."

My eyes widened and tears came. Then the door opened and the wind blew in with Papa, and I went to stir the stew. Papa put his arms around me and put his nose in my hair.

"Nice soapy smell, that stew," he said.

I laughed. "That's my hair."

Caleb came over and threw his arms around Papa's neck and hung down as Papa swung him back and forth, and the dogs sat up.

"Cold in town," said Papa. "And Jack was feisty." Jack was Papa's horse that he'd raised from a colt. "Rascal," murmured Papa, smiling, because no matter what Jack did Papa loved him.

I spooned up the stew and lighted the oil lamp and we ate with the dogs crowding under the table, hoping for spills or handouts.

Papa might not have told us about Sarah that night if Caleb hadn't asked him the question. After the dishes were cleared and washed and Papa was filling the tin pail with ashes, Caleb spoke up. It wasn't a question, really.

"You don't sing anymore," he said. He said it harshly. Not because he meant to, but because he had been thinking of it for so long. "Why?" he asked more gently.

Slowly Papa straightened up. There was a long silence, and the dogs looked up, wondering at it.

"I've forgotten the old songs," said Papa quietly. He sat down. "But maybe there's a way to remember them." He looked up at us.

"How?" asked Caleb eagerly.

Papa leaned back in the chair. "I've placed an advertisement in the newspapers. For help."

"You mean a housekeeper?" I asked, surprised.

Caleb and I looked at each other and burst out laughing, remembering Hilly, our old housekeeper. She was round and slow and shuffling. She snored in a high whistle at night, like a tea kettle, and let the fire go out.

"No," said Papa slowly. "Not a housekeeper." He paused. "A wife."

Caleb stared at Papa. "A wife? You mean a mother?"

Nick slid his face onto Papa's lap and Papa stroked his ears.

"That too," said Papa. "Like Maggie."

Matthew, our neighbor to the south, had written to ask for a wife and mother for his children. And Maggie had come from Tennessee. Her hair was the color of turnips and she laughed.

Papa reached into his pocket and unfolded a letter written on white paper. "And I have received an answer." Papa read to us:

Dear Mr. Jacob Witting,

I am Sarah Wheaton from Maine as you will see from my letter. I am answering your advertisement. I have never been married, though I have been asked. I have lived with an older brother, William, who is about to be married. His wife-to-be is young and energetic.

I have always loved to live by the sea, but at this time I feel a move is necessary. And the truth is, the sea is as far east as I can go. My choice, as you can see, is limited. This should not be taken as an insult. I am strong and I work hard and I am willing to travel. But I am not mild mannered. If you should still care to write, I would be interested in your children and about where you live. And you.

Very truly yours,
Sarah Elisabeth Wheaton

P.S. Do you have opinions on cats? I have one.

No one spoke when Papa finished the letter. He kept looking at it in his hands, reading it over to himself. Finally I turned my head a bit to sneak a look at Caleb. He was smiling. I smiled, too.

"One thing," I said in the quiet of the room.

"What's that?" asked Papa, looking up.

I put my arm around Caleb.

"Ask her if she sings," I said.

Caleb and Papa and I wrote letters to Sarah, and before the ice and snow had melted from the fields, we all received answers. Mine came first.

Dear Anna,

Yes, I can braid hair and I can make stew and bake bread, though I prefer to build book shelves and paint.

My favorite colors are the colors of the sea, blue and gray and green, depending on the weather. My brother William is a fisherman, and he tells me that when he is in the middle of a fog-bound sea the water is a color for which there is no name. He catches flounder and sea bass and bluefish. Sometimes he sees whales. And birds, too, of course. I am enclosing a book of sea birds so you will see what William and I see every day.

Very truly yours,
Sarah Elisabeth Wheaton

Caleb read and read the letter so many times that the ink began to run and the folds tore. He read the book about sea birds over and over.

"Do you think she'll come?" asked Caleb. "And will she stay? What if she thinks we are loud and pesky?"

"You *are* loud and pesky," I told him. But I was worried, too. Sarah loved the sea, I could tell. Maybe she wouldn't leave there **after all to** come where there were fields and grass and **sky and not** much else.

"What if she comes **and doesn't** like our house?" Caleb asked. "I told her it **was small.** Maybe I shouldn't have told her it was small."

"Hush, Caleb. Hush."

Caleb's letter came **soon after,** with a picture of a cat drawn on the envelope.

Dear Caleb,

> *My cat's name is Seal because she is gray like the seals that swim off shore in Maine. She is glad that Lottie and Nick send their greetings. She likes dogs most of the time. She says their foot prints are much larger than hers (which she is enclosing in return).*

> *Your house sounds lovely, even though it is far out in the country with no close neighbors. My house is tall and the shingles are gray because of the salt from the sea. There are roses nearby.*

> *Yes, I do like small rooms sometimes. Yes, I can keep a fire going at night. I do not know if I snore. Seal has never told me.*

> *Very truly yours,*
> *Sarah Elisabeth*

"Did you really ask her about fires and snoring?" I asked, amazed.

"I wished to know," Caleb said.

He kept the letter with him, reading it in the barn and in the fields and by the cow pond. And always in bed at night.

One morning, early, Papa and Caleb and I were cleaning out the horse stalls and putting down new bedding. Papa stopped suddenly and leaned on his pitchfork.

"Sarah has said she will come for a month's time if we wish her to," he said, his voice loud in the dark barn. "To see how it is. Just to see."

Caleb stood by the stall door and folded his arms across his chest.

"I think," he began. Then, "I think," he said slowly, "that it would be good—to say yes," he finished in a rush.

Papa looked at me.

"I say yes," I told him, grinning.

"Yes," said Papa. "Then yes it is."

And the three of us, all smiling, went to work again.

The next day Papa went to town to mail his letter to Sarah. It was rainy for days, and the clouds followed. The house was cool and damp and quiet. Once I set four places at the table, then caught myself and put the extra plate

away. Three lambs were born, one with a black face. And then Papa's letter came. It was very short.

Dear Jacob,

I will come by train. I will wear a yellow bonnet. I am plain and tall.

Sarah

"What's that?" asked Caleb excitedly, peering over Papa's shoulder. He pointed. "There, written at the bottom of the letter."

Papa read it to himself. Then he smiled, holding up the letter for us to see.

Tell them I sing was all it said.

A Family Secret

by Damián Fernández

I never dared tell anyone in the family. It would have convinced them that Grandpa was crazy, and that was not the case at all. Mama and Aunt Margot used to whisper about how Grandpa was losing his mind. Every night, as they scraped the grease off the black pans in the kitchen, they would tell lies about him. Well, it was true that sometimes he still talked to Grandma as he rocked back and forth on the dark porch. Once in a while, I would hide behind the door to listen to him tell her about the family and about their old friends, and he even would ask her questions. It scared me. Because you see, Grandma was dead and he still talked to her. But that doesn't mean he was crazy, does it?

Grandpa was seventy-three years old. He was strong and healthy and he didn't need a cane to walk. He had a small shoe repair shop near my school. Every day, around 3:15, after school was dismissed, I would go to his shop. Along the way, I would buy a cold bottle of soda with a dime Mama gave me. The shop was a white woodshed behind an old house. Inside, it seemed it was always snowing, because of the dust particles floating in the air. It smelled of clean, recently cut leather. Grandpa, wearing his glasses, would be there hammering the black high heel of Mrs. Herrera's shoe, pressing lightly on a tiny nail between his lips, or he would be there cementing the soles of some brown penny-loafers. As soon as he saw me arrive, he would lay down whatever he was doing. Smiling, he would listen to me tell him how the substitute teacher cried again in class, or why Miss Moyer made us repeat "Empty vessels make the most sounds." Grandpa would laugh like a child, but with deep and hearty chuckles, as we sat there drinking our soda. At five o'clock he would say *"Se terminó lo que se daba,"* and he would kiss Grandma's photograph before he locked the uneven doors of the shop. He kissed her photographs after she died. You see, Grandpa loved her a lot. He used to call her *mi viejita* in his native Spanish. When she died, they wouldn't let me go to the funeral.

I heard them say that it wasn't healthy for kids to see dead people. I didn't see Grandpa cry once during those days, although he was silent. But afterwards, he acted as if nothing had changed. That's why they thought he was crazy.

Now you know why I never told them about what happened on his birthday, nine months after Grandma's death. Mother had baked him a cake and everyone bought him a present. But not me. I made him a nice wooden frame for one of Grandma's pictures. He hugged me when I gave it to him. Grandpa was always warm and hairy and smelled of cologne and white starched shirts. That night, I was lying in bed ready to sleep when Grandpa quietly comes to my side and whispers that he has something important to show me. A special gift he had received. We tiptoed to his room and he closed the door behind us. From under the bed, he pulled a small, flat box which he handed to me. "Open it," he said. I found two white handkerchiefs embroidered in Spain.

"Grandpa, they are nice," I told him, and he smiled.

"Read the letter," he whispered. So I picked up the piece of notebook paper from inside the box and read it. I looked up at him and met his brown eyes staring slowly at me.

"Grandpa," I said. I couldn't say any more.

"*Mi viejita* didn't forget me, *no me olvidó*," he said in a low voice. "She still remembers my birthday."

Between my fingers I felt the soft, delicate cloth of the handkerchiefs. "She wouldn't forget you, Grandpa," I told him. He came closer, almost smiling, and hugged me tightly.

514

Think About It

1. What do you think singing came to mean for the characters in "A New Song"?
2. What expectations do you think Papa, Caleb, Anna, and Sarah have about their life together?
3. Why do you think Damian's grandfather in "A Family Secret" continued talking to his wife after her death?
4. Where do you think the handkerchiefs and the note came from? What makes you think this?
5. Who tells each of these stories? How do the storytellers' feelings affect the way they tell the stories?

Create and Share   Describe your feelings about a member of your own family who is as special to you as Grandfather is to Damian. Include one or more incidents that show the relationship you have with this person.

Explore   If you liked "A New Song," you may want to read the rest of Patricia MacLachlan's *Sarah, Plain and Tall*. This author also wrote *Arthur for the Very First Time* and *Cassie Binegar*. Look in the library card catalog or in the fiction section for her last name to see what is available.

BREAK DOWN

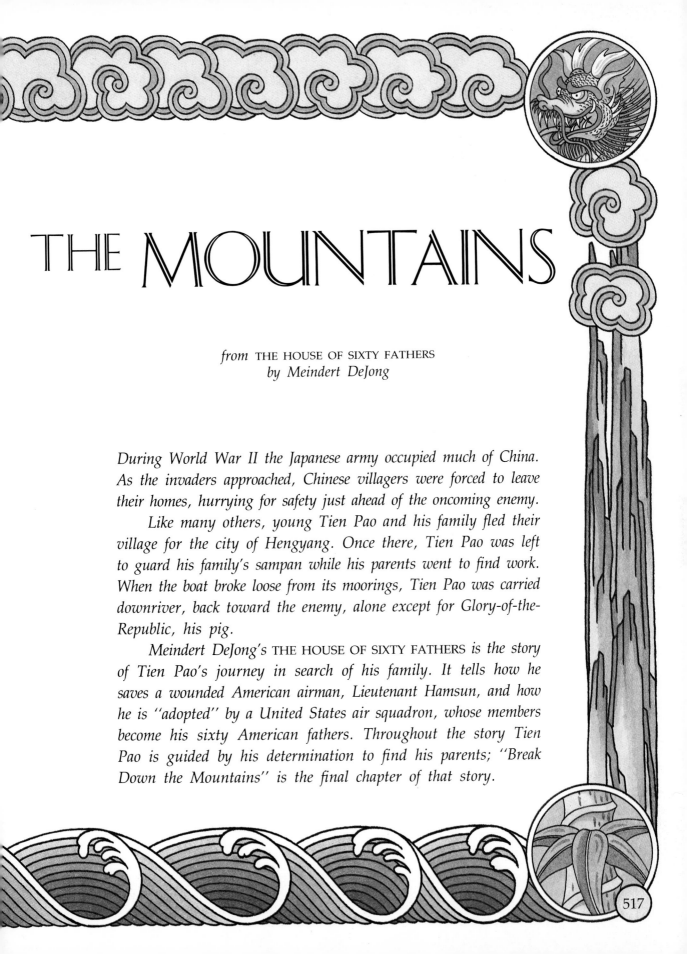

THE MOUNTAINS

from THE HOUSE OF SIXTY FATHERS
by Meindert DeJong

During World War II the Japanese army occupied much of China. As the invaders approached, Chinese villagers were forced to leave their homes, hurrying for safety just ahead of the oncoming enemy.

Like many others, young Tien Pao and his family fled their village for the city of Hengyang. Once there, Tien Pao was left to guard his family's sampan while his parents went to find work. When the boat broke loose from its moorings, Tien Pao was carried downriver, back toward the enemy, alone except for Glory-of-the-Republic, his pig.

Meindert DeJong's THE HOUSE OF SIXTY FATHERS is the story of Tien Pao's journey in search of his family. It tells how he saves a wounded American airman, Lieutenant Hamsun, and how he is "adopted" by a United States air squadron, whose members become his sixty American fathers. Throughout the story Tien Pao is guided by his determination to find his parents; "Break Down the Mountains" is the final chapter of that story.

Tien Pao stared after the plane with amazed mouth wide open. The interpreter and some of the sixty men came running out of the house, but Glory-of-the-Republic had scuttled under the jeep.

"It is called buzzing the barracks," the interpreter called out to Tien Pao in Chinese, proud of his knowledge of such things.

Tien Pao hardly heard him. He stared toward where the plane had disappeared almost in the wink of an eye— that quick, that fast. And now there stirred in Tien Pao a great new idea.

He laid an urgent hand on Lieutenant Hamsun's arm. Totally forgetting that the man couldn't understand him, he talked earnestly, rapidly, his words tumbling over each other because of the great hope and the great thought that had come to him out of the roaring swiftness of the silver plane that had scraped over the house and had been gone before its sound was gone. Lieutenant Hamsun listened as intensely as Tien Pao talked. Without taking his eyes from Tien Pao's face, he motioned to the interpreter to come close. "It is this." Tien Pao began all over again without interrupting the flood of his words. "It is the hope the swift plane gave me, and if it should fail, then I will gladly be the adopted son of these sixty men, for they are like fathers to me, and the good doctor, too . . .

"Yesterday as I watched from the rock, the last stragglers passed from Hengyang, and now there will be no more, for I was told that the Japanese have all of Hengyang and are coming on.

"But those who passed in the night and those who

passed that whole day while I lay sleeping on the rock are still walking somewhere, and a plane in all its swiftness could overtake them in moments.

"Oh, I am asking much, I know . . . But it's my father and my mother, and my little sister. Could then the Lieutenant Hamsun take me in a plane down the railroad track until we come to such a point that the refugees have not yet reached? Then I would know. Isn't there still enough daylight left, even after the sun sets, that if my father and mother were not on the railroad track—would it—couldn't the plane still follow the other roads from Hengyang?"

Tien Pao was out of breath and aghast at his own desperate boldness to make such an enormous request. All the men were standing around . . . "It is not that I'm ungrateful," he mumbled, although the interpreter was busy translating what he had said. Then, overcome by the enormity of what he had done, he stared stony-faced at the floor of the jeep while the interpreter's strange words that were *his* words went on and on.

Then words flew between Lieutenant Hamsun and the doctor standing beside the jeep. Tien Pao did not dare look up. Oh, he wasn't ungrateful! He was almost bursting with gratitude, and with happiness at seeing Lieutenant Hamsun, but the plane had come over, and the thoughts had come, and the hope . . .

The interpreter must have seen Tien Pao's face turn colors as the two men argued, for he said in a low voice: "Lieutenant Hamsun wants to do just what you said—right now. But the doctor won't let him because of his hurt leg, even though the doctor agrees that it ought to be done.

519

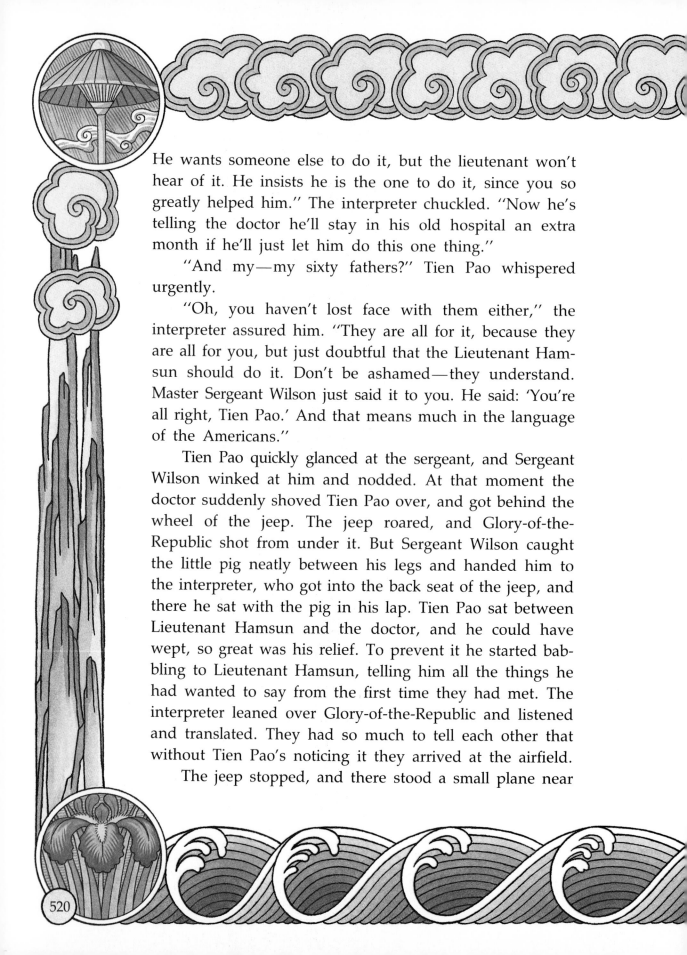

He wants someone else to do it, but the lieutenant won't hear of it. He insists he is the one to do it, since you so greatly helped him." The interpreter chuckled. "Now he's telling the doctor he'll stay in his old hospital an extra month if he'll just let him do this one thing."

"And my—my sixty fathers?" Tien Pao whispered urgently.

"Oh, you haven't lost face with them either," the interpreter assured him. "They are all for it, because they are all for you, but just doubtful that the Lieutenant Hamsun should do it. Don't be ashamed—they understand. Master Sergeant Wilson just said it to you. He said: 'You're all right, Tien Pao.' And that means much in the language of the Americans."

Tien Pao quickly glanced at the sergeant, and Sergeant Wilson winked at him and nodded. At that moment the doctor suddenly shoved Tien Pao over, and got behind the wheel of the jeep. The jeep roared, and Glory-of-the-Republic shot from under it. But Sergeant Wilson caught the little pig neatly between his legs and handed him to the interpreter, who got into the back seat of the jeep, and there he sat with the pig in his lap. Tien Pao sat between Lieutenant Hamsun and the doctor, and he could have wept, so great was his relief. To prevent it he started babbling to Lieutenant Hamsun, telling him all the things he had wanted to say from the first time they had met. The interpreter leaned over Glory-of-the-Republic and listened and translated. They had so much to tell each other that without Tien Pao's noticing it they arrived at the airfield.

The jeep stopped, and there stood a small plane near

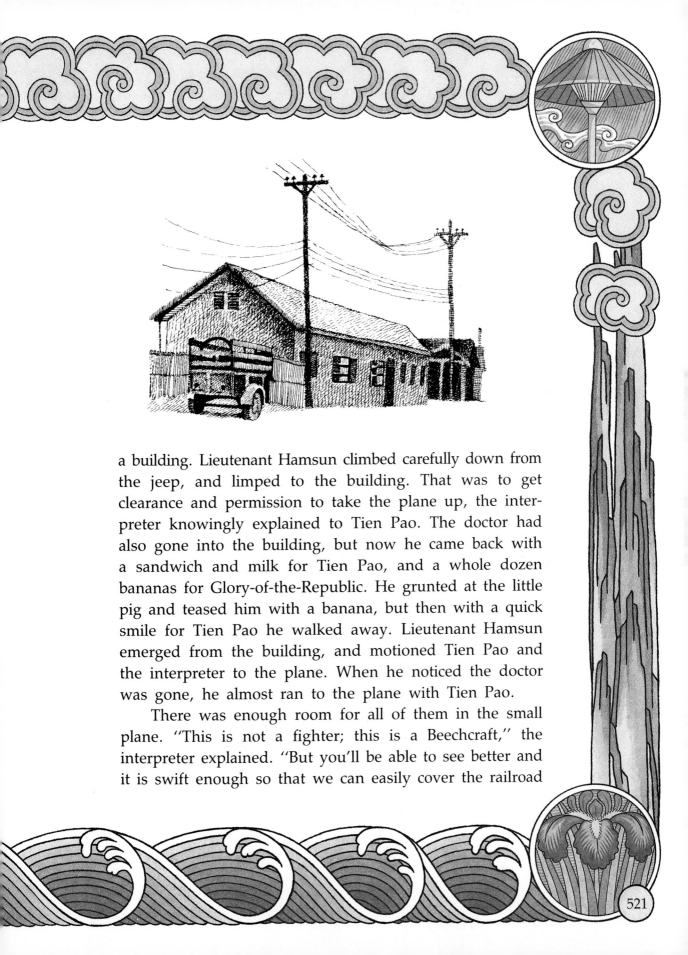

a building. Lieutenant Hamsun climbed carefully down from the jeep, and limped to the building. That was to get clearance and permission to take the plane up, the interpreter knowingly explained to Tien Pao. The doctor had also gone into the building, but now he came back with a sandwich and milk for Tien Pao, and a whole dozen bananas for Glory-of-the-Republic. He grunted at the little pig and teased him with a banana, but then with a quick smile for Tien Pao he walked away. Lieutenant Hamsun emerged from the building, and motioned Tien Pao and the interpreter to the plane. When he noticed the doctor was gone, he almost ran to the plane with Tien Pao.

There was enough room for all of them in the small plane. "This is not a fighter; this is a Beechcraft," the interpreter explained. "But you'll be able to see better and it is swift enough so that we can easily cover the railroad track and also the two dirt roads leading from Hengyang long before darkness falls."

Lieutenant Hamsun was busy in the pilot's seat. Glory-of-the-Republic was busy eating the last peel of the last banana, but when the plane's motor suddenly roared, the little pig scuttled between Tien Pao's feet and flattened himself so tightly against the floor, Tien Pao almost had to pry him loose. He hoisted the little pig to his lap. By that time the plane was already running like a possessed thing across the flat field. Tien Pao held Glory-of-the-Republic up to the window. The little pig got a wild look in his eyes, and shrank back when he saw the speed at which a building, standing trucks, and a mountainside rushed by. He had clenched his teeth down on the banana peel in his first scare. It still hung limp from his mouth, and his scared ears flapped as limply as the banana peel.

Tien Pao's own throat felt too narrow and too full as suddenly the plane bounced up, took another higher bounce, and was a thing of earth no more. Now just as a rooftop was beside them for a second, the next second the tip of a mountain, but already it fell away, and then there were clouds. Earth had dropped away; now the clouds too fell away as the plane broke through them. Tien Pao clenched his teeth and closed his eyes, for a sickness rose, and his stomach seemed to rush up faster than the plane rushed up from the earth.

The interpreter poked Tien Pao, shoved a stick of gum at his clenched mouth, and motioned him to chew hard. Tien Pao dared hardly unclench his teeth for fear his stomach would pop out. He closed his eyes again.

Again the interpreter poked him. Lieutenant Hamsun wanted them to come forward. To Tien Pao's amazement, he could walk over the floor as if the plane were a level, flat, standing thing and not something hurtling through air. Lieutenant Hamsun motioned Tien Pao to the seat beside him. The interpreter stood behind them, leaning over Tien Pao's shoulder, looking and looking. Now Lieutenant Hamsun pointed down.

Tien Pao gasped in surprise. The airfield was gone. Below them was a village—why, this must be the village where the interpreter had gone to buy him shoes and underwear. They were flying low over the village, following the crooked market street. The street was full of people— it must be market day in the village. Down below, a rickshaw boy was shouting and clearing a path for himself and his rickshaw down the packed street. Tien Pao could see him yelling.

A crowd had gathered at the corner of the market street and an alley. They stood around a dentist, who had a man in a chair and was pulling his teeth. The man sat head tilted back, his agonized eyes stared into the sky. Tien Pao looked down into his wide-open mouth. For a moment it was as if he and Tien Pao were staring into each other's eyes. Tien Pao gave no thought to the man, but hugged himself in utter relief. Oh, it would be easy! If he could look into a mouth, even though it was just for a flash, he could surely recognize his father and mother, for that would not even take a flash. He hugged himself again. You saw so clearly, even though it was just for a moment. It would need only a moment, an instant.

Already the village was long gone, and now below them stretched two narrow steel bands, glinting in the rays of the evening sun. The railroad track! But it stretched empty, straight, and deserted before them.

"Lieutenant Hamsun will first fly along the railroad toward Hengyang as far as it is safe to go," the interpreter explained beside Tien Pao's ear. "Then he'll turn and fly in the other direction until there is not a single refugee anywhere along the track."

Tien Pao nodded and leaned forward over the pig in his lap. Glory-of-the-Republic began finishing the banana peel he found clenched between his teeth. The little pig was already used to flying. Tien Pao laughed. He was laughing! The sickness was gone with the laugh. His stomach had slid back to where it had always been and where it belonged. Oh, flying was wonderful and effortless and easy and swift!

Down below, the railroad track lay absolutely empty, and now the plane rose higher, still higher. Then far below them, far in the misty distance, rose a town, row on row of roofs. A silver ribbon coiled crookedly through the town among the straight rows of buildings. But where the river crawled, the blackened buildings had no roofs, yawned empty at the sky. Tien Pao gave a start of recognition. "Hengyang?"

Lieutenant Hamsun nodded.

The plane was banking, turning, and now it flew away from Hengyang. Flew back along the empty railroad track. Again that start of recognition jerked Tien Pao upright—why, there already was the rock on which he had watched yesterday. They were back! It was unbelievable, the speed of an airplane—here they were back and even on a train it had taken a whole night, and on foot—oh, his father and mother could have walked days and nights on end, but the airplane in moments would overtake all their walking.

Tien Pao leaned hard over his pig, sat rigid, eyes riveted on the two steely ribbons of track. He mustn't miss them—it needed but a moment, but he mustn't look away even for a moment, he mustn't miss a single person down there on the track.

Now the plane started down from its height and the track rose and neared. Here people plodded down below, and the plane levelled off and swept over them. Here again were the strung-out stragglers. Again the start of recognition came over Tien Pao. There was the little family—the last ones—the man walking on ahead with long strides. He looked up at the plane. But the old toothless man Tien Pao had seen was nowhere—he must be eating and resting in some village.

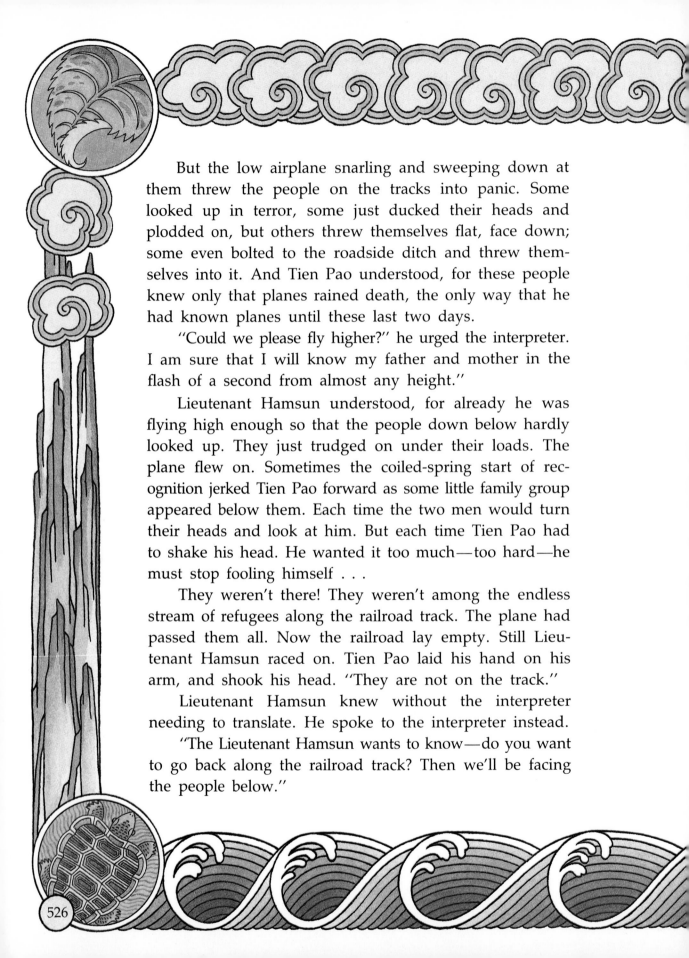

But the low airplane snarling and sweeping down at them threw the people on the tracks into panic. Some looked up in terror, some just ducked their heads and plodded on, but others threw themselves flat, face down; some even bolted to the roadside ditch and threw themselves into it. And Tien Pao understood, for these people knew only that planes rained death, the only way that he had known planes until these last two days.

"Could we please fly higher?" he urged the interpreter. I am sure that I will know my father and mother in the flash of a second from almost any height."

Lieutenant Hamsun understood, for already he was flying high enough so that the people down below hardly looked up. They just trudged on under their loads. The plane flew on. Sometimes the coiled-spring start of recognition jerked Tien Pao forward as some little family group appeared below them. Each time the two men would turn their heads and look at him. But each time Tien Pao had to shake his head. He wanted it too much—too hard—he must stop fooling himself . . .

They weren't there! They weren't among the endless stream of refugees along the railroad track. The plane had passed them all. Now the railroad lay empty. Still Lieutenant Hamsun raced on. Tien Pao laid his hand on his arm, and shook his head. "They are not on the track."

Lieutenant Hamsun knew without the interpreter needing to translate. He spoke to the interpreter instead.

"The Lieutenant Hamsun wants to know—do you want to go back along the railroad track? Then we'll be facing the people below."

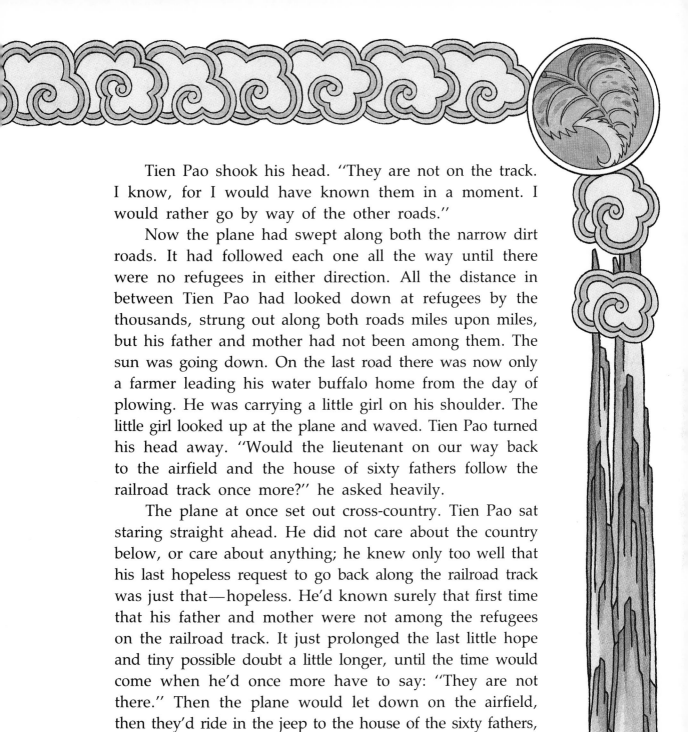

Tien Pao shook his head. "They are not on the track. I know, for I would have known them in a moment. I would rather go by way of the other roads."

Now the plane had swept along both the narrow dirt roads. It had followed each one all the way until there were no refugees in either direction. All the distance in between Tien Pao had looked down at refugees by the thousands, strung out along both roads miles upon miles, but his father and mother had not been among them. The sun was going down. On the last road there was now only a farmer leading his water buffalo home from the day of plowing. He was carrying a little girl on his shoulder. The little girl looked up at the plane and waved. Tien Pao turned his head away. "Would the lieutenant on our way back to the airfield and the house of sixty fathers follow the railroad track once more?" he asked heavily.

The plane at once set out cross-country. Tien Pao sat staring straight ahead. He did not care about the country below, or care about anything; he knew only too well that his last hopeless request to go back along the railroad track was just that—hopeless. He'd known surely that first time that his father and mother were not among the refugees on the railroad track. It just prolonged the last little hope and tiny possible doubt a little longer, until the time would come when he'd once more have to say: "They are not there." Then the plane would let down on the airfield, then they'd ride in the jeep to the house of the sixty fathers, and then there'd be no more hope. There'd just be emptiness and the final hard fact, which was that he was lucky, among all these thousands upon thousands of the homeless,

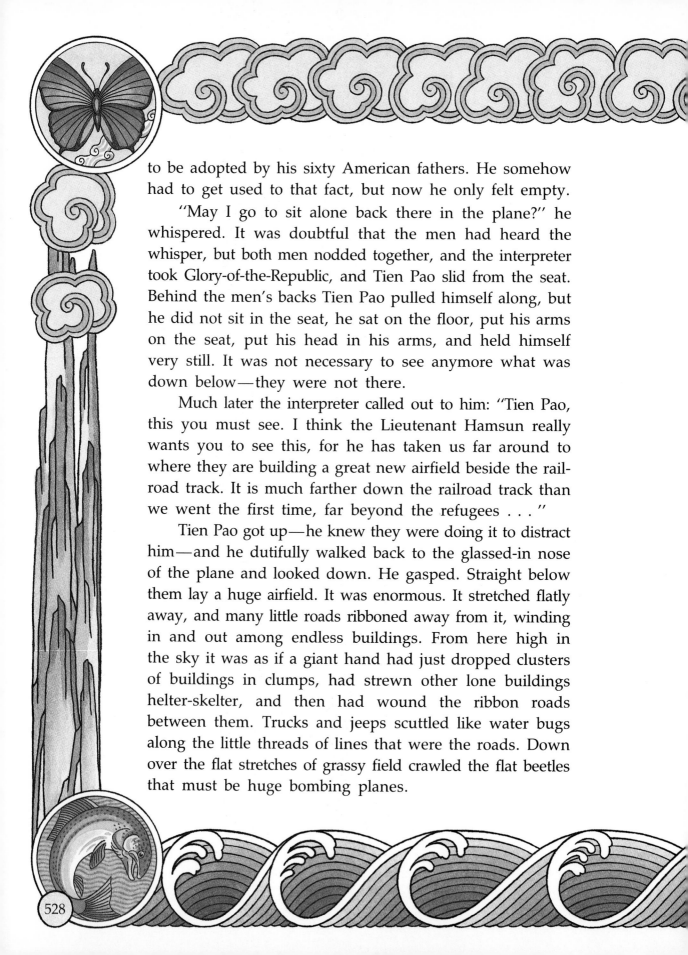

to be adopted by his sixty American fathers. He somehow had to get used to that fact, but now he only felt empty.

"May I go to sit alone back there in the plane?" he whispered. It was doubtful that the men had heard the whisper, but both men nodded together, and the interpreter took Glory-of-the-Republic, and Tien Pao slid from the seat. Behind the men's backs Tien Pao pulled himself along, but he did not sit in the seat, he sat on the floor, put his arms on the seat, put his head in his arms, and held himself very still. It was not necessary to see anymore what was down below—they were not there.

Much later the interpreter called out to him: "Tien Pao, this you must see. I think the Lieutenant Hamsun really wants you to see this, for he has taken us far around to where they are building a great new airfield beside the railroad track. It is much farther down the railroad track than we went the first time, far beyond the refugees . . . "

Tien Pao got up—he knew they were doing it to distract him—and he dutifully walked back to the glassed-in nose of the plane and looked down. He gasped. Straight below them lay a huge airfield. It was enormous. It stretched flatly away, and many little roads ribboned away from it, winding in and out among endless buildings. From here high in the sky it was as if a giant hand had just dropped clusters of buildings in clumps, had strewn other lone buildings helter-skelter, and then had wound the ribbon roads between them. Trucks and jeeps scuttled like water bugs along the little threads of lines that were the roads. Down over the flat stretches of grassy field crawled the flat beetles that must be huge bombing planes.

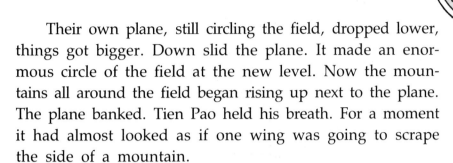

Their own plane, still circling the field, dropped lower, things got bigger. Down slid the plane. It made an enormous circle of the field at the new level. Now the mountains all around the field began rising up next to the plane. The plane banked. Tien Pao held his breath. For a moment it had almost looked as if one wing was going to scrape the side of a mountain.

The last rays of the evening sun lay against the mountainside. Tien Pao could see the shadow of their plane sliding along the mountain. It slid over men working on the mountainside. They did not even look up as the shadow slid over them; they kept swinging big hammers. Some leaped from one pile of rocks to another pile, nimbly—like the little black goats of the mountains.

Tien Pao grabbed Lieutenant Hamsun's arm. "My mother told me of this," he jabbered in excited Chinese. "At the great field for airplanes at Hengyang that I never saw. She said my father and the men were like goats of the mountains. She said my father and the men broke down the mountains with great dynamite blasts, and then they broke up the rocks from the blasts to make crushed stone for runways for the airplanes. And look! It is just what these men are doing. This isn't Hengyang, but, oh, my mother told me of this, and then she promised me that the next day I would go along to see it, too, but the river took me."

The mountain was gone, the plane was cruising along another part of the endless field. It dipped still lower, and now there were women working below—an endless file of women, each one with a carrying pole from which hung

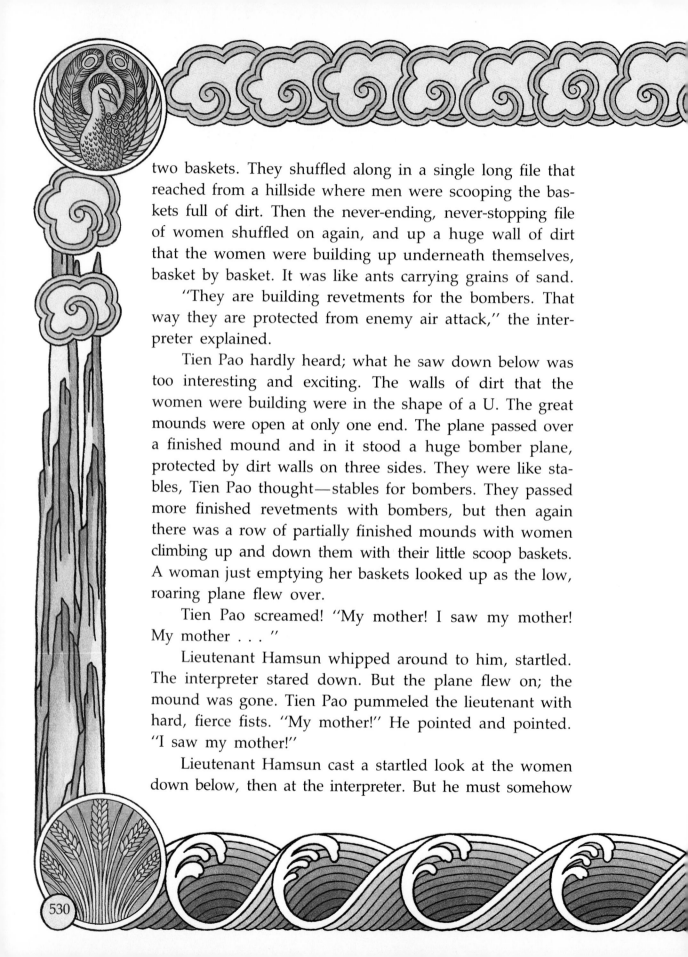

two baskets. They shuffled along in a single long file that reached from a hillside where men were scooping the baskets full of dirt. Then the never-ending, never-stopping file of women shuffled on again, and up a huge wall of dirt that the women were building up underneath themselves, basket by basket. It was like ants carrying grains of sand.

"They are building revetments for the bombers. That way they are protected from enemy air attack," the interpreter explained.

Tien Pao hardly heard; what he saw down below was too interesting and exciting. The walls of dirt that the women were building were in the shape of a U. The great mounds were open at only one end. The plane passed over a finished mound and in it stood a huge bomber plane, protected by dirt walls on three sides. They were like stables, Tien Pao thought—stables for bombers. They passed more finished revetments with bombers, but then again there was a row of partially finished mounds with women climbing up and down them with their little scoop baskets. A woman just emptying her baskets looked up as the low, roaring plane flew over.

Tien Pao screamed! "My mother! I saw my mother! My mother . . . "

Lieutenant Hamsun whipped around to him, startled. The interpreter stared down. But the plane flew on; the mound was gone. Tien Pao pummeled the lieutenant with hard, fierce fists. "My mother!" He pointed and pointed. "I saw my mother!"

Lieutenant Hamsun cast a startled look at the women down below, then at the interpreter. But he must somehow have understood what Tien Pao was screaming and the interpreter forgot to translate. His eyes were searching along the revetments. "No, Tien Pao," Lieutenant Hamsun said. "You couldn't have seen your mother. There's hardly a chance."

It did not matter what the lieutenant said, or in what language, Tien Pao did not hear him. The plane was going over buildings now. Never, never in all this enormous complicated field would they find that one revetment again. Tien Pao tried to keep the revetment in sight. He couldn't. It was gone. He sank down in a sobbing heap on the floor of the plane. He beat the floor with his hands. He had lost his mother. For a moment there she had been, but he had lost her.

"Tien Pao! Tien Pao! We'll go look. We'll go in for a landing, grab a jeep and race out there . . . But you've got to understand—this isn't a wheelbarrow, I can't just let go of the handles and set it down. We're going in now, then we'll grab a jeep and find your revetment."

The lieutenant talked and talked. Tien Pao did not listen. Lieutenant Hamsun spoke impatient words to the interpreter; the interpreter hastily told Tien Pao what Lieutenant Hamsun had said. Tien Pao did not listen; he did not care what they said—he had seen his mother and he had lost her. Never, never in all this huge complicated field would they find that one particular revetment. Darkness would fall. The workers on the field would go home . . .

The plane was down. Then Tien Pao and Lieutenant Hamsun, in spite of his bad leg, were running to a jeep standing beside a building. The interpreter came running behind—only he had remembered Glory-of-the-Republic. They jumped into the jeep without anybody's permission. Lieutenant Hamsun started the motor. A soldier came dashing out of the building, shouted at them, but Lieutenant

Hamsun just shouted something over his shoulder and kept going.

Lieutenant Hamsun looked at Tien Pao and said things.

"The lieutenant says you mustn't build your hopes too high," the interpreter said weakly.

Tien Pao did not hear him, he stared straight ahead. Never in all this horrible long bouncing and weaving among all these half-finished little roads would they find the revetment. Already Tien Pao was utterly confused; he hadn't the slightest idea which way they'd have to go. But then the jeep screeched around a short corner and they were on a wider road. They shot past built-up revetments that had bombers standing in them. They passed some low ones that were just going up. And then . . . and then the jeep roared right up to the high one on which his mother had been! Oh, Lieutenant Hamsun knew; he'd known all the time. He could see things from the air and know just where they were on the ground and how to get to them. Tien Pao could have bawled with relief. He jumped up in the moving jeep, and Lieutenant Hamsun hastily stopped it.

As they were getting out of the jeep, a bomber in one of the great revetments across the road began a thundering roar. The wind from the huge propeller almost knocked Tien Pao against the jeep. It scared Glory-of-the-Republic so, he leaped from the interpreter's arms and bowled away as if blown by the terrific wind. The interpreter chased after him. Tien Pao did not wait, but raced up the mound of dirt past the row of shuffling women going down with their empty baskets. Lieutenant Hamsun came right behind him. And then Tien Pao stood in the exact spot where his mother had stood when she had looked up at the plane! He knew. He knew. Here she had stood and had looked up at him, but of course, she didn't know.

With the lieutenant, Tien Pao examined each stooped woman as she trudged wearily up the mound with her loaded scoop baskets. They had their heads so bowed against the weight and the climb, it was hard to see their faces in the gathering evening dusk until they emptied the baskets. Lieutenant Hamsun stopped a woman who was emptying her basket at his toes. He stuffed some yen into her hand, then with an apologetic grin he pulled out his handkerchief and tied it to her yoke pole. He pointed it out to Tien Pao. "As if you wouldn't know your mother a mile off! But I've got to prove it to you if she isn't here. When at last this woman makes the circle you'll know we've seen them all. And oh, I dread seeing that moment come." Tien Pao did not seem to be aware that the lieutenant was talking; he kept searching the faces. Soon it would be dark, and they'd all go home. "Come soon now, Mother. Come soon." It kept saying itself over and over inside of him, as if it would hurry her on.

There were hundreds and hundreds of women, and always they came on, a few shuffling slow steps behind each other, backs bent, heads stooped, chins on chest. And then at last Lieutenant Hamsun saw the white handkerchief. Slowly it came up the line, slowly it climbed the mound. The lieutenant took Tien Pao's hand and held it tightly in his own.

Now the woman was emptying her basket right before Tien Pao's feet. But Tien Pao would not give up. He turned his back on her, and from the high mound searched the other revetments. The long night shadows were filtering down on the field, but still the work went on. At a sudden sound of singing, Tien Pao glanced down the field. And there came some hundred chanting women, pulling a huge stone roller that was crushing the fine rock into a hard road for a new runway. An overseer marched beside the mass of tugging women leaning in the ropes. He chanted, the women chanted back, and as they chanted they strained forward and tugged the roller ahead.

Tien Pao's hand jerked nervously in the lieutenant's grasp. Then with a loud, wild yell he jerked himself free, plunged down the revetment, plunged unseeing past the interpreter coming up with Glory-of-the-Republic, and tore madly across the crushed stone roadway straight at the roller. He plunged among the mass of tugging, chanting women. The roller stopped. There was an alarmed cackle of voices. The overseer barked loud, fierce words at the excited women, but the roller stood still. Tien Pao flung himself at a woman in the midst of the group. "MY MOTHER!"

The overseer ranted and shrieked. It made no matter. The women stood twisted in the ropes; they huddled around a kneeling, weeping woman who sobbed herself out against her son's chest. The women wept with her, laughed, asked bewildered questions that no one heard and no one answered.

Then Lieutenant Hamsun was there. He yelled something fierce at the ranting Chinese overseer, and behind him the interpreter with the little pig stopped to explain things to the overseer to calm him down. But Lieutenant Hamsun elbowed his way in among the women, waded into the heap of kneeling women. Tien Pao's mother, her eyes streaming, looked blindly up at him. "The father! The father!" she chattered wildly. "He is there on the mountain; he too must know it is Tien Pao."

"I'll go get the jeep," Lieutenant Hamsun shouted. Nobody heard him.

Tien Pao's mother wrenched herself out of the harness rope, grabbed Tien Pao's hand, and together they broke out of the heap of excited, chattering women. Tien Pao, not knowing what he was doing, pulled away from her, dashed to the interpreter, grabbed the little pig, and tore back to his mother. Together, hand in hand, they started running toward the distant, darkening mountain.

From far down the runway Lieutenant Hamsun shouted after them: "The jeep, the jeep! What's the jeep for? You can't run all that way . . . "

They didn't hear him, and Lieutenant Hamsun turned and went on a limping run for the jeep. He forgot about the interpreter waiting near the roller, he forgot about roads and runways, he set out after Tien Pao and his mother across the rough field. He caught up with them. He almost had to lift Tien Pao's mother bodily into the jeep; she was too bewildered in her happy, delirious joy to be able to comprehend anything. The lieutenant set out for the mountain. He couldn't reach it. The strewn jagged rocks and enormous boulders hurled below the mountainside by dynamite blasts forced him to stop far from the foot of the dug-away mountain. But Tien Pao's mother jumped up in the jeep, and in the fierce strength of her joy she lifted Tien Pao high and screamed a terrible scream at the mountain. "It is Tien Pao! It is Tien Pao!"

Her cry rang up the mountainside. Men stopped and looked down, and one man halfway up the rocky hill let his huge sledge hammer fall from his hand. He just stood. But then he bellowed it out: "It is Tien Pao!"

He came plunging down. He came straight down, straight toward the jeep. He used no paths. But he could not run that fast, not down a mountain. He fell. He struggled up again, and fell. He leaped up. All around him the men were shouting at him, running toward him. He half turned to them as he lunged on. "It is Tien Pao," he bellowed, and that answered all and explained all, and he came on in terrible plunging strides.

Tien Pao's mother sank down on her seat, her strength suddenly all gone. Her whole body trembled, she clung fiercely to Tien Pao, and she cried. Softly she cried, and Tien Pao cried with her as they watched his plunging father. And in his happiness he had to tell Lieutenant Hamsun, who could not understand. "Oh, it was my mother, and I knew it. She had been on the revetment, but they called the younger women down to pull the roller to finish the job before dark. Oh, I knew it, I knew it. And my little sister is with neighbors in a little village near this airfield." Suddenly he remembered his little pig. He grabbed up Glory-of-the-Republic; he hugged him.

And as Tien Pao finished talking, his mother looked and looked her gratitude at the lieutenant. "It is Tien Pao," she softly told the lieutenant as if it were a wholly new and unbelievable thing. "It is Tien Pao." And in her gratitude this timid, shy Chinese woman leaned forward and laid her hand on the lieutenant's arm and talked to him in earnest Chinese, and the tears rolled unheeded down her cheeks.

"It is Tien Pao," she said again. "And tomorrow and tomorrow and tomorrow—and all the days to come—there will still be my little son. And the house won't be too empty and the anxious heart too full . . . Ah, tomorrow, and tomorrow, and then will come a day when there will be no more shooting, and no more running from the shooting, and no war. There will come a day when the little family of Tien will go back to their little village, and live in peace. Ah, tomorrow and tomorrow. Ah, ah, ah."

She had no more words. She choked on them and her tears streamed. And there came his father, and his mother was clutching him fiercely again. There sat the lieutenant half turned, and he did not understand what his mother had said. Ah, but he did understand. He understood! The heart understands without words.

Think About It

1. Why did Lieutenant Hamsun go out of his way to help Tien Pao?
2. How does the way Tien Pao felt about his 60 American fathers compare to the way he felt about his parents and sister? Which details from the story support your answer?
3. Tien Pao's reunion with his family was an emotional climax to the story. Describe the feelings of Tien Pao, his parents, Lieutenant Hamsun, and your own feelings at that moment.
4. What does Glory-of-the-Republic add to the story?
5. How are the selections in FAMILY TIES alike? In what ways are they different?

Create and Share   Think about a time when you were lost or separated from your family. If you have never had this experience, imagine how it would feel. Write a short story about someone who is lost, and how that person searches for his or her family before they are finally reunited. Put lots of action in your story to make it exciting.

Explore   This story was taken from *The House of Sixty Fathers*. You may want to read this book or others by the author Meindert DeJong, such as *Hurry Home Candy*, *Shadrach*, or *The Wheel on the School*. For other books about family relationships, see FAMILY LIFE and FAMILY LIFE—FICTION.

I must go down to the seas again, to the
lonely sea and sky . . .

from SEA FEVER
by John Masefield

Up From the Sea

The Singing Float

by Monica Hughes

*T*he singing woke Melissa, high, clear notes like those of a violin, at the very edge of hearing. She sat up in bed. The cabin was silent, the only light a strip of pure white between the not-quite-closed curtains across the window.

She slipped out of bed and padded to the window, her toes curling away from the chill of the floor. She pushed the drape aside and looked out. Beyond the fringe of pines the land dropped abruptly to the beach, and she could see, framed by the dark strokes of the trees, a line of silver stretching clear to the horizon.

It rippled like a bolt of silk flung down from the sky toward her feet. She stood, frozen in its magic, until the moon sailed out from behind an obscuring pine and the silken path became only its reflection on the still surface of the sea. She shivered, scampered back to bed, and lay in a ball, warming her feet with her hands, until she fell asleep.

When Melissa woke, the sun was shining in an ordinary sort of way. The tide was out and the memory of the singing and of the white moon's path was like a dream. She pulled on shorts and a T-shirt, made her bed neatly, and dusted her collection of shells with a tissue. That did not take long. She had collected only five, but each of them was perfect, without a flaw or a chip.

When everything was in order she ran into the living room, which was really living and dining room and kitchen all in one, with a fireplace where you could roast marshmallows and a big window overlooking the Pacific.

"Good morning, Half Pint."

"Morning, Daddy." She gave him a kiss and got her special hug in return. "Good morning, Mum. What's for breakfast?"

"Sausages and scrambled eggs. If you and Dad do the dishes."

"Worth it. I'm starving." She stood by the stove and carried the plates to the table as Mum filled them.

"Full moon last night. Extra high tide. Good pickings on the shore today, Lissa."

"Oh, I do hope so. Do you realize that we've only got two more days? Only *two*. I can't believe it."

"Me neither."

When breakfast was eaten and the dishes put away, Melissa picked her way carefully down the path to the beach. There were steps roughly carved between tree roots, and at the bottom was a tangle of weather-whitened timbers, painful to bare feet. She crossed it with care and then did what she did every morning: raced as fast as she could across the sand to the very edge of the sea.

Only then, standing with her toes dug into the wet sand, the sea foaming at her insteps, did she turn and look back along the beach. This was the magic moment. The moment of choice. Where shall I look today? Where is the best shell hiding? Above all, *will* there at last be a glass float?

Glass floats were as rare as hens' teeth, Daddy said, now that the Japanese fisherfolk had started using plastic floats of gaudy green and pink to hold up their gill nets and mark their traps, instead of the smoky iridescent globes of blown glass the size of a large grapefruit.

"Only two more days," she said as she stood with the water dragging at her toes. "Only *two* more days." She looked at the rocky headland to the north and along the white beach that curved around to the southern headland.

"Where, oh where, do I begin today?"

Into her mind came the high, clear note she had heard in the night. Slowly she followed the sound, walking over strands of shining brown kelp and pale half-buried logs and tree roots smoothed by the sea. She walked without thought toward a tangle of seaweed at the uppermost limit of last night's tide.

There, among fat cords and shiny ribbons and air bladders, was the faint glint of a rainbow. She dropped to her knees and gently loosened the strands one by one.

There it was, perfect, like a huge frozen soap bubble. She lifted it out and cradled it in the palms of her hands. The singing in her head had stopped, and the whole morning was still.

"You beauty, oh you beauty," she whispered. For a brief second it seemed that something flickered in the depths of the glass globe. Then the sun dazzled on its curve and she blinked. When she looked again she could see nothing inside.

She got to her feet and began to walk slowly back toward their cabin, holding the float carefully in both hands.

"What have you got?" Mum turned as the screen door banged.

"Just look!"

"Oh, what a beauty."

"Clever girl."

Was I? she wondered. It had been more like being led than finding. She wadded some tissues in the center of the table and set the float down upon them. "Isn't it the most perfect thing in the whole world? I don't care if we have to go home in two days. I wouldn't care if we had to go tomorrow. Right now, even."

"Well, I would." Mum laughed. "I'm counting on two more days' fun with you and Dad. What's the plan, Phil, now Melissa has done her beachcombing?"

"I thought we might drive up to Tofino and take the boat out to look at the seals. Maybe even get a peek at a whale."

"Great idea. I've already packed lunch. Lissa, get your shoes and socks on. And better take a jacket. It might be cool on the water."

"But . . . " Melissa looked longingly at her float. Like a rainbow, she thought. Of my very own.

"Dear girl, you can't sit in here all day. The sun's shining. Go get your shoes, quick!"

"But . . . " she said as she went.

"*And* your jacket. Phil, have you got the thermos? And I've got the basket. Oh, Lissa, *do* wake up!"

Melissa followed them reluctantly out of the cabin. In the shadowy living room the globe glowed.

"Oh, I forgot to lock the door!" she cried out, halfway to Tofino. "Dad, we have to go back. My float . . . "

"It won't walk away. And I did check the door. My goodness, Lissa, I think you must be bewitched."

Perhaps I am, she thought, and kneeled on the backseat of the car, watching the road unwind between the pines, taking them farther and farther away from the cabin.

At any other time the boat ride to the seal rocks and beyond, almost out to the salmon fishing grounds, would have been the high point of the holidays. Indeed, part of Melissa enjoyed every moment. But the other part of her kept looking back to the low line of the shore and thinking: There is the bay. And there must be our cabin, and in it, on the table . . .

She gripped the aft railing so tightly that her knuckles went white. For one crazy minute she'd actually wanted to dive into the water and swim ashore, *she* who could barely make it across the school pool.

She jumped when Mum touched her shoulder.

"Melissa, Mrs. White would like to talk to you. She owns a gift shop in town. She's very interested in your float."

Melissa turned, her face lighting up. "It's so perfect," she said. "About *this* big. And like a rainbow."

"Will you sell it to me?" Mrs. White said abruptly.

"Huh?"

"I'll give you . . . ten dollars."

Melissa shook her head.

"You can buy a lot of candy with ten dollars."

"Candy's bad for your teeth."

"Books then. Whatever." The woman smiled. Melissa didn't like her smile. It wasn't quite real. She shook her head again.

"Twenty dollars. My last word. That's a lot of money for a young girl."

Melissa looked at Mum, but for once she was no help at all. "It's your find, love. Your decision." She walked away and left the two of them together.

"N-no," Melissa stammered. "Thank you."

The smile became fixed. "Thirty dollars," the woman snapped. "Oh, come on now. If it's as good as you say, I'll make it thirty-five. Think what you could do with thirty-five dollars!"

Melissa went on shaking her head dumbly.

"They're fragile things, these floats. You might not even get it home in one piece. Suppose you drop it? What have you got then? Nothing. Better take my offer."

Melissa was no longer listening. The boat had turned for shore, and she could hear the singing once again, high, sweet, piercing.

On the drive home Mum suddenly said, "That woman, what's-her-name, Mrs. White, said you were rude to her, Melissa."

"Was I?" said Melissa vaguely. "I didn't think I was."

As soon as Dad had parked she ran along the path. "Oh, hurry, where's the key?"

"My goodness, but you're jumpy." Mum unlocked the door with maddening slowness.

Melissa rushed into the living room. "It's still there."

"Of course it is, Silly Billy. Tell me, how much *did* that woman offer you for the float?"

"Thirty-five dollars." Melissa dropped into a chair and, elbows on the table, chin on hands, stared into the iridescent glass. She didn't notice the expression on her parents' faces.

"Thirty-five dollars!"

Dad whistled. "Which I suppose means she could sell it for twice that. That's an expensive bauble, Melissa. You'd better take care of it!"

They all stared at the float. Then . . . "I almost thought—but that's ridiculous." Mum shook her head as if to clear it. "Look, let's have a proper bake-out on the beach. That salmon we bought in Tofino. Will you get a fire started, Phil? I'll make a salad. Melissa, that thing's making me nervous. Will you please put it safely in your room?"

Melissa lifted the float from its bed of tissues and gasped.

"Hey, careful! You nearly dropped it then. Want me to look after it for you?"

"No, thanks, Dad. It's fine." Melissa walked quickly out of the room. The glass float was suddenly as hot as a baked potato. She put it safely on her dressing table and rubbed her hands. The palms were pink and puffy. She stared at the float. Deep inside it something glittered and moved. She ran out of the room, her heart thumping, and went to help Mum dry the lettuce.

Sitting with her back against a log, Melissa licked the last of the salmon off her fingers and stared vaguely out to sea. The sun had set, and the dark was creeping up the beach with the incoming tide. Far out past their headland she could see the rhythmic flash–flash of a lighthouse. The wind rose and she shivered suddenly.

"Time to go in. Hot chocolate by the fire and then bed."

"Our last day tomorrow. I wish we could come back here for ever and ever."

"I second that." Dad kissed the top of her head. He began to pick up the remains of their meal, and Mum shook out the rug. Melissa followed them up to the cabin, suddenly reluctant to face whatever it was that moved within the float.

Mum lit the fire, and Dad stirred chocolate on the stove. Beyond the uncurtained window the blackness was broken only by the comforting lighthouse signal. Melissa drank her chocolate in very small sips. It was almost cold by the time she got to the bottom.

"Enough hanging around," Mum said at last. "Teeth and bed. Off you go." And she had to kiss them good night and go into her room.

She walked over to the dressing table and touched the float with a fingertip. It was as cool as . . . as cool as glass. In the semidarkness it was just a smoky glass globe, so fragile she could crash it just like *that*. She found she was holding it in the palm of her hand, her fingers closed tightly about it. She hadn't even remembered deciding to pick it up. She put it down with a gasp, tore into her pajamas, and jumped into bed.

She fell asleep and into a muddled dream in which she was a princess, imprisoned by a magic spell in a tiny spherical house. Each day she grew weaker and weaker. One day she would be too weak to shine anymore and would cease to be . . .

The singing woke her and she sat up, shivering, still in the sadness of her dream. From the dressing table came a faint rosy glow. She could see its reflection in the mirror. Surely she wouldn't have imagined *that*?

"What is it?" she whispered desperately. "What do you *want*?"

Freedom . . . The word slid into her mind, and it was the right word, the word behind the singing and the dream.

"How?"

You know how. In her mind was the picture of her hand holding the float, her fingers tight about it, crushing.

"Break it? I couldn't. Not possibly." She buried her head in the pillow and pulled the covers over her ears to muffle the sound of singing. Or was it weeping?

Next morning, after making her bed and dusting her shells—she didn't feel up to touching the float—Melissa had breakfast and ran down the beach until the sea seethed around her bare toes and the tide tugged at her ankles. Then she turned to look along the shore. The very last day. Where shall I go? What shall I find?

But the magic was quite gone. Suddenly it didn't matter whether she walked south or north. It wasn't important to find another perfect shell. Nothing mattered.

In the end she walked south along the creamy edge of the sea, scuffing the wet sand with her toes, her hands in her pockets. She trudged all the way to the southern headland, which was covered with barnacles and mussels and great red and purple starfish. Then she turned and trudged slowly back.

All the colors seemed to have drained out of the sea and the sand. Melissa shivered and looked up at the sky. The sun was shining steadily, and there wasn't a cloud in sight. Then the singing began again, very faintly, as if whoever it was had moved farther away. Or was, perhaps, becoming weaker.

She sat on a log with her head in her hands. "What am I to do? Oh, I wish I'd sold it to that horrid woman. Then I'd have the thirty-five dollars and none of this worry." But she knew, as soon as she said it, that her wish wasn't true. Mrs. White wasn't the kind of person to pay attention to the singing, even if she could hear it. And she would *never* let the float go.

"Neither can I," thought Melissa desperately.

Then she heard Dad calling her and she had to run along the beach with a happy smile on her face and be very excited about a trip down the coast to Ucluelet.

They had a splendid dinner out, to celebrate the last night of the holidays, and for whole minutes at a time Melissa was able to forget. But eventually they drove up the dark, winding road to the cabin, and Melissa had to open her bedroom door and go in.

There was no color at all in the globe tonight, and the singing was fainter than the sound of the sea. "If I just hang on," she told herself, "it'll stop altogether and then I'll just have a beautiful float."

No you won't, a small voice inside said coldly. It'll be a coffin. For something. For someone.

She sighed heavily, got into her pajamas, and brushed her teeth and kissed Mum and Dad good night. Then she sat up in bed with the pillow at her back and her arms tightly around her knees, waiting. She knew exactly what had to be done.

The quiet voices of Mum and Dad stopped at last. A long time later a silveriness at her window told Melissa that the moon must be high over the sea. She got out of bed and put on her slippers. Then she picked up the float and quietly opened the front door.

The path to the beach was striped with moonshine and shadow. She held the float in both hands until she was safely down on the sand. The tide had reached the high mark. There was no wind, and the water was almost still, with just a faint swell like the breathing of a giant. The silken path of the moon lay from the horizon almost to her feet.

It was the right time and the right place. She held the float with a tissue around it to protect her hand. Then she shut her eyes and squeezed.

It took much more pressure than she had expected. I can't, she thought. I can't. Then, quite suddenly, it collapsed. She had a flash of intense happiness and opened her eyes in time to see something dart into the moon's white path.

For an instant she saw clearly a beautiful face, small and pale as carved ivory. The lips smiled and the dark eyes glowed with joy. "Wait!" Melissa called, and her voice

was shockingly loud in the stillness of the turning of the tide. "Tell me who you are."

The figure paused on its upward flight, and the gossamer robes curved about it in a prism flash of rainbow colors. You are a princess, Melissa found herself thinking, imprisoned by a Japanese ogre. How many years ago? She imagined her bobbing helplessly across the ocean, singing her sad song, until the day when at last wind and tide brought her to this beach and drew Melissa to her.

I set her free. Melissa drew a deep breath and savored the happiness that tingled through her whole body, making her feel more alive than she had ever felt before, so that she could understand the voice of the sea and the breeze, and smell each separate scent of salt and iodine, seaweed and pine tree, moonlight and night.

Then a small cloud slid for a moment across the moon. At once the white path was gone and with it the fairy princess. Melissa was alone, shivering and sad, with her hands full of shards of rainbow-shot glass. She wrapped the pieces carefully in the tissue and walked slowly back to the cabin and put them in the wastebasket in her room. She got into bed and turned her back on the moonlit stripe that lay between the not-quite-shut curtains.

Melissa woke to the bustle of packing. Breakfast was cereal and rolls, so as to dirty no more dishes than necessary.

" . . . and give me your glass float, Lissa, and I'll pack it among all our soiled clothes. It'll be as safe as houses there."

Melissa tried to swallow a piece of roll that had turned into a lump of concrete as all the misery of the night before came flooding back. "It's broken. I broke it."

"Oh, Lissa . . . " Mum began, then stopped. "Never mind, love. Bring me your other treasures, and I'll see they get home safely."

It began to rain as they started out. By the time they had reached the main road, the wipers were going full speed. Melissa sat in the back surrounded by bags and leaned her forehead against the seat in front. She tried to recapture that tiny moment of joy, but she couldn't. All that was left was this black heaviness.

I don't have my float, and I'll never find another. I don't even have the thirty-five dollars. I've got nothing.

She shut her eyes and tried to remember the rainbow colors that appeared and vanished as you turned the float in the light. Maybe she should have saved the pieces. Maybe in them would have been a tiny memory . . .

"Oh, look, Melissa!" Mum suddenly cried, "Did you ever see anything so beautiful!"

She looked up. The rain clouds had been torn apart and the sun had appeared in the gap. Directly ahead of them, arching from the headland to the sea, was a perfect double rainbow.

Think About It

1. What makes this story a fantasy?
2. What first made you feel there was something mysterious about the float?
3. What keeps Melissa from selling the float?
4. What was the relationship of the glass float to the rainbow?
5. Do you think Melissa ever tells her parents about the princess? Why or why not?

Create and Share

You are the voice inside the float. What powerful message will you send to Melissa? Write a poem or song to beg for your freedom. Tell what you will do when you escape and explain what Melissa will gain by freeing you.

Explore

If you like this fantasy, you may want to read others in the collection it came from, *Dragons and Dreams*, edited by Jane Yolen. Or you may want to find another fantasy to stir your imagination. Look in the card catalog under FANTASY, GHOST STORIES, and SUPERNATURAL—FICTION.

Greyling

a folktale from the Shetland Islands
by Jane Yolen

Once upon a time when wishes were aplenty, a fisherman and his wife lived by the side of the sea. All that they ate came out of the sea. Their hut was covered with the finest mosses that kept them cool in the summer and warm in the winter. And there was nothing they needed or wanted except a child.

Each morning, when the moon touched down behind the water and the sun rose up behind the plains, the wife would say to the fisherman, "You have your boat and your nets and your lines. But I have no baby to hold in my arms." And again, in the evening, it was the same. She would weep and wail and rock the cradle that stood by the hearth. But year in and year out the cradle stayed empty.

Now the fisherman was also sad that they had no child. But he kept his sorrow to himself so that his wife would not know his grief and thus double her own. Indeed, he would leave the hut each morning with a breath of song and return each night with a whistle on his lips. His nets were full but his heart was empty, yet he never told his wife.

One sunny day, when the beach was a tan thread spun between sea and plain, the fisherman as usual went down to his boat. But this day he found a small grey seal stranded on the sand bar, crying for its own.

The fisherman looked up the beach and down. He looked in front of him and behind. And he looked to the town on the great grey cliffs that sheared off into the sea. But there were no other seals in sight.

So he shrugged his shoulders and took off his shirt. Then he dipped it into the water and wrapped the seal pup carefully in its folds.

"You have no father and you have no mother," he said. "And I have no child. So you shall come home with me." And the fisherman did no fishing that day but brought the seal pup, wrapped in his shirt, straight home to his wife.

When she saw him coming home early with no shirt on, the fisherman's wife ran out of the hut, fear riding in her heart. Then she looked wonderingly at the bundle which he held in his arms.

"It is nothing," he said, "but a seal pup I found stranded in the shallows and longing for its own. I thought we could give it love and care until it is old enough to seek its kin."

The fisherman's wife nodded and took the bundle. Then she uncovered the wrapping and gave a loud cry. "Nothing!" she said. "You call this nothing?"

The fisherman looked. Instead of a seal lying in the folds, there was a strange child with great grey eyes and silvery grey hair, smiling up at him.

The fisherman wrung his hands. "It is a selchie," he cried. "I have heard of them. They are men upon the land and seals in the sea. I thought it was but a tale."

"Then he shall remain a man upon the land," said the fisherman's wife, clasping the child in her arms, "for I shall never let him return to the sea."

"Never," agreed the fisherman, for he knew how his wife had wanted a child. And in his secret heart, he wanted one, too. Yet he felt, somehow, it was wrong.

"We shall call him Greyling," said the fisherman's wife, "for his eyes and hair are the color of a storm-coming sky. Greyling, though he has brought sunlight into our home."

And though they still lived by the side of the water in a hut covered with mosses that kept them warm in the winter and cool in the summer, the boy Greyling was never allowed in the sea.

He grew from a child to a lad. He grew from a lad to a young man. He gathered driftwood for his mother's hearth and searched the tide pools for shells for her mantel. He mended his father's nets and tended his father's boat. But though he often stood by the shore or high in the town on the great grey cliffs, looking and longing and grieving his heart for what he did not really know, he never went into the sea.

Then one wind-wailing morning, just fifteen years from the day that Greyling had been found, a great storm blew up suddenly in the North. It was such a storm as had never been seen before; the sky turned nearly black and even the fish had trouble swimming. The wind pushed huge waves onto the shore. The waters gobbled up the little hut on the beach. And Greyling and the fisherman's wife were forced to flee to the town high on the great grey cliffs. There they looked down at the roiling, boiling sea. Far from shore they spied the fisherman's boat, its sails flapping like the wings of a wounded gull. And clinging to the broken mast was the fisherman himself, sinking deeper with every wave.

The fisherman's wife gave a terrible cry. "Will no one save him?" she called to the people of the town who had

gathered on the edge of the cliff. "Will no one save my
own dear husband who is all of life to me?"

But the townsmen looked away. There was no man
there who dared risk his life in that sea, even to save a
drowning soul.

"Will no one at all save him?" she cried out again.

"Let the boy go," said one old man, pointing at
Greyling with his stick. "He looks strong enough."

But the fisherman's wife clasped Greyling in her arms
and held his ears with her hands. She did not want him
to go into the sea. She was afraid he would never return.

"Will no one save my own dear heart?" cried the fisherman's wife for a third and last time.

But shaking their heads, the people of the town edged to their houses and shut their doors and locked their windows and set their backs to the ocean and their faces to the fires that glowed in every hearth.

"I will save him, Mother," cried Greyling, "or die as I try."

And before she could tell him no, he broke from her grasp and dived from the top of the great cliffs, down, down, down into the tumbling sea.

"He will surely sink," whispered the women as they ran from their warm fires to watch.

"He will certainly drown," called the men as they took down their spyglasses from the shelves.

They gathered on the cliffs and watched the boy dive down into the sea.

As Greyling disappeared beneath the waves, little fingers of foam tore at his clothes. They snatched his shirt and his pants and his shoes and sent them bubbling away to the shore. And as Greyling went deeper beneath the waves, even his skin seemed to slough off till he swam, free at last, in the sleek grey coat of a great grey seal.

The selchie had returned to the sea.

But the people of the town did not see this. All they saw was the diving boy disappearing under the waves and then, farther out, a large seal swimming toward the boat that wallowed in the sea. The sleek grey seal, with no effort at all, eased the fisherman to the shore though the waves were wild and bright with foam. And then, with a final salute, it turned its back on the land and headed joyously out to sea.

The fisherman's wife hurried down to the sand. And behind her followed the people of the town. They searched up the beach and down, but they did not find the boy.

"A brave son," said the men when they found his shirt, for they thought he was certainly drowned.

"A very brave son," said the women when they found his shoes, for they thought him lost for sure.

"Has he really gone?" asked the fisherman's wife of her husband when at last they were alone.

"Yes, quite gone," the fisherman said to her. "Gone where his heart calls, gone to the great wide sea. And though my heart grieves at his leaving, it tells me this way is best."

The fisherman's wife sighed. And then she cried. But at last she agreed that, perhaps, it was best. "For he is both man and seal," she said. "And though we cared for him for a while, now he must care for himself." And she never cried again.

So once more they lived alone by the side of the sea in a new little hut which was covered with mosses to keep them warm in the winter and cool in the summer.

Yet, once a year, a great grey seal is seen at night near the fisherman's home. And the people in town talk of it, and wonder. But seals do come to the shore and men do go to the sea; and so the townfolk do not dwell upon it very long.

But it is no ordinary seal. It is Greyling himself come home—come to tell his parents tales of the lands that lie far beyond the waters, and to sing them songs of the wonders that lie far beneath the sea.

All the Names of Baby Hag

by Patricia MacLachlan

Listen. Do you hear it? That soft wet sound when the waves come in and slide back again? It is the whisper of the sea hags, soft and sly. An every-so-often whisper as they come up from the sea and disguise themselves—a rest from the tiresome peace under the water, the boring rise and fall, in and out of the tides. You have seen the hags, yes you have, don't shake your head. The leather-faced, chicken-legged women with gold chains yelling, "Stop throwing sand, Dwight. This very minute. I meeean it!" Sea hags. The old man with the bucket belly who sleeps with his face to the sun, mouth open, awakening suddenly with a drool. A sea hag. The silent child who visits your beach blanket and eats up your french fries before you notice. Sea hag.

Baby Sea Hag was born in the stillness of a slack tide. She was round and the pale-green color of a sea urchin, with delicate diaphanous fins and tidy webbed feet.

"Lovely hag," Mother Hag murmured. "Like the others."

Father Hag nodded, his long whiskers trailing in the sea. Baby Hag reached out to touch one.

"I wonder what she will choose for her name," mused Father Hag.

"She will find the special name, all her own, just for her," said Mother Hag. "All sea hags do, after all. She will, too."

Baby Hag's brothers and sisters, dozens of them, came from the eel grasses and tidal pools and marshes to see her. They filled the water with breath bubbles that brushed her nose and made her sneeze. Like Baby Hag they were all perfect and pale-green-round, with fins and webbed feet. But Baby Hag was different. She smiled from the moment

she was born, for one thing. And she laughed out loud before a full day had passed, unusual for hags. They are generally purposeful and serious-minded creatures. Not frivolous. Certainly not cheerful on a daily basis.

"All the time she's happy!" exclaimed Baby Hag's sister, Snow White Hag. She had found her name when she was disguised as a child, sitting on the edge of a blanket with other children. She had listened to tales read from a book, eating soft white-bread sandwiches with the crusts cut off, seven sweet pickles, and the last lemon sour ball. She had loved that story of human creatures and the sound of the two words that would become her name. The two words that meant the same. Snow. White.

"I thought she was your sister," one boy complained to the other after she'd gone.

"*Mine!* Isn't she *yours?* She ate all the pickles!"

Rex, the oldest of the hag children, swam in circles while Baby Hag trailed behind. "Special she may be," he said, "but she will have to find her own name the way we all did. Up on the land." Rex had spent one lively morning with a large loping black Labrador whose tag read: *Rex is ours. Send him home. We love him.* Rex had loved the dog's sweet, sloppy nature. He had taken him home. And at the end of the day slipped back to the sea with his name.

"Land is far better than the sea for names," said Beach Pea shyly. "Nothing is nameless on land. Children, build-ings—humans often name their houses, do you believe it?— and their boats!" Often, when the blooms came, Beach Pea went up to the shore, disguised as a toad or a child, a sand flea or a grandmother, to peer at the pink-lavender bloom of the beach pea. "Even cars they name," she added. "Chevrolet. Chev-ro-lay. Lovely, don't you think, Chevrolet?"

Baby Hag smiled.

"She likes it!" cried Beach Pea.

"She does," said Mother Hag, matter-of-factly. "She likes Mirabelle, Clothilde, and Veronica, too. And Baby Bernice."

"All of them?" asked Father Hag, amazed.

"All of them."

"What about Olivia?" suggested Beach Pea. "I met an Olivia once when I was a hungry human standing in line for a hamburger."

"Ah, hamburger," said Father Hag softly, remembering his time ashore. He had taken the form of a parking attendant. "I once ate seven. Odd things, hamburgers."

"Mirabelle?"

"Clothilde?"

"Veronica?"

Baby Hag smiled at the names.

"Olivia?"

"Hamburger?" Father Hag's suggestion.

Baby Hag smiled.

"Pippit? A lively and restless name."

"Grandma Meeker? She fished at night by lantern light."

"Elizabeth Margaret Bernadette Mary O'Shaughnessy? She was very bad mannered. She licked all the sandwiches and had to sit the afternoon on a towel."

Still Baby Hag smiled.

"She likes all the names," said Mother Hag. "Strange. Or worse, unnatural."

Father Hag touched Baby Hag very lightly with a fin. "She likes one name as well as another, it seems," he said.

And she did. So the other young hags, the dozens of brothers and sisters, all of them generally purposeful and

567

serious-minded hags, went back to their generally purposeful and serious-minded lives. And Baby Hag did not have a name. She didn't have one name, that is. She answered to any and all names. Names that the sea hags had heard on land, crouched in the dune grass, listening; lying on the beach blankets, pretending sleep; standing in food lines with handfuls of human food with the strange names. *Onion ring. Chili dog. Submarine. Shake.*

Each day Mother Hag tried out new names.

"Dilly?"

"What?"

"Trixie?"

"Here I am."

"Cousin Coot!"

"Coming!"

"This is impossible," said Mother Hag, crossly. "There is no living hag without a name. Never in hag history has there been a nameless hag!"

"There is now," said Father Hag very softly.

"It cannot go on," said Mother Hag. "It will not go on!"

But it did. The tides rose and fell with magical monotony, and Baby Hag rose and fell, slept and wakened with them. She was left with the lovely light of the sea at dawn, and the dark of it at night. With no names. With *all* names. *Melissa, Sandcastle, Nanny, Umbrella, Myna, Sunrise . . .*

One season led to another—autumn to winter with dark seas and wind, and the rumble of rocks beneath the waves. *Gloria, Alice-Iris, Zoe, Aunt Zell, Sunset . . .*

Not many creatures roamed the land when it was winter; only someone walking now and then, a dog or two or three, and the raccoons at nighttime. Once there was a kite flyer, high in the dunes, and Snow White Hag went up to ask her name. One moment there was nothing but sea and rocks and a great wave. The next moment there was a small, pale child bundled up against the cold.

"My name? Doodoo Schwartz the Third," the kite flyer told Snow White Hag without looking. "*Doo* Schwartz the Third for short." Above, the kite whirled and dipped and fluttered in the winter wind. When she looked again to see who'd asked for her name there was no child. *No child at all.*

"Doodoo Schwartz is nice," Baby Hag told Snow White Hag. "Third is nice, too." She swam in circles, upside down, so that the late sunlight warmed her pale underbelly. "All nice."

"She *is* different, Baby Hag is," said one hag to another. "Liking all those names, not one her own . . . and all that cheer!"

"She will change," said Mother Hag, worried.

"Maybe," said Father Hag. He did not look worried, but he was. Sea hags, purposeful and serious minded, always worried.

Winter turned to spring and spring to summer, with the great warm sea surrounding Baby Hag. Father Hag watched Baby Hag closely. He swam with the currents, Baby Hag following always, and went about his life thinking about names. He thought very hard, as if one name—just one name of all the names—might float like a bubble into Baby Hag's mind. Or heart. *Chloe, Afton, Wild Annie . . .*

Rex went up to land as a beagle, his face to the ground, sniffing out names like a dog nosing for food. Beach Pea went, too, though no one knew what form she took. She visited a garden.

"How about Runner Bean?" she suggested. "Or Rosa Ragosa—wild blooms by the sea. Or . . . " She swam close to whisper to Baby Hag, "Eggplant! Luminous during the full moon, and firm bodied."

Baby Hag liked Luminous.

Rex returned breathless after two days. He had raced the beaches and sea roads with two dogs, in and out of the wild honeysuckle, up and down the dunes, back and forth through steaming compost heaps; sending up flocks of quail, chasing cats whose hair stood in ridges along their backs. At dusk chewing on old bones.

Rex sighed and treaded water wearily.

"A waste of time," he announced. "One was a tiresome terrier whose name you wouldn't want. The small one was too low to the ground and had a flat forehead. Lady? Scruffy?"

Baby Hag shook her head.

Snow White Hag sighed.

"You must have a name," she said sadly. "A name that means you."

"*My* name means me," said Beach Pea thoughtfully. "Sometimes, just before sleep, I think about the color of the wild blooms against the sand. And the soft feel of them."

"I think about Rex on land even in daylight," said Rex. "I see him in the eye of my mind stalking cars, rolling by the water in the carcass of a dead cod; twitching his legs in his dreams.

"I know," said Baby Hag, nodding her head up and down. "Lots of names mean me. All names. If I have one name, you know, I cannot have another. If I am Veronica, I can't be Eggplant. And if I come when you call Clothilde, I can't when you call Pippit."

"No," said Mother Hag fiercely. "I am weary of this. It is not the way of hags. One hag, one name. And that is that!"

There was a silence that grew slowly like the full-moon tide filling a marsh. Even Rex, sometimes as easygoing as a mutt, was silent and serious.

"The first fair day," said Mother Hag firmly, "you will go up to land and find a name. There will be a long, warm shore full of names."

"Many names," agreed Baby Hag cheerfully. "All names."

At this Mother Hag lost all reason.

"Not all names!" she cried. With every word a burst of bubbles came forth. "The first name you hear. *That* will be your name. Then you will return to the sea and we'll all live in peace." She looked at Baby Hag and her face softened a bit. "And you will have one name. One name that means you."

The sun had faded long ago. Night moved overhead, and slowly, without a word, the other hags swam off. They would return with the sun.

One name. Only one name Mother Hag wanted for Baby Hag; Baby Hag wished for all names. Impossible. One name. All names. It became a song that sang in Father Hag's head, over and over. He closed his eyes and rocked gently in the sea. One name. All names. *The first name she heard.* Impossible. *Or was it?* Suddenly Father Hag opened his eyes in the darkness. He smiled. It was strange to him, the smiling, though it felt familiar like a sudden smell from the past, a glimpse of something nearly, but not quite, forgotten. The night rains came, and the soft dropping on the water finally lulled him to sleep. He smiled all through his dreams.

Morning bloomed bright. There were dogs by the sea, and children with their pants rolled, chasing waves.

"Now," Mother Hag said to Baby Hag. "Quickly before the other hag children come. Go up to land for your name."

Father Hag smiled at Baby Hag and nodded his head.

Baby Hag peered at him. There was something. Something about his eyes that made her smile, too.

"Will you come with me?" she asked.

Father Hag shook his head.

"You will be fine. Remember, the first name you hear."

Baby Hag nodded, and with a quick flash of fin she swam to the surface of the sea. Into the first rise of wave she went, over and onto the next, and to the next. Six waves she rode, and then, with a great rush of foam and rolling wave and the barest whisper of sound, she tumbled onto wet sand—a small child blinking in the sunlight. It was strange on land, warm and bright. There was no safe darkness of the sea, no brothers and sisters. For the first time she felt earth beneath her feet.

Nearby sat a child, building a sand castle, humming to herself; another was throwing sand; a mother asleep, a father calling. Baby Hag turned around with a start, and there stood a child staring at her. The child's hair was short, and it was hard to tell if it was a boy child or girl. The child moved closer, closer, until it stood a breath away, arms folded, a small string of jingle shells strung in a bracelet on one wrist. Baby Hag tried to look away. But there was something about the child's eyes. Suddenly the child reached out and touched Baby Hag lightly, very lightly, and the string of jingle shells made a soft sweet noise. *Something about the eyes.* Baby Hag stared at the child. She took a deep breath. And she spoke.

"What is your name?"

She had never heard her own voice out of the sea. It seemed to fly away like spindrift.

The child smiled.

"Guess," said the child.

Guess.

In that moment the wind died and there was a great stillness between one wave and another. Baby Hag smiled at the child. And with a small sound, with the next wave, Baby Hag was gone.

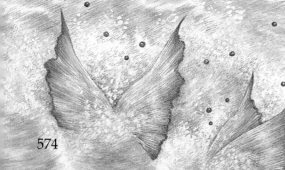

"Was that a child?" called a woman nearby, looking alarmed. "Where did that child go?"

A man shook his head.

"Who was she? What was her name?"

They both turned to ask the other child. But the other child was gone, too. *There was no child at all.*

Her name? Baby Hag heard the question and swam wave past wave past wave, slipping down again through the cool waters of her home. Down where her family waited for her.

"What is it?" called Rex, excited.

"Your name?" asked Mother Hag.

Baby Hag smiled at them.

"Guess," she said.

"Clothilde?"

"Martine?"

"No," said Baby Hag, shaking her head. "Guess."

"Lila?"

"Lizzie?"

A slight brush of fins touched Baby Hag then, and her father was there beside her.

"She has told you her name," he said. "It is not Clothilde or Francine, Lila or Lizzie. Her name," he said slowly, "is Guess."

There was a silence. Rex was the first to speak.

"Guess," he said. He laughed. "Guess."

"One name," said Mother Hag softly.

"One name for those who know her," said Father Hag. "But from those who ask her, she will always hear all the names she loves."

Baby Hag . . . Guess . . . turned to look at Father Hag, and she smiled suddenly at what she saw. Around one fin, so delicate that it moved in the currents of the water, hung a string of white jingle shells.

There it is, that whisper again! Hush, and you may hear another. It may be a child who appears suddenly, silently behind you, or a dog who grins. If the dog follows you, quickly tell him your name and he will trot away. If the child asks your name, do not say Guess. There is already a Guess who smiles and dreams beneath the sea. She lives with the lovely light of the sea at dawn, and the dark of it at night. With one name. With all names. And one thing more. Around her neck she wears a slim thread necklace of jingle shells.

Think About It

1. What are the sea hags' special powers and what are their habits?
2. What is Baby Hag's problem? What happens later to solve her problem?
3. Describe what you would do if you were a sea hag looking for a name.
4. What magical, mysterious elements were in each selection you read in UP FROM THE SEA?
5. Why do you think people are fascinated with mysterious stories about the sea?

Create and Share   You are walking alone on the beach one day when you experience something fantastic or mystical. Write a short story that describes the incident.

Explore   For more stories about the sea, look under these headings in the library card catalog: OCEAN, SEA MONSTERS, and SEA STORIES. A sea fantasy you might enjoy is *The Wreck of the Zephyr*, by Chris Van Allsburg. Look for it in your library.

Glossary

Full pronunciation key* The pronunciation of each word is shown just after the word, in this way: **ab·bre·vi·ate** (ə brē ′ vē āt).

The letters and signs used are pronounced as in the words below.

The mark ′ is placed after a syllable with a primary or heavy accent, as in the example above.

The mark ′ after a syllable shows a secondary or lighter accent as in **ab·bre·vi·a·tion** (ə brē′vē ā′shən).

a	hat, cap	**k**	kind, seek	**TH**	then, smooth
ā	age, face	**l**	land, coal	**u**	cup, butter
ä	father, far	**m**	me, am	**u̇**	full, put
b	bad, rob	**n**	no, in	**ü**	rule, move
ch	child, much	**ng**	long, bring	**v**	very, save
d	did, red	**o**	hot, rock	**w**	will, women
e	let, best	**ō**	open, go	**y**	young, yet
ē	equal, be	**ô**	order, all	**z**	zero, breeze
ėr	term, learn	**oi**	oil, voice	**zh**	measure, seizure
f	fat, if	**ou**	house, out	**ə**	represents:
g	go, bag	**p**	paper, cup		*a* in about
h	he, how	**r**	run, try		*e* in taken
i	it, pin	**s**	say, yes		*i* in pencil
ī	ice, five	**sh**	she, rush		*o* in lemon
j	jam, enjoy	**t**	tell, it		*u* in circus
		th	thin, both		

*Pronunciation Key and respellings are from *Scott, Foresman Intermediate Dictionary*, by E. L. Thorndike and Clarence L. Barnhart. Copyright © 1983 by Scott, Foresman and Co. Reprinted by permission.

A

ac·ces·si·ble (ak ses′ə bəl) *adj.* easy to reach or approach (Since it was next door, the store was *accessible* to me.)

ac·ci·dent-prone (ak′sə dənt prōn′) *adj.* likely to have accidents (an *accident-prone* person)

ac·tiv·i·ty (ak tiv′ə tē) *n.* an act of physical or mental exercise (Baseball is an outdoor *activity;* reading is an indoor *activity.*) *pl.* **activities**

ad·mon·ish·ment (ad mon′ ish mənt) *n.* disapproval or criticism of a fault, usually given in a kind and gentle way

ad·van·tage (ad van′tij) *n.* anything that is helpful or profitable (The wind was an *advantage* to the sailors.)

a·ghast (ə gast′) *adj.* struck with surprise or horror (I was *aghast* when I saw the tornado headed my way.)

air pressure (er presh′ ər) *n.* the force that air exerts on a surface that it touches

al·leg·ed·ly (ə lej′id lē) *adv.* reportedly; supposedly; as has been said to be the truth but has not been proved (That tree is *allegedly* the oldest in town.)

am·pu·tate (am′ pyə tāt) *v.* to cut off; especially, to cut off a part of the body **amputated, amputating**

an·chor (ang′kər) *n.* **1.** a heavy weight that is attached to a chain or rope and is dropped into the water to keep a ship from moving **2.** the person in a television news program who is the chief, or main, broadcaster

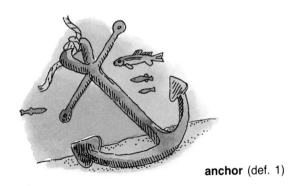

anchor (def. 1)

an·tic·i·pate (an tis′ə pāt) *v.* to look forward to **anticipated, anticipating**

ap·pease (ə pēz′) *v.* to calm, make quiet, or satisfy by giving what is wanted (A lion tamer *appeases* the animals with a tasty bit of fresh meat.) **appeased, appeasing**

ar·du·ous (är′ jü əs) *adj.* hard to do; requiring much energy to do

ar·ro·gant (ar′ ə gənt) *adj.* exaggerating one's own importance in a proud manner (The *arrogant* princess wanted everyone to bow before her.)

at·mo·sphere (at′ mə sfir) *n.* **1.** all the air surrounding the earth **2.** the air at a particular place or area **3.** a mood or feeling in a place (The *atmosphere* in the spooky old house was scary.)

at·tend·ant (ə ten′dənt) *n.* someone who waits on another person

awe (ô) *n.* great wonder, often combined with fear

B

ban (ban) *v.* to prohibit; to forbid (Some restaurants *ban* smoking.) **banned, banning**

ban·ish (ban′ish) *v.* **1.** to force to leave a country or place of residence (Rulers sometimes *banish* their enemies.) **2.** to drive away; to remove (*Banish* all sorrow.)

bar (bär) *v.* **1.** to put bars across **2.** to keep out; to prevent or forbid (The rules *bar* students from bringing pets to school.) **barred, barring**

bar·row (bar′ ō) *n.* a large mound of earth or stone placed over a grave (*Barrows* marked the spots where ancient Vikings were buried.)

bau·ble (bô′bəl) *n.* a showy toy, piece of jewelry, or other object, that has little use or value

bay (bā) *n.* a position in which an animal or person is unable to retreat and must face danger (The hunter's dog kept the fox at *bay*.)

beach·comb (bēch′kōm′) *v.* to search the beach for useful or attractive items tossed up by the waves (They like to *beachcomb* for pretty shells.)

be·wil·der (bi wil′ dər) *v.* to confuse completely; to puzzle (The strange noise *bewildered* me.)

broach (brōch) *v.* to begin to talk about something

C

ca·nine (kā′ nīn) *adj.* having to do with a dog; doglike *n.* a dog

can·o·py (kan′ ə pē) *n.* **1.** a covering fixed over a bed or throne **2.** a covering; shelter; shade (The trees formed a *canopy* over the path.) *pl.* **canopies**

canopy (def. 1)

cat·a·pult (kat′ ə pult) *n.* **1.** a machine that hurls objects, such as stones (In ancient times, *catapults* were used as weapons.) **2.** a slingshot *v.* to throw; to hurl

a hat / ā age / ä far / e let / ē equal / ėr term / i it / ī ice / o hot / ō open / ô order / oi oil / ou out / u cup / u̇ put / ü rule / ch child / ng long / sh she / th thin / ᴛʜ then / zh measure / ə a in about, e in taken, i in pencil, o in lemon, u in circus

cat·e·go·ry (kat′ə gôr′ ē) *n.* a group or class of things; a class in a system of grouping (Pines are one *category* of trees.) *pl.* **categories**

cen·sus (sen′səs) *n.* a counting of the people who live in a particular place at a particular time (Every ten years, the United States government takes a *census* of all the people living in the country.)

chain mail (chān māl) *n.* armor made of metal rings that are connected like links in a chain

chain mail

chant (chant) *v.* to sing, mostly in one tone *n.* a simple song sung mostly in one tone

co·he·sive (kō hē′ siv) *adj.* sticking together (*cohesive* group of friends.)

com·mence (kə mens′) *v.* to begin (In a few minutes, the ceremony will *commence.*) **commenced, commencing**

com·mit (kə mit′) *v.* **1.** to do; to do something wrong (Did he *commit* the crime?) **2.** to hand over for safekeeping or imprisonment (The judge *committed* the criminal to prison.) **3.** to promise to do something (Josh *committed* himself to delivering the newspapers every Saturday.) **committed, committing**

com·mon sense (kom′ən sens) *n.* natural good judgment or understanding

com·pen·sa·tion (kom′ pən sā′shən) *n.* something given to make up for something else (My parents took us to the movies as *compensation* for the rained-out picnic.)

com·post (kom′ pōst) *n.* a mixture that is made up mainly of once-living material, such as leaves and grass, and is used to fertilize plants

com·pre·hend (kom′ pri hend′) *v.* to understand (Since I do not speak French, I could not *comprehend* what the French woman was saying.)

con·coc·tion (kon kok′shən) *n.* a mixture of ingredients (a *concoction* of rice, meat, and tomatoes)

con·fine·ment (kən fīn′mənt) *n.* the act of being shut up or imprisoned

con·jure (kon′jər) *v.* to summon by a magic spell (When Aladdin rubs the magic lamp, he *conjures* up the genie.) **conjured, conjuring** *n.* the knowledge of how to summon by magic

con·sec·u·tive (kən sek′yə tiv) *adj.* following one after the other (April, May, and June are *consecutive* months.)

con·struc·tive·ly (kən struk′tiv lē) *adv.* in a manner that is helpful or useful (to criticize someone *constructively*)

con·tam·i·nat·ed (kən tam′ ə nā təd) *adj.* made impure by coming into contact with something harmful; polluted

con·trap·tion (kən trap′shən) *n.* a device; a mechanical gadget

con·vey·or (kən vā′ər) *n.* something that carries things from one place to another

581

cor·re·spond·ent (kôr′ ə spon′dənt) *n.* a person who exchanges letters with another person (Mary has received 20 letters from one *correspondent*.)

cor·rupt (kə rupt′) *v.* to cause to behave in an evil way

cra·dle (krā′dl) *v.* to hold closely **cra-dled, cradling** *n.* a baby's bed, usually on rockers

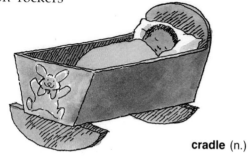

cradle (n.)

cre·a·tive (krē ā′tiv) *adj.* able to think of new ideas; having a good imagination

D

de·cline (di klīn′) *v.* **1.** to refuse (A person who does not want to go to a party *declines* the invitation.) **2.** to grow less; to decrease (As the sun set, the temperature *declined* some.) **declined, declining** *n.* a downward slope (a steep *decline*)

de·cree (di krē′) *v.* to command; to order (The king *decreed* that everyone must pay higher taxes.) **decreed, decreeing** *n.* an order, usually having the force of law (the ruler's *decree*)

de·fend·ant (di fen′dənt) *n.* a person who is on trial in a court of law; a person against whom a legal action is brought

de·fi·ant (di fī′ənt) *adj.* disobedient; openly against authority

de·scend·ant (di sen′dənt) *n.* the child, grandchild, and so on of specific people (Ellen is the *descendant* of people who came to this country in 1909.)

des·pe·ra·tion (des′ pə rā′shən) *n.* panic; readiness to try anything because of fear (She saw the bull charging and in *desperation* jumped into the river.)

dif·fuse (di fyüz′) *adj.* widely scattered *v.* to scatter **diffused, diffusing**

din (din) *n.* a loud, confused noise that keeps on going

dis·dain·ful (dis dān′fəl) *adj.* showing disrespect; looking down on; showing dislike for

dis·pute (dis pyüt′) *n.* an argument or debate *v.* to disagree with; to say a statement is false (Jake *disputes* the umpire's call.) **disputed, disputing**

dis·taste·ful (dis tāst′fəl) *adj.* unpleasant; displeasing

du·bi·ous (dü′bē əs) *adj.* doubtful or uncertain

E

eer·ie (ir′ ē) *adj.* strange; weird; mysterious (an *eerie* wailing noise) **eerier, eeriest**

---

a hat / ā age / ä far / e let / ē equal / ėr term / i it / ī ice / o hot / ō open / ô order / oi oil / ou out / u cup / ù put / ü rule / ch child / ng long / sh she / th thin / ŦH then / zh measure / ə *a* in about, *e* in taken, *i* in pencil, *o* in lemon, *u* in circus

em·i·grant (em′ə grənt) *n.* a person who leaves his or her country to settle in another

en·coun·ter (en koun′ tər) *v.* to meet unexpectedly (The hikers *encountered* a bear in the forest.)

en·ter·prise (en′ tər prīz) *n.* a project; an important plan (The success of the *enterprise* depended on Joe's hard work.)

ex·ist (eg zist′) *v.* to live; to be (Dinosaurs no longer *exist.*)

ex·pi·ra·tion (ek′ spə rā′ shən) *n.* the closing or ending of something (the *expiration* of a magazine subscription)

ex·ploit (ek′ sploit) *n.* a bold or daring act (the *exploits* of the brave knight)

ex·tor·tion (ek stôr′ shən) *n.* the act or crime of getting money, information, or anything else by using threats or force

---

F

fa·nat·ic (fə nat′ ik) *n.* someone who has unusually strong feelings about something (Sarah is a *fanatic* about baseball; she never misses a game.)

fer·ment (fər ment′) *v.* to cause a chemical change in which sugar is changed to alcohol, as in the process of making wine; to go through such a chemical change

flinch (flinch) *v.* to draw back from difficulty or pain

flour·ish (flèr′ ish) *v.* to grow strong; to do well; to thrive

friv·o·lous (friv′ ə ləs) *adj.* not serious; silly

G

gaunt·let (gônt′ lit) *n.* **1.** an iron glove that was part of the armor of a medieval knight **2.** a heavy glove with a flaring cuff that covers the wrist and part of the arm

gauntlet (def. 2)

ge·ne·al·o·gy (jē′ nē al′ə jē) *n.* a record of the members of a family over several generations; a record of a person's parents, grandparents, great-grandparents, and so on

goad (gōd) *v.* to urge; to prod (Nathan *goaded* Pat into diving off the high board.) *n.* something used to prod or urge (Fear was the *goad* that made her run fast.)

gos·sa·mer (gos′ ə mər) *n.* **1.** a spider web **2.** cloth that is as light, delicate, and airy as a web *adj.* light, delicate, and airy (the *gossamer* wings of the butterfly)

H

har·di·ness (här′ dē nis) *n.* strength; ability to stay alive or keep on existing under unfavorable conditions

hu·mane (hyü mān′) *adj.* kind; not cruel or brutal (Stray animals should be treated in a *humane* manner.)

im·ma·ter·i·al (im' ə tir' ē əl) *adj.* not important

im·pair (im per') *v.* to damage or to weaken

im·per·cep·ti·ble (im' pər sep' tə bəl) *adj.* very slight; not able to be seen or felt (The growth of plants is so slow that it is *imperceptible* to the human eye.)

in·di·ca·tor (in' də kā' tər) *n.* a person or thing that points out or shows something (A red traffic light is an *indicator* that cars should stop.)

in·dig·nant (in dig' nənt) *adj.* angry at something that seems to be unfair or mean (Carlos was *indignant* when he saw the boys teasing his little sister.)

in·ev·i·ta·ble (in ev' ə tə bəl) *adj.* sure to happen; not to be avoided (It is *inevitable* that spring will follow winter.)

in·flict (in flikt') *v.* to give or to cause something that is unwelcome, such as a wound or pain

in·gre·di·ent (in grē' dē ənt) *n.* one of the parts of a mixture

in·sig·nif·i·cant (in' sig nif' ə kənt) *adj.* having little meaning or importance

in·sur·mount·a·ble (in' sər moun' tə bəl) *adj.* not able to be overcome (an *insurmountable* problem)

in·ter·pret·er (in tẻr' prə tər) *n.* **1.** a person who explains the meaning of something (He is an *interpreter* of dreams.) **2.** a person who translates the words spoken in a foreign language (Because she speaks German, she is an *interpreter* at those meetings.)

in·tro·mit·tent (in trə mit' ənt) *adj.* having been put in; designed to be put in; sending in

ir·i·des·cent (ir' ə des' nt) *adj.* showing the colors of the rainbow (In the sun, a soap bubble is *iridescent*.)

joust·ing (joust' ing) *n.* fighting between knights, armed with spears, on horseback

kelp (kelp) *n.* a large brown seaweed

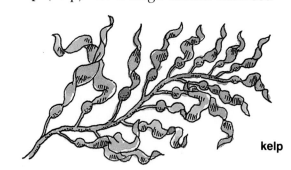

kelp

ker·nel (kẻr' nl) *n.* a seed of certain types of plants; a grain (*kernel* of wheat)

lance (lans) *n.* a long wooden spear with a sharp iron head

---

a hat / ā age / ä far / e let / ē equal / ẻr term / i it / ī ice / o hot / ō open / ô order / oi oil / ou out / u cup / u̇ put / ü rule / ch child / ng long / sh she / th thin / ŦH then / zh measure / ə a in about, e in taken, i in pencil, o in lemon, u in circus

lec·ture (lek′chər) *n.* **1.** a planned speech (a *lecture* on butterflies) **2.** a long warning or scolding (a *lecture* on being neat) *v.* **1.** to give a speech **2.** to scold **lectured, lecturing**

li·be·rat·ed (lib′ə rā′ təd) *adj.* freed; set free

lin·e·age (lin′ē ij) *n.* the ancestors of a person in a direct line from parent to grandparent to great-grandparent, and so on

lin·tel (lin′tl) *n.* a horizontal beam or stone over a door or opening

lintel

lob·by (lob′ē) *v.* to try to influence lawmakers about some special interest **lobbied, lobbying** *n.* an entrance hall *pl.* **lobbies**

lu·mi·nous (lü′mə nəs) *adj.* giving off light; bright (the *luminous* stars)

M

main·te·nance (mān′ tə nəns) *n.* the upkeep of property or equipment

man·u·al (man′yü əl) *n.* a small book of instructions *adj.* done with the hands

me·an·der (mē an′dər) *v.* **1.** to wind (The river *meanders* through the city.) **2.** to wander aimlessly; to stroll without a destination (She *meandered* through the park.)

mech·a·nism (mek′ə niz′ əm) *n.* **1.** a machine (A wristwatch is a small *mechanism* used for telling time.) **2.** the parts of a machine that make it work (They checked the clock's *mechanism*.)

me·men·to (mə men′tō) *n.* an object that helps a person remember something (The seashells are *mementos* of our trip to the beach.) *pl.* **mementos**

me·te·o·rol·o·gist (mē′ tē ə rol′ ə jist) *n.* a person who makes a scientific study of the weather

me·thod·i·cal·ly (mə thod′ə kə lē) *adv.* carefully; in a way that follows a particular manner of doing something

mi·cro·bi·ol·o·gy (mī′ krō bī ol′ ə jē) *n.* the scientific study of living things so small that they can be seen only through a microscope

mid air (mid′er′) *n.* a point in the middle of the air

min·er·al (min′ər əl) *n.* **1.** any substance that is not of plant or animal origin, such as gold, silver, or rocks **2.** any substance that is obtained by digging in the earth, such as coal, salt, iron, or petroleum

mi·nor·i·ty (mə nôr′ə tē) *n.* **1.** a part of something that is less than half of the whole (While most of the children wanted to play soccer, a *minority* wanted to play baseball.) **2.** a part of a population that is different in some way—such as race, religion, or national origin—from others in the same population (*Minorities*, such as black Americans and Jewish Americans, have played an important part in the history of the United States.) *pl.* **minorities**

mire (mīr) *n.* deep mud *v.* to sink or stick in mud **mired, miring**

mo·not·o·ny (mə not′n ē) *n.* sameness; lack of variety; a state in which the same thing happens over and over

mo·ti·va·tion (mō tə vā′shən) *n.* a reason for doing something; something that makes a person want to take action (His *motivation* for calling his aunt was to wish her a happy birthday.)

N

ne·go·ti·a·tion (ni gō′ shē ā′shən) *n.* the act of talking things over in order to reach an agreement

nose (nōz) *v.* to push or investigate with the nose; to find by using the sense of smell **nosed, nosing**

nurse (nėrs) *v.* to treat with special care; to make well (She *nursed* the weak bird back to health.) **nursed, nursing** *n.* a person who is trained to take care of sick people

nu·tri·ent (nü′ trē ənt) *n.* a food; an ingredient that is necessary for a living thing to grow or do well (*nutrients* in the soil)

O

o·blit·e·rate (ə blit′ ə rāt′) *v.* to erase; to remove all traces of (The waves *obliterated* the footprints in the sand.) **obliterated, obliterating**

oc·cur·rence (ə kėr′ əns) *n.* a happening; an event

odds (odz) *n.* the chance of something happening (The *odds* were against our side because our pitcher was sick.)

of·fen·sive (ə fen′ siv) *adj.* **1.** attacking (the *offensive* team in football) **2.** disagreeable; unpleasant (an *offensive* odor)

op·ti·mism (op′tə miz′əm) *n.* a tendency to expect the best possible thing to happen

o·rig·i·nate (ə rij′ ə nāt) *v.* to begin; to come into being (Noodles probably *originated* in ancient China.) **originated, originating**

P

pains·tak·ing (pānz′ tā′ king) *adj.* taking great care; very careful

par·a·pher·nal·ia (par′ ə fər nā′lyə) *n.* the equipment used in or associated with an activity (The coach will bring the balls, bats, and other *paraphernalia* for the game.)

pen·nant (pen′ənt) *n.* **1.** a long, narrow flag **2.** the yearly championship of each of the two major leagues in professional baseball

pennant (def. 1)

---

a hat / ā age / ä far / e let / ē equal / ėr term / i it / ī ice / o hot / ō open / ô order / oi oil / ou out / u cup / u̇ put / ü rule / ch child / ng long / sh she / th thin / ᴛʜ then / zh measure / ə *a* in about, *e* in taken, *i* in pencil, *o* in lemon, *u* in circus

per·son·nel (pėr′ sə nel′)   *n.* the whole group of people working in a business or organization

pre·ced·ing (prē sē′ ding)   *adj.* going before; coming before   (The day *preceding* Tuesday is Monday.)

pre·serv·ing (pri zėrv′ing)   *n.* the saving of something; the act of keeping something from harm

pro·ces·sion (prə sesh′ ən)   *n.* a group of persons, animals, cars, or any other thing, moving along in a line

a graduation **procession**

pro·duc·er (prə dü′ sər)   *n.* the person who supervises the making of, or provides the money for, a play, a television program, a movie, or something similar

pro·long (prə long′)   *v.* to make last longer   (Don't *prolong* your speech, because I need to leave soon.)

pro·posed (prə pōzd′)   *adj.* suggested; recommended   (the *proposed* change)

pros·e·cu·tion (pros′ ə kyü′shən)   *n.* the government officials that, in a law court, try to show that the accused person, the defendant, is guilty of a crime

pros·the·sis (pros′thē sis)   *n.* an artificial part of the body that replaces a part missing because of an accident, illness, or other cause   *pl.* **prostheses**

pro·to·zo·an (prō′ tə zō′ ən)   *n.* any of a large group of one-celled living creatures that are usually too small to be seen without a microscope   *pl.* **protozoa**

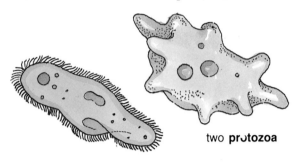

two **protozoa**

pry (prī)   *v.* to raise up by force   (She will *pry* the lid off that bottle.)   **pried, prying**

pur·pose·ful (pėr′pəs fəl)   *adj.* having a purpose or reason for doing something; deliberate; planned

R

re·as·sure (rē′ ə shūr′)   *v.* to bring back courage or confidence; to convince   (Sally *reassured* her father that she hadn't forgotten her lunch.)   **reassured, reassuring**

re·cep·tion·ist (ri sep′ shə nist)   *n.* someone who meets and welcomes callers or guests

re·fract (ri frakt′)   *v.* to bend from a straight path   (When raindrops *refract* light, a rainbow often forms.)

re·luc·tant (ri luk′ tənt)   *adj.* unwilling; not wanting to do something

re·me·di·al (ri mē′ dē əl)   *adj.* helping to do better or curing poor habits   (People having trouble with math must sometimes take a *remedial* course.)

re·morse (ri môrs′) *n.* a deep, painful regret for having done something unkind or wrong

re·pro·duce (rē′ prə düs′) *v.* **1.** to make or do again (Scientists must be able to *reproduce* their experiments.) **2.** to produce children; to make more of your own kind of living thing

rep·u·ta·tion (rep′ yə tā′shən) *n.* what people think and say about the character of a person; the character of a person in the opinion of other people

res·o·lu·tion (rez′ ə lü′ shən) *n.* **1.** something decided upon (The Merloni family made a *resolution* to visit Acadia National Park.) **2.** the act of solving something

re·solve (ri zolv′) *v.* to make up the mind; to decide **resolved, resolving**

res·pite (res′ pit) *n.* a short period of rest or relief

re·vet·ment (ri vet′mənt) *n.* an embankment or barricade to give shelter or protection

ri·vet (riv′ it) *v.* to fix firmly *n.* a metal bolt with a head on each end used to fasten things together

S

scav·en·ger (skav′ ən jər) *n.* **1.** a living thing that feeds on dead plants or animals **2.** someone who searches through discarded objects for something that is useful or valuable

se·date (si dāt′) *adj.* calm; serious

seethe (sēᴛH) *v.* to foam as though boiling (The fast-moving boat made the water *seethe*.) **seethed, seething**

sen·sor (sen′sər) *n.* an instrument that receives and responds to light, temperature, or some other signal (The gas gauge in a car is a *sensor* that shows how full the gas tank is.)

sen·sor·y probe (sen′sər ē prōb) *n.* a small, thin instrument that picks up signals from its surroundings

se·rene (sə rēn′) *adj.* peaceful; quiet; calm (In spite of the crisis, Mary seemed *serene*.)

se·ver·i·ty (sə ver′ə tē) *n.* harshness; sternness

sim·u·la·tor (sim′yə lā′ tər) *n.* a device that copies or imitates the looks, conditions, or sounds of something (The *simulator* produced a sound similar to a human voice.)

skein (skān) *n.* a small bundle of yarn or thread (Becky needed several *skeins* of green yarn for the sweater she was knitting.)

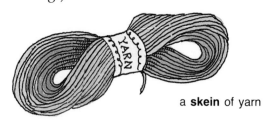

a **skein** of yarn

slew (slü) *v.* to twist; to turn (The car's wheels did not go straight but *slewed* to the right.) **slewed, slewing**

---

a hat / ā age / ä far / e let / ē equal / ėr term / i it / ī ice / o hot / ō open / ô order / oi oil / ou out / u cup / ù put / ü rule / ch child / ng long / sh she / th thin / ᴛH then / zh measure / ə *a* in about, *e* in taken, *i* in pencil, *o* in lemon, *u* in circus

spec·trum (spek′trəm)   *n.* the bands of colors seen when a beam of light is broken up   (A rainbow is a *spectrum*.) *pl.* **spectra** or **spectrums**

spher·i·cal (sfir′ə kəl)   *adj.* having the shape of a globe or ball

spin·ney (spin′ē)   *n.* a small woods or forest area

spinney

stalk (stôk)   *v.* **1.** to follow in such a way as to avoid being seen   **2.** to walk in a stiff, slow, haughty way

stam·mer (stam′ər)   *v.* to repeat the same sound several times when speaking   ("I d-d-did n-n-not g-g-go," he *stammered*.)

sta·tis·tic (stə tis′tik)   *n.* a numerical fact about something, such as the number of people who live in cities, the highest and lowest yearly temperatures in an area, and so forth   (According to the *statistics*, President John F. Kennedy received 34,227,096 votes in the 1960 election.)

stud·y (stud′ē)   *n.* **1.** the act of trying to learn, usually by reading carefully   **2.** a careful examination of something (They made a *study* of butterflies.)   **3.** the written explanation of such an examination   (They read a *study* on butterflies.) *pl.* **studies** *v.* **1.** to try to learn by reading carefully   (*study* the

history lesson)   **2.** to make a careful examination   **studied, studying**

sub·stance (sub′stəns)   *n.* material; matter; what something is made of (Some *substances* in a loaf of bread are flour, water, yeast, and air.)

sum·mon (sum′ən)   *v.* to call; to send for (*summon* the doctor)

sur·face ten·sion (sėr′fis ten′shən)   *n.* a condition that exists on the outside of a liquid that acts like a weak skin to hold the surface together

sur·veil·lance (sər vā′ləns)   *n.* a close watch over somebody or something (The spies had the fort under *surveillance*.)

sus·pense (sə spens′)   *n.* uncertainty; anxiety

swag·ger (swag′ər)   *v.* to walk with a boastful air; to strut   *n.* a strutting walk

T

team·ster (tēm′stər)   *n.* a person whose work is to drive a team of horses

tempt (tempt)   *v.* to try to persuade a person to do something

tour·ney (tėr′nē)   *n.* a contest between two groups of knights on horseback

tourney

u

un·cul·ti·vat·ed (un kul′tə vā′ tid) *adj.* having no planted crops; undeveloped; not tended; wild (*uncultivated* land)

v

vale (vāl) *n.* a valley; a low area between mountains or hills

vale

ven·om·ous (ven′ ə məs) *adj.* able to poison; giving out a poison

view·er (vyü′ ər) *n.* a person who watches

vin·dic·tive (vin dik′tiv) *adj.* having a grudge; wanting revenge; wanting to harm someone you dislike

vis·u·al·ize (vizh′ ü ə līz) *v.* to see a mental picture (Can you *visualize* what your room will look like after you've rearranged the furniture?)

w

wit (wit) *n.* (*usually pl.*, **wits**) the ability to understand; sense (In spite of the danger, she kept her *wits.*)

wretch·ed (rech′id) *adj.* **1.** very sad; very unhappy; miserable (the wet, *wretched* cat) **2.** very bad (a *wretched* movie)

---

a hat / ā age / ä far / e let / ē equal / ėr term / i it / ī ice / o hot / ō open / ô order / oi oil / ou out / u cup / u̇ put / ü rule / ch child / ng long / sh she / th thin / ŦH then / zh measure / ə a in about, e in taken, i in pencil, o in lemon, u in circus

592